THE POLITICAL ECONOMY OF HUNGER

The Political Economy of Hunger

Edited by

JEAN DRÈZE AND AMARTYA SEN

Volume 3

Endemic Hunger

CLARENDON PRESS · OXFORD
1991

Oxford University Press, Walton Street, Oxford OX2 6DP

Oxford New York Toronto
Delhi Bombay Calcutta Madras Karachi
Petaling Jaya Singapore Hong Kong Tokyo
Nairobi Dar es Salaam Cape Town
Melbourne Auckland

and associated companies in
Berlin Ibadan

Oxford is a trade mark of Oxford University Press

Published in the United States
by Oxford University Press, New York

British Library Cataloguing in Publication Data
The political economy of hunger. – (WIDER studies in
development economics).
Vol. 3
1. Food supply
I. Drèze, Jean II. Sen, Amartya III. Series
363.8
ISBN 0–19–828637–6

Library of Congress Cataloging in Publication Data
(Revised for vol. 3)
The Political economy of hunger.
(WIDER studies in development economics)
Includes bibliographical references and indexes.
Contents: v. 3. Endemic hunger.
1. Famines—Africa, Sub-Saharan—Case studies. 2. Food relief—
Africa, Sub-Saharan—Case studies. 3. Famines—South Asia—Case
studies. 4. Food relief—South Africa—Case studies. 5. Hunger—
Case studies. I. Drèze, Jean. II. Sen, Amartya Kumar.
III. Series.
HC800.Z9F37 1991 363.8′83′0967 90-7663
ISBN 0–19–828637–6

Typeset by Rowland Phototypesetting Ltd
Bury St Edmunds, Suffolk
Printed and bound in
Great Britain by Bookcraft (Bath) Ltd,
Midsomer Norton, Avon

In fond memory of
Sukhamoy Chakravarty

FOREWORD

The first fruits of WIDER's programme in the theme area of 'Hunger and Poverty—The Poorest Billion' initiated in 1985 were presented in August 1986 at a research conference in Helsinki on 'Food Strategies'. The research was co-ordinated by WIDER's Research Adviser on this theme, Amartya Sen, now Lamont University Professor at Harvard University. The focus of the research project was on identifying 'what feasible opportunities exist' for changing a situation where inordinately large numbers of people go hungry.

A common background to many of the papers presented at the conference was provided by an approach that sees famine and hunger as arising not primarily from a lack of availability of food but from failure of entitlement to food. Another key focus of the conference was on the public intervention issue, namely, how does a country with a low per capita income reach high levels of physical quality of life in terms of literacy rates, life expectancy, and infant mortality. Besides the country studies, other issues addressed in the research include strategies of famine prevention, international interdependence, gender inequalities, the role of food production, and the functions of an active press.

The conference papers have been brought together in three volumes, edited by Jean Drèze and Amartya Sen, of which this is the third. In addition to editing these three volumes, Jean Drèze and Amartya Sen have themselves written a separate monograph entitled *Hunger and Public Action* (Oxford University Press, 1989), which closely relates to the themes and concerns of this book.

Lal Jayawardena
Director, WIDER
August 1989

PREFACE

This collection of twenty-six papers, presented in three volumes, represents the result of work undertaken at and for the World Institute for Development Economics Research (WIDER) in Helsinki. This programme of joint research was initiated in the summer of 1985. The first versions of most of the papers were presented at a WIDER conference on 'food strategies' held in Helsinki in July 1986. The papers as well as the research programme as a whole were subjected to close scrutiny at that conference. Those discussions strongly influenced the work that followed—both extensive revisions of the papers presented and the undertaking of new studies, which are also included in these volumes.

The objective of this programme has been the exploration of a wide range of issues related to hunger in the modern world. The papers are concerned with diagnosis and causal analysis as well as policy research. The focus is particularly on Africa and Asia, but there are also two papers on hunger and deprivation in Latin America and a few contributions on more general theoretical issues. The full list of papers in the three volumes can be found at the beginning of each volume. Our 'Introduction' to the three volumes, discussing the papers and their interrelations, is included in full in volume 1, but the parts relevant for the subsequent volumes are also included in the respective volumes, i.e. volumes 2 and 3.

The tasks of revising the papers and carrying out the follow-up studies proved to be quite challenging, and the entire project has taken much longer than we had hoped. We are extremely grateful to the authors for their willingness to undertake substantial—and in some cases several rounds of —revisions, and for putting up with long lists of suggestions and requests. The revisions have been enormously helped by the contributions of the discussants who participated in the 'food strategies' conference in July 1986, including Surjit Bhalla, Susan George, Keith Griffin, S. Guhan, Iftekhar Hussain, Nurul Islam, Nanak Kakwani, Robert Kates, Qaiser Khan, Henock Kifle, Stephen Marglin, Siddiq Osmani, Martin Ravallion, Sunil Sengupta, Mahendra Shah, Nick Stern, Paul Streeten, Megan Vaughan, and Samuel Wangwe. Carl Eicher's comments and suggestions contributed greatly to the improvement of a number of papers. Very helpful comments and suggestions were also received after the conference from Sudhir Anand, Susan George, Judith Heyer, Nurul Islam, Robert Kates, B. G. Kumar, and François-Régis Mahieu.

For their participation in the conference, and their help in planning these studies, we are also grateful to Frédérique Apffel-Marglin, Juha Ahtola, Tuovi Allén, Lars-Erik Birgegaard, Pekka Harttila, Cynthia Hewitt de Alcantara, Eric Hobsbawm, Charles Kindleberger, Michael Lipton, Kaarle

Nordenstreng, Kimmo Pulkinnen, Shlomo Reutlinger, Tibor Scitovsky, Darrell Sequiern, Heli Sirve, Marjatta Tolvanen, Matti Tuomala, Tony Vaux, and Hannu Vesa.

For editorial and logistic assistance, we are greatly in debt to Nigel Chalk, Robin Burgess, Pekka Sulamaa, Jacky Jennings, Shantanu Mitra, Sanjay Reddy, Sangeeta Sethi, Asad Ahmed, and Anna-Marie Svedrofsky. We would also like to thank Judith Barstow for preparing the subject index.

Finally, we are grateful to WIDER for its generous support. We owe special thanks to Lal Jayawardena, the Director, for being immensely helpful at every stage of this project.

J.D.
A.S.
November 1989

CONTENTS

LIST OF PAPERS

Volume 1: Entitlement and Well-Being

Volume 2: Famine Prevention

Volume 3: Endemic Hunger

LIST OF CONTRIBUTORS

SUDHIR ANAND is University Lecturer in Quantitative Economic Analysis at the University of Oxford, and Fellow and Tutor at St Catherine's College.

KAUSHIK BASU is Professor of Economics at the Delhi School of Economics, and currently Visiting Professor of Economics at Princeton University.

PARTHA DASGUPTA is Professor of Economics at the University of Cambridge, and Professor of Economics and Philosophy at Stanford University.

MEGHNAD DESAI is Professor of Economics at the London School of Economics.

JEAN DRÈZE formerly Lecturer in Development Economics at the London School of Economics, is now an Associate of the London School of Economics.

CHRISTOPHER HARRIS is University Lecturer in Public Economics at the University of Oxford, and a Faculty Fellow of Nuffield College.

BARBARA HARRISS is University Lecturer in Agricultural Economics at Queen Elizabeth House, University of Oxford, and Fellow of Wolfson College.

JUDITH HEYER is Lecturer in Economics at the University of Oxford, and Fellow and Tutor at Somerville College.

FRANCIS IDACHABA is Vice-Chancellor of the University of Agriculture, Makurdi, on leave of absence from the Department of Agricultural Economics, University of Ibadan.

S.M. RAVI KANBUR is Editor of the World Bank Economic Review and Senior Adviser of the Social Dimension of Adjustment at the World Bank, on leave from Professorship in Economics at the University of Warwick.

B. G. KUMAR is Associate Fellow at the Centre for Development Studies, Trivandrum, Kerala, India.

S. R. OSMANI is Research Fellow at the World Institute for Development Economics Research, Helsinki, Finland.

KIRIT S. PARIKH is Director of the Indira Gandhi Institute of Development Research, Bombay, and from 1980 to 1986 was Program Leader at the Food and Agriculture Program of the International Institute for Applied Systems Analysis, Austria.

JEAN-PHILIPPE PLATTEAU is Professor of Economics at the Facultés Universitaires, Namur, Belgium.

N. RAM is Associate Editor of *The Hindu*, a leading national daily newspaper in India, based in Madras.

MARTIN RAVALLION is Senior Economist in the Agricultural Policies Division of the World Bank, Washington DC, on leave from the Australian National University, Canberra, Australia.

DEBRAJ RAY is Professor, Planning Unit, Indian Statistical Institute, New Delhi.

CARL RISKIN is Professor of Economics at Queens College, City University of New York, and Senior Research Scholar at the East Asian Institute, Columbia University.

IGNACY SACHS is Professor at the Écoles des Hautes Études en Sciences Sociales, and Director of its Research Centre on Contemporary Brazil in Paris.

AMARTYA SEN is Lamont University Professor at Harvard University.

REHMAN SOBHAN was formerly the Director of the Bangladesh Institute of Development Studies, Dhaka, with which he is still associated.

PETER SVEDBERG is a Senior Research Fellow at the Institute for International Economic Studies, Stockholm.

SAMUEL WANGWE is Professor of Economics at the University of Dar es Salaam.

ANN WHITEHEAD is Lecturer in Social Anthropology at the University of Sussex, England.

LIST OF TABLES

Introduction[1]

Jean Drèze and Amartya Sen

The facts are stark enough. Despite the widespread opulence and the unprecedentedly high real income per head in the world, millions of people die prematurely and abruptly from intermittent famines, and a great many million more die every year from endemic undernourishment and deprivation across the globe. Further, hundreds of millions lead lives of persistent insecurity and want.

While all this is quite obvious, many things are unclear about the characteristics, causation, and possible remedies of hunger in the modern world. A great deal of probing investigation—analytical as well as empirical—is needed as background to public policy and action for eradicating famines and eliminating endemic undernutrition. In this collection of twenty-six papers in three volumes, serious attempts have been made to address many of these momentous issues.

0.1. Organization and structure

These studies were initiated in 1985 when the World Institute for Development Economics Research (WIDER) was established in Helsinki. First versions of most of the papers were presented at a conference on 'food strategies' held at WIDER in July 1986. In that meeting there were extensive discussions of the analyses presented in the various papers, and some of the debates continued well beyond the conference. The papers have been revised in the light of these exchanges, and of further discussions among the authors and the editors. A few new studies were also undertaken during 1986–8 to fill some identified gaps. This book of three volumes represents the fruits of these efforts. It is meant to be a wide-ranging investigation of the causal antecedents, characteristic features, and policy demands of hunger in the modern world. The focus is primarily on sub-Saharan Africa and South Asia, but the experiences of several other countries—from China to Brazil—have also been examined.

Though three of our own essays are included in these volumes, our role has been primarily organizational and editorial. We have, however, also written a monograph of our own, *Hunger and Public Action*,[2] which deals with related issues, and there is a clear connection between the two works. The planning

---

[1] This Introduction draws on the fuller and more general Introduction to the set of three volumes presented in vol. 1.

[2] Also published by Oxford University Press in the series of WIDER Studies in Development Economics: Drèze and Sen (1989).

and the design of these three volumes of essays, *The Political Economy of Hunger*, have been closely related to the approach explored and developed in *Hunger and Public Action*, and in turn, in that book, we have drawn on the results of the studies presented in these three volumes.

We should, however, emphasize the obvious. We, as editors, must not be identified with all the views that have been expressed in these essays. These three volumes of essays, which are mainly revised conference papers, present investigations and conclusions that deserve, in our view, serious consideration. But although we have been involved at every stage of these studies, and have also presented our critical comments on the various versions, it was not our aim to soldier on with requests for revision until we all agreed. The analyses and the views are those of the respective authors.

0.2. *Political economy*

The essays in the first volume deal with 'general matters'—including the nature and diversity of the problem of world hunger. They set the background for the analysis of government policy and public action. The second volume includes studies of famines and of anti-famine strategies, and altogether there is an attempt here to identify what is needed for the eradication of famines. The third volume takes up endemic deprivation and undernourishment, discusses successes and failures of different lines of action, and investigates the lessons for public policy aimed at eliminating persistent hunger. The different volumes, thus, deal with distinct but interrelated aspects of what we have called 'the political economy of hunger'.

The meaning of the expression 'political economy' is not altogether unambiguous. To some it simply means economics. It is indeed the old name of the discipline, common in the nineteenth century, and now rather archaic. To others, political economy is economics seen in a perspective that is a great deal broader than is common in the mainstream of the modern tradition. In this view, the influences of political and social institutions and ideas are taken to be particularly important for economic analysis and must not be pushed to the background with some stylized assumptions of heroic simplicity. Political economy thus interpreted cannot but appear to be rather 'interdisciplinary' as the disciplines are now standardly viewed.

Even though the two interpretations are quite distinct, there is a clear connection between them in the sense that the dominant tradition of economics is much narrower now than it was in the classical political economy of Adam Smith, Robert Malthus, David Ricardo, Karl Marx, John Stuart Mill, and others.[3] Thus the old and archaic term for economics as such is also a reminder of the breadth of the earlier tradition of the subject. Many of the analyses of the kind that are now seen as interdisciplinary would have appeared to Smith or

---

[3] On this issue, see Sen (1984, 1989).

Mill or Marx as belonging solidly to the discipline of political economy as a subject.

It does not, of course, really matter whether political, social, and cultural influences on economic matters are counted inside or outside the discipline of economics, but it can be tremendously important not to lose sight of these influences in analysing many profoundly important economic problems. This is particularly the case with the problem of hunger. The title of the book, *The Political Economy of Hunger*, is meant to be an explicit reminder of the need to adopt a broad perspective to understand better the causation of hunger and the remedial actions that are needed.

0.3. *Endemic undernourishment and deprivation*

As was mentioned earlier, the essays included in the first volume of this book deal with rather general matters that serve as background to policy analysis. The topics covered include the characteristics and causal antecedents of famines and endemic deprivation, the interconnections between economic and political factors, the role of social relations and the family, the special problems of women's deprivation, the connection between food consumption and other aspects of living standards, and the medical aspects of undernourishment and its consequences. Several contributions also address the political background of public policy, in particular the connection between the government and the public, including the role of newspapers and the media, and the part played by political commitment and by adversarial politics and pressures.[4]

The second volume of the book is concerned with famine prevention issues, with special attention paid to sub-Saharan Africa. Three of the six chapters provide detailed case-studies of famine prevention in different countries of Africa and South Asia, including both successes and failures. The other papers deal with more general strategic issues. These include, *inter alia*, the question of 'early warning', the interconnections between public policy and market responses, and the long-term rehabilitation of rural African economies.

This third volume deals with the challenge of combating persistent want and hunger. Two cases of notable success—China and Sri Lanka—are discussed in some detail. In both these cases a major reduction of deprivation and expansion of life expectancy and related indicators have been achieved despite very low gross national product per capita.

In another book (Drèze and Sen 1989), we have compared and contrasted two different—though not unrelated—general strategies for eliminating endemic undernourishment and deprivation. The approach of 'growth-mediated security' involves rapid economic expansion, including that of GNP per head, and the use of this achievement to eradicate regular hunger and privation. In this general strategy, the fruits of growth are widely shared partly through a

[4] On these questions see also Drèze and Sen (1989).

participatory growth process (involving, in particular, a rapid and sustained expansion of remunerative employment), but also through the use of the resources generated by economic growth to expand public support of health, nutrition, education, and economic security for the more deprived and vulnerable. In contrast, the approach of 'support-led security' involves going in for public support measures without waiting for the country to become rich through economic growth. Examples of support-led security include, in addition to China and Sri Lanka, such countries as Costa Rica, Cuba, Chile, Jamaica, and the State of Kerala in India.

There is a real contrast between these two strategies, but it is important to recognize that the extensive use of public support measures plays a crucial role in both. While public support is the primary and immediate instrument of action in the strategy of support-led security, it is also an important ingredient of the success of growth-mediated security. Indeed, in the absence of public involvement to guarantee that the fruits of growth are widely shared, rapid economic growth can have a disappointingly poor impact on living conditions.[5] The distinctiveness of the strategy of support-led security is not the *use* of public support to improve living conditions, but the *temporal priority* that is attached to this instrument of action even when the country in question is still quite poor.

It may be asked how poor countries can *afford* to have extensive public support systems. Part of the answer lies in the labour intensive nature of many of these measures of public delivery—particularly in health care and education—making them cheaper in poorer economies. But some of the explanation also relates to the scope for reorienting the focus of delivery away from providing an enormous lot—expensive and advanced services—to a few (the relatively affluent) to securing minimal basic services for all (including the worst off).[6] Indeed, the fractions of their relatively low GNP per head devoted to public programmes of health care and education in China, Sri Lanka, Kerala, Cuba, and other adopters of the general strategy of support-led security have not been remarkably higher than in countries that have treated education and medicine as the entitlement of the rich and the privileged.

0.4. *China's record*

Chapter 1 is an illuminating account by Carl Riskin of China's experience in combating hunger since the revolution.[7] While a problem of undernourishment in many rural areas continues to exist, China has been in general

---

[5] On the role of public support measures in the recent experiences of growth-mediated security, see Drèze and Sen (1989: ch. 10).

[6] There are many other factors involved in this complex question. On this and related matters (including the considerations involved in the choice between the two general strategies), see Drèze and Sen (1989: chs. 10–12).   [7] See also Riskin (1987).

remarkably successful in reducing the reach and magnitude of undernourishment across the country. Food production has generally grown faster than population over these years, but between the 1950s and the reforms of 1979, not by very much.[8] China's success in reducing deprivation is particularly connected with public policies involving relatively egalitarian distribution and widespread public support of health and nutrition. Riskin also discusses in some detail the mechanisms of food distribution in China—between the provinces, between the urban and rural areas, and between different families and persons.

One terrible blot in China's otherwise impressive record is the occurrence of a large famine during 1959–61, in the wake of the failure of the so-called Great Leap Forward. Riskin discusses the factors that contributed to this calamity, including the limited information that the central government had about food production and consumption in the provinces.

The fact that China could have such a famine despite its excellent general record in the reduction of endemic deprivation and normal mortality underlines the need to see the battle against hunger as one with many facets. It also indicates that the eradication of hunger benefits not only from having a dedicated and determined government committed to that objective, but also from having a system that permits participatory and adversarial involvement of the general public.[9] Given the recent developments in China, the relevance of these considerations may extend well beyond the limited field of anti-hunger policy.

0.5. *Public support in Sri Lanka*

Sri Lanka's achievements in raising life expectancy and the related aspects of quality of life have been the subject of much attention among economists (even though these achievements are in some danger of being overshadowed by the violence and strife into which Sri Lanka has recently been plunged). A life expectancy of 70 years for a country with the low GNP per head that Sri Lanka has is no mean feat. Indeed, its life expectancy is still marginally *higher* than that of South Korea despite the latter's remarkable economic expansion leading to a GNP per capita many times that of Sri Lanka.

Sri Lanka's use of public support measures goes back a long way. Expansion of primary education took place early in the century. A rapid expansion of

---

[8] Oddly, in the post-reform period, between 1979 and the mid-1980s, while agricultural and food production per head have rapidly increased, the decline of mortality seems to have been halted (on this see Banister 1987). These changes are not yet fully studied, but among the factors implicated are general financial stringency and some withdrawal of wide-coverage rural health services, and the introduction of compulsory birth control measures, leading to a neglect (if not worse) of female children. These matters have been discussed in Drèze and Sen (1989: ch. 11).

[9] On this see also Drèze and Sen (1989). Also ch. 6 in vol. 1, and chs. 1 and 2 in vol. 2.

health services occurred in the mid-1940s. Sri Lanka moved to a system of free or subsidized distribution of rice in 1942. Between 1940 and 1960, its crude death rate fell from above 20 per thousand to around 8 per thousand.

Sri Lanka's radical and innovative public support measures have played a substantial part in its achievements.[10] In Chapter 2, Sudhir Anand and Ravi Kanbur have provided a probing account of that connection. By using time-series data pertaining to the relevant variables, they have indicated how and when direct public intervention has contributed to reducing deprivation and to enhancing the quality of life in Sri Lanka. These lessons have considerable bearing on future policy as well, since public support measures have been under severe scrutiny in Sri Lanka—as elsewhere—on the grounds of their being expensive, and there has been some withdrawal (also analysed by Anand and Kanbur) from an interventionist strategy in recent years.

Anand and Kanbur's econometric analysis suggests that the expansion of health services has been rather more effective than food subsidies in bringing about mortality decline in Sri Lanka. The policy issues to be faced in Sri Lanka—and elsewhere—not only concern the recognition of the role of public support measures in general, but also call for a discriminating assessment of the choices to be faced *within* a general strategy of public intervention. Anand and Kanbur have provided a far-reaching account of the diagnostic and policy issues concerning one of the most interesting experiences of combating hunger and deprivation in a poor country.

0.6. *Brazil and unaimed opulence*

While Sri Lanka provides an example of what can be achieved even with a low real income per head and moderate economic growth, Brazil provides an illustration of how little can happen in removing poverty and deprivation even with remarkably rapid growth of GNP per head. In Chapter 3, Ignacy Sachs provides a lucid account of this contrary experience.

Brazil's economic growth has not only been fast, it has also been sustained and technologically rich (with widespread use of modern technology). Brazil has also emerged as one of the largest exporters of industrial products in the

---

[10] Some observers (e.g. Bhalla and Glewwe 1986, Bhalla 1988) have argued that Sri Lanka's high level of life expectancy and other achievements may not have been related to its public support measures and in support of this view they have pointed to its unexceptional expansion of life expectancy and other indicators in the period *since 1960* (compared with other countries). Aside from some methodological problems in the analysis (on which see Isenman 1987, Pyatt 1987, Ravallion 1987b, among others), this line of argument overlooks the fact that the expansion of public support measures in Sri Lanka substantially *predates* 1960, and that in the period of rapid expansion of public support (particularly from the mid-1940s) Sri Lanka's death rate did fall quite fast. On this and related matters, see Drèze and Sen (1989: ch. 12).

world, and the incomes generated in production for domestic and foreign markets have raised the level of average income in the country to levels that are very much higher than obtained a few decades ago. And yet there is a good deal of endemic undernutrition in Brazil and there is persistent poverty affecting a substantial section of the population. Sachs discusses how and why rapid economic growth has failed to improve the lives of so many million Brazilians, and why their entitlements have been so little influenced by the newly generated incomes. Identifying inequality as the major villain in all this, Sachs has also briefly explored the scope for 'growth with redistribution' in Brazil.

As we discussed earlier in this Introduction (and more fully in Drèze and Sen 1989), growth of GNP *can be* a major contributor to removing undernourishment and deprivation, and the strategy of 'growth-mediated security' specifically focuses on this connection. But that recognition should not be confused with the claim that growth of GNP per head must invariably and automatically bring about removal of deprivation across the board. What is at issue is not merely the quality of growth—in particular its participatory nature—but also the willingness of the government to use the fruits of growth to provide public support with comprehensive coverage—guaranteeing basic health services, education, and other basic amenities to all sections of the population, including the most vulnerable and deprived groups. In both these respects the experience of growth-mediated security in, say, South Korea contrasts sharply with the 'unaimed opulence' of Brazil.[11]

0.7. *Latin American poverty and undernourishment*

While Sachs concentrates on Brazil, Chapter 4 by Ravi Kanbur has a much wider coverage. Kanbur identifies the extent of undernourishment in Latin America, which is obviously much less severe than in South Asia or sub-Saharan Africa, but which is far from negligible in magnitude.[12]

Kanbur goes on to discuss the extent to which economic growth on its own can be expected to eliminate undernourishment in the Latin American countries. Here Kanbur's broader analysis supplements the more concentrated study of Brazil by Sachs. Kanbur shows that the 'crossover time' (i.e. the number of years required for the average poor person to cross the poverty line if his or her income grows at the average rate of growth of per capita GNP of the past twenty years) tends to be remarkably high. This takes Kanbur to the

[11] The contrast between 'growth-mediated security' and 'unaimed opulence' is discussed in Drèze and Sen (1989: ch. 10).

[12] While the proportion of people in poverty in Latin America is comparable to that in East Asia in terms of income deprivation, Latin America's record is much worse than that of East Asia in terms of living conditions, including expectation of life.

question of the *aiming* of economic expansion and the *targeting* of the increase of incomes and consumptions. He outlines some necessary characteristics of a well-targeted policy for alleviating poverty and undernourishment.

Crucial to Kanbur's analysis is his identification of the contrasts between socio-economic groups in terms of vulnerability to deprivation. Throughout Latin America, the incidence of poverty is much higher in the rural areas than in the urban (though the urban slum dwellers form one of the more deprived groups). Within the rural areas, the landless workers and those with tiny holdings are most prone to suffer. Kanbur finds the size of the family to be an important parameter as well, indicating the relevance of population policy. His analysis of targeting in removing undernourishment draws on the results of these diagnostic analyses. The important issue is to replace 'unaimed opulence' by using growth as a mediator of security.

0.8.   *The extent of undernourishment in sub-Saharan Africa*

Peter Svedberg in Chapter 5 is concerned with the diagnostic question as to how much undernourishment exists in sub-Saharan Africa. Svedberg deals with both methodological and substantive issues. He argues that the methodologies used to measure the extent of undernourishment in sub-Saharan Africa have frequently been faulty and have involved the use of unreliable data. He also indicates that the extent of undernourishment has been very often exaggerated.

Svedberg makes extensive use—*inter alia*—of anthropometric evidence to establish his substantive conclusions. There are interpretational problems here too, but Svedberg's critical assessment of the unreliability of the usual high estimates is certainly quite robust. It is important not to read his conclusions as grounds for smugness, since even his own estimates indicate a substantial problem of deprivation and undernourishment in sub-Saharan Africa.

Svedberg's chapter can be seen as an argument for not exaggerating what is in any case quite a momentous problem. It can be added that, by exaggerating the extent of the problem, well-meaning scholars have sometimes inadvertently encouraged a sense of hopelessness and fatalism about hunger in sub-Saharan Africa. This can be changed by a more realistic assessment of the extent of the challenge, followed by determination to deal with it effectively. Svedberg's essay serves this dialectic purpose in addition to the methodological and diagnostic functions on which he himself concentrates.

0.9.   *Institutions and policies for sub-Saharan Africa*

In removing the true—unexaggerated—prevalence of endemic undernourishment in sub-Saharan Africa, the expansion of its agriculture will undoubtedly play an important part. This is not merely because food comes primarily from agriculture, but also because the entitlements of the majority of Africans depend—directly or indirectly—on the functioning of the agricultural sector, and this situation can change only relatively slowly. Despite the importance of distinguishing between the problems of food entitlement and those of food production as such, the crucial contributory role of food production in particular and agricultural production in general can scarcely be denied.

In Chapter 6 Francis Idachaba has provided a broad-ranging analysis of ailments of sub-Saharan agriculture and the policy options that exist. Rather than concentrating on some simple 'remedies', Idachaba surveys the whole gamut of specific issues—social institutions, technological research, rural infrastructure, agricultural prices. It is in this wide setting that he assesses what the governments can do and what policies seem most promising.[13] Idachaba also considers the role of external assistance and the parts—negative as well as positive—played by international institutions such as the World Bank.

0.10. *Kenyan agriculture and food deprivation*

While Idachaba takes on the whole of sub-Saharan Africa as his field of investigation, Judith Heyer looks specifically in Chapter 7 at smallholder agriculture in Kenya. The incidence of poverty among people engaged in smallholder agriculture in Kenya is, of course, very high, and Heyer considers the ways in which this situation can be changed.

Although Heyer examines various internal reforms within smallholder agriculture, she comes to the conclusion that, in bringing about a major change, an important part will have to be played by developments *outside* the sector—in non-agricultural activities and in large-scale farming. Heyer identifies intersectoral interconnections that are important, but which are frequently overlooked in viewing smallholder agriculture on its own. Her argument for a broader economic analysis with an eye to social consequences can be seen as a corrective of some of the prevailing preconceptions in this field.

0.11. *The industrial connection*

Chapter 8 by Samuel Wangwe has close links with Judith Heyer's broad-based approach. Wangwe looks specifically at the contribution of industry to combating hunger (in this his concentration is rather narrower than that of Heyer), but he does not confine his analysis to any particular country (his focus is, in that respect, broader than that of Heyer).

---

[13] There is a discussion in Drèze and Sen (1989: ch. 9) of these issues, including the importance of diversification and the balance of food production *vis-à-vis* the production of cash crops and industrial goods.

Given the importance of employment in securing entitlements, Wangwe devotes a good deal of attention to the need for generating opportunities of employment—in off-farm activities and in industry in addition to farm employment. Another industrial connection that receives much attention in Wangwe's paper is the part played by the production, acquiring, and use of agricultural equipment. He also goes on to discuss the role of industry in agricultural processing.

The contributions of Heyer and Wangwe supplement the analysis presented by Idachaba, and help to underline the important fact that the solution of the so-called 'food problem' in sub-Saharan Africa will require a good deal more than a concentration on internal problems of the food-producing sector. The persistence of endemic undernourishment in sub-Saharan Africa calls for a wide range of remedial actions involving institutional changes and economic reforms both within the food sector and outside it.[14]

0.12. *Hunger in Bangladesh*

Sub-Saharan Africa is not only plagued by endemic deprivation, it also suffers from the persistence of recurrent famines. In this respect the situation in South Asia is rather less desperate in that famines have rarely occurred in recent years in any of the South Asian economies. The one exception is Bangladesh which experienced a major famine in 1974.[15] But despite this relative absence of famines, the extent of regular undernourishment seems to be, if anything, *larger*—even in proportion to its population—in South Asia than in sub-Saharan Africa.[16]

Among the major countries in South Asia, Bangladesh is not only the poorest, it also has the largest proportion of hungry and undernourished people according to most estimates. In Chapter 9, Siddiq Osmani has provided a helpful and authoritative account of the problems of undernourishment and famines in Bangladesh. Despite the international perception of the enormous and seemingly incurable nature of Bangladesh's problems (it has frequently been referred to as 'a basket case'), Bangladesh's achievements are far from negligible. It has achieved a growth rate of per capita income of about 2 per cent per year over the fourteen years or so since the famine of 1974,[17] and it has successfully avoided famines despite natural calamities of rather larger dimension than in 1974 (including the widespread and severe flooding of 1988).

---

[14] See also Mellor *et al.* (1987), Lipton (1987), Eicher (1988). Drèze and Sen (1989).

[15] On this see Alamgir (1980) and Sen (1981: ch. 9).

[16] This is so even according to standard estimates (see ch. 4 below for some comparative figures). Svedberg's criticisms have the effect of indicating that the actual extent of undernourishment is less in sub-Saharan Africa than these estimates suggest.

[17] On this see also Osmani (1989).

Osmani discusses the changes that have taken place and the major tasks that remain.

Osmani comes to the conclusion that, despite actually avoiding famines since 1974, Bangladesh's vulnerability to them remains. There is a lack of system in famine prevention and too much reliance on muddling through.[18] As far as endemic hunger is concerned, Osmani also argues that current food policies have the effect of accentuating rather than relieving this problem. The relatively successful overall economic growth has not been adequate in eliminating regular undernourishment.[19]

It is interesting that despite a much faster overall growth of aggregate real income compared with the growth of food production and consumption (nutritional intake per head has not materially increased over the last two decades), food prices have not risen relative to other prices (in fact, the contrary has happened[20]). This is one result of the fact that Bangladesh's continuing problems have much to do with the persistence—even accentuation—of inequality, and the distribution of ownership and power that lead to unequal results. Osmani discusses the lines of reform that would be needed to meet the major challenge of continuing hunger in Bangladesh.

0.13.   *Public support and South Asia*

While Chapter 9 concentrates on Bangladesh, Chapter 10, by Kaushik Basu, considers the problems of South Asia as a whole. The inadequacy of relying only on overall economic growth resurfaces here again in this context. Basu outlines the need for—and the actual possibility of—effective policies of 'direct action' to remove poverty and regular deprivation.

Basu illustrates his arguments with empirical illustrations from the experiences of Sri Lanka, India, and Bangladesh. He also provides a probing scrutiny of various 'poverty alleviation programmes' in use in South Asia, including 'food-for-work' schemes. While many of these programmes have failed in diverse ways, Basu outlines the promising nature of some of these policies if they are effectively planned and implemented.

The 'direct action' programmes take the form of economic action, but their success depends greatly on their political background—in particular the ability to remove the political constraints that often make them ineffective or degenerate. In addition to providing economic analysis of poverty removal, Chapter 10 goes into the political requirements of entitlement protection and

---

[18] It is also possible to argue that the more restricted nature of adversarial politics in Bangladesh compared with India is a factor that keeps the former country more vulnerable to famines arising from the lack of alertness and speed in anti-famine public policy.

[19] There has, however, been a considerable reduction in mortality, morbidity, and clinically diagnosed undernourishment in Bangladesh, connected with better delivery of health services.

[20] On this see Osmani (1989).

promotion. Both Osmani and Basu go explicitly into the political factors on which the effectiveness and success of economic policies significantly depend.[21] Here again political economy, in the broader sense outlined earlier, becomes the crucial analytical apparatus.

[21] On this see also Drèze and Sen (1989: esp. ch. 13).

References

ALAMGIR, M. (1980), *Famine in South Asia* (Cambridge, Mass.: Oelgeschlager, Gunn & Hain).

BANISTER, JUDITH (1987), *China's Changing Population* (Stanford, Calif.: Stanford University Press).

BHALLA, SURJIT (1988), 'Is Sri Lanka an Exception? A Comparative Study in Living Standards', in Srinivasan, T. N., and Bardhan, P. K. (eds.), *Rural Poverty in South Asia* (New York: Columbia University Press).

——and GLEWWE, PAUL (1986), 'Growth and Equity in Developing Countries: A Reinterpretation of the Sri Lankan Experience', *World Bank Economic Review*, 1.

DRÈZE, JEAN (1988), 'Social Insecurity in India', paper presented at a Workshop on Social Security in Developing Countries held at the London School of Economics, July.

——and SEN, AMARTYA (1989), *Hunger and Public Action* (Oxford: Oxford University Press).

————(1990), 'Public Action for Social Security', in Ahmad, S. E., Drèze, J. P., Hills, J., and Sen, A. K. (eds.) (forthcoming), *Social Security in Developing Countries* (Oxford: Oxford University Press).

EICHER, CARL (1988), 'Food Security Battles in Sub-Saharan Africa', paper presented at the VIIth World Congress of Rural Sociology, Bologna, 25 June–2 July.

ISENMAN, PAUL (1987), 'A Comment on "Growth and Equity in Developing Countries: A Reinterpretation of the Sri Lankan Experience" by Bhalla and Glewwe', *World Bank Economic Review*, 1.

LIPTON, MICHAEL (1987), 'Limits of Price Policy for Agriculture: Which Way for the World Bank?', *Development Policy Review*, 5.

MELLOR, J. W., DELGADO, C. L., and BLACKIE, C. L. (eds.) (1987), *Accelerating Food Production in Sub-Saharan Africa* (Baltimore, Md.: Johns Hopkins).

OSMANI, SIDDIQ (1989), 'Food Deprivation and Undernutrition in Rural Bangladesh', paper presented at the 9th World Congress of the International Economic Association, Athens, Aug.

PYATT, GRAHAM (1987), 'A Comment on "Growth and Equity in Developing Countries: A Reinterpretation of the Sri Lankan Experience" by Bhalla and Glewwe', *World Bank Economic Review*, 1.

RAVALLION, MARTIN (1987a), *Markets and Famines* (Oxford: Oxford University Press).

——(1987b), 'Growth and Equity in Sri Lanka: A Comment', mimeo (Washington, DC: World Bank).

RISKIN, CARL (1987), *China's Political Economy: The Quest for Development since 1949* (Oxford: Oxford University Press).

SEN, AMARTYA (1981), *Poverty and Famines* (Oxford: Oxford University Press).

——(1984), *Resources, Values and Development* (Oxford: Basil Blackwell).

——(1989), 'Economic Methodology: Heterogeneity and Relevance', *Social Research*, 56.

1

Feeding China

The Experience since 1949

Carl Riskin

China's approach to feeding its 22 per cent of the world population has varied considerably during the thirty-six years of the People's Republic, as have the results. In the late 1970s its leadership began repudiating much of the country's earlier experience. While food policy since 1978 has moved along new paths, there are nevertheless close links between recent accomplishments and the earlier record.

The purpose of this chapter is to survey the experience of food policy under the People's Republic in a comprehensive manner and in historical context. The first two sections present background information on China's agricultural economy and a chronology of important institutional developments since 1949. Section 1.3 then discusses food supply and nutrition in terms of national averages. The fourth section takes up in some detail the famine of 1959–62, and this is followed in section 1.5 by a general discussion of food policy problems before the reforms that began in the late 1970s. Issues of regional and personal distribution of food are examined in the sixth section. Finally, there is a brief summary and conclusion.

1.1. *Background features*

The central fact of the Chinese food supply situation is the relative scarcity of arable land. John Lossing Buck (1956: 165) estimated in the 1930s that about 362,000 square miles were under cultivation in the main agricultural areas of China, which would make the cultivated area only about 10 per cent of a gross land area of about 3.7 million square miles. Dominated by arid grasslands in the north-west, high plateaux and massive mountain ranges in the west, and uneven hills in the south and south-west, the topography of China begrudges its people good farm land.

What there is of it is limited almost entirely to five specific areas (*Geography of China* 1972: 6–9): (1) the North-East or Heilongjiang Plain, which is China's principal producer of *gaoliang* (sorghum) and soybeans: (2) the North China Plain, earliest and largest of China's farm regions, dominated by the Yellow River and producing winter wheat, *gaoliang*, maize, and cotton; (3) the Middle

I would like to thank Thomas P. Bernstein, Jean Drèze, Keith Griffin, Mark Selden, and an anonymous referee for valuable comments on an earlier draft of this chapter. I alone am responsible for remaining errors as well as for interpretations of the data.

and Lower Changjiang (Yangtse) Plain, a major rice area; (4) the Chengdu Plain, a fertile rice-growing basin in western Sichuan; and (5) various south China valleys (especially the Pearl River Delta of southern Guangdong) that are ribbons of rice and subtropical cultivation amidst the prevailing hills.

This physical geography explains why 90 per cent of China's population lives on only one-sixth of the total land area. In fact, the last four of these regions account for about three-quarters of the population.

Official figures for cultivated acreage indicate a reduction from 108 million hectares in 1952 to 99.5 million in 1979 (Xue Muqiao 1981/2: vi–9).[1] The downward trend is explained by the fact that the 17 million hectares known to have been reclaimed between the late 1950s and late 1970s were more than offset by some 27 million hectares abandoned to new housing, factories, and road construction (Lardy 1983a: 3). Moreover, the lost acreage was on average more fertile than the marginal land brought under cultivation.

Arable land per capita thus declined by half between the early years of the PRC and the late 1970s, when it came to 0.1 hectares. Table 1.1 shows China's arable land–population ratio in comparison with that of several other countries. It is evident that China ranks lower in the amount of land available to its farm population than in its overall land availability.

Tables 1.2 and 1.3 look somewhat more closely at physical conditions. From the former it can be seen that the ratio of sown to cultivated area yields a multiple cropping index of about 1.5. This was pushed past the point of negative marginal returns in some areas in the late 1960s and early 1970s; it subsequently declined slightly. About 45 per cent of China's farmland is irrigated (Table 1.3), half of this by power machinery. The major increases in irrigated area occurred before 1975. Since 1978 neither total nor power irrigated area has increased (State Statistical Bureau 1984b: 26).

Table 1.1 Arable land per capita, mid-1970s: international comparison

	Arable land per capita (ha)	Arable land per farm population (ha)
China	0.10	0.12
World	0.38	1.82
Asia (exc. China)	0.24	0.44
S. Korea	0.07	0.15
India	0.27	0.44
Japan	0.05	0.27
US	0.97	27.50

Source: Perkins and Yusuf (1984: 52).

[1] The statistical authorities warn that actual cultivated acreage in the early 1980s probably exceeded official estimates by as much as one-quarter to one-third. See World Bank (1985: 28).

Table 1.2 Relation between land, population, and labour force, China, 1952–1987

	Population (m.)	Agricultural labour force (m.)	Arable land (m. ha)	Sown area (m. ha)	Multiple cropping index	Arable land per capita (ha)	Arable land per agricultural worker (ha)
1952	575	173	107.9	141.3	1.3	0.19	0.62
1957	647	193	111.8	157.2	1.4	0.17	0.58
1965	725	234	103.6	143.3	1.4	0.14	0.44
1975	920	295	99.7	149.5	1.5	0.11	0.34
1984	1,035	309	98.4[a]	144.2	1.5	0.10	0.32
1987	1,081	317	95.9	144.9	1.5	0.09	0.30

[a] Estimate for 1983. But see n. 1 above.

Sources: Lardy (1983a: 4, 5); State Statistical Bureau 1984b, 1985c, 1988). World Bank (1985: 30).

Table 1.3 Irrigated area, China, 1952–1987

	Irrigated area (m. ha)		Irrigated area as % of cultivated area
	Total	% power irrigated	
1952	19.96	1.6	18.5
1957	27.34	4.4	24.4
1965	33.06	24.5	31.9
1975	43.30	n/a	43.4
1979	45.00	56.3	45.2
1984	44.45	56.4	45.2
1987	44.40	55.9	46.3

Source: Perkins and Yusuf (1984: 52); World Bank (1985: 30); State Statistical Bureau (1985*c*: 41; 1988: 233).

1.2. *The institutional framework*

Most of China's agriculture consisted of peasant smallholdings until 1955. Land reform, which lasted from the late 1940s to 1952, resulted in a fairly even distribution of land holdings. Nevertheless, remaining inequality, together with the great density of farm population, left less than half an acre of farm land per capita for the poorest three deciles of the rural population. The average 'poor peasant' farm of 1½ acres in southern Jiangsu Province could provide its owners with only about 1,500 kilocalories per day each (Ash 1976: 529). Some leaders, notably Mao Zedong, feared that the evident unviability of poor peasant farms implied that repolarization was inevitable. For that reason, as well as to make surplus extraction easier and to substitute large-scale organization of labour for capital investment, Mao moved quickly in the mid-1950s to collectivize agriculture. Between 1954 and 1956 virtually all of China's more than 100 million farm households joined collectives.[2] After a breathing period in 1957, the trend of rapid institutional change resumed in 1958 with the 'Great Leap Forward' and the formation of 'rural people's communes'.

The commune underwent several years of adjustment under the trying circumstances of the famine that ended the 'Leap'. By 1962 it had attained the form that, in large part, was to last almost two decades. It consisted of three levels of formal organization—the commune level at the top, the production team at the bottom, and between them the production brigade—plus the household economy below. The team consisted of 20 to 30 households and was the 'basic accounting unit', meaning that it organized ordinary farm labour and

---

[2] At the autumn harvest of 1954 only 2% of farm households were in small lower-stage co-operatives (in which land was still owned privately and yielded rent to its owners). By late 1956, 88% of households were in larger collectives and private ownership had been abolished. Despite the rapidity of this transition, the myth persists of a golden age of gradual, voluntary formation of co-operatives up to mid-1955.

distributed its net income among its members. The brigade distributed important inputs to the teams, including power, irrigation water, and the use of larger machines, and ran social services such as health clinics and primary schools. It was composed of an average of 7 or 8 teams. Brigades also had militia units, which were often thrown into construction projects.

The commune level, made up of 8–12 brigades, ran larger-scale enterprises, including small industries, and some operated hospitals and secondary schools. The commune was the basic level of state government in the country-side and it accordingly had governmental institutions such as People's Bank branches, tax collection and grain management offices, and supply and marketing co-operatives.

The household economy remained a crucial part of agricultural organization for most of the duration of the commune. Private plots and family sideline production provided a large share of cash income and of vegetables and other subsidiary foods.

This quadripartite division of labour was convenient for organizing produc-tion and capital construction work (such as water conservancy projects) at whichever level was called for by the required scale of work. It also facilitated the transmission of technological innovations from central research institutes to the villages.

Income was distributed in this system according to the number of 'work-points' earned in labour. Two basic methods of workpoint assignment were used: one based on evaluating the worker, the other the task. In the first, the individual was given a workpoint rating based on strength and skill (and later, on political 'attitude') and then earned that rating by putting in a full day's work. In the second, each task was rated and workers earned points by carrying out tasks. When the harvest was in, the team's net income—after deductions of anticipated production costs, agricultural tax, and contributions to an accumulation fund for capital purchases and a welfare fund to help indigent members—was divided by the total number of workpoints accumulated to derive the money value of a workpoint, and income was distributed accord-ingly. During the year, grain was usually made available on a per capita basis to member households; the money value of this grain was deducted at the time of distribution. This was an important factor in bringing about a relatively equal income distribution within individual teams and in putting a floor under rural income (see section 1.6 below).

Neither workpoint system replicated the incentive furnished by the problem of survival itself in private farming. Both presented problems of allocative efficiency, for there was no immediate individual payoff for doing the right thing at the right time (as opposed to doing the task that brought the highest workpoints). Both also presented incentive problems *per se*, for they lengthened considerably the link between work and income, while putting a big premium on the values of co-operation and collective solidarity. The effectiveness of both systems thus depended heavily upon the strength of these values in a particular team, which in turn depended on the quality of team leadership and on the general social and political environment that shaped and limited team operations. In retrospect, the deterioration of that environment in the decade beginning with the Cultural Revolution (1966–9) doomed whatever chance the Chinese form of collective farming might have had to take advantage of its inherent strengths (e.g. in 'farmland capital construction') and achieve a high per capita rate of growth.

From the viewpoint of the reform government that came to power after 1978, the commune system suffered from a fatal flaw: because the commune itself was both the lowest level of state administration and the highest level of collective organization, it lent itself to government dictation to the farmers as if the production teams were state farms. Autocratic and sometimes corrupt behaviour by shielded state cadres, as well as compromise of the teams' collective autonomy in matters of production (e.g. decisions about what to plant) and distribution (e.g. putting arbitrary caps on distributed income), were quite common and are blamed for destroying the initiative of the farmers under the commune system. The egalitarian quality of intrateam distribution is also faulted, but it is difficult to know what to make of this criticism in view of the obvious link between the incentive implications of a given distribution and the fairness of the surrounding environment.

Starting about 1978 the government encouraged and then required the dissolution of the commune system in favour of a 'household responsibility system' (HRS), in which land was contracted out to individual households. The system of HRS that came to predominate allowed the household to keep all produce above an amount due to the 'collective' for meeting its tax and quota sales obligations and contributing to its accumulation and welfare fund. Workpoints were thus abolished, as was collective organization of much ordinary farm work. Some farm tasks, however, such as planting and harvesting, are often still done collectively (Bernstein 1986), as are capital construction projects, irrigation management, and other infrastructural work.[3]

The term 'quota sales' in the preceding paragraph refers to an essential institution in China's food supply system from the mid-1950s until 1985. Farmers or their collectives in areas producing more than their subsistence needs of grains and some other crops were obligated to sell a portion of the surplus to the state at below-market 'quota prices'. The sales obligation was calculated as a fraction of 'normal yield' and was kept constant for several years as an incentive to improve yields. The treatment of above-quota output varied over time; in recent years it was divided into two categories, one of which would bring 'above-quota' prices and the other still higher 'negotiated' prices from the state. The state also undertook to resell grain at quota prices to grain-deficient areas. Standards for rural grain distribution varied by region.

---

[3] On the post-1978 reforms see, *inter alia*, Bernstein (1984*b*, 1986); Domes (1982); Khan and Lee (1983); Lin (1983); Shue (1984); Watson (1983); Zweig (1982).

In the cities, however, grain was strictly rationed; besides stretching tight supplies, urban rationing was a crucial element in the control of rural–urban migration.

In 1985 the state abolished the mandatory quota system. Now farmers contract their sales to the state and sell surplus on the open market. This change was carried out under conditions of relative grain abundance. Total grain purchases had risen more than proportionally with the rapid post-reform increases in output, going from 51 MMT in 1978 to 117 MMT in 1984 (*State Statistical Bureau* 1985a: 480).[4] Since the state makes losses on its grain trade as a means of subsidizing urban consumption, this development entailed a growing financial burden (see section 1.6 below).

The immediate effect of the shift from mandatory quotas to contract purchases was to lighten this burden by relieving the state of the obligation to purchase at premium prices all above-quota grain offered to it. In 1985 the state purchased only 75 MMT of rice, wheat, and corn (Erisman 1986: 20). Peasants must now dispose of extra grain on the open market and the state will intervene only if the market price falls below a set trigger level. Grain production responded in 1985 with the first decline in several years, a sharp fall of 28 MMT, or 7 per cent.[5]

Aside from lightening the state's burden, it seems that the contract system as now practised differs little from the previous quota system. Local cadres often assign 'contractual obligations' as they once assigned quotas, although in some cases more genuine negotiations occur (Oi 1986). Since the state continues to set 'quota' and 'above-quota' prices (70 per cent of contract sales are supposed to take place at the latter price) and purchase targets, the system clearly embodies a mix of plan and market elements.

1.3. *National food supply and nutrition*

Since 1950 foodgrains (which in Chinese statistics include soybeans, tubers at 5 : 1 weight ratio, and pulses) have supplied some 86–89 per cent of available energy and 80–85 per cent of available protein (Piazza 1983: 17–18). The grain harvest has thus been a major determinant of the overall food situation.

---

[4] Data are in 'trade grain', i.e. rice and millet are measured in husked form, other grains in unprocessed form.

[5] While bad weather also affected the grain crop in 1985, policies, including the sudden disappearance of market security for grain producers and a structure of relative prices that distinctly favours industry, trade, and sideline activity over crop growing, probably played a major role. CIA analysts argue that 'much of the decrease in grain production in 1985 probably can be attributed to the new rural policies' (US Central Intelligence Agency 1986: 9). However, given severe storage and disposal problems that occurred in 1984 and the underdevelopment of a grain-using animal husbandry industry, reducing grain production was quite a rational course of action for the farmers to take.

Table 1.4 Aggregate and per capita foodgrain
production, China, 1952–1985

Year	Aggregate output (MMT)	Per capita output (kg)
1952	163.92	288.00
1953	166.83	287.00
1954	169.52	285.00
1955	183.94	302.00
1956	192.75	310.00
1957	195.05	306.00
1958	200.00	306.00
1959	170.00	255.00
1960	143.50	215.00
1961	147.50	223.00
1962	160.00	240.50
1963	170.00	249.00
1964	187.50	269.00
1965	194.53	272.00
1966	214.00	291.00
1967	217.82	289.00
1968	209.06	270.00
1969	210.97	265.00
1970	239.96	293.00
1971	250.14	297.00
1972	240.48	279.00
1973	264.94	300.50
1974	275.27	305.50
1975	284.52	310.50
1976	286.31	307.50
1977	282.73	299.50
1978	304.77	318.50
1979	332.12	342.50
1980	320.56	326.50
1981	325.02	327.00
1982	354.50	351.50
1983	387.28	379.50
1984	407.31	395.50
1985	378.98	362.18

Sources: State Statistical Bureau (1983*a*; 1985*a*; 1986*a*: 27, 33).

Foodgrain output from 1952 to 1985 is shown in Table 1.4.[6] Over the entire period aggregate grain production increased about 1½ times, for an average annual growth rate of 2.8 per cent. From 1957 to 1977, however, the growth rate was only 1.8 per cent, while it rose to 3.9 per cent during 1978–85. On a per capita basis, food production averaged 0.9 per cent growth over the entire period. The two decades 1956–77 saw only a 0.2 per cent growth rate, but since 1978 it has averaged 2.6 per cent. Both production and consumption per capita fluctuated substantially from year to year, although the use of stocks and imports and the treatment of commercial uses of foodgrain as a residual reduced fluctuations in consumption relative to those in production (see Fig. 1.1). It is also apparent that annual variability in consumption was greater during 1958–73 than in the years of relative normalcy that preceded and followed that turbulent period.

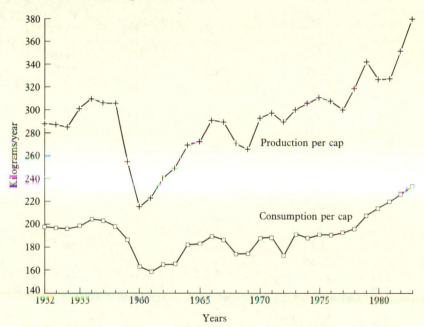

Fig. 1.1. Cereal production and consumption per capita, China, 1952–1984

[6] A word needs to be said about the accuracy of Chinese official statistics. Checks of internal consistency and other considerations have convinced most independent scholars that government statistics during most of the post-1949 years have been accurate expressions of what the Chinese government believed to be true. The community of foreign scholars has generally found them usable on this basis (see Eckstein 1980). The government has often not released information available to it; there have been periods, especially during the Great Leap Forward, when politically motivated distortion of information has occurred; the bases and/or definitions of statistics are frequently not made clear; capacity to collect and process accurate information has fluctuated quite sharply, and methods (e.g. sampling methods) are sometimes flawed. Thus, to say that deliberate falsification has rarely occurred is not to confirm the accuracy of official information. The problems of using such information, however, and the need for suitable caution are generally well known and accepted by students of the Chinese economy.

Table 1.5 Daily per capita availability of energy, protein, and fat, China, 1952–1982

Year	Total energy (Kcal)	Annual change in energy (%)	Total protein (g)	Total fat (g)
1952	1,861		51	24
1953	1,879	1.0	50	23
1954	1,895	0.9	50	24
1955	2,005	5.8	53	25
1956	2,051	2.3	53	24
1957	2,045	−0.3	55	24
1958	2,053	0.4	54	26
1959	1,722	−16.1	46	22
1960	1,453 (1,875)	−15.6	39	16
1961	1,558	7.2	43	16
1962	1,660	6.5	45	17
1963	1,776	7.0	46	19
1964	1,934	8.9	50	22
1965	1,967	1.7	53	22
1966	2,078	5.6	53	23
1967	2,042	−1.7	52	23
1968	1,931	−5.4	49	22
1969	1,881	−2.6	48	22
1970	2,076 (2,131)	10.4	52	23
1971	2,082	0.3	51	23
1972	2,006	3.7	49	24
1973	2,160	7.7	53	25
1974	2,194	1.6	54	24
1975	2,210	0.7	55	24
1976	2,220	0.5	56	24
1977	2,236	0.7	56	25
1978	2,360	5.5	58	25
1979	2,562	8.6	65	31
1980	2,487 (2,611)	−2.9	64	32
1981	2,517 (2,650)	1.2	65	33
1982	2,729	8.4	68	38

Note: The source notes that figures in parentheses show estimates of energy availability based only upon a 20% wastage rate for grain, as assumed by the Chinese government. The World Bank estimates are based on commodity-specific deductions for seed, feed, waste, and manufacturing use.

Source: World Bank (1984: 164), based on methodology of Piazza (1983).

Estimates of the average daily per capita availabilities of energy, protein, and fat between 1952 and 1982 are shown in Table 1.5 and Figs. 1.2 and 1.3. Energy availability has trended upward with per capita grain production, and has been subject to similar fluctuations. Estimates have been made of per capita

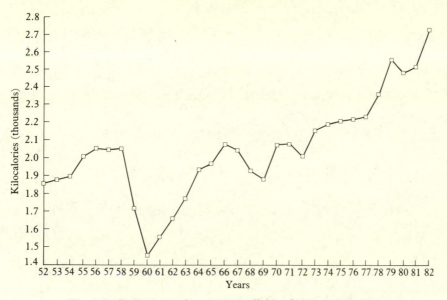

Fig. 1.2. Daily per capita energy available, China, 1952–1982

requirements of energy and protein in China for 1953 and 1979.[7] Energy availability in 1953 fell short of estimated requirements (put at 2,023 Kcal) by 5 per cent. In 1979 availability exceeded the higher requirements of that year (2,185 Kcal) by 18 per cent.

Protein availability appears to have exceeded safe requirements substantially throughout the entire period. However, Piazza (1983: 23–7) provides alternative estimates that take into account protein quality (which determines the degree of absorption and utilization of amino acids). Much protein consumed in China is derived from grain and is of low quality. Accordingly, Piazza's estimates of 'net protein utilization' fall significantly short of requirements in 1950, 1951, and the years 1960–2. Shortfalls might have been greater in those years and might have existed in other years when energy availability did not meet requirements; under such circumstances protein sources may be utilized by the body for energy rather than for protein (Piazza 1983: 23, 27).[8] Lardy (1983a: 156) believes that average protein availability must have been lower in 1976–8 than in 1957 because of the marked decline in per capita soybean production between those two dates; and that this presented a serious nutritional problem in rural areas: 'Widespread anemia among children has been attributed by Chinese medical sources to protein deficiency in the diet,

[7] See World Bank (1984: 169–72). The estimates use WHO/FAO standards and data on age-specific average body weights, age distribution, and assumptions about activity levels.

[8] On the other hand, Piazza's estimates ignore protein complementarity, and thus *understate* to some degree the quality of protein consumption (1983a: 27).

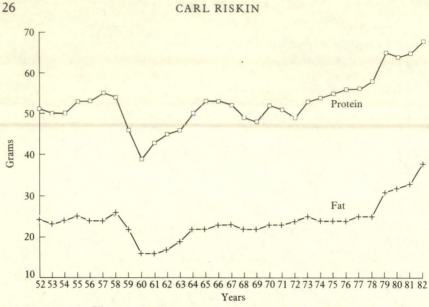

Fig. 1.3. Daily protein and fat, China, 1952–1982

because anemia is widespread except in the traditional soybean-growing areas of the Northeast' (Lardy, 1983a: 156).[9]

Evidence of secular improvements in nutrition up to the early 1980s is limited. One of China's most noteworthy accomplishments, namely the steady rise in estimated life expectancy at birth[10] from 34 years in 1952 to 69 years in 1982 (World Bank 1984: 113), was influenced by many factors besides nutrition. There were marked gains between 1957 and 1977 in height for age of school-age children in some urban and prosperous suburban areas, notably suburban Shanghai, Beijing, and Guangzhou (Canton), but hardly any longitudinal data are available from areas more representative of the conditions of most Chinese (Jamison and Trowbridge 1984; World Bank 1984: 19–20).

Anthropometric surveys from 1975 and 1979 reveal evidence of little malnutrition in urban areas but a continuing problem in rural ones. There is also considerable regional variation in the incidence of malnutrition. The 1979 survey of 16 provinces and centrally administered municipalities found that a national average of 2.6 per cent of urban and 12.7 per cent of rural 7-year-old boys were stunted.[11] Provincial rural rates (not including suburbs of municipalities) ranged up to 37.1 per cent in Sichuan. In seeking to explain these results, World Bank analysts argue that diarrhoeal diseases remain much more

[9] Lardy (1983a) reports an experiment in which the incidence of anaemia among children in one region was rapidly and sharply reduced by adding a small amount of beans to their diet.

[10] This 'steady' rise was interrupted by the famine of 1959–62. Life expectancy fell from 38 years in 1957 to 25 in 1960, according to World Bank estimates, before resuming its upward trend.

[11] However, the rural figure is biased downward because it includes suburban areas of major cities.

prevalent in rural than urban areas, and they also cite urban–rural differences in the quantity and quality of the diet (World Bank 1984: 31). No significant difference in incidence of stunting was found between males and females (World Bank 1984: 30, 32).

As a result of the agricultural reforms beginning in 1978, including rises in farm prices, encouragement of trade and diversification, and long-term household contracting of production, per capita consumption of food began to increase at substantially higher rates, as is shown in Tables 1.6, 1.7. Grain consumption per capita grew by almost 4 per cent between 1977 and 1984, compared with prior long-term rates of well under 1 per cent. Although absolute consumption levels of meat, fish, eggs, and other non-cereals are still

Table 1.6 Per capita consumption, various foods, selected years, China, 1952–1984 (kg)

Year	Grain	Edible oil	Pork	Beef, mutton	Poultry	Fresh eggs	Aquatic products
1952	197.67	2.05	5.92	0.92	0.43	1.02	2.67
1957	203.06	2.42	5.08	1.11	0.50	2.51	2.34
1962	164.63	1.09	2.22	0.79	0.38	1.53	2.96
1965	182.84	1.72	6.29	1.02	0.36	2.84	3.33
1970	187.22	1.61	6.02	0.82	0.32	2.64	2.94
1975	190.52	1.73	7.63	0.72	0.35	3.26	3.26
1976	190.28	1.60	7.38	0.66	0.35	3.52	3.52
1977	192.07	1.56	7.25	0.71	0.36	3.70	3.23
1978	195.46	1.60	7.67	0.75	0.44	3.94	3.50
1979	207.03	1.96	9.66	0.82	0.57	4.15	3.22
1980	213.81	2.30	11.16	0.83	0.80	4.54	3.41
1981	219.18	2.94	11.08	0.85	0.83	4.87	3.57
1982	225.46	3.54	11.76	1.03	1.02	5.05	3.85
1983	232.23	4.03	12.35	1.11	1.18	5.92	4.02
1984	251.34	4.70	13.02	1.25	1.35	7.81	4.36

Note: Grain is measured in 'trade grain'. 'Edible oil' refers to vegetable oil and includes the oil equivalent of oil-bearing crops.
Source: State Statistical Bureau (1985a: 576).

Table 1.7 Average annual growth rate of per capita consumption, various foods, selected years, China, 1952–1984 (%)

Years	Grain	Edible oil	Pork	Beef, mutton	Poultry	Fresh eggs	Aquatic products
1952–7	0.5	3.4	−3.0	3.8	0.03	19.7	26.6
1965–77	0.4	−0.8	1.2	−3.0	0.00	2.2	0.0
1977–84	3.9	17.3	8.7	8.6	21.50	11.6	4.5

Source: Table 1.6.

very low, their differentially high growth over recent years offers hope that the Chinese diet can finally begin to escape from its overwhelming dependence on cereals.

1.4. The famine of 1959–1962: extent and measurement

Fluctuations around the trend in food supply have created periods of extreme national shortage. The most serious such event was the famine of 1959–62, perhaps the greatest famine on record in terms of scale of loss of life. After rising by 2.6 per cent in 1958, foodgrain output fell sharply for the following two years to reach a 1960 nadir some 29 per cent below the 1958 peak (Table 1.4). The average per capita level of grain consumption in the countryside fell from 204 kg in 1957 to only 154 kg in 1961 (Table 1.9) and one estimate of national average per capita daily caloric intake in 1960 put it at only 1,453 calories (Table 1.5).[12]

Chinese reports at the time mentioned the existence of malnutrition, 'serious famine', and even 'starvation' (Walker 1977: 559) but did not report the magnitude of loss of life. More recent foreign analyses, based upon newly released mortality and fertility statistics for the years in question (see Table 1.8) as well as the population age distribution emerging from the 1964 and 1982 censuses, suggest an appalling loss (Aird 1980, 1982: Ashton *et al.* 1984; Coale 1981, 1984; Sun Yefang 1981). The increases in official mortality rates alone during 1959–61 imply deaths above the 'normal' level (defined by the 1957 mortality rate) numbering over 15 million. One estimate, that of Ashton *et al.* (1984), is almost twice this figure.[13] There remain many unanswered questions about the sources and quality of the statistics, which describe a period in which the statistical system itself was in disarray.[14] At this point no exact estimate of famine mortality can be accepted with confidence, but available information leaves little doubt that it was very large.

Both natural conditions and socio-political factors contributed to the situation, although their relative shares of the blame cannot be assessed with

[12] The method of estimation used by the Chinese government yields a higher calorie intake of 1,875 Kcal for 1960 (see Note to Table 1.5). Ashton *et al.* (1984: 622) put it at 1,535 Kcal for that year.

[13] This estimate, of 29.5 million premature deaths, also has problems associated with it. It results in part from an unrealistically low estimate of 'normal' deaths obtained by applying normal infant mortality rates to the abnormally small number of births that took place during the crisis. Furthermore, the ratio of child to adult mortality fluctuates in ways that are hard to explain. Unreported deaths are also assumed to fluctuate sharply—from 28 to 47% of actual deaths during the famine years.

[14] The fact that the regime which released these figures had an interest in discrediting its predecessor has led some to discount the figures themselves. My own view is that to have manufactured such enormous mortality statistics in order to attack the previous government would have been political overkill. To say that the figures were unlikely to have been deliberately inflated, however, is not to say that they are necessarily accurate. The fact is, nothing concrete is known about how they were arrived at.

confidence. Natural disasters were widespread, especially in 1960 (Freeberne 1962), but state policy undoubtedly contributed to the shortages, doing both short- and long-run damage to agriculture, as well as complicating and delaying relief measures. Construction of dams and reservoirs without prior assessment of their impact on the water table led to salinization and alkaliniza- tion of the soil. Such damage is not easily reversed and helps to explain why the collective grain output of the three North China Plain provinces of Henan, Hebei, and Shandong did not regain its previous peak level until the late 1960s (Walker 1977: 558). Innovations such as deep ploughing and close planting, promoted by the centre beyond the bounds of rationality, also reduced output, as did the excessive drain of labour out of agriculture and into small-scale industry and transport. The military organization of farm production and confiscation of peasants' personal property, especially in the earlier part of the Leap, the elimination in many places of farmers' private plots, the overcentral- ized and redistributive character of the early communes, and the adoption of a public dining hall system featuring free food all harmed peasant incentives.

Great Leap policies not only helped create the crisis but also caused costly delays in responding to it. The politically motivated exaggeration of harvest size and destruction of objective reporting systems kept the leadership in the dark about real supply conditions: 'Leaders believed in 1959–60 that they had 100 MMT more grain than they actually did' (Bernstein 1984a: 13). Some local cadres, their reputations dependent upon meeting impossibly high output commitments, failed to seek relief or even sealed their localities to keep news of real conditions from getting out.

Table 1.8 Demographic crisis and state procurement of foodgrains, China, 1955–1965

	Crude birth rate	Crude death rate	Natural increase rate	Grain output	State procurement		% of output procured	
					Total	Net	Total	Net
1955	32.60	12.28	20.32	183.9	50.7	36.2	27.6	19.7
1956	31.90	11.40	20.50	192.7	45.4	28.7	23.6	14.9
1957	34.03	10.80	23.23	195.0	48.0	33.9	24.6	17.4
1958	29.22	11.98	17.24	200.0	58.8	41.7	29.4	20.9
1959	24.78	14.59	10.19	170.0	67.4	47.6	39.7	28.0
1960	20.86	25.43	−4.57	143.5	51.1	30.9	35.6	21.5
1961	18.02	14.24	3.78	147.5	40.5	25.8	27.4	17.5
1962	37.01	10.02	26.99	160.0	38.1	25.7	23.8	16.1
1963	43.37	10.04	33.33	170.0	44.0	28.9	25.9	17.0
1964	39.14	11.50	27.64	187.5	47.4	31.8	25.3	17.0
1965	37.88	9.50	28.38	194.5	48.7	33.6	25.0	17.3

Note: 'Net' procurement refers to gross procurement minus resales to deficit areas in the countryside.

Source: State Statistical Bureau (1984c: 83, 370).

Excessive procurement of grain was a prime contributor to shortages in the countryside (Bernstein 1984a; Lardy 1983a). Under the mistaken belief that harvests had broken all records, the government in 1958, 1959, and 1960 procured 22 per cent, 40 per cent, and 6 per cent, respectively, more than in 1957 (Table 1.8). In 1957 gross procurement had come to 24.6 per cent of the harvest; by 1959 it had gone up to 39.7 per cent, and in the year of greatest crisis, 1960, it was 35.6 per cent of output. Even after resales to deficit rural areas it remained a full 10 percentage points higher in 1959 and 4 points higher in 1960 than in 1957. Rural areas were the chief sufferers: as Table 1.9 and Fig. 1.4 show, government efforts to keep the cities adequately supplied succeeded in suppressing rural per capita grain supplies well below urban supplies, where they stayed right up to the 1980s.[15] Substantial grain imports, designed to supply the coastal cities and relieve pressure on the countryside, finally began in 1961, two years late.[16]

Table 1.9 Annual per capita grain supply and daily food energy, China, 1957–1964

Year	Annual average per capita consumption of grain (kg)	
	National	(Rural)
1957	203	(204)
1958	198	(201)
1959	187	(183)
1960	164	(156)
1961	159	(154)
1962	165	(161)
1963	165	(160)
1964	182	(178)

Note: Data are in 'trade grain' and labelled 'pingjun meiren shenghuo xiaofei liang' (average per capita amount of consumption).

Source: State Statistical Bureau (1984a: 27).

[15] State Statistical Bureau (1984a: 27). State Statistical Bureau (1983b: 509) shows urban–rural differentials in calorie consumption ranging from 380 to 490 Kcal per day for every year from 1978 to 1982, whereas Fig. 1.4 indicates that rural inhabitants had a growing advantage in grain consumption from 1980 on. It is likely that city dwellers maintained their superiority with respect to non-grain foods, however.

[16] These imports, together with reduced procurement pressure on the countryside and the belated organization of relief measures—including stringent conservation measures, emergency food-growing campaigns, and vigorous redistribution to affected regions—probably provide a sufficient explanation for the fall in mortality after 1960 despite continued low levels of consumption and energy intake through 1963. Note also that the energy (Table 1.5) and per capita grain consumption (Table 1.9) series are from different sources; there is no immediate explanation for the fact that the former rises from 1960 to 1961 while the latter falls.

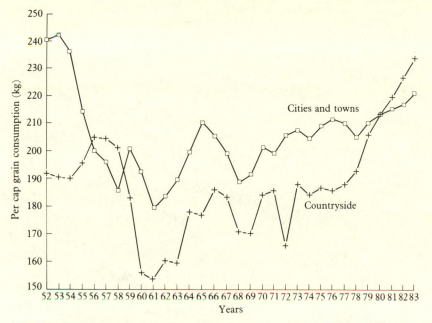

Fig. 1.4. Grain consumption per capita, urban vs. rural areas, China, 1952–1983

Party and government decisions worsened the crisis in more general ways, as well. Thus, Mao was in the process of moderating the policies of the Great Leap in 1959 when the popular Defence Minister and veteran revolutionary Peng Dehuai criticized them and thus indirectly challenged Mao's leadership at a meeting of the Party Central Committee. The purge of Peng Dehuai resulted in a resurrection of the excessive policies he had attacked, which must have deepened and prolonged the famine. Moreover, as Mao himself later acknowledged, preoccupation from late 1959 with the growing polemic with the Soviet Union slowed the leadership's perception of and response to the domestic crisis (Bernstein 1984a: 31; MacFarquhar 1983: parts iii and iv).[17]

In the 1959–61 famine, then, there was a complementarity between short-falls in supply, on the one hand, and deprivation of food entitlements, on the other. Policy was itself partly responsible for the fall in supply, as well as for the allocation of the resulting burden. The process of depriving those affected of their entitlements began with the wrecking of the food production system during the Great Leap Forward, continued with the abandonment of objective statistical reporting, which prevented remedial measures (including imports) from being undertaken until quite late, and ended with the state's overprocure-ment of grain to protect the cities and the leadership's preoccupation with domestic and foreign political matters.

Ordinarily, one would expect that in times of scarcity a greater than normal

[17] Much in the above paragraphs on the famine is taken from Riskin (1987: ch. 6).

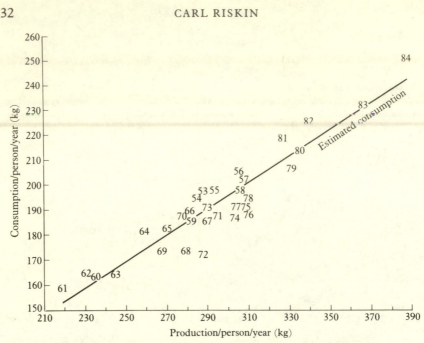

Fig. 1.5. Grain production and consumption, China, 1953–1984

proportion of food output would be eaten, as waste and non-food uses of grain are reduced and stocks consumed. Fig. 1.5 plots the regression of consumption on (half-year lagged) production (both per capita).[18] The bad years, 1960–2, are above the line as expected, but very close to it, while 1959 (probably because of the exceptionally large fraction of waste in the 1958 output) lies virtually on the line. More unexpectedly, other bad years, such as 1968, 1969, 1972, and 1977 (see Fig. 1.1), show consumption well *below* the line.

Part of the explanation may lie in a pronounced downward time trend through the 1970s—not captured in Fig. 1.5—in the fraction of lagged per capita production consumed. Fig. 1.6 shows this trend, and the fluctuations of the annual observations around it. The crisis years now emerge starkly, the fraction of output consumed rising well above the trend line. For subsequent bad years, especially 1968 and 1972, however, the unexpected outcome of Fig. 1.5 is accentuated, for these observations lie well below the trend line.

This suggests that stocks were not used very effectively to even out consumption over the harvest cycle during the chaotic period 1966–76, despite substantial annual food imports. Consumption seems to have been cut back at the first signs of an impending poor harvest. It then recovered whether the next harvest was better or not (in the latter event, 1969 being a case in point,

[18] The regression is of consumption on the average of current and previous year's output (since much of consumption is of the previous year's harvest): $C_t = a + \frac{1}{2}b(P_t + P_{t-1})$, where C = annual foodgrain consumption per capita, P = annual foodgrain production per capita, and t = year. The results are as follows: constant $a = 36.19$; production coefficient $b = 0.53$; $R^2 = 0.89$.

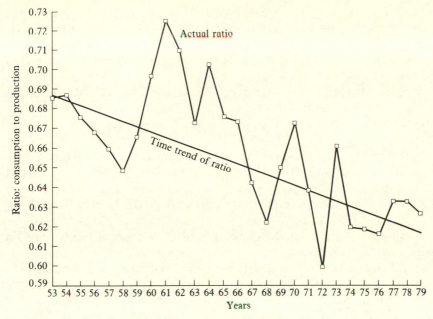

Fig. 1.6. Grain consumption per capita/production per capita, actual and trend, China, 1952–1979

presumably because stocks had been drawn down). We know that the capacity of the government to redistribute food spatially declined over the 1960s and 1970s (see section 1.6 below); it seems that its ability to redistribute temporally may also have suffered.

1.5. *Problems of food policy before the reform*

Chinese statistics show that per capita grain production levels of 1956–8 were not attained again until 1973 (see Table 1.4), and per capita grain 'livelihood consumption'[19] levels of 1956 were equalled again only in 1979 (State Statistical Bureau 1984a: 27). World Bank estimates of per capita calorie consumption find the 1958 level being matched in 1970 (Table 1.5). Although discussion of the standards and criteria that must lie behind evaluation —especially in a comparative context—is beyond the scope of this paper, it is hard to avoid the conclusion that the record of China's food provision up to the end of the 1970s suffered in some respects from deeply flawed policies (and, during the height of the factional strife throughout the 1966–76 decade, from the *absence* of coherent policy).

---

[19] As measured in 'trade grain'. 'Livelihood consumption' probably excludes grain consumed in the form of meat.

This impression is strengthened by the great success of agriculture in the years after 1977. Between that year and 1984, per capita foodgrain output increased by 31 per cent (Table 1.4) while other sectors of agriculture were growing even more quickly. It is widely believed that the basis for this rapid advance was laid in the 1960s and 1970s by such improvements as the extension of irrigated area, the adoption of improved varieties of wheat, rice, and other grains, the development of chemical fertilizer and pesticide industries, and the levelling and terracing of fields via winter 'farmland capital construction' work.

These positive developments of the collective era were prevented from bearing fruit in growing per capita supplies of food by policies that weakened farm incentives. The speed with which output bounded forward when incentives were restored implies that resources already in place were being productively reallocated.

Chief among the negative policies pre-1978 was that of local foodgrain self-sufficiency. Government policy strongly encouraged all regions to be self-sufficient in grains, including those with a long history of specialization in raising economic crops or livestock or in other non-grain activities. Because the state monopolized the grain trade and could withhold grain from areas that resisted abandoning their specialities, the localities had no choice but to comply. The result was that grain basket areas were deprived of their markets, while non-grain regions produced grain inefficiently.

Both objective circumstance and ideological predilection contributed to the policy of foodgrain self-sufficiency. Through much of the period in question, China's leaders felt threatened, first from the US, which was at war with Vietnam on China's border, then from the USSR. Local self-sufficiency was seen as part of a strategy of defence in depth against a threat from abroad. In addition, however, it seems that Mao Zedong and his followers in the leadership were intent on developing a form of economic organization that would minimize the bureaucratic hierarchies and rigidities associated with central administrative planning, yet without developing the role of the market as a substitute. As part of this quest, Mao had waged political war on the planning system and its upholders in the party and government, largely disabling it by the 1970s. The state in the end had neither the capacity nor the will to implement the complex redistribution of goods that would have been necessary had regional specialization and division of labour been encouraged. Local food self-sufficiency was, in the end, a principle dictated by necessity.[20]

The maintenance of low purchase prices for farm products was another policy that hurt production incentives. Table 1.10 shows official estimates of the commodity terms of trade between agriculture and industry from the 1930s until 1979. It is acknowledged in China that a 'scissors gap' has existed since the early days of the PRC and has functioned as a virtual tax on agriculture (the

---

[20] This thesis is argued in detail in Riskin (1987).

Table 1.10 Terms of trade between agriculture and industry, China, 1930–1936 to 1979 (official estimates)

Year	1950 = 100			Terms of trade (1936 = 100)
	Agricultural prices (1)	Industrial prices (2)	Terms of trade (1)/(2)	
1930–6 (av.)	49.6	37.6	131.9	100.0
1944	—	—	50.1	38.0
1948	—	—	79.1	60.0
1951	119.6	110.2	108.5	82.3
1952	121.6	109.7	110.8	84.0
1957	146.2	112.1	130.4	98.9
1962	193.4	126.6	152.8	115.8
1965	185.1	118.4	156.3	118.5
1975	208.7	109.6	190.4	144.4
1978	207.3	109.8	188.8	143.1
1979	265.5	109.9	241.6	183.1

Notes: Reprinted from Riskin (1987: Table 10.11), where sources are given. 'Agricultural prices' are 'purchase prices of agricultural and subsidiary products' and 'industrial prices' are 'retail prices of industrial goods in the countryside'.

actual tax having declined in importance since the early 1950s). Table 1.10 appears to show the gap narrowing substantially between the 1950s and late 1970s. Yet, despite the fact that one yuan of agricultural earnings apparently purchased 74 per cent more industrial goods in 1978 than in 1951, there were renewed complaints in the late 1970s that the scissors gap remained wide, and some even claimed it had widened, creating difficulties for the farmers and depressing their living standards.

The explanation for this apparent anomaly may lie in flaws in the price indices used in Table 1.10. The industrial index seems to be composed of the prices of traditional goods, such as kerosene, salt, sugar, and matches, and to omit highly priced modern producer goods, such as farm chemicals and machinery (Yang and Li 1980: 207). Prices of the latter kinds of goods were very high in China relative to their international levels. A kilogram of rice exchanged in China for less than half the amount of fertilizer it could command on the world market, and it took five or six times as much rice to purchase a tractor of given horsepower in China as in Japan (ibid.). These prices imposed heavy burdens on farmers who were increasingly dependent on modern inputs to overcome diminishing returns to scarce land. A national survey found that, between 1962 and 1976, production costs per hectare for six grain crops grew by 305 yuan, exceeding the gain in output value per hectare of Y249, and causing net income per hectare to fall (Yang and Li 1980: 207–8).

Farm prices also fared poorly against those of industrial consumer goods. A sample of the low exchange rate of rice against various consumer goods, relative to Hong Kong prices, is given in Table 1.11. Low farm prices not only hurt production incentives; they also contributed to the urban–rural gap in income and entitlement to food over much of the period (Fig. 1.4).

Table 1.11 Terms of trade between rice and selected industrial goods, Guangzhou and Hong Kong, mid-1970s

	No. of kg of husked, polished rice required to buy one unit in		Ratio: Guangzhou– Hong Kong
	Guangzhou	Hong Kong	
Portable radio (Guangzhou)	14.0	6.0	2.3
Thermos bottle (Guangzhou)	15.5	3.5	4.4
Sewing machine (Shanghai)	616.5	124.0	5.0
Bicycle (Shanghai)	582.0	110.5	5.3
Camera (Shanghai)	462.5	59.0	7.8
Alarm clock (Shanghai)	75.5	7.5	10.1

Note: Cities in parentheses indicate place of manufacture. Data refer to identical brands sold in Guangzhou and Hong Kong.
Source: Liu (1980: 5–6).

In 1978, the Central Committee raised farm prices sharply. Grain quota purchase prices were increased by 20 per cent, beginning with the summer harvest of 1979, and an additional 50 per cent premium was set for above-quota sales. Purchase prices of cotton, oil-bearing crops, sugar, and other farm and sideline products were also raised. The average price increase for all agricultural purchases was about 22 per cent (Cheng Zhiping 1983: 19). Smaller price hikes followed in subsequent years, and the proportion of state purchases at above-quota and negotiated prices also rose from negligible levels in 1977 to reach 60 per cent in 1981 (Travers 1984: 242). The resulting average purchase price increases in the years 1980–4 for farm and subsidiary goods were as follows (State Statistical Bureau 1986*b*: 623):

1980	7.1%
1981	5.9%
1982	2.2%
1983	4.4%
1984	4.0%

However, industrial prices also rose during the first half of the 1980s (Lardy 1983*a*: 192); agricultural means of production sold by state commercial organs rose 18 per cent between 1978 and 1984 (State Statistical Bureau 1985*a*: 533). It is thus unclear in what direction the commodity terms of trade moved after 1980.

However, farm purchasing power might be better gauged by either the single factoral or the income terms of trade.[21] Farm output and labour productivity both grew rapidly between 1978 and 1984. Their growth must have outpaced any conceivable decline in agriculture's commodity terms of trade, as farmers used their new freedom to select more profitable output mixes, and as the new incentives spurred them to greater effort and efficiency. Agriculture's income and single factoral terms of trade must therefore have improved, and with them farmers' access to industrial goods.[22]

Linked to the abandoned policies of grain self-sufficiency and low farm prices was that of state dictation to the communes. Nominally, the communes and their subunits were collectively owned, and policy should have been made by their members. The team leaders, in particular, were not state cadres but were paid out of team income. Like other commune cadres but more so, they owed their success not only to the ability to satisfy higher authorities, but also to their rapport with the villagers. The degree to which rural leaders exercised development initiative and also protected their constituents from the more arbitrary demands of the higher levels has probably been underestimated in recent indictments of the commune system.

However, it is also true that the ambiguous identity of the commune, which was the lowest level of state administration as well as a collective economic organization, facilitated the practice of the government issuing direct orders to the farmers. In the 1960s and 1970s this became common. Cropping patterns, technological choices, and income distribution all became subject to government determination. Not only did the workpoint system tend to produce a highly even intravillage distribution to minimize the social friction that differentiation would produce, but caps were put on personal income as a matter of state policy. Thus, even solidary collectives with relatively equal distribution could not hope to raise personal incomes commensurately with productivity.

Rhetorically, the post-1978 reforms were committed to respecting peasant and collective autonomy. The abandonment of the commune institution was justified because it removed the state from direct political control of farm production activities. The substitute *xiang* or township government is a purely political body. The death of the commune also meant the weakening of the structures of egalitarian distribution in the countryside. Individual household farming, under the encouragement of state policy favouring 'letting some get rich first', has encouraged those with superior skills, labour power, or political access to forge ahead of their less well-endowed neighbours. Collective

[21] The commodity terms of trade index N is here simply P_a/P_i (where P_a and P_i are price indexes for agricultural and industrial goods). The single factoral terms of trade, here $N \times Z_a$ (where Z_a is an index of farm labour productivity), measure changes in the command over industrial goods of a unit of agricultural labour. The income terms of trade, here $N \times Q_a$ (where Q_a is an index of agricultural output), measure changes in agriculture's overall access to industrial goods.

[22] I am indebted to Keith Griffin for this point.

autonomy and individual differentiation are two quite separate issues; China seems to have moved between the extremes of state-controlled collectives and family farms, bypassing autonomous collectives.[23]

1.6.   *Distribution of food*

Rationing, an ethic of relative equality as well as frugality, and powerful state organization have been credited with stretching meagre food supplies over China's enormous population so that the most extreme deprivation to be found in many other poor countries was on the whole avoided most of the time (the major exception, of course, being 1959–1961). Impressive statistics on life expectancy and infant mortality are consistent with this picture, and it is not contradicted by the observations of international observers.

The subject of food distribution is a good deal more complex than this, however, and the record has also varied substantially over time. The question of urban–rural differentials in food availability has already been touched on. This section will discuss the interprovincial and interpersonal dimensions of the Chinese approach to distribution.

(*a*).   *Variations by province*

Published reports in China in the late 1970s and early 1980s stated that in 1978 100 million peasants had yearly per capita grain rations of less than 150 kg (Jiang *et al.* 1980: 53); if ration is interpreted to mean consumption (it is probably lower than consumption),[24] this implies a daily intake of only 1,500 calories (Lardy 1982*a*: 161 n. 9). Such widespread want of food is not known to have existed in the 1950s. If in fact it was a new phenomenon, food distribution must have become more erratic[25] between that decade and the 1970s, since average per capita food availability (i.e. output plus imports) did not decrease. Indeed, the state's capacity to redistribute grain, especially between surplus and deficit provinces, may well have declined.

Interprovincial transfers of food are in the first instance a function of the overall 'commercialization rate', meaning the fraction of total output extracted from the producer by means of tax, quota sales, or market sales. Of this fraction, most is redistributed within the province of origin, but a portion

[23] This sentence oversimplifies a complex situation. Bernstein (1986: 2) brought back from his field study of rural structural reform a dominant impression that 'party, government and collective economic organizations continue to play a major role in the rural economy and indeed, in the ongoing reform process'.

[24] The term 'rations' (*kouliang*) is used in the source. 'Rations' are usually lower than total grain consumption (see Walker 1982: 578–82). The calorie figure in the text might thus underestimate actual consumption in the affected regions.

[25] Not necessarily more unequal. Declining ability to supply enough food to particular deficit regions can be compatible with growing average equality (as measured, e.g., by the coefficient of variation of provincial per capita consumption). This indeed is what seems to have happened, as the text below argues.

crosses provincial boundaries to feed major cities and deficit provinces and for export abroad.

Free market sales of basic foodgrains were illegal from the mid-1950s until the late 1970s; during that period virtually all 'marketed' grain (except an indeterminate amount that entered the black market) was procured by the government through tax and purchase quotas. From the late 1970s on, however, grain was increasingly available on the free market. Total purchases (including tax extraction, and measured in trade grain) rose from 51 million metric tons in calendar 1978 to 117 MMT in 1984 (State Statistical Bureau 1985a: 480); although a growing portion of this took the form of direct sales by farmers to the non-agricultural population,[26] the great bulk was bought by the state, which was accordingly subject to a growing financial and logistical burden. In 1985, the state shed its role of guaranteed buyer of last resort, limiting its purchase to 75 MMT of rice, wheat, and corn, and the rest of the surplus was sold on the market (Erisman 1986: 20).

The declining role of the state in redistributing foodgrain is pictured in Table 1.12. Total tax plus purchases declined as a fraction of grain output from 25–30 per cent in the 1950s to only 20–1 per cent in the 1970s (col. 5). Out of this, an average of 18 per cent of total output was kept during the First Plan period of 1953–7 to feed the cities and build up stocks. This category had slipped to about 16 per cent during the 1962–77 period (col. 6). The last column shows what was resold to deficit areas of the countryside. Never a large share of output, it nevertheless fell from an average of 8.6 per cent during the First Plan period to 5.7 per cent during the years 1966–76. If indeed 100 to 150 million people were unable to provide themselves with sufficient food, the small fractions of the harvest available for state relief would not seem to have been enough to meet the need.

In the 1950s, vigorous government commerce in grain played a role in evening out provincial consumption. Table 1.13 gives K. Walker's estimates of the provincial distributions of per capita net output and consumption for the First Plan period. Output varied from Hebei's 195 kg to Heilongjiang's 756, a range of 3.9. The coefficient of variation was 35 per cent. After state redistribution, the range for consumption was reduced to 2.2 and the coefficient of variation to 20 per cent.

Table 1.14, columns 1 and 2, presents the provincial distributions for 1979 of per capita "availabilities' of grain and total energy. Unfortunately, these estimates unlike Walker's do not take into account interprovincial (or international) trade; to the degree that trade redistributed food among provinces, therefore, the term 'availability' is a misnomer.

Grain imports (shown in Table 1.15 and Fig. 1.7, along with exports) have

---

[26] Chinese grain trade statistics are ambiguous as to coverage. They explicitly include the agricultural tax, purchases by state commercial, industrial, and other departments, and direct purchases by the non-agricultural population from peasants. They appear to exclude direct market transactions within agriculture, e.g. market purchases by non-grain-growing farmers.

Table 1.12 Foodgrain procurement (unprocessed grain), China, 1952–1984

Grain year[a]	Output (MMT)	Marketing[b] Total (MMT)	Net[c] (MMT)	Annual increase in marketing	Gross marketing ratio (2)/(1)	Net marketing ratio (3)/(1)	Proportion of output resold to countryside (5) − (6)
	(1)	(2)	(3)	(4)	(5)	(6)	(7)
1952	163.92	33.3	28.19		0.20	0.17	0.03
1953	166.83	47.5	35.89	42.7	0.28	0.22	0.07
1954	169.52	51.8	31.59	9.2	0.31	0.19	0.12
1955	183.94	50.7	36.18	−2.1	0.28	0.20	0.08
1956	192.75	45.4	28.70	10.5	0.24	0.15	0.09
1957	195.05	48.0	33.87	5.7	0.25	0.17	0.07
1958	200.00	58.8	41.73	22.3	0.29	0.21	0.09
1959	170.00	67.4	47.57	14.7	0.40	0.28	0.12
1960	143.50	51.1	30.90	−24.3	0.36	0.22	0.14
1961	147.50	40.5	25.81	−20.7	0.27	0.17	0.10
1962	160.00	38.2	25.72	−5.7	0.24	0.16	0.08
1963	170.00	44.0	28.92	15.2	0.26	0.17	0.09
1964	187.50	47.4	31.85	7.9	0.25	0.17	0.08
1965	194.53	48.7	33.60	2.7	0.25	0.17	0.08
1966	214.00	51.6	38.24	5.9	0.24	0.18	0.06
1967	217.82	49.4	37.74	−4.3	0.23	0.17	0.05
1968	209.06	48.7	37.87	−1.4	0.23	0.18	0.05
1969	210.97	46.7	33.83	−4.1	0.22	0.16	0.06
1970	239.96	54.4	42.02	16.6	0.23	0.18	0.05
1971	250.14	53.0	39.82	−2.6	0.21	0.16	0.05
1972	240.48	48.3	33.92	−8.9	0.20	0.14	0.06
1973	264.94	56.1	41.01	16.2	0.21	0.15	0.06
1974	275.27	58.1	43.98	3.5	0.21	0.16	0.05
1975	284.52	60.9	43.98	4.8	0.21	0.15	0.06
1976	286.31	58.3	40.72	−4.3	0.20	0.14	0.06
1977	282.73	56.6	37.56	−2.8	0.20	0.13	0.07
1978	304.77	61.7	42.71	9.1	0.20	0.14	0.06
1979	332.12	72.0	51.70	16.6	0.22	0.16	0.06
1980	320.56	73.0	47.97	1.4	0.23	0.15	0.08
1981	325.02	78.5	48.77	7.5	0.24	0.15	0.09
1982	354.50	91.9	52.02	17.0	0.26	0.15	0.11
1983	387.28	119.9	85.27	30.5	0.31	0.22	0.09
1984	407.31	141.7	94.61	18.2	0.35	0.23	0.12

[a] The grain year runs from 1 Apr. to the following 31 Mar.
[b] 'Marketing' includes tax procurements, state quota purchases and above-quota purchases, and free market sales.
[c] 'Net' refers to total marketing less state resales to the countryside.

Source: State Statistical Bureau (1983b: 393; 1985a: 482).

Table 1.13 Walker's estimates of provincial rural per capita net grain production and consumption in China (averages for 1953–1957)

	Net output per capita (kg)	Grain consumption per capita (kg)
North-east		
Liaoning	348	297
Jilin	562	355
Heilongjiang	756	424
North		
Hebei	195	195
Shanxi	254	196
Inner Mongolia	433	249
East		
Jiangsu	291	230
Zhejiang	338	271
Anhui	313	262
Fujian	307	259
Jiangxi	375	278
Shandong	233	210
Central south		
Henan	233	204
Hubei	343	297
Hunan	307	258
Guangdong	327	276
Guangxi	294	234
South-west		
Sichuan	294	240
Guizhou	277	213
Yunnan	296	247
North-west		
Shaanxi	282	229
Gansu	269	217
Qinghai	267	233
Xinjiang	271	227
Average	327.71	255.04
Range	3.9	2.2
Coefficient of variation	35%	20%

Notes: Estimates of consumption are based on production and procurement data, and are net of estimated seed and livestock feed uses as well as of loss from storage. Tibet is omitted.

Source: Walker (1984*b*: 107).

Table 1.14 Per capita food supply by province, China, 1979 and 1984

	1979			1984		
	Grain 'availability' (kg) (1)	Energy (Kcal) (2)	Grain output per capita (kg) (3)	Total output of grains (MMT) (4)	Population (m.) (5)	Grain output per capita (kg) (6)
North-east						
Liaoning	186.11	2,139	338	14.26	36.55	390.15
Jilin	222.69	2,476	408	16.34	22.84	715.41
Heilongjiang	259.59	2,888	462	17.57	32.95	533.23
North						
Hebei	206.38	2,313	325	18.70	54.87	340.81
Shanxi	184.40	2,041	294	8.72	26.00	335.38
Inner Mongolia	159.00	1,882	253	5.95	19.85	299.50
East						
Jiangsu	255.38	2,888	402	33.54	61.71	543.43
Zhejiang	249.22	2,863	393	18.17	39.93	455.05
Anhui	205.62	2,394	315	22.03	51.03	431.61
Fujian	182.96	2,318	308	8.51	26.77	317.71
Jiangxi	241.90	2,735	379	15.49	34.21	452.79
Shandong	203.91	2,549	330	30.40	76.37	398.06
Central south						
Henan	182.33	2,106	292	28.94	76.46	378.43
Hubei	243.25	2,758	368	22.63	48.76	464.11
Hunan	254.76	2,906	411	26.13	55.61	469.88
Guangdong	183.55	2,313	303	19.73	61.66	319.90
Guangxi	202.93	2,434	331	12.13	38.06	318.71

	Col. 1	Col. 2	Col. 3	Col. 4	Col. 5	Col. 6
South-west						
Sichuan	194.85	2,364	321	40.80	101.12	403.43
Guizhou	134.05	1,577	234	7.58	29.32	258.53
Yunnan	149.95	1,758	269	10.05	33.62	298.93
Tibet	154.45	1,926	232	0.50	1.97	251.27
North-west						
Shaanxi	197.22	2,190	293	10.24	29.66	345.08
Gansu	152.21	1,722	251	5.40	20.16	267.61
Qinghai	147.04	1,865	238	1.01	4.02	251.24
Ningxia	181.13	1,995	315	1.54	4.06	379.31
Xinjiang	197.45	2,228	306	4.97	13.44	369.79
Central cities						
Beijing				2.18	9.47	229.67
Shanghai				2.53	12.05	209.54
Tianjin				1.32	7.99	164.58
Average	197.40	2,293.38	321.96	38.50		384.21
Standard deviation	35.90	381.97	59.19			104.08
Coefficient of variation	18.2%	16.7%	18.4%			27.1%
Maximum	259.59	2,906	462			715.41
Minimum	134.05	1,577	232			251.24
Range	1.94	1.84	1.99			2.85

Notes: Col. 1: Piazza (1983: 115). Provincial grain output net of processing, waste, seed use, and other non-human food end uses. Figures exclude interprovincial and international trade in grains.

Col. 2: World Bank (1984: 166). Figures exclude interprovincial and international trade.

Col. 3: Walker (1984b: 169). Refers to average for 1978–80. Figure for Tibet estimated from output given in Chang Zizhong and Luo Hanxian (1982: 55) and provincial population given in Hu Qiaomu (1980: 114).

Cols. 4–5: State Statistical Bureau (1985a: 19, 38).

Col. 6: col. 4 divided by col. 5.

Table 1.15 Foodgrain imports and exports,
China, 1952–1984 (m. metric tons)

Year	Imports	Exports
1950	0.06	1.23
1951	0.00	1.97
1952	0.00	1.53
1953	0.01	1.83
1954	0.03	1.71
1955	0.18	2.23
1956	0.15	2.67
1957	0.17	2.09
1958	0.22	2.88
1959	0.00	4.16
1960	0.07	2.72
1961	5.81	1.35
1962	4.92	1.03
1963	5.95	1.49
1964	6.57	1.82
1965	6.41	2.42
1966	6.44	2.89
1967	4.70	2.99
1968	4.60	2.60
1969	3.79	2.24
1970	5.36	2.12
1971	3.17	2.62
1972	4.76	2.95
1973	8.13	3.89
1974	8.12	3.64
1975	3.74	2.81
1976	2.37	1.76
1977	7.34	1.67
1978	8.83	1.88
1979	12.36	1.65
1980	13.43	1.62
1981	14.81	1.26
1982	16.12	1.25
1983	13.44	1.96
1984	10.45	3.57
1985	5.97	9.33

Source: State Statistical Bureau (1983*b*: 422, 438; 1985*a*:
510, 517; 1986*b*: 569, 572).

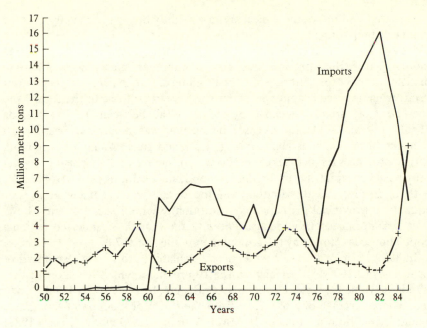

Fig. 1.7. Foodgrain imports and exports by volume, China, 1950–1984

gone chiefly to feed the coastal cities, especially Beijing, Tianjin, and Shanghai.[27] Their omission therefore has minor impact on the distribution. As for interprovincial trade, this has been declining since the 1950s. The number of provinces that shipped grain out declined from 15 in 1965 to 8 in 1978 (Piazza 1983: 41). Interprovincial cereal exports appear to have dropped from 7.85 MMT in 1953 (5.5 per cent of national output) to 4.7 MMT in 1965 (2.8 per cent of output); in 1978 they were only 2.05 MMT (less than 1 per cent of output), of which all but about 0.325 MMT were destined for export abroad (Lardy 1982*b*). This trend was closely connected to the grain self-sufficiency policy, the reasons for which were discussed in section 1.5 above. In short, for both ideological and practical reasons, and because Mao's assault on the central planning structure effectively disabled it, the central government largely abandoned the business of shipping grain between provinces.

If the state had only a minimal effect on the provincial distribution of grain in 1979, then the range (1.94) and coefficient of variation (18.2 per cent) of provincial grain 'availability' shown in Table 1.14 represent fairly well the distribution of provincial per capita consumption even after state

---

[27] Omitting the effects of trade, therefore, causes consumption in these cities to be grossly underestimated; they have therefore been left out of Table 1.14. These three municipalities have the status of provinces. They are therefore not part of other provinces and their omission does not distort the other figures.

intervention.[28] Both of these measures are slightly below their 1950s level for grain consumption (Table 1.13).

On average, then, it seems that the interprovincial grain distribution became more equal.[29] But this was due not to improved mechanisms for state distribution of output but rather to the levelling of provincial per capita output itself: while average output was about the same in 1979 as in the 1950s, the coefficient of variation declined by almost a half between the two periods (Tables 1.13 and 1.14). In this case, the levelling was mostly downward, with high producers, such as Heilongjiang, Jilin, and Inner Mongolia, declining and no provinces rising to take their place. The net result of increasingly equal provincial per capita output, on the one hand, and declining state involvement with interprovincial distribution, on the other, was a somewhat greater equality of provincial per capita consumption. Such a rise in equality, however, was not necessarily inconsistent with the growth of underfed regional populations, as claimed by the government in the late 1970s.

In 1979, to increase per capita energy availability to Piazza's standard of sufficiency (2,160 Kcal per day) in the 10 provinces which fell short of that standard (Table 1.14, col. 2), and to bring Beijing, Shanghai, and Tianjin up to the national average of 2,600 Kcal from their own production of foodgrain, would have required a total of 10 MMT of unprocessed wheat (Piazza 1983: 43). This amount is approximately equal to China's net grain import in 1979. Even without interprovincial redistribution, therefore, China could have met minimum standards in all provinces (disregarding problems of intraprovincial distribution) on the basis of local production plus imports. It is likely, however, that imports served rather to raise urban standards well above the national average, and that poor provinces such as Guizhou, Gansu, Yunnan, and Qinghai were left short.

The picture changed greatly in 1984 (Table 1.14, col. 6). The average provincial output per capita was substantially above that of the 1950s. While the coefficient of variation rose above that of 1979, it remained below the 1950s level; moreover, every province but one (Guangxi) experienced growth in per capita output between 1979 and 1984. In addition, the proportion of the much larger harvest resold to deficit areas of the countryside also rose—from 7 per cent of national output in 1979 to 12 per cent in 1984 (Table 1.12, col. 7). Thus, the increase in provincial inequality in per capita production would seem to be a small price to pay for advance along a wide front and the redistribution of greater surpluses. Indeed, if a combination of state commercial organs and the market can handle the task of supplying grain-deficit regions, then the goal of

[28] Table 1.14 also gives provincial figures for per capita energy availability and grain output. As can be seen, the magnitudes of relative variation are closely similar for all three variables.

[29] This conclusion is tentative because the data for the two periods are not strictly comparable, while the differences between the two ranges and coefficients of variation may be too small to be of much significance.

provincial specialization and division of labour would seem more effective in feeding China than that of provincial grain self-sufficiency.

(*b*)   *Personal distribution*

There are no published data on personal distribution of food, or of cereal, as far as I am aware. Income data have been used by the World Bank to construct estimates of the distribution of personal income in urban and in rural China. Their estimate of the Gini coefficient for the rural income distribution in 1982 is 0.225, well below the Ginis of other South Asian countries (0.30–0.35). Substantial remaining inequality is largely interregional. The Bank characterizes urban inequality as 'uniquely low . . . with virtually no extreme poverty in urban areas' (World Bank 1985: Main Report, p. 29); the estimated Gini coefficient for 1981 is 0.16 (World Bank 1981: 59).[30] One can infer similar degrees of equality in distribution of food entitlements, but direct data are lacking.

This discussion is therefore confined to the changing methods, with their implications for the personal distribution, by which individuals have gained entitlement to food. In the villages, before the return of family farming (practices after the reforms are discussed below), peasants received rations in two basic ways (see below). They paid an agricultural tax, largely in grain, and were obliged to sell to the state quotas (and above-quota amounts) that were calculated on output above a subsistence ration. The state undertook to resell grain at quota prices to food-deficit localities. Because most redistribution in recent years has been *intra*provincial (and of this much may have been confined within smaller administrative units, such as the district), the guaranteed minimum consumption standard has varied geographically, a common figure being 200 unprocessed kg in rice regions (providing about 1,400 Kcal and 25 grams of protein) and 150 kg elsewhere (if wheat this would provide about 1,250 Kcal and 35 grams of protein) (World Bank 1984: 80).

Land reform and collectivization in the 1950s probably resulted in a marked gain in equality of food distribution in rural areas, both among regions and among individuals within a locality, because these institutional changes eliminated property income, the largest source of intraregional income inequality, and established institutions for food redistribution. The policies of the 1960s and 1970s, on the other hand, may have increased disparities among localities[31] while maintaining (and possibly increasing) equality of distribution *within* localities.

There were two basic methods of grain distribution to members of a production team. First, grain was distributed on a per capita basis according to the age and sex of each family member. This grain (called 'basic grain') was

---

[30] China's overall distribution is less impressive than that of either of these components, however, because of the remaining sizeable urban–rural gap.

[31] However, the discussion of section 1.6*a* above concluded that disparities among *provinces* seem to have further narrowed on average, but not to the benefit of at least some poor regions.

debited to the family's account with the collective, and in principle had to be paid for at the post-harvest settling of accounts. Second, grain distribution was tied to workpoint earnings, and thus to earning power. A small amount of grain might also be distributed in exchange for household manure.

The relative importance of basic grain and workpoint grain in total grain distribution varied greatly among localities. Villages stressing basic grain tended to have more equal food distribution and greater security for their poor members. In practice, going into debt to the collective for basic grain and postponing repayment was one method by which families in difficult circumstances could survive. Villages where work-point grain was stressed in order to promote work incentives tended to have less equal distribution. 'The proportion of basic or work-point grain is then a matter of intense and volatile debate, with local systems changing with the current political wind and with the changing needs and desires of team members and their leaders' (Parish and Whyte 1978: 66).[32] The Cultural Revolution of the late 1960s brought about a move to equal distribution, the reaction of the early 1970s a return to more workpoint grain. Parish and Whyte (1978: 69–70) found a link between village affluence and reliance on 'basic grain'. In their sample of villages, higher income, consumption, and land–labour ratios were associated with greater willingness to share food equally.

Basic and workpoint grain seem to have disappeared as a result of the reforms. Now, grain-growing households keep the excess of their output above what is due in tax, contracted sales (formerly quota sales), and contribution to the collective accumulation and welfare funds. Non-grain-growing households commonly are allotted 'ration land' (*kouliang tian*), on which to grow food for their own needs, in addition to their contract land (Bernstein 1986). Presumably, households unable to grow enough food must buy it with their earnings on the open market, unless they are 'five-guarantee' or 'hardship' households that qualify for public assistance.

The rural elderly do not have access to a government pension system, as do full-status workers and staff in state enterprises. In the villages grown children (sons, in practice, since daughters marry out of the village) are expected to care for their aged parents. Those without grown sons to support them may become 'five-guarantee households' (guaranteed food, clothing, housing, medical care, and burial expenses by their collective). The collective usually tries to provide them with sideline employment and a plot of land as a means of supplementing their incomes.

In the 37 Guangdong production teams studied by Parish and Whyte in the 1970s, only 1.24 persons per team, or 6 per cent of all people over age 60, received five-guarantee help. This system persists into the post-reform era: a

---

[32] This discussion of rural distribution depends heavily on Parish and Whyte (1978) in its depiction of the pre-1978 situation. See below for discussion of the changes brought about by household contracting.

Shandong village of 283 households visited in 1985 by T. Bernstein had three five-guarantee households. Each got 200 kg of grain, 200 yuan in cash, free medical care, and 500 yuan for funeral expenses (Bernstein 1986: 16).

Assistance has been available through various channels to ordinary households in difficulty because of injury, illness, or simply lack of labour power. The team or village might provide extra employment to the children or elderly in the family, make available low-cost loans or direct grants, or permit a household to overdraw indefinitely on its grain account. Much help has also taken the more traditional form of informal assistance based on kinship (Parish and Whyte 1978: 76–7).

With the transformation of the old commune system and the adoption of household farming, collective welfare services broke down in some places. Beggars, some of them peasant migrants, again appeared at railway stations and thoroughfares. The government has put renewed stress on helping poor areas and households. Bernstein (1986: 16) was told that 5 to 6 per cent of households in Anhui Province were classified as hardship cases eligible to receive assistance. The approach taken was to help such households achieve self-sufficiency and avoid long-term dependence on welfare. Policies include reduction or remittance of taxes, provision of low-interest loans, priority in purchasing output and in supplying improved seed and other farm inputs, subsidies to buy such inputs, and provision of technical education and advice (FBIS, 7 Jan. 1985: K17).[33] Cadres in some areas have taken it upon themselves to help indigent families work out plans to overcome their problems (Hinton 1983: 22; *Beijing Review*, 3 (1981) and 5 (1982); Jing Wei 1983: 20–1). A good deal of pressure seems to have been put on the new village entrepreneurs to develop their philanthropic impulses, and stories abound of the emerging élite privately building old-age homes, establishing local schools, or subsidizing the electrification of their village.[34] Chinese commentators point out that, even amidst the general advance of recent years, 'comparatively speaking, poverty-stricken "pockets" exist everywhere. In the whole nation, there are tens of millions of people whose problems regarding food and clothing have not been completely solved' (*Renmin Ribao*, 8 Feb. 1986, trans.

[33] Curiously, the Minister of Civil Affairs, discussing aid to the poor in Jan. 1985, 'pledged' that 'his ministry would continue to raise money to support the poorer peasants', making it sound more like a private charitable organization than one funded by the state budget.

[34] A recent article on combating poverty in China's richest county, Wuxi (Jiangsu Province), captures the flavour of current policy: 'In the work to help poor households, the county adopted a method of state subsidies, collective assistance, and mutual help among the masses in order to collect funds through various channels. . . . The county's civil affairs, grain, and supply and marketing departments also did what they could to make things easy for this work in financial affairs and material supply as well as in production and sales . . . (V)arious areas have . . . adopted various measures such as giving priority to poor households to work in the town and township enterprises or in initiating social welfare work. . . . At the same time, they also enthusiastically encourage all kinds of specialized households to encourage poor households and to let the rich help the poor' (*Guangming Ribao* (Beijing), 8 Feb. 1986, trans. FBIS, 24 Feb. 1986, p. K17).

Table 1.16 Grain rations, Chengdu, 1982 (kg/month)

Category	Ration
Age	
Below 1 year	4.0
1 year	5.5
2 years	6.5
3 years	7.5
4 years	8.5
5 years	9.0
6 years	10.0
7 years	10.5
8 years	11.0
9 years	12.0
10 years	12.5
Senior middle school students	16.0
University students	17.2
'Ordinary persons'	13.5
Office worker	14.0
Manual labourer	22.5–25

Note: Rations vary somewhat by location. Thus, a male office worker in Beijing was entitled to 17 kg rather than 14, a female office worker to 15 rather than 14. The vegetable oil and sugar rations in all three locations noted by the World Bank were 0.25 kg each.

Source: World Bank (1984: 168).

FBIS, 24 Feb. 1986, p. K16).[35] But detailed statistics on the extent of the problem have not been published.

In urban areas, formal rationing of cereals and edible vegetable oils has existed since 1955. A grain ration schedule from Chengdu, in Sichuan Province, is given in Table 1.16. Rationing has undoubtedly served to equalize food distribution within urban areas. With grain relatively scarce during much of China's recent history, urban rationing also served to assure a stable and equitable supply for city residents. Under more recent conditions of relative grain abundance and a growing free market in grain, and given the unusual degree of income equality in urban China, urban rationing may have lost much of its rationale. It may also have contributed to exacerbating the urban–rural gap by safeguarding the urban population's access to relatively stable supplies of cheap grain while giving rise to wider annual fluctuations in per capita supplies in the countryside.

Certainly, the state subsidy of urban grain consumption, occasioned by the rising spread between state purchase and sales prices since the mid-1960s, has

[35] There is some evidence that recent policy has in fact exacerbated the situation of many rural poor by eliminating collective food supports and in various other ways rendering their economic position more precarious. See Unger and Xiong (1990).

been a significant contributor to the urban–rural income differential. State losses from this spread averaged 4 billion yuan per year between 1974 and 1978. They came to almost 2 per cent of national income in the latter year or over 179 yuan per state employee (almost 30 per cent of the average annual wage) (Lardy 1983b: 193). Moreover, as farm procurement prices were raised after 1978 and the state bought increasing percentages of the harvest at above-quota and high negotiated prices, the subsidy of urban consumption grew rapidly. Lardy estimates that all urban food subsidies in 1981 (including those on imported grain and on non-staple foods) amounted to 6.4 per cent of official national income (roughly net domestic material product), or 30.5 per cent of the total wage bill of state workers, or one quarter of revenue of all levels of government (1983b: 194–5). These large subsidies were available to only 16–17 per cent of the population. Their contribution to government budget deficits in the late 1970s and early 1980s was a principal reason for the decontrol of non-staple food prices in 1985 and the switch from mandatory quotas to contract purchases from the peasants.

1.7. *Conclusion*

Certain points in this broad survey deserve a summary reprise.

1. The discussion of institutional development found that the rural collective institutions in place until the end of the 1970s played a role in bringing about the growth of food production and, through relatively egalitarian distribution methods *within* collectives, in ensuring the adequacy of food consumption of poor members. However, the 'workpoint' system of distribution was bound to lose its motivational efficacy as the national political atmosphere became fractious and national policies toward the countryside became increasingly inequitable. Rural communes also suffered from the propensity of the party and government to administer them as if they were state institutions, and to adopt policies, such as those of low farm prices and local foodgrain self-sufficiency, that imposed hardships on both advanced and backward regions.

2. Average per capita food energy availability fluctuated around a flat trend for two decades after 1952, then began rising. China did not exceed the peak 1950s level of average calorie consumption until the early 1970s. Foodgrain production per capita exceeded the 1956–8 level only in 1973. From 1978 to 1984, grain consumption per capita grew quite rapidly, and the diet began to diversify as a result of differentially high growth rates of meat, dairy, and aquatic products.

3. Available evidence indicates that the famine which occurred in 1959–61 was of calamitous proportions. Official government mortality statistics imply a total excess mortality of more than 15 million during those years, and some Western estimates run considerably higher. However, many questions remain about the famine itself and the statistics concerning it, and no precise estimate of mortality can be made with confidence. State policy contributed to the

severity and duration of the crisis in both direct and indirect ways. In this famine, the deprivation of food entitlements began with the destructive effects of state policy on food production itself; later, mistaken distribution policies (such as overprocurement of grain from the peasants) contributed to the disaster.

4. The rapid advances in food production and consumption after 1978 owed much to the elimination of negative incentive policies in place earlier, and of the institutional framework supporting such policies. At the same time, these advances were also due to infrastructural developments and the equalization of access to land that occurred during the era of collective agriculture.

5. Malnutrition appears to be only a slight problem in urban China, but may be a much more substantial one in the countryside, where it is also subject to great regional variation.

6. Food distribution has developed differently, according to which of its several dimensions is examined. Average variation among provinces in per capita grain consumption declined between the 1950s and the 1970s, but in a manner that apparently permitted the growth of large underfed regional populations—not a happy result of greater equality. Conversely, general but differentially rapid growth from 1978 to 1984, together with a more vigorous government redistributive role, seems to have significantly reduced regional insufficiency of food supply.

With respect to the personal distribution of food, very low Gini coefficients in the early 1980s for urban and rural income distributions, taken separately, may imply similarly great equality in food availability, but direct data are lacking. The elimination of the collective system of distribution in the countryside, and the erosion of collective welfare institutions that accompanied the reversion to household farming, created new hardships for some households ill equipped to cope with the new conditions. The Chinese government has stressed the need to provide aid in such cases, but the extent and degree of success of its assistance programmes is not yet known.

Space does not permit an exploration of many other issues relevant to China's food situation, e.g. the record of state investment in agriculture; the government's plans for price reform; the unexpectedly sharp inflation in non-staple food prices brought about by decontrol in 1985; the expressed plan drastically to reduce the fraction of the labour force in agriculture by the end of the century; the intent to adopt and popularize Western types of processing and fast food services. Through these various issues runs the basic and still unresolved question of how to combine planning and state control with family farming and a free market. In the urban industrial sector a viable plan–market mix is even farther from achievement; yet agriculture depends increasingly on industry for inputs and on the cities for markets. Despite the early success of the reforms, China's food problem is far from solved.[36]

---

[36] Grain output has fallen short of the 1984 peak in all subsequent years up to 1989.

What is notable about China's experience is its extraordinary range. When Mao Zedong was the pre-eminent force in the country, he had and used the authority to implement unprecedented experiments in organization and distribution. At the same time, the existence of major differences within the leadership has meant that economic policy, including food policy, changed dramatically when the balance of power within the party shifted. As a result, a great variety of organizational and institutional forms have been tried in the quest for growth and equity. After early progress there was an extended period in which improvements in the quantity and quality of diet were not forthcoming, and the population at times paid a very high price for ill-considered experiments. The mixed record of the reform years since 1978 leaves very much open the question whether the lessons of almost four decades of experience will be used to devise vigorous yet equitable policies capable of bringing food security to China's people.

References

AIRD, JOHN S. (1980), 'Reconstruction of an Official Data Model of the Population of China' (US Department of Commerce, Bureau of the Census, May).

——(1982), 'Population Studies and Population Policy in China', *Population and Development Review*, 8.

——(1983), 'The Preliminary Results of China's 1982 Census', *China Quarterly*, 96.

——(1984), 'Age Distribution of China's Population', *Beijing Review*, 3.

ASH, ROBERT (1976), 'Economic Aspects of Land Reform in Kiangsu, 1949–52', *China Quarterly*, 66 (June) and 67 (Sept.).

ASHTON, BASIL, HILL, KENNETH, PIAZZA, ALAN, and ZEITZ, ROBIN (1984), 'Famine in China, 1958–61', *Population and Development Review*, 10.

BANISTER, JUDITH (1984a), 'An Analysis of Recent Data on the Population of China', *Population and Development Review*, 10.

——(1984b), 'Population Policy and Trends in China, 1978–83', *China Quarterly*, 100.

BERNSTEIN, THOMAS P. (1984a), 'Stalinism, Famine, and Chinese Peasants', *Theory and Society*, 13.

——(1984b), 'Reforming China's Agriculture', paper prepared for the conference 'To Reform the Chinese Political Order', June 1984, Harwichport, Mass., sponsored by the Joint Committee on Chinese Studies of the ACLS and the SSRC.

——(1986), 'Local Political Authorities and Economic Reform: Observations from Two Counties in Shandong and Anhui, 1985', paper prepared for presentation at the Conference on Market Reforms in China and Eastern Europe, Santa Barbara, Calif. 8–11 May.

BUCK, JOHN LOSSING (1956), *Land Utilization in China* (New York: Paragon Book Reprint Corporation).

CHANG ZIZHONG and LUO HANXIAN (eds.) (1982), *Zhongguo Nongye Nianjian 1980* (Agricultural Yearbook of China), excerpts with tables translated, in Joint Publications Research Service, *China Report, Agriculture*, No. 192, JPRS 80270, Mar.

CHEN KAIGUO (1982), 'A Tentative Inquiry into the Scissors Gap in the Rate of Exchange between Industrial and Agricultural Products', *Social Sciences in China*, 2.

CHEN, S. C., and RIDLEY, CHARLES P. (1969), *The Rural People's Communes in Lien-chiang* (Stanford, Calif.: The Hoover Institution).

CHENG ZHIPING (Director of State Price Bureau) (1983), Interview in *Beijing Review*, 35 (29 Aug.).

COALE, ANSLEY J. (1981), 'Population Trends, Population Policy, and Population Studies in China', *Population and Development Review*, 7/1 (Mar.).

——(1984), *Rapid Population Change in China, 1952–1982*, Report no. 27 (Committee on Population and Demography, Washington, DC: National Academy Press).

'Communiqué of the Third Plenary Session of the 11th Central Committee of the Communist Party of China', *Peking Review*, 52.

Communist Party of China Central Committee (1981), 'Zhonggong zhongyang banfa "guanyu jinyibu jiachiang he wanshan nongye shengchan zerenzhide jige wentide tongzhi"' (Directive of the Central Committee of the Chinese Communist Party on several questions concerning further strengthening and perfecting of the production responsibility system in agriculture), *Zhong Gong Nian Bao* (Yearbook on Chinese Communism) (Taibei).

Communist Party of China Central Committee (1983), 'Some Questions Concerning Current Rural Economic Policies', Document No. 1, 1983, excerpted in Foreign Broadcast Information Service, 13 Apr.

——(1984a), 'Certain Questions Concerning the Current Rural Economic Policy', Document No. 1, 1 Jan. 1984, trans. Foreign Broadcast Information Service, 13 June; also trans. in *China Quarterly*, 101.

——(1984b), Zhonggong zhongyang guanyu yijiubasi nian nongcun gongzuo de tongzhi' (Directive of the Central Committee of the Chinese Communist Party concerning rural work in 1984), *Renmin Ribao*, 12 June.

DELFS, ROBERT (1984), 'Agricultural Yields Rise, but the Boom Cannot Last', FEER, 13 Dec.

DOMES, JURGEN (1982), 'New Policies in the Communes: Notes on Rural Societal Structures in China, 1976–1981', *Journal of Asian Studies*, 41/2.

DONNITHORNE, AUDREY (1970), *China's Grain: Output, Procurement, Transfers and Trade* (Hong Kong: The Chinese University of Hong Kong, Economic Research Centre).

DU RUNSHENG (1985), 'Second-Stage Rural Structural Reform', *Beijing Review*, 25.

ECKSTEIN, ALEXANDER (ed.) (1980), *Quantitative Measures of China's Economic Output* (Ann Arbor, Mich.: University of Michigan Press).

ERISMAN, LEW (1986), 'The Grain Challenge', *China Business Review*, Mar.–Apr.

FREEBERNE, MICHAEL (1962), 'Natural Calamities in China, 1949–1961', *Pacific Viewpoint*, 3.

HINTON, WILLIAM H. (1983), 'A Trip to Fengyang County: Investigating China's New Family Contract System', *Monthly Review*, Nov.

HU QIAOMU (ed.) (1980), *Zhongguo Baihe Nianjian* (Annual Encyclopedia of China) (Beijing: China Great Encyclopedia Publishers).

JAMISON, DEAN T., and TROWBRIDGE, F. L. (1984), 'The Nutritional Status of Children in China: A Review of the Anthropometric Evidence' (PHN Technical Note GEN 17), Supplementary Paper No. 8 of World Bank (1984).

JIANG JUNCHEN, ZHOU ZHAOYANG, and SHEN JUN (1980), 'Lun shengchan he shenghuode guanxi wenti' (On the relations between production and livelihood), *Jingji Yanjiu*, 9.

JING PING (1985), 'Contract Purchasing of Grain is a Major Reform', *Red Flag*, 10, trans. JPRS-CRF-85-015, *China Report*, 26 July.

JING WEI (1982), 'Responsibility System Revives Jiangsu Countryside', *Beijing Review*, 48 (28 Nov.).

KHAN, AZIZUR RAHMAN, and LEE, EDDY (1983), *Agrarian Policies and Institutions in China after Mao* (Bangkok: ILO, ARTEP).

LARDY, NICHOLAS R. (1982a), 'Food Consumption in the People's Republic of China', in Barker, Randolph, Sinha, Radha, and Rose, Beth (eds.), *The Chinese Agricultural Economy* (Boulder, Colo.: Westview).

——(1982b), 'Prices, Markets and the Chinese Peasant', Center Discussion Paper No. 428, Yale Economic Growth Center.

——(1983a), *Agriculture in China's Modern Economic Development* (New York and Cambridge: Cambridge University Press).

——(1983b), 'Subsidies', *China Business Review*, 10/6.

——(1984), 'Consumption and Living Standards in China, 1978–83', *China Quarterly*, 100.

LIN ZILI (1983), 'The New Situation in the Rural Economy and Its Basic Direction', *Social Sciences in China*, 3.

LIU, JUNG-CHAO (1980), 'A Note on China's Pricing Policies', paper presented to Workshop of the Dept. of Economics, SUNY Binghampton, 19 Mar.

MACFARQUHAR, RODERICK (1983), *Origins of the Cultural Revolution, ii: The Great Leap Forward 1958–1960* (New York: Columbia University Press).

MAO ZEDONG (1977), 'On the Cooperative Transformation of Agriculture', in Mao, *Selected Works*, v (Beijing: Foreign Languages Press, 1977; originally pub. 1955).

OI, JEAN C. (1986), 'Peasant Grain Marketing and State Procurement: China's Grain Contracting System', *China Quarterly*, 106.

PARISH, WILLIAM F., and WHYTE, MARTIN KING (1978), *Village and Family in Contemporary China* (Chicago Ill.: University of Chicago Press).

PERKINS, DWIGHT H. (1969), *Agricultural Development in China, 1368–1968* (Chicago, Ill.: Aldine).

——and YUSUF, SHAHID (1984), *Rural Development in China* (Baltimore, Md.: Johns Hopkins).

PIAZZA, ALAN (1983), 'Trends in Food and Nutrient Availability in China, 1950–81', World Bank Staff Working Paper No. 607 (Washington, DC: World Bank).

Policy Research Office (1979), *Zhongguo Nongye Jiben Qingkuang* (Basic situation in Chinese agriculture) (Beijing: Ministry of Agriculture, Nongyechubanshe).

RISKIN, CARL (1987), *China's Political Economy: The Quest for Development since 1949* (Oxford: Oxford University Press).

ROLL, CHARLES R. (1974), 'The Distribution of Rural Incomes in China', Ph.D. dissertation, Harvard University, Cambridge, Mass.

SCHRAN, PETER (1969), *The Development of Chinese Agriculture, 1950–1959* (Urbana, Ill.: University of Illinois Press).

SELDEN, MARK (1981), 'Cooperation and Socialist Transition in China's Countryside', in Selden and Lippit (1981).

——and LIPPIT, VICTOR (eds.) (1981), *The Transition to Socialism in China* (Armonk, NY: M. E. Sharpe).

SEN, AMARTYA (1981), *Poverty and Famines: An Essay on Entitlement and Deprivation* (Oxford: Oxford University Press).

——(1982), 'How is India Doing?', *New York Review of Books*, 16 Dec.

SHUE, VIVIENNE (1984), 'The Fate of the Commune', *Modern China*, 10/3.

State Security Office (1962), 'Nongcun renmin gongshe gongzuo tiaoli (xiuzheng cao'an)' (Work regulations for the rural people's communes (revised draft)) (Taiwan).

State Statistical Bureau (1983a), *Statistical Yearbook of China* (Hong Kong: Economic Information & Agency).

——(1983b), *Zhongguo Tongji Nianjian, 1983* (Statistical Yearbook of China, 1983) (Beijing: Chinese Statistical Publishing House).

——(1983c) *Zhongguo Tongji Zhaiyao* (Statistical Abstract of China) (Beijing: Chinese Statistical Publishing House, repr. with translations of table headings in Joint Publications Research Service 84111).

——(1984a), *Zhongguo Maoyi Wujia Tongji Ziliao, 1952–1983* (Statistics on China's commerce and prices, 1952–1983) (Beijing, Office of Commerce and Price Statistics: Chinese Statistical Publishing House).

——(1984b), *Zhongguo nongyede guanghui chengjiu, 1949–1984* (Brilliant accomplishments of China's agriculture, 1949–1984), Office of Agricultural Statistics, State Statistical Bureau (Beijing: Chinese Statistical Publishing House).

——(1984c), *Zhongguo Tongji Nianjian* (Statistical Yearbook of China) (Beijing: Chinese Statistical Publishing House).

——(1985a), *Statistical Yearbook of China* (Oxford: Oxford University Press).

——(1985b), *Zhongguo Tongji Zhaiyao, 1985* (Statistical Abstract of China, 1985) (Beijing: Chinese Statistical Publishing House).

——(1985c), *Zhongguo Tongji Nianjian* (Statistical Yearbook of China) (Beijing: Chinese Statistical Publishing House).

——(1986a), 'Communiqué on the Statistics of 1985 Economic and Social Development', *Beijing Review*, 12.

——(1986b), *Zhongguo Tongji Nianjian* (Statistical Yearbook of China) (Beijing: Chinese Statistical Publishing House).

——(1988), *Zhongguo Tongji Nianjian* (Statistical Yearbook of China) (Beijing: Chinese Statistical Publishing House).

STAVIS, BENEDICT (1978), *The Politics of Agricultural Mechanization in China* (Ithaca, NY: Cornell University Press).

STONE, BRUCE (1985), 'The Basis for Chinese Agricultural Growth in the 1980s and 1990s: A Comment on Document No. 1, 1984', *China Quarterly*, 101.

STRONG, ANNA LOUISE (1964), *The Chinese People's Communes—and Six Years After* (Peking: New World Press).

SUN YEFANG (1981), 'Jiaqiang tongji gongzuo, gaige tongji zhidu' (Strengthen statistical work, reform the statistical system), *Jingji Guanli*, 2, 15 Feb., trans. Foreign Broadcast Information Service, 26 Mar.

TIAN JIYUN (1985), 'Price System Due for Reform', *Beijing Review*, 4.

TRAVERS, LEE (1982), 'Bias in Chinese Economic Statistics: The Case of the Typical Example Investigation', *China Quarterly*, 91.

——(1984), 'Post-1978 Rural Economic Policy and Peasant Income in China', *China Quarterly*, 98.

UNGER, JONATHAN, and XIONG, JEAN (1990), 'Life in the Chinese Hinterlands under the Rural Economic Reforms', *Bulletin of Concerned Asian Scholars*, 22/2 (Apr.–June).

US Central Intelligence Agency (1986), 'China: Economic Performance in 1985', report presented to the US Congress, Joint Economic Committee, Subcommittee on Economic Resources, Competitiveness, and Security Economics, 17 Mar. (typescript).

US Congress, Joint Economic Committee (1982), *China under the Four Modernizations*, parts i and ii (Washington, DC: US Government Printing Office).

WALKER, KENNETH R. (1965), *Planning in Chinese Agriculture* (Chicago, Ill.: Aldine).

——(1977), 'Grain Self-Sufficiency in North China', *China Quarterly*, 71.

——(1982), 'Interpreting Chinese Grain Consumption Statistics', *China Quarterly*, 92.

——(1984a), 'Chinese Agriculture during the Period of the Readjustment, 1978–83', *China Quarterly*, 100.

——(1984b), *Food Grain Procurement & Consumption in China* (Cambridge: Cambridge University Press).

WAN LI (1985), 'Developing Rural Commodity Production', *Beijing Review*, 9.

WATSON, ANDREW (1983), 'Agriculture Looks for "Shoes that Fit": The Production Responsibility System and Its Implications', *World Development*, 11.

WEI, LIN, and CHAO, ARNOLD (1982), *China's Economic Reforms* (Philadelphia, Penn.: University of Pennsylvania Press).

WIENS, THOMAS (1980), 'Agricultural Statistics in the People's Republic of China', in Eckstein (1980).

World Bank (1983), *China: Socialist Economic Development*, vols. i–iii (Washington, DC: World Bank).

——(1984), *China: The Health Sector* (Washington, DC: World Bank).

——(1985), *China: Long-Term Development Issues and Options* (Baltimore, Md., and London: Johns Hopkins).

WREN, CHRISTOPHER (1984), 'Despite Rural China's Gains, Poverty Grips Some Regions', *New York Times*, 18 Dec.

WU XIANG (1980), 'The Open Road and the Log Bridge: A Preliminary Discussion on the Origins, Advantages and Disadvantages, Nature and Future of the Fixing of Farm Output Quotas for Each Household', *Renmin Ribao*, 5 Nov., trans. Foreign Broadcast Information Service, 7 Nov.

XUE MUQIAO (ed.) (1981/2), *Zhongguo Jingji Nianjian* (Economic Yearbook of China 1981) (Beijing: Jingji guanli chubanshe).

YANG JIANBAI and LI XUEZENG (1980), 'The Relations between Agriculture, Light Industry and Heavy Industry in China', in *Social Sciences in China*, 2.

ZHAO ZIYANG (1985a), 'Loosen Control over the Prices of Farm Products to Promote the Readjustment of the Production Structure in Rural Areas', *Hong Qi*, 3, trans. Foreign Broadcast Information Service, 31 Jan.

——(1985b), 'The Current Economic Situation and the Reform of the Economic Structure', Report on the Work of the Government, 27 Mar., in *Beijing Review*, 16.

ZWEIG, DAVID (1982), 'National Élites, Rural Bureaucrats and Peasants: Limits on Commune Reform', in *The Limits of Reform in China* (Washington, DC: The Wilson Center)

2

Public Policy and Basic Needs Provision: Intervention and Achievement in Sri Lanka*

Sudhir Anand and S. M. Ravi Kanbur

2.1. Introduction

In academic and policy discussions of development strategy, Sri Lanka has become a test case. It is well known that the country has exceptionally high achievements in the areas of health and education. The life expectancy at birth of a Sri Lankan is almost 70 years, which is a figure approaching that found in industrial market economies, and much higher than that typical of developing countries at similar or even considerably higher levels of per capita income. Infant mortality rates in Sri Lanka are below 40 per 1,000 live births, which compares with figures in excess of 100 for most countries at similar levels of per capita income. Literacy rates are 80 per cent or more, compared with the developing countries' average of around 50 per cent.

Assuming that one of the major objectives of development is to enhance the quality of life along the dimensions of health, education, and other basic needs, Sri Lanka appears to have been remarkably successful. Yet the growth of its per capita income has been modest in comparison with other developing countries, and it remains part of the 'low-income' group of developing countries. The remarkable record in achievement is attributed by some to a systematic and sustained policy of government intervention in the areas of health, education, and food over a long period. The counter to this position comes in several forms, which can perhaps best be summarized in the statement that the intervention was, or has become, 'excessive' relative to the achievement. It should be clear, therefore, why Sri Lanka is seen as a test case—a verdict on whether or not intervention was excessive in that country will have implications for other countries deciding on levels of intervention. The intensity of debate on Sri Lanka as a test case has been further heightened by the fact that in 1977 the government explicitly introduced changes which were seen as a retreat on intervention. The post-1977 experience in Sri Lanka is thus also of great importance to the 'intervention and achievement' debate.

The object of this chapter is to examine the role of public policy in basic

* An earlier version of this paper was presented at a seminar at WIDER, Helsinki, in Aug. 1986. We are grateful to Saman Kelegama and Madhura Swaminathan for research assistance, and to Jean Drèze, Keith Griffin, Lal Jayawardena, Heather Milne, Martin Ravallion, Abhijit Sen, and Amartya Sen for comments.

needs provision in Sri Lanka. How much does Sri Lanka's enviable record owe to direct intervention by the state? The next section provides an overview of the historical development of public policy and intervention in the areas of health, education, and food, taking in both the pre-independence and post-independence periods. It also considers long-term trends in Sri Lanka's health and education indicators, and recent developments in indicators related to food intake. Section 2.3 moves from the descriptive to the econometric method. We assess the recent literature on linking intervention and achievement in the area of basic needs, which is based on evidence from a cross-section of countries. After a critique of some aspects of this literature, we move to a direct analysis of intervention and achievement using time-series evidence for Sri Lanka for the post-independence period. Section 2.4 concludes the chapter.

2.2. *Intervention and achievement: historical overview*

Sri Lanka has a long record of government intervention in the field of social welfare. The record includes intervention in health, education, and other social services, as well as in the area of food subsidies. In most areas intervention predates independence in 1948; in some areas it even predates the granting of universal adult franchise in 1931. The origins of intervention in Sri Lanka lie in legislation to regulate the living conditions of Indian immigrant workers on the estates, with the pressure for these regulations coming from the (colonial) Government of India. Tinker (1974) has analysed the role of the Government of India in regulating the process of indentured labour migration to Ceylon and to other areas of the British Empire, including the West Indies, Mauritius, and Malaya. He documents the conflicting concerns of the government in balancing the requirements of employers for cheap labour, its own perception that such migration was a useful way of easing population pressure in India, and its self-perceived duty to protect its citizens' conditions of passage and work. Revelations of the appalling treatment of indentured labour *en route* to estates and plantations led to the establishment of inspectorates at ports of origin and destination.

Further requirements, e.g. on working conditions, were often seen as an intrusion into the internal affairs of the colonies concerned, and Tinker gives a fascinating account of how the India Office and the Colonial Office in London mediated these conflicts. However, the demand for labour was such that the employers usually gave way. It would be beyond the scope of this chapter to document in detail this intricate bargaining process in the case of labour migration to Ceylon. But Orde Browne (1943: 20–1) summarizes the process well:

Conditions of service had begun to receive the attention of the Legislature far back in the last century (the Ordinance on Contracts for Hire and Service dates from 1866), but the main impetus to improve living conditions came from the gradually increasing requirements of the Government of India. (The Ordinance relating to Estate Labour (Indian) was passed in 1889 and amended in 1890, 1909, 1921, 1927, 1932, and 1941.) Early improvements were chiefly connected with housing and medical attention, but the standard and scope of requirements grew, until employers were called upon to provide hospitals, schools, maternity arrangements, creches, and various other amenities, representing, as a whole, considerable responsibility and expense . . .

While the employer's responsibility for the welfare of his work-people may be fully admitted, there is something anomalous about an arrangement whereby the supervision and management of such institutions as a school or a hospital must be undertaken by an estate manager . . . Consequently, the existing waste of money, effort, and efficiency in maintaining numerous small schools and hospitals could largely be eliminated by grouping these around central institutions, which would admit a higher standard of inspection and supervision by the appropriate Government Officers.

Orde Browne thus hints at the next logical stage in the process, a shift in responsibility from the employers to the Government of Ceylon—a transition in which the employers themselves had no small interest and which had in any case already begun, as we shall see. The main point of interest for us is that the provision of 'basic needs' goes back a long way in Sri Lanka and began with immigrant workers on the estates, i.e. among workers who are today the least well off in terms of satisfaction of basic needs. While the process of indentured labour migration may only be a part of the explanation (for instance it cannot explain the different developments in the former colonies during the post-independence period), it nevertheless provides a backdrop to the consistent intervention of government in basic needs provision in the modern period.

In what follows we will examine in greater detail the historical record of intervention and achievement under the headings of health, education, and food subsidies.

(a) Health

Table 2.1 provides some indicators for the health sector from 1926 onwards. As Alailima (1985) notes, the date 1926 is significant for the fact that the first Health Unit in Sri Lanka was established in this year, providing primary health care, including control of infectious diseases.[1] Before this date the network of hospitals was in the main restricted to the estate sector and the urban areas. In 1926 a total of 98 hospitals in Sri Lanka served the entire population, implying a figure of around 50,000 persons per hospital, and 605 persons per bed. There were 285 doctors for the then population of 4.9 million. The formal training of doctors had started in 1870 and that of nurses in 1878. By 1926 there were 437 nurses—one per 11,213 persons.

While we have figures for nominal government expenditure on health from

---

[1] Perera (1985) gives an intriguing historical account of health care systems in Sri Lanka from 300 BC to the present. A detailed overview of health and development in Sri Lanka in the modern period is provided by Gunatilleke (1985).

Table 2.1 Selected statistics for the health sector in Sri Lanka, 1926–1984

Year	Total no. of hospitals[a]	Persons per hospital	Persons per bed	No. of doctors	Persons per doctor	Total no. of nurses	Persons per nurse
1926	98	50,000	605	285	17,193	437	11,213
1927	98	51,020	599	308	16,234	499	10,020
1928	107	47,664	592	321	15,888	545	9,358
1929	108	48,148	575	337	15,302	569	9,139
1930	112	46,429	549	341	15,249	605	8,595
1931	112	47,321	562	341	15,543	612	8,660
1932	113	47,788	566	339	15,929	611	8,838
1933	112	48,214	572	338	15,976	613	8,809
1934	111	50,451	600	333	16,817	613	9,135
1935	112	50,000	471	339	16,519	618	9,061
1936	112	50,000	478	342	16,374	632	8,861
1937	114	50,000	473	367	15,531	688	7,884
1938	115	50,435	564	366	15,847	723	8,022
1939	120	49,167	482	403	14,640	730	8,083
1940	126	47,619	490	404	14,851	744	8,065
1941	129	48,062	507	426	14,554	791	7,838
1942	132	46,970	507	455	13,626	848	7,311
1943	134	47,015	515	450	14,000	895	7,039
1944	141	45,390	514	459	13,943	n/a	n/a
1945	153	43,137	425	514	12,938	769	8,583
1946	189	35,979	408	559	12,261	n/a	n/a
1947	223	31,390	385	n/a	n/a	n/a	n/a
1948	246	29,268	381	689	10,334	948	7,595
1949	256	28,906	376	643	11,594	1,124	6,584
1950	263	29,278	385	674	11,392	1,165	6,609
1951	266	29,699	388	752	10,529	1,762	4,484
1952	268	30,224	388	768	10,486	1,729	4,685
1953	268	30,970	388	773	10,724	1,938	4,283
1954	270	31,555	368	814	10,447	2,105	4,038
1955	274	31,835	358	952	9,163	2,210	3,936
1956	278	32,118	350	984	9,074	2,304	3,863
1957	279	32,849	347	947	9,678	2,587	3,556
1958	282	33,290	341	1,128	8,323	2,767	3,397
1959	283	34,010	345	1,172	8,212	3,129	3,068
1960	289	34,242	332	1,173	8,436	3,232	3,063
1961	291	34,941	340	1,236	8,226	3,547	2,848
1962	292	35,763	318	1,345	7,764	3,270	3,180
1963	295	36,088	329	1,436	7,413	4,420	2,398
1964	294	37,085	329	1,454	7,498	3,435	3,086
1965	296	37,716	330	1,494	7,472	3,642	2,993
1966	297	38,515	342	1,512	7,565	3,499	3,258
1967	298	39,271	328	1,598	7,323	3,999	2,926

1968	302	39,708	332	1,613	7,434	4,382	2,738
1969	310	39,522	332	1,841	6,655	4,734	2,577
1970	455	27,503	320	1,932	6,477	5,542	2,256
1971	450	27,617	320	1,983	8,840	5,003	2,518
1972	457	28,490	325	2,038	6,388	4,955	2,603
1973	456	29,055	329	2,089	6,342	6,234	2,101
1974	451	29,067	332	2,127	6,295	5,288	2,496
1975	458	29,506	332	2,138	6,356	5,653	2,388
1976	460	29,848	334	2,248	6,108	5,640	2,429
1977	469	29,723	340	2,168	6,429	6,266	2,234
1978	484	29,326	352	2,258	6,286	6,169	2,286
1979	480	29,961	342	2,263	6,394	6,673	2,173
1980	480	30,704	340	2,051	7,186	6,227	2,361
1981	488	30,713	340	2,233	6,712	6,805	2,204
1982	479	31,710	350	2,036	7,460	6,931	2,193
1983	483	31,917	350	1,951	7,902	7,114	2,165
1984	484	32,229	n/a	2,822	5,528	7,216	2,162

Notes: *a* Includes maternity homes.
n/a denotes not available.

Source: Rasaputra (1986: Statistical Appendix, Table 11).

1926 onwards (Rasaputra 1986: Statistical Appendix, Table 11), the problem is that we do not have an adequate deflator to express these in real terms before 1951. Intertemporal comparisons and trend calculations are therefore not possible between 1926 and 1950 in so far as *real* expenditure is concerned. However, an indication that this must have risen is provided by the large increase in the number of hospitals (from 98 to 263), doctors (from 285 to 674), and nurses (from 437 to 1,165). Sri Lanka's population was also rising over this period, of course, but the population per hospital bed, for example, fell from 605 to 385, while the population per nurse fell from 11,213 to 6,609.

A major feature of the 1926–50 period was the campaign against malaria. In terms of expenditure this was reflected in a substantial increase in *nominal* per capita expenditure on health after the mid-1930s—from Rs. 3.49 in 1935 to Rs. 8.34 in 1950 (Rasaputra 1986: Statistical Appendix, Table 11). While these nominal figures do not allow for price changes, they do reflect institutional evidence of the concerted effort to combat malaria after the 1935 epidemic, when deaths from malaria were responsible for 23 per cent of all deaths. The system of health units was also expanded, and in the later 1940s DDT was used. The results were dramatic. The mortality rate from malaria fell from 187.3 per 100,000 of the population in 1946 to 66.1 in 1947, and then to 32.8 in 1949 and 20.6 in 1953.[2] The morbidity rate similarly fell from 41,200 per

[2] In his review of health and development in Sri Lanka, Gunatilleke (1985: 112) notes that 'The year 1947 marks a very significant turning point. The infant mortality rate dropped steeply from 141 per thousand to 101 and the crude death rate from 19.8 to 14. This steep decline in mortality recorded in the period of one year was described by WHO as "an unparalleled achievement in world demography".'

100,000 of the population in 1946 to 19,600 in 1947, 9,900 in 1949, and 5,800 in 1951 (Rasaputra 1986: Table 22, p. 62). By 1960 malaria had become insignificant as a cause of morbidity and mortality. The campaign against tuberculosis also showed success. From a level of 62 per 100,000 in 1940, the mortality rate from this disease fell to 57 in 1948; by 1960 it had reached a figure of 16 (Rasaputra 1986: 63). These specific campaigns had a major effect on overall mortality rates. As Table 2.2 shows, the crude death rate fell from 22.9 per 1,000 in 1934 to 21.8 in 1936 (during the malaria epidemic of 1935 it reached a high of 36.6). By 1946–50 it averaged 14.6, and in the late 1950s it had fallen to below 10.

Thus despite certain shortcomings in the data, primarily the lack of a series on real health expenditures, the link between intervention and achievement can be documented with some confidence for the two decades before independence. From 1951 onwards, we can use the GDP deflator to calculate year-to-year movements in real health expenditure, and indeed real values of other categories of social expenditure. Table 2.3, based on Alailima (1985: Table 8), shows real per capita expenditure from 1950/1 to 1982 on different categories of social services—health, education, food, and other. For the same period, Table 2.4 expresses these categories of expenditure, as well as total social expenditure, as a percentage of GNP. These figures provide a picture of the evolution of the level and pattern of social expenditure in Sri Lanka in the 1950s, 1960s, and 1970s. We turn now to a detailed examination of the record on health over these three decades.

After 1950 real social expenditure per capita on health continued to increase from a figure of Rs. 8.80 in 1950/1 to Rs. 15.86 in 1960/1 (except for very small declines between 1953/4 and 1954/5, and between 1958/9 and 1959/60). After that a decline set in, and real expenditure did not overtake the 1960/1 level until the turn of the decade, when it reached just over Rs. 16. There was again a sharp decline till the trough of 1974 (Rs. 11.63) and then a rise to the all-time peak of Rs. 16.54 in 1979. However, while the 1979 figure is the highest per capita real expenditure on health in the three decades between 1950/1 and 1982, the figures in Table 2.4 indicate that expenditure on health has *not* risen as fast as GNP. From the mid-1950s to the end of the 1960s, health expenditure was equal to or exceeded 2 per cent of GNP. After this it hovered around 1.5 per cent in the mid-1970s and fell to 1.3 per cent in 1982.

It is particularly interesting to note that in the 'post-liberalization' years after 1977, real health expenditure per capita did *not* fall. If anything, it increased relative to the immediate pre-liberalization years. Average real health expenditure per capita for the five years 1973–7 was Rs. 13.16 while the average for the next five years 1978–82 was Rs. 15.48—some 17 per cent higher. Similarly, as a fraction of GNP, health expenditure averaged 1.44 per cent during 1973–7, and fell only to 1.38 per cent during 1978–82. Whatever the implications of the post-1977 period of adjustment for other items of social expenditure, it does seem as though health expenditure was protected in real terms.

We have already noted the dramatic improvements in health-related indicators during the quarter-century before 1950. These improvements were consolidated during the next three decades. Between 1952 and 1981 the death rate declined at an average annual rate of 1.60 per cent (see Table 2.5). In fact, the bulk of the improvement appears to have come in the early part of this period, which suggests a link with the rapid increases in health expenditure in the 1950s. If we consider just the subperiod 1952–60, the rate of decline is 3.12 per cent per annum (not shown in Table 2.5), compared with 1.60 per cent per annum for the full period. Similarly, the infant mortality rate (IMR) declined at an average annual rate of 3.57 per cent in the earlier period (not shown in Table 2.5), compared with a rate of decline over the whole period of 2.50 per cent per annum.

To suggest further the link between intervention and achievement, we note that these declines in mortality rates were underpinned by a steady improvement in the indicator of persons per doctor, which stood at 10,486 in 1952 and at 6,712 in 1981 (see Table 2.1). While the ratio has fluctuated somewhat from year to year, this long-run fall of 35 per cent over three decades must indicate a significant improvement in the provision of medical services to the population, especially when added to the fact that the number of persons per nurse fell from 4,685 to 2,204 over this period (an improvement of more than 50 per cent). A Ministry of Plan Implementation report (1985: 21) gives some indication of the quality of treatment when it notes that deaths in government hospitals fell from 229.1 per 100,000 population in 1965 to 174.1 in 1983. Of course, such figures have to be treated with caution as indicators of quality, since the deaths could instead have been occurring outside government hospitals if the system was contracting; but we know that the system was not contracting. The same report gives figures for hospital morbidity: the cases discharged from government hospitals per 100,000 population increased from 14,773.9 in 1965 to 15,471.9 in 1983. Again, this has to be seen in the context of an expanding service, where it can be interpreted as reaching out to more people, rather than as increased morbidity *per se*.

We end, however, with a note of caution. While the achievements in health at the all-island level have been remarkable, the picture is by no means uniform. Although the crude death rate and the infant mortality rate have come down for Sri Lanka as a whole, the rates are much higher for the estates than for the rest of the island. Thus, in 1970, the estate sector mortality rate was 11.9 per 1,000 while the all-island rate was 7.5 (Gunatilleke 1985: Table 4). In 1980, the all-island death rate had fallen to 6.1 while the estate sector rate was still 11.4. Similarly, in the estate sector, infant mortality rates persisted at above 100 per 1,000 live births throughout the 1950s and 1960s, and were about 85 in the 1970s; for Sri Lanka as a whole they were already below 50 in the 1970s, and down to 38 by 1979 (see Table 2.2 and Gunatilleke 1985: Table 4). An interesting cross-district regression analysis of infant mortality rates in 1953, 1963, and 1971 is reported in Fernando (1985: Table 9). Fernando

Table 2.2 Population, crude birth and death rates, infant mortality rate, and life expectancy, Sri Lanka, 1900–1984

Year	Population (mid-year) (m.)	Crude birth rate (per 1,000)	Crude death rate (per 1,000)	Rate of natural increase (%)	Infant mortality rate (per 1,000 live births)	Life expectancy at birth Male	Female
1900	3.9	38.6	28.7	1.0	178	n/a	n/a
1901	4.0	37.5	27.6	1.0	170	n/a	n/a
1902	4.1	39.1	27.5	1.2	173	n/a	n/a
1903	4.1	40.0	25.9	1.4	164	n/a	n/a
1904	4.2	38.6	24.9	1.4	174	n/a	n/a
1905	4.3	38.6	27.7	1.1	176	n/a	n/a
1906	4.4	36.5	35.1	0.1	198	n/a	n/a
1907	4.5	33.6	30.7	0.3	186	n/a	n/a
1908	4.5	40.8	30.1	1.1	183	n/a	n/a
1909	4.5	37.5	31.0	0.7	202	n/a	n/a
1910	4.6	39.0	27.3	1.2	176	n/a	n/a
1911	4.7	38.0	34.8	0.3	218	n/a	n/a
1912	4.8	33.3	32.4	0.1	215	n/a	n/a
1913	4.8	38.6	28.4	1.0	189	n/a	n/a
1914	4.8	38.2	32.2	0.6	213	n/a	n/a
1915	4.9	37.0	25.2	1.2	171	n/a	n/a
1916	5.0	39.0	26.8	1.2	184	n/a	n/a
1917	5.0	40.1	24.7	1.5	174	n/a	n/a
1918	5.1	39.2	31.9	0.7	188	n/a	n/a
1919	5.2	36.0	37.6	−0.2	223	n/a	n/a
1920	5.2	36.5	29.6	0.7	182	n/a	n/a
1921	5.3	40.7	31.1	1.0	192	n/a	n/a
1922	5.4	39.1	27.6	1.2	188	n/a	n/a
1923	5.4	38.7	30.3	0.8	212	n/a	n/a
1924	5.4	37.5	25.8	1.2	186	n/a	n/a
1925	5.5	39.9	24.3	1.6	172	n/a	n/a
1926	4.9	42.0	25.3	1.8	174	n/a	n/a
1927	5.0	41.0	22.6	1.8	160	n/a	n/a
1928	5.1	41.9	26.0	1.6	177	n/a	n/a
1929	5.2	38.3	26.1	1.2	187	n/a	n/a
1930	5.2	39.0	25.4	1.4	175	n/a	n/a
1931	5.3	37.4	22.1	1.5	158	n/a	n/a
1932	5.4	37.0	20.5	1.7	162	n/a	n/a
1933	5.4	38.6	21.2	1.7	157	n/a	n/a
1934	5.6	37.2	22.9	1.4	173	n/a	n/a
1935	5.6	34.4	36.6	−0.2	263	n/a	n/a
1936	5.6	34.1	21.8	1.2	166	n/a	n/a
1937	5.7	37.8	21.7	1.6	158	n/a	n/a
1938	5.8	35.9	20.2	1.6	161	n/a	n/a

1939	5.9	36.0	20.9	1.5	166	n/a	n/a
1940	6.0	35.8	19.9	1.6	149	n/a	n/a
1941	6.2	36.5	18.3	1.8	129	n/a	n/a
1942	6.2	36.7	18.5	1.8	120	n/a	n/a
1943	6.3	40.6	21.3	1.9	132	n/a	n/a
1944	6.4	37.1	21.0	1.6	135	n/a	n/a
1945	6.6	36.7	21.4	1.5	139	47.2	42.5
1946	6.8	38.4	19.6	1.9	141	43.8	41.5
1947	7.0	39.4	13.8	2.6	101	52.7	51.0
1948	7.2	40.6	12.7	2.8	92	54.9	53.0
1949	7.4	39.0	12.6	2.6	87	56.1	54.8
1950	7.7	39.6	12.6	2.7	82	56.4	54.8
1951	7.9	39.8	12.9	2.7	82	56.1	54.0
1952	8.1	38.8	12.0	2.7	78	57.6	55.5
1953	8.3	38.7	10.1	2.9	71	58.8	57.5
1954	8.5	35.7	10.4	2.5	72	60.3	59.4
1955	8.7	37.3	11.0	2.6	71	58.1	57.1
1956	8.9	36.3	9.8	2.7	67	59.9	58.7
1957	9.2	36.4	10.1	2.6	68	59.1	57.9
1958	9.4	35.8	9.7	2.6	64	59.8	58.8
1959	9.6	37.0	9.1	2.8	58	60.9	60.1
1960	9.9	36.6	8.6	2.8	57	61.9	61.4
1961	10.1	35.8	8.0	2.8	52	63.0	62.4
1962	10.4	35.5	8.5	2.8	53	61.9	61.4
1963	10.6	34.1	8.5	2.6	56	62.8	63.0
1964	10.6	33.2	8.7	2.5	55	63.0	63.6
1965	10.9	33.1	8.2	2.5	53	63.7	65.0
1966	11.4	32.3	8.3	2.4	54	63.6	65.0
1967	11.7	31.6	7.5	2.4	48	64.8	66.9
1968	12.0	32.0	7.8	2.4	50	64.0	66.8
1969	12.2	30.4	8.0	2.2	53	n/a	n/a
1970	12.5	29.4	7.5	2.2	47	n/a	n/a
1971	12.6	32.7	8.2	2.4	45	64.0	66.9
1972	12.9	30.0	8.1	2.2	46	n/a	n/a
1973	13.1	28.0	8.7	1.9	46	n/a	n/a
1974	13.2	27.5	9.0	1.9	51	n/a	n/a
1975	13.5	27.8	8.5	1.9	45	n/a	n/a
1976	13.7	27.8	7.8	2.0	44	n/a	n/a
1977	14.0	27.9	7.4	2.1	42	n/a	n/a
1978	14.1	28.5	6.6	2.2	37	67.1	71.2
1979	14.5	28.7	6.5	2.2	38	67.2	71.2
1980	14.7	27.6	6.1	2.2	34	67.0	71.2
1981	15.0	28.0	6.0	2.2	29.5	n/a	n/a
1982	15.2	26.8	6.1	2.1	n/a	n/a	n/a
1983	15.4	26.2	6.1	2.0	n/a	n/a	n/a
1984	15.6	24.8	6.5	1.8	n/a	n/a	n/a

Source: Rasaputra (1986: Statistical Appendix, Table 10).

Table 2.3 Real GDP per capita and real public expenditure per capita on social
services, Sri Lanka, 1950/1–1982 (Rs. at 1959 prices)

Year	GDP per capita	Education expenditure per capita	Health expenditure per capita	Food subsidy expenditure per capita	Other social welfare expenditure per capita
1950/1	617.59	14.60	8.80	n/a	2.05
1951/2	629.63	16.47	10.51	31.38	2.30
1952/3	619.40	16.96	10.78	15.73	2.54
1953/4	623.65	15.96	10.84	1.45	2.34
1954/5	648.85	16.51	10.67	4.23	2.32
1955/6	634.94	17.84	11.40	9.50	2.60
1956/7	622.72	19.88	11.87	11.76	2.70
1957/8	619.15	22.09	12.90	12.22	3.26
1958/9	617.71	24.84	14.72	15.55	3.55
1959/60	641.41	24.14	14.28	20.25	3.81
1960/1	646.34	29.64	15.86	25.57	4.17
1961/2	649.81	30.31	14.56	23.56	4.57
1962/3	655.75	31.44	14.77	23.99	4.31
1963/4	697.83	32.27	13.82	34.28	4.17
1964/5	694.04	33.38	13.98	25.01	4.04
1965/6	688.95	32.49	14.45	24.44	4.04
1966/7	705.56	30.53	14.38	16.13	3.65
1967/8	744.75	30.13	14.74	22.23	3.41
1968/9	767.87	32.26	15.99	23.15	3.16
1969/70	786.16	33.33	16.10	21.96	3.10
1970/1	780.63	32.42	16.16	34.19	3.08
1971/2	786.43	33.67	15.62	31.42	3.79
1973	802.60	31.03	13.80	34.25	2.35
1974	825.15	24.44	11.63	35.72	2.03
1975	883.11	25.89	12.63	44.18	3.33
1976	842.48	28.66	14.28	31.05	7.29
1977	860.07	25.17	13.45	39.51	4.47
1978	924.96	25.25	15.42	54.46	3.51
1979	956.14	29.78	16.54	62.29	0.62
1980	997.82	32.29	15.84	34.38	2.92
1981	1,034.60	30.93	14.08	24.31	2.77
1982	1,073.03	33.97	15.54	20.72	5.02

Note: Before 1973 the financial year covered the period from 1 Oct. to 30 Sept. With effect from 1973 the financial year was changed to coincide with the calendar year. All the estimates in this table refer to a period of 12 months. (This has been accomplished by multiplying the expenditure figures for the 15-month period from 1 Oct. 1971 to 31 Dec. 1972 by the factor 12/15.)

Sources: The GDP per capita figures are calculated from Rasaputra (1986: Statistical Appendix, Table 1), which gives GDP at 1959 factor costs, and the mid-year population estimates in our Table 2.2. The social expenditure figures are taken from Alailima (1985: Table 8).

Table 2.4 Social expenditure as a percentage of GNP, Sri Lanka, 1950/1–1982

Year	Education	Health	Food subsidies	Other social welfare	Total social expenditure
1950/1	2.5	1.5	n/a	0.3	n/a
1951/2	3.0	1.9	5.3	0.4	10.6
1952/3	3.1	2.0	2.8	0.5	8.4
1953/4	2.9	1.9	0.3	0.4	5.5
1954/5	2.7	1.8	0.8	0.4	5.7
1955/6	3.2	2.0	1.5	0.5	7.2
1956/7	3.5	2.1	2.1	0.5	8.2
1957/8	3.8	2.2	2.2	0.6	8.8
1958/9	4.1	2.4	2.6	0.6	9.7
1959/60	3.8	2.2	3.1	0.6	9.7
1960/1	4.7	2.5	3.9	0.7	11.8
1961/2	4.7	2.2	3.5	0.7	11.1
1962/3	4.7	2.2	5.1	0.6	11.0
1963/4	4.8	2.0	5.1	0.6	12.5
1964/5	4.9	2.1	3.6	0.6	11.2
1965/6	4.7	2.1	3.6	0.6	11.0
1966/7	4.6	2.2	2.4	0.6	9.8
1967/8	4.1	2.0	3.0	0.5	9.6
1968/9	4.3	2.1	3.1	0.4	9.9
1969/70	4.6	2.1	2.8	0.4	9.9
1970/1	4.3	2.1	4.5	0.4	11.3
1971/2ᵃ	4.4	2.6	4.1	0.5	11.6
1973	3.5	1.5	3.8	0.3	9.1
1974	2.8	1.3	4.0	0.2	9.3
1975	2.8	1.4	4.8	0.4	9.4
1976	3.1	1.6	3.4	0.8	8.9
1977	2.7	1.4	4.1	0.5	8.7
1978	2.7	1.5	5.3	0.3	9.8
1979	2.7	1.5	5.7	0.1	10.0
1980	2.9	1.4	3.1	0.3	7.7
1981	2.7	1.2	2.1	0.2	6.2
1982	2.9	1.3	1.8	0.4	6.4

Notes: GNP for 1951–6 obtained from National Accounts of the Department of Census and Statistics. GNP for 1956 onwards obtained from Central Bank Annual Reports.
  Expenditure figures obtained from Treasury Estimates.
ᵃEstimated from 15 months' expenditure and GNP figures.

Source: Alailima (1985: Table 7).

Table 2.5 Average annual rate of change in infant mortality rate, death rate, and birth rate, Sri Lanka, 1952–1981

Indicator	Annual rate of change 1960–78 (%)	Annual rate of change 1952–81 (%)
Infant mortality rate (IMR)	−1.72	−2.50
Death rate (DR)	−0.55	−1.60
Birth rate (BR)	−1.58	−1.28

Note: For each time period, the annual rates of change reported in this table have been estimated by means of a semi-logarithmic regression of the variable in question on time. The data on IMR, DR, and BR are from Table 2.2.

(1985: 83) also reports the results of another study relating to 1971 which shows that 83 per cent of the interdistrict variation in IMR is accounted for by the following variables: the proportion of the district population that is Indian Tamil, the proportion of employed females, and the proportion of females aged 15–19 with more than five years of education. The last of these highlights another factor which may be important in determining the course of IMR —education—and it is to this factor that we now turn.

(h) Education

As with health, government intervention in education in Sri Lanka predates independence. Education became the responsibility of central government with Education Ordinance No. 1 in 1920. This was the culmination of a process which began with the disclosure in the Census Report of 1901 that only 218,479 children out of a total of 867,103 between the ages of 5 and 14 years were actually receiving formal education (Alailima 1985: 6). The period after 1920 saw a steady increase of government responsibility in the field of education, and a corresponding increase in expenditure. In 1926, the expenditure on education was only 0.5 per cent of GNP; thereafter, the ratio rose to 1.5 per cent in 1946 following the adoption of free education (calculated from Rasaputra 1986: Statistical Appendix, Tables 1 and 7).

Selected educational indicators for Sri Lanka are provided in Table 2.6. Between 1926 and 1950 the number of pupils in the country rose from 10.1 per cent of the population to 17.7 per cent (calculated from Tables 2.2 and 2.6). Of course, these figures have to be interpreted with care—there are other reasons why this number may increase than an expansion of education to the previously uncovered population. However, the institutional details of the development of education in Sri Lanka corroborate these figures. As Alailima (1985: 8) notes:

In 1931 universal adult suffrage was granted and under the new Constitution there was provision for an elected Minister of Education. For the first time a man who was from the people and knew their problems was put in charge of the education of their children. The electorate was transformed from a restricted literate and property owning minority and the Minister and his Executive Committee of elected representatives had to be responsive to their needs. This change had an immediate effect on the sphere of education. After the General Elections of 1931 and 1936 (the first conducted under the new Constitution) the state assumed much greater responsibility for the provision of education. Enrollment in government schools increased from 216,067 (39% of total enrollment) in 1931 to 378,861 (44%) in 1945 and the number of government schools almost doubled from 1,341 to 2,391 over this period . . . Due to the inability of some private schools to pay their teachers during the depression, the state also took on the direct payment of these teachers.

While we have figures for nominal expenditures on education before 1950 (Rasaputra 1986: Statistical Appendix, Table 7), we do not—as noted in the previous section—have an appropriate index to account for price changes during this period. After 1950 the GDP deflator can be used to convert nominal figures to real magnitudes, and these are shown in our Table 2.3. We turn to a discussion of the post-1950 period.

An examination of the movements of real per capita expenditure on education in the post-independence period shows that there was a doubling of such expenditure in the decade of the 1950s, followed by a gradual increase in the 1960s until a peak was reached in 1969/70 (Table 2.3). Thus, real per capita expenditure on education rose from Rs. 14.60 in 1950/1 to Rs. 29.64 in 1960/1, and reached Rs. 35.53 in 1969/70. There was a sharp decline of over 20 per cent between 1973 and 1974, and real per capita expenditure did not recover its 1971/2 value until 1982. The five-year average for 1973–7 was Rs. 27.04 while that for 1978–82 was Rs. 30.44. As in the case of health, real educational expenditure per capita seems to have been protected in the post-1977 reform period.

In the thirty years from 1952 to 1981, the number of pupils more than doubled (Table 2.6). In light of this increase, the decrease in the pupil–teacher ratio from an average of 33.3 in the 1950s to an average of 25.6 during 1980–4 can perhaps be seen as an indicator of improved quality of education. The problem with this interpretation, as with interpretations of other educational indicators, is that such indicators should really be viewed as 'inputs' rather than 'outputs'. The problem lies in specifying an appropriate 'output' of the educational system beyond such obvious indicators as literacy rates. In fact, as Table 2.7 shows, literacy rates have improved dramatically in Sri Lanka since the turn of the century. They increased from 26.4 per cent in 1901 to 39.9 per cent in 1921, and by 1953—the start of our three-decade modern period—the literacy rate was already 65.4 per cent. By 1981, it was as high as 86.5 per cent.

Of course, since the maximum literacy rate is 100 per cent it is inappropriate to compare percentage changes over time—it is easier to get large percentage

Table 2.6 Number of schools, teachers, and pupils, Sri Lanka, 1926–1984

Year	Total no. of schools	Total no. of teachers	Total no. of pupils	Pupil–teacher ratio
1926	4,523	16,606	494,004	29.7
1927	4,512	17,787	515,221	29.0
1928	4,741	19,162	532,894	27.8
1929	4,941	18,571	562,550	30.3
1930	5,219	17,934	578,999	32.3
1931	5,304	18,242	593,437	32.5
1932	5,183	17,947	613,210	34.2
1933	5,145	18,131	631,122	34.8
1934	5,327	18,516	653,509	35.3
1935	5,351	19,243	717,287	37.3
1936	5,749	20,019	726,502	36.3
1937	6,029	20,553	783,905	38.1
1938	6,151	20,628	802,853	38.9
1939	6,100	21,570	828,090	38.4
1940	n/a	n/a	n/a	n/a
1941	n/a	n/a	n/a	n/a
1942	5,746	22,163	606,051	27.3
1943	5,568	22,698	611,529	26.9
1944	5,686	24,308	833,670	34.3
1945	5,726	25,281	867,309	33.9
1946	5,945	27,693	944,508	34.1
1947	6,097	28,977	1,036,134	35.8
1948	6,409	33,668	1,192,423	35.4
1949	6,447	35,084	1,260,667	35.9
1950	6,487	39,256	1,366,742	34.8
1951	6,708	42,558	1,454,773	34.2
1952	6,636	45,508	1,502,107	33.0
1953	6,731	47,426	1,578,349	33.3
1954	6,894	49,283	1,625,742	33.0
1955	6,755	48,342	1,637,008	33.8
1956	6,844	50,186	1,693,879	33.7
1957	7,119	55,410	1,833,074	33.0
1958	7,406	59,679	1,962,243	32.8
1959	7,586	66,113	2,098,941	31.7
1960	7,860	69,658	2,192,379	31.4
1961	8,434	69,859	2,140,698	30.6
1962	8,765	76,353	2,267,564	29.6
1963	9,327	81,109	2,482,613	30.6
1964	9,434	95,137	2,540,913	26.7
1965	9,550	91,981	2,556,191	27.7
1966	9,560	90,515	2,565,891	28.3
1967	9,585	93,673	2,588,502	27.6
1968	9,801	92,982	2,633,637	28.3
1969	9,955	95,117	2,670,099	28.0

1970	9,931	96,426	2,716,187	28.1
1971	9,502	93,539	2,717,719	29.0
1972	9,417	95,281	2,265,241	26.9
1973	8,952	102,649	2,698,854	26.3
1974	9,645	102,656	2,622,424	25.1
1975	9,629	104,043	2,543,641	24.6
1976	9,683	110,563	2,571,984	23.2
1977	9,701	117,735	2,566,381	21.7
1978	9,726	n/a	3,083,725	25.0
1979	9,626	142,207	3,208,191	22.5
1980	9,794	141,185	3,389,776	24.0
1981	9,789	135,869	3,451,358	25.6
1982	9,901	133,802	3,484,661	26.0
1983	9,947	134,299	3,553,027	26.5
1984	9,914	140,190	3,625,897	25.9

Source: Rasaputra (1986: Statistical Appendix, Table 7).

Table 2.7 Literacy rate for population over 10 years of age, Sri Lanka, 1901–1981 (%)

Year	Female	Male	All
1901	8.5	42.0	26.4
1911	12.5	47.2	31.0
1921	21.2	56.4	39.9
1946	43.8	70.1	57.8
1953	53.6	75.9	65.4
1963	63.2	79.3	71.6
1971	70.9	85.6	78.5
1981	82.4	90.5	86.5

Source: Alailima (1985: Table 4).

increases when the absolute level is low. Rather, we can ask what percentage of the *shortfall* between the base value of the literacy rate and the upper bound of 100 per cent is made up in any period (Sen 1981: 292). Using this measure for the period 1921–53, the shortfall of 60.1 per cent in 1921 was reduced to a shortfall of 34.6 per cent in 1953, i.e. a proportionate decline of 42.4 per cent over the 32-year period, or 1.7 per cent a year. Between 1953 and 1981 the shortfall was reduced further to 13.5 per cent, which was a decrease of 61.0 per cent over the 28-year period, or 3.3 per cent a year. Viewed in this way, the improvements in the literacy rate are seen as being much faster in the post-independence period, although of course the movement had gathered some momentum by the time independence came.

In the case of mortality rates in the post-independence period, we saw that declines were much faster in the 1950s than in the 1960s and 1970s. Is the same true of the improvement in the literacy rate? We know that in 1963 the average literacy rate stood at 71.6 per cent. Thus, in the 10-year period 1953–63 the literacy shortfall was reduced from 34.6 per cent to 28.4 per cent—a proportionate decline of 17.9 per cent, or 2.0 per cent a year. In the 18-year period 1963–81 the shortfall decreased from 28.4 per cent to 13.5 per cent, a proportionate decline of 52.5 per cent, or 4.0 per cent a year. It does seem, then, as if the momentum towards greater literacy was not only maintained but intensified in the later post-independence period. In contrast to the behaviour of health indicators, the improvement in literacy is much faster during the 1960s and 1970s.

As with health indicators, the overall satisfactory level of all-island literacy rates masks important sectoral differences. From Rasaputra (1986: Table 18, p. 54) it is clear that literacy rates in the estate sector are much lower than those in other parts of the island. Moreover, most of the improvement in literacy rates seems to have come about in the non-estate sectors, with the estate sector in fact registering a slight worsening in literacy.

(c) Food subsidies

Food subsidies in Sri Lanka were first introduced as the food ration scheme in 1942, a wartime relief measure. The scheme guaranteed the supply of basic food items at low prices. Rice was the most important component of this scheme and in what follows we will concentrate on rice. After a description of the rice ration schemes in the post-war period, we will discuss food subsidy expenditure. Having established the nature of the intervention, we will then proceed to a consideration of the achievements, in so far as the data permit us to do so.

A brief history of rice subsidies is provided in Tables 2.8 and 2.9. Before 1954 the rationed quantity varied between adults, children, and infants. In 1954 all individuals became entitled to two measures of rationed rice per week at a low price (a measure is equal to two pounds avoirdupois). In June 1959 a price differential was introduced between the two measures allowed under the ration—the first measure was priced at Rs. 0.25 while the second was priced at Rs. 0.45. In April 1960 *both* measures were priced at Rs. 0.25. This price remained constant until December 1966.

In December 1966 the scheme was changed again. The rationed quantity was halved to only one measure, but this measure was provided *free*. The rest of an individual's or a household's consumption could be made up in the open market. In 1970 there was a shift back to the June 1959 pattern of differential pricing—the first measure was still free but the second measure now cost Rs. 0.75. In December 1972 a very important distinction of principle was introduced, that between income tax payers and non-income tax payers. The argument for 'targeting' was therefore accepted in principle. While non-income tax payers still received their basic ration of one measure free, the income tax payers had to pay Rs. 1.00 for this measure. The additional ration of

Table 2.8 Rice ration distribution, Sri Lanka, 1950–1966

	Ration quantity (measures per week)					Price (Rs. per measure)
	Adults	Children	Infants	Manual workers	Income tax payers	
Dec. 1950–	1.25	1.00	0.75	1.25	1.25	0.25
Sept. 1952–	1.00	0.75	0.50	1.25	1.00	0.25
July 1953–	1.25	1.00	0.75	2.00	1.25	0.70
Oct. 1953–	1.25	1.00	0.75	2.00	1.25	0.55
Nov. 1954–	2.00	2.00	2.00	2.00	2.00	0.55
May 1955–	2.00	2.00	2.00	2.00	2.00	0.50
May 1956–	2.00	2.00	2.00	2.00	2.00	0.40
June 1958–	2.00	2.00	2.00	2.00	2.00	0.35
June 1959–	2.00	2.00	2.00	2.00	2.00	0.25 (1st measure)
						0.45 (2nd measure)
Apr. 1960–	2.00	2.00	2.00	2.00	2.00	0.25 (1st measure)
Dec. 1966						0.25 (2nd measure)

Note: A measure is equal to two pounds avoirdupois.

Source: Rasaputra (1986: Appendix A, Table A-6).

one measure cost both groups of people Rs. 1.00.[3] This basic structure was maintained, with changes in ration quantities and prices, until after the major reforms of 1977—and it is to these that we now turn.

As discussed in Anand and Sen (1984) (see also Jayawardena *et al.* 1987 and Kelegama 1990) the newly elected government of July 1977 began to introduce a programme of liberalization and adjustment. A devaluation of currency took place and this immediately increased the cost of imported food, and hence the cost of the food subsidy, measured in local currency terms. Over the next two years the subsidy was modified fundamentally by a series of policy changes. In April 1977, before the changes, the basic ration was half a measure per week, which was free to non-income tax payers and cost Rs. 2.00 per measure to income tax payers. The additional ration was 1½ measures a week at Rs. 2.00 per measure for everyone. In February 1978, the ration was restricted to households with an income of less than Rs. 300 per month. Some adjustments were made to allow for household size: for households with more than five members, each additional member increased the income ceiling by Rs. 60, subject to a maximum of Rs. 750 per month. These new rules are estimated to have restricted the recipients of rationed rice to 7.6 million persons, around half the population (Ministry of Plan Implementation 1982).

[3] See Gavan and Chandrasekera (1979: 27–9) for details of changes in the food subsidy scheme between 1952 and 1977.

Table 2.9 Rice ration distribution, Sri Lanka, 1966–1979

	Basic ration			Additional ration	
	Quantity (measures per week)	Price (Rs. per measure)		Quantity (measures per week)	Price (Rs. per measure)
		Non-income tax payers	Income tax payers		
19 Dec. 1966–	1.00	Free	Free	—	—
26 Sept. 1970–	1.00	Free	Free	1.00	0.75
10 Nov. 1971–	1.00	Free	Free	1.00	1.00
4 Dec. 1972–	1.00	Free	1.00	1.00	1.00
19 Feb. 1973–	1.00	Free	1.60	1.00	1.60
12 Mar. 1973–	1.00	Free	1.40	1.00	1.40
1 Oct. 1973–	0.50	Free	2.00	—	—
29 Oct. 1973–	0.50	Free	2.00	0.50	2.00
11 Nov. 1973–	0.50	Free	2.00	—	—
10 Dec. 1973–	0.50	Free	2.00	0.50	2.00
1 Feb. 1974–	0.50	Free	2.00	—	—
18 Feb. 1974–	0.50	Free	2.00	0.50[a]	2.00
18 Mar. 1974–	0.50	Free	2.00	1.00	2.00
15 Apr. 1974–	0.50	Free	2.30	1.00	2.30
29 Apr. 1974–	0.50	Free	2.30	0.50	2.30
6 May 1974–	0.50	Free	2.30	1.00[b]	2.30
15 July 1974–	0.50	Free	1.50	1.00[b]	2.50
5 Aug. 1974–	0.50	Free	2.20	1.00[b]	2.20
6 Nov. 1975–	0.50	Free	2.00	1.00[b]	2.00
4 Apr. 1977–	0.50	Free	2.00	1.50	2.00
May 1977–	0.50	Free	2.00	2.00	2.00
Feb. 1978[c]–	1.00	Free	—	1.50	2.00
May 1978[c] – Sept. 1979	0.50	Free	—	1.50	2.00

Notes: A measure is equal to two pounds avoirdupois.
[a] Colombo and suburbs only.
[b] In 21 deficit districts. Additional ration was half a measure for the rest of the country.
[c] Restricted to households with income less than Rs. 300 per month; some adjustment made for households of size greater than five.

Source: Rasaputra (1986: Appendix A, Table A-7).

In September 1979, the government introduced a food stamp scheme to replace the rationing system which had been in operation in Sri Lanka since 1942. Those families receiving income of Rs. 300 or less per month (excluding the income support of Rs. 50 per month given to the unemployed) were eligible for food stamps, which could be used to purchase a specified basket of goods. Families in receipt of an income in excess of Rs. 300 but less than Rs. 750 per month were also eligible for food stamps, the number of people eligible depending on the income and size of the family and the value of stamps received depending on the age-composition of the family (Ministry of Plan Implementation 1982).

In the final phase of the post-1977 reforms beginning in 1980, price subsidies on rice, flour, and sugar were removed and their prices raised to reflect costs. The most striking feature of the new food stamp scheme was that the value of stamps received was not indexed to inflation. A total of Rs. 1,800 million, fixed in nominal terms, was allocated from the annual budget to meet the cost of food (and kerosene) stamps. It has been estimated that by 1984 the real value of this expenditure had been eroded by inflation to such an extent that a nominal expenditure of Rs. 3,200 million (nearly 7 per cent of the government budget) would have been required in that year to maintain the real value.

What seems to have happened, then, is that a major component of savings for the government budget in the post-1977 period has come not from retargeting but from the post-1979 erosion of real expenditure on food stamps. The strain on the budget has, of course, been a major theme of discussions on food subsidy policy ever since the first rationing scheme was introduced over four decades ago. Tables 2.3 and 2.4 show the real value of food subsidy expenditure per capita, and food subsidies as a percentage of GNP, respectively. As can be seen, the early period is characterized by a sharp fall in real food subsidy expenditure per capita from a high of Rs. 31.38 in 1951/2 to Rs. 1.45 in 1953/4 (at 1959 prices). The high values were the result of increases in the price of imported rice as a consequence of the Korean War. The low value was the result of a policy decision effectively to end all subsidies on food. The decision led to 'food riots', and the government changed. The new government reversed the policy, and real expenditure on food subsidies began a steady increase to Rs. 34.28 in 1963/4, which was more than its 1951/2 value. The rise during the ten-year period from 1953/4 to 1963/4 was the longest sustained increase or decrease in the post-independence period. After the peak of 1963/4, real expenditure per capita fluctuated with a three- or even two-year cycle —troughs in 1966/7, 1969/70, 1971/2, and 1976, and peaks in 1968/9, 1970/1, 1975, and 1979. By 1982 real per capita expenditure on food subsidies had fallen to Rs. 20.72, a value comparable with that of the late 1950s (in the middle of the long period of sustained increase).

This brief account shows that government intervention in the area of food subsidy has been extensive. What have been its achievements? Fairly clearly, the record in achievements in the area of food has to be seen in terms of the extent to which food consumption—on average and for the poor—has changed over the years. We can consider real food consumption in aggregate, or the consumption of particular commodities. More directly, we can analyse how the nutritional status of the population—measured in terms of its calorie intake for example—has changed over time. A particularly serious problem is faced if we are interested in measuring intertemporal variations of the nutritional status of the *poor* in the country. For this we would need data on the joint distribution of food consumption and the variable with respect to which poverty is defined. To match the annual figures for food subsidy expenditure, we would require corresponding distributional data for each year during the past three decades. Such data are simply not available for Sri Lanka.

What we have are a small number of surveys, undertaken at different points in time over the previous twenty years. There are the Consumer Finance Surveys (CFSs) conducted by the Central Bank of Ceylon for 1953, 1963, 1973, 1978/79, and 1981/82. Other surveys that have been used in the literature are the 1969/70 and 1980/81 Socio-Economic Surveys conducted by the Department of Census and Statistics. The major problem that arises in using these surveys as seven observations spanning the post-independence period is their comparability. As Pyatt (1987: 518) notes, the Socio-Economic Surveys differ from the Consumer Finance Surveys in a number of respects which make comparisons difficult. Moreover, even if we stick to the Consumer Finance Surveys, for example, there is some question about comparability of the later surveys with the 1953 and 1963 ones, and about the quality of the data in the earlier period (see Anand and Harris 1985).

Given these problems, we will restrict ourselves to a comparison of the results of the 1973, 1978/79, and 1981/82 Consumer Finance Surveys. Anand and Harris (1985: 53–82) have argued for the comparability of these surveys in terms of their income and expenditure concepts, definition of unit of enumeration, continuity of Central Bank staff participation, etc. The 1978/79 and 1981/82 surveys also span the major food policy change in Sri Lanka—the removal of the generalized food subsidy scheme and its replacement by a targeted food stamp scheme. As discussed above, the change in structure was accompanied by a sharp decline in the real value of transfers to the poor accomplished through the scheme. We will, first of all, examine the changes in real food consumption and calorie intake between these two years, and then move on to a comparison with 1973.

Anand and Harris (1985) have constructed food price indices based on detailed food price and quantity data from the 1978/79 and 1981/82 surveys. Using these, they show that real food consumption per capita increased by 2.2 per cent for Sri Lanka as a whole between the survey years. But this aggregate increase hides major sectoral differences. While the urban sector increased its real food consumption per capita by 5.5 per cent, and the rural sector by 3.2 per cent, the estate sector experienced a fall of 8.7 per cent. A possible explanation is that while urban workers were protected from the decrease in food subsidy through cost-of-living related wage increases, and the rural sector benefited from higher paddy prices, the estate sector lost out in the changeover from the ration to the food stamp scheme (perhaps because of relatively easy to monitor money incomes from estates' wage registers).

So much for change in average real food consumption per capita. What happened at the lower end of the food consumption distribution? Anand and Harris (1985) calculate the incidence of food poverty for two poverty lines —monthly food expenditure per capita in 1978/79 of Rs. 70 and Rs. 60, respectively. (These poverty lines are adjusted to take account of both *intersectoral* and *intertemporal* price differences.) Taking first the higher of the two poverty lines, they find that the incidence of poverty fell from 22.7 per cent to 21.9 per cent for Sri Lanka as a whole. Again, this overall small improvement conceals a significant improvement in the urban sector (24.4 per cent to 19.6 per cent), a minor improvement in the rural sector (23.8 per cent to 23.2 per cent), and a major deterioration in the estate sector (8.9 per cent to 13.8 per cent).

The above results are perhaps to be expected given the movements in average real food consumption per capita for Sri Lanka as a whole and for the sectors taken separately. However, results for the *lower* poverty line indicate some interesting changes at the bottom end of the distribution. With the Rs. 60 poverty line, the incidence of food poverty in Sri Lanka goes *up* from 12.9 per cent to 13.3 per cent. This increase in all-island incidence is driven largely by an increase in rural sector incidence from 12.8 per cent to 13.6 per cent; a small positive contribution is also made by the rise in estate sector incidence from 3.6 to 5.8 per cent, but this is more than offset by the fall in urban incidence from 14.3 to 12.4 per cent.

The results for real food consumption are supported by Sahn's (1987) calculation of the percentage of individuals with a calorie intake per adult equivalent below certain levels. (Household calorie intake was derived from the CFSs by converting food quantities into calorie equivalents using food composition factors estimated by the Medical Research Institute of Sri Lanka.) Sahn (1987: Table 5, p. 818) shows that between 1978/79 and 1981/82 the percentage of individuals who belong to households with a daily intake per adult equivalent below 2,200 calories stayed constant at 31.1 per cent. But there was an increase in the percentage of individuals with an intake below 2,000 calories per day from 20.8 to 22.7 per cent. The percentage with an intake below 1,800 calories rose more sharply between 1978/79 and 1981/82, from 12.6 to 15.5 per cent. However, if an even lower cut-off of 1,600 calories per day is used, the increase (from 7.0 to 10.2 per cent) is even more pronounced—the incidence of undernutrition goes up by 45 per cent.

An indirect method of looking at the distribution of calorie intake is to consider the calorie intake of those who are poor in terms of income or total expenditure. This is the strategy followed by Edirisinghe (1987: Tables 22 and 23, pp. 38–9) in his analysis of the CFS 1978/79 and 1981/82 data. His Table 22 shows that between 1978/79 and 1981/82 mean calorie consumption in the island as a whole—and in the urban and estate sectors—fell, while in the rural sector it rose. Furthermore, his Table 23 shows that the mean calorie consumption of the bottom three all-island deciles fell between the survey years. A recent paper by Anand and Harris (1987) also estimates changes in nutrition in Sri Lanka between 1978/79 and 1981/82. Although critical of the methodology used—and the cleaning of CFS data—by Edirisinghe (1987), it nevertheless confirms the decline in per capita calorie intake by the lowest 30 per cent of the all-island population.[4] At the sectoral level, however, the findings of Anand and Harris (1987) are significantly different: they find an increase in per capita calorie intake in the urban and rural sectors—and in the island as a whole —and a decrease only in the estate sector.[5]

Between 1979 and 1982 real government expenditure per capita on food subsidies fell from Rs. 62.29 to Rs. 20.72 (Table 2.3). While it would be difficult, given the other forces at play and the nature of the available data, to establish a clear and unambiguous link between this cut and food consumption of the population—the results are at the very least suggestive. The food stamp scheme replaced the earlier ration scheme in September 1979 and, despite leakages, the burden of real cuts in the food subsidy budget is likely to have fallen disproportionately on the poor. The increase in food poverty using the Anand and Harris (1985) low poverty line corroborates this suggestion, as does the increase in the percentage of individuals with calorie intake below a low cut-off.

In order to investigate further the link between food subsidy expenditure and poverty, it would be instructive to compare 1979 with an earlier period. This is possible using the CFS 1973 data. Although there are no distributions of calorie intake available for that year,[6] Anand and Harris (1985) have calculated the change in food poverty between 1973 and 1978/79. Using the poverty line of Rs. 70 (at 1978/79 prices), there was a fall in the incidence of poverty from 27.6 per cent to 22.7 per cent. The same trend is seen with the Rs. 60 (at 1978/79 prices) poverty line—the incidence of poverty fell from 15.0 per cent in 1973 to 12.3 per cent in 1978/79. Given that real food subsidy

[4] Another indication of the deteriorating nutritional status of the population emerges from the anthropometric data collected in two surveys on pre-school children undertaken in 1975/76 and 1980/82. The 1975/76 survey was conducted by the Ministry of Health in Sri Lanka, with technical assistance from the US Center for Disease Control in Atlanta, Georgia. The 1980/82 survey was conducted by the Food and Nutrition Policy Planning Division of the Ministry of Plan Implementation, Sri Lanka. The findings of these surveys have been reviewed in, *inter alia*, Ministry of Plan Implementation (1983?: ch. II), Ratnayake (1985), and Sahn (1987). The conclusion of Sahn (1987: 813) is that 'The percentage of children suffering from acute malnutrition was higher in 1980/82 than in 1975/76. Overall, there was a 64 per cent increase in wasting in the rural sector from one survey to the next. The increase was especially high among the 6–11 month old age cohort. This undoubtedly reflects a combination of a decline in dietary intake, more episodes of infection, and less favourable birth outcomes conditioned by the mother's health and nutritional status. The prevalence of concurrent wasting and stunting is also higher in 1980/82 than in 1975/76 . . .'

[5] Anand and Harris (1987) identify several problems with the Edirisinghe (1987) methodology for estimating mean calorie consumption by decile and sector. (These are apart from problems with his cleaning of the CFS 1978/79 and CFS 1981/82 food quantity files, and with ensuring the comparability of food items between the two surveys.) For example, Edirisinghe (1987: 37–9) estimates per capita daily calorie consumption as an *unweighted* mean across households of household per capita calorie consumption. Obviously this is *not* a meaningful average of *individual* calorie intakes. For details of the biases caused by this and other problems with the Edirisinghe methodology, see Anand and Harris (1987).

[6] As noted in Anand and Harris (1985), the detailed food quantities file of the CFS 1973 data is unfortunately no longer available.

expenditure per capita increased from Rs. 34.25 in 1973 to Rs. 62.29 in 1979 (see Table 2.3), this would tend to confirm the link between intervention and achievement. However, before entertaining such a conclusion, we should note that both estate and urban sector poverty increased during this period, no matter which poverty line is chosen. The causes of poverty are manifold, and without further detailed investigation of the pattern of food subsidy distribution, we cannot so easily draw a firm connection between food subsidy expenditure and poverty. Nevertheless, we would argue that there is a prima-facie case for the link between intervention and achievement given this description of the historical record in Sri Lanka.

2.3. *Intervention and achievement: an econometric analysis*

The previous section has provided a historical overview of intervention and achievement in Sri Lanka. The discussion is suggestive of the link between intervention and achievement. It cannot be more than suggestive as we have not established a statistically significant relationship between them. This is where econometric analysis comes in. While such an analysis cannot do justice to the institutional detail of the historical development, it does provide a framework for testing relationships between variables in a stochastic setting.

Given the importance of Sri Lanka as a test case, it should not be surprising that much is written about the country in the applied econometric literature. In a series of papers, Isenman (1980, 1987), Sen (1981, 1988), Bhalla and Glewwe (1986), Glewwe and Bhalla (1987), Pyatt (1987), Ravallion (1987), and Bhalla (1988a, 1988b) have all contributed to a debate on whether Sri Lanka's achievements are exceptional, and the links of these achievements to intervention. A characteristic feature of this literature is that it is based on econometric analysis of a cross-section of countries, Sri Lanka being one of them. The debate centres around establishing Sri Lanka as an 'outlier' in the sample, and around the interpretation of its outlier status.[7]

Our major concern in this chapter is with examining intervention and achievement in Sri Lanka over time. Accordingly, we wish to investigate the link by means of econometric analysis of *time-series* data for Sri Lanka. In doing so we circumvent many of the problems that are peculiar to the cross-section framework. Section 2.3(a) provides a brief review of the cross-section evidence, focusing on why a time-series approach is more appropriate. Section 2.3(b) proceeds to the time-series analysis.

---

[7] A non-econometric but nevertheless 'cross-country' approach is also employed by Caldwell (1986). Using World Bank data he shows that 'some countries reach health levels far above those that would be dictated by their economies and others fall far below. Thus the superior health achievers are characterized by average per capita income levels one-ninth of those of the poor health achievers, but, nevertheless, record half the infant mortality level and an expectation of life at birth ten years higher.' (Caldwell 1986: 173)

(a)   A critique of the cross-section literature

In our brief excursion into the cross-section literature, we will adopt the basic notation used by Bhalla and Glewwe (1986: equation (4), p. 39). They posit the following model to explain some measure of living standard, H_{it}, for country i at time t:

$$H_{it} = \alpha_t + \beta Y_{it} + \delta E_{it} + \lambda_i + u_{it}'' \qquad (2.1)$$

where Y_{it} is per capita income; E_{it} is social welfare expenditure; α_t is a time-specific but country-invariant effect assumed to reflect technological advances (e.g. disease eradication techniques); λ_i is a country-specific and time-invariant 'fixed effect'; δ is the marginal impact of social expenditure on living standards; and u_{it}'' is a random error term.[8]

If we had data on all the variables of (2.1), then of course we could estimate the equation directly. However, data on E_{it} and λ_i are typically not available for a cross-section of countries, and Isenman (1980), Sen (1981), and others usually estimate

$$H_{it} = \alpha_t + \beta Y_{it} + e_{it} \qquad (2.2)$$

for a cross-section of countries at a given point in time. They find that Sri Lanka is an outlier, having much higher values of H than predicted by the estimated relationship. This they attribute to Sri Lanka's record in intervention on basic needs. Comparing (2.1) and (2.2) we see that

$$e_{it} = \delta E_{it} + \lambda_i + u_{it}'' \qquad (2.3)$$

so that a large positive residual for a country could be attributed either to a large E_{it} (assuming $\delta > 0$) or to a large λ_i, or to some combination of the two. This is the crux of the Bhalla and Glewwe (1986) and Bhalla (1988a, 1988b) criticism of the Isenman–Sen analysis. Of course, a large λ_i may itself be due to past expenditures on social welfare, but presumably the focus is on the period in question.

In order to control for the effect of λ_i, Bhalla and Glewwe (1986: equation (5), p. 39) suggest the first-difference model

$$\Delta H_{it} = \Delta \alpha_t + \beta \Delta Y_{it} + u^* \qquad (2.4)$$

where, for a variable x, Δx_t is defined as

$$\Delta x_t = x_{t+1} - x_t.$$

---

[8] It should be stated at the outset that this specification has a number of problems other than the ones which we deal with below. For example, the distribution of income as well as its average level may be expected to influence social indicators; and there may be *interaction* effects between Y and E. Furthermore, dynamic considerations and the role of the 'stock' of E, as opposed to its flow, may also be important. These shortcomings are recognized in the literature, but the bulk of the discussion is organized around the Bhalla-Glewwe specification given in equation (2.1). A major problem with the more complete specification is that the data requirements—e.g. on the distribution of income and the stock of E—are greater.

A comparison of (2.1) and (2.4) shows that

$$u^* = \delta\Delta E_{it} + \Delta u''_{it}, \tag{2.5}$$

Bhalla and Glewwe (1986: 40) argue that 'It is the residual of equation [2.4], and not the residual of equation [2.2], that may be useful in assessing country performance over time'. They estimate equation (2.4) for a cross-section of countries, with $t = 1960$ and $t + 1 = 1978$. They argue that for *this* regression Sri Lanka is no longer an outlier.

Let us return to the basic model in (2.1). We are interested in the sign and magnitude of the coefficient δ, and also its magnitude relative to the coefficient β. It is this comparison which allows us to comment on the efficacy or otherwise of the direct and indirect (i.e. income-growth) route to improving living standards. If we do not have data on E_{it} and estimate (2.2), can we nevertheless infer the sign and magnitude of δ from the residual of the cross-section regression?

If the regression is as in (2.2), and we denote the estimated value of the residual as $\hat{e}_{it}$, then

$$E(\hat{e}_i) = (Y_i - \bar{Y})(\beta - E(\hat{\beta})) + \delta(E_i - \bar{E}) + (\lambda_i - \bar{\lambda}) \tag{2.6}$$

where the t-subscript has been suppressed because the regression is cross-section, $\hat{\beta}$ is the ordinary least squares (OLS) estimate of β, and a bar over a variable indicates its sample mean.[9] As can be seen from (2.6) it is more likely that the residual for a country i will be large and positive in expectation if: (1) $\delta > 0$ and $E_i > \bar{E}$, which is the Isenman–Sen argument; or (2) $\lambda_i > \bar{\lambda}$, which is the Bhalla–Glewwe critique; or (3) $(Y_i - \bar{Y})(\beta - E(\hat{\beta})) > 0$, a possibility which is not entertained to any great extent by either Isenman–Sen or Bhalla–Glewwe. It is easy to show that in the OLS estimate $\hat{\beta}$ of β in (2.2) the bias arising from the omitted variables (E_i and λ_i) is

$$\beta - E(\hat{\beta}) = -\delta \, \frac{\Sigma_i(Y_i - \bar{Y})(E_i - \bar{E})}{\Sigma_i(Y_i - \bar{Y})^2} - \frac{\Sigma_i(Y_i - \bar{Y})(\lambda_i - \bar{\lambda})}{\Sigma_i(Y_i - \bar{Y})^2}.$$

Assume for the moment that the correlation between λ_i and Y_i is zero; we have little reason to suppose otherwise. Then if $\delta > 0$ and E_i and Y_i are positively

---

[9] Dropping the t-subscript, the OLS regression of (2.2) yields the residual

$$\hat{e}_i = H_i - \hat{H}_i$$
$$= \alpha + \beta Y_i + \delta E_i + \lambda_i + u''_i - \hat{\alpha} - \hat{\beta} Y_i$$

using (2.1) and $\hat{H}_i = \hat{\alpha} + \hat{\beta} Y_i$. But since the OLS regression passes through the sample means $\bar{Y}$, $\bar{H}$, we have

$$\hat{\alpha} = \bar{H} - \hat{\beta}\bar{Y}$$
$$= \alpha + \beta\bar{Y} + \delta\bar{E} + \bar{\lambda} + \bar{u}'' - \hat{\beta}\bar{Y}$$

using (2.1). Substituting in the equation above for $\hat{e}_i$, and taking expectations, gives the expression (2.6) for $E(\hat{e}_i)$.

correlated,[10] we have $\beta - E(\hat{\beta}) < 0$. Now from (2.6), if $Y_i < \overline{Y}$ (country i's income is less than the sample average) then we will get an upward bias in the residual $\hat{e}_i$. Of course, a non-zero correlation between λ_i and Y_i will also confound the inference that can be drawn from the residual $\hat{e}_i$.

What if we estimate the Bhalla–Glewwe first-difference model (2.4)? What can be inferred from *its* estimated residual $\hat{u}^*$? Analogously to (2.6), we get

$$E(\hat{u}^*) = (\Delta Y_i - \overline{\Delta Y})(\beta - E(\hat{\beta})) + \delta(\Delta E_i - \overline{\Delta E}) \qquad (2.7)$$

where $\hat{\beta}$ is now the OLS estimate of β in (2.4) and the bias depends on the correlation between ΔE_i and ΔY_i. As can be seen from (2.7), even though there is no $(\lambda_i - \overline{\lambda})$ term, an insignificant value of $\hat{u}^*$ does *not* necessarily imply that δ is zero. A zero value for $E(\hat{u}^*)$ is quite consistent with a positive value for δ. For example, if there is no bias in $\hat{\beta}$, i.e. $\beta = E(\hat{\beta})$, then $\Delta E_i = \overline{\Delta E}$ will give a zero value for $E(\hat{u}^*)$ even with $\delta > 0$, and this is indeed a line of defence adopted by Sen (1988: 550–2).

Sen argues that during the period under consideration (1960–78), the increment in social welfare expenditure in Sri Lanka was not exceptional relative to the sample; thus, it is not surprising that the increment in H is not exceptional. In order to adjudicate on this issue we would need fuller data on ΔE_i in the sample, and this is indeed the problem—if we had those data we could estimate the relationship directly and not have to rely on the residual method to give us an indication of the value of δ.

Thus, our conclusion is that while the Isenman–Sen method may be open to certain criticisms, the Bhalla–Glewwe alternative *cannot* resolve the basic question of the relative magnitudes of δ and β. Given the lack of cross section data on social welfare expenditures it is difficult to see how it could, in fact, be resolved. However, with time-series data for a particular country, we can obtain estimates of δ and β directly for that country. It so happens that Sri Lanka is indeed a country for which such data are available. In the next section we proceed to utilize these data in an econometric analysis of the relationship between intervention and achievement. This corresponds to the 'explicit approach' of Sen (1988: 550):

The common wisdom of the approach is based on the idea that we cannot really measure the impact of a policy of social welfare programs without explicitly incorporating it as a variable in a causal framework and testing its effect.

(b)   Time-series evidence for Sri Lanka

For our time-series investigation, we retain the Bhalla–Glewwe (1986) specification given in equation (2.1). We focus attention on Sri Lanka for the Bhalla–Glewwe period 1960–78, but also discuss the longest time period for

---

[10] In fact, Bhalla seems committed to such a positive correlation between E_i and Y_i. In the course of formulating his living standards model, Bhalla (1988a: 101) specifies the relationship $E_{it} = \beta' Y_{it} + e'_{it}$, which with $\beta' > 0$ will in general imply a positive correlation between E_i and Y_i. By contrast, Isenman (1980; 1987) and Sen (1981; 1988) are not committed to any such correlation.

which a consistent series is available, namely 1952–81. Relevant measures of social expenditure E_{it} are explicitly included for each year.

Our data for this purpose are drawn almost exclusively from the paper by Alailima (1985), 'Evolution of Government Policies and Expenditure on Social Welfare in Sri Lanka during the 20th Century', which is extensively referred to and used by Bhalla–Glewwe (1986) and Bhalla (1988a, 1988b). Alailima's Table 8, on which our Table 2.3 is based, gives a 32-year series from 1950/1 to 1982 for real per capita expenditure on social services (separately for education, health, food subsidies, and other social welfare).

Alailima (1985: Table 8) calculates real expenditures by using the GDP deflator, which includes social welfare expenditure as a component. She calculates per capita expenditure by using population estimates from the Department of Census and Statistics. Finally, her Table 3 presents vital statistics data from the same source for the period 1900 to 1981. This series consists of estimates of the crude birth rate, the crude death rate, and the infant mortality rate. The same information is available, but up to 1984, in Rasaputra (1986: Statistical Appendix, Table 10), and this is reproduced in our Table 2.2. Rasaputra's paper (1986: Statistical Appendix, Table 1) also contains a *consistent* series for real GDP at factor cost from 1950 onwards, using the same GDP deflator (with 1959 = 100) as Alailima does for her series on real social welfare expenditures. It is important to use this *comparable* income series for GDP at factor cost because, as is well known, the GNP series in Sri Lanka has been revised twice—in 1958 and 1970—and the new series is not consistent with the old one. Real GDP per capita has been calculated by us using the same mid-year population figures (Table 2.2) as Alailima (1985: Table 8) uses to calculate her per capita social expenditures. These real GDP per capita estimates are shown in our Table 2.3.

We are now ready to estimate the Bhalla–Glewwe specification of the living standards relationship

$$H_{it} = \lambda_i + \alpha_t + \beta Y_{it} + \delta E_{it} + u''_{it} \tag{2.1}$$

where

country i = Sri Lanka, fixed in the sample
$\quad H_{it}$ = some measure of living standard such as infant mortality rate (IMR), death rate (DR), or birth rate (BR) in year t
$\quad \lambda_i$ = country-specific intercept term for Sri Lanka
$\quad \alpha_t$ = technical progress term, specified simply as $\alpha.t$ (with α constant)
$\quad Y_{it}$ = real GDP per capita in year t
$\quad E_{it}$ = real social expenditure per capita in year t (separately for health, education, and food).

In their cross-section analysis, Bhalla–Glewwe (1986) and Bhalla (1988a) consider six indicators of living standard—life expectancy, primary school enrolment, adult literacy rate, infant mortality rate, death rate, and total fertility rate. Given the time-series data available to us, we are obliged to restrict attention to the infant mortality rate (IMR), the death rate (DR), and the birth rate (BR). Since the H_{it} variables are bounded below by zero, we use them in logarithmic form—as ln H—so that the dependent variable in equation (2.1) can be negative (to minus infinity) for negative realizations of the right-hand side. Since the H_{it} variables are also bounded *above* by 1,000 (IMR, DR, and BR are all measured per 1,000 population), we can allow unbounded variation upwards (to plus infinity) of the dependent variable by *subtracting* ln (1,000 − H) from ln H, i.e. by using H_{it} in the *logistic form* ln [$H/(1,000 − H)$]. We have not done this here because the sample values of H_{it} occur in a region much closer to zero than to 1,000; hence the further transformation is unlikely to affect significantly the estimates of the coefficients of the independent variables (excepting, of course, the intercept term). In any case, this has been confirmed by doing the regressions in logistic form (not reported here).

Table 2.10 presents the results of our time-series regressions. The right-hand side independent variables (except t) have been entered in both *linear* (non-log) and *logarithmic* form; t is always entered in *linear* form. The 'A' and 'B' equations in Table 2.10 refer respectively to these forms. First we report results for the Bhalla–Glewwe period 1960–78, for which the authors claim that Sri Lanka is *not* an outlier. This is followed by results for the full three-decade period 1952–81 for which a consistent time series was available. We have entered the real per capita health and food subsidy expenditures separately—as the variables HEXP and FEXP. There are two interrelated reasons for doing this. First, the impact of health and food subsidy expenditures may be expected to be different from one another. Secondly, the food subsidy accounts for a relatively small proportion of total food consumption, so that variations in it will not reflect corresponding variations in the total food consumed by the population. By contrast, the coverage of health is more nearly universal, so that variations in health expenditure will more closely track health provision for the population. Current and capital expenditures on health have been aggregated in the variable HEXP. A similar procedure is followed for real per capita education expenditure, EEXP, which is also introduced into the regressions separately to allow for possible differential effects.

For the period 1960–78, the results (equations (1A) and (1B) in Table 2.10) show that health expenditure HEXP has a very significant negative effect on IMR, but that FEXP, EEXP, and PCY (real GDP per capita) are insignificant.[11] What is important about the results is that direct intervention, as reflected in government health expenditure, has a statistically significant beneficial impact on IMR. Note that our procedure based on time-series data

---

[11] The significance level chosen for the discussion here is 5%.

Table 2.10 Time-series estimates of living standard equations, Sri Lanka, 1960–1978 and 1952–1981

Dependent variable	Equation number	Time period	Intercept	HEXP	FEXP	EEXP	PCY	t (year)	F-statistic	SEE	Mean of dependent variable	R^2	Log of likelihood function
Ln IMR	(1A)	1960–78	44.54 (2.14)	−0.0381 (−3.21)	−0.002900 (−1.33)	0.00599 (1.33)	0.000412 (0.52)	−0.02060 (−1.90)	17.84	0.0471	3.89	0.873	34.72
		1952–81	24.27 (2.30)	−0.0322 (−2.79)	0.001970 (1.63)	−0.00117 (−0.28)	−0.000982 (−3.01)	−0.00975 (−1.77)	90.16	0.0572	3.94	0.949	46.63
	(1B)	1960–78	44.99 (2.46)	−0.5620 (−3.36)	−0.054400 (−0.91)	0.20200 (1.62)	0.274000 (0.47)	−0.02130 (−1.91)	17.20	0.0478	3.89	0.869	34.42
		1952–81	25.97 (2.18)	−0.4300 (−2.42)	0.018300 (0.82)	−0.04250 (−0.35)	−0.764000 (−2.22)	−0.00802 (−1.10)	75.35	0.0622	3.94	0.940	44.08
Ln DR	(2A)	1960–78	11.43 (0.46)	−0.0460 (−3.23)	0.001380 (0.53)	0.00795 (1.47)	−0.000229 (−0.24)	−0.00446 (−0.34)	3.52	0.0565	2.09	0.575	31.24
		1952–81	8.53 (0.79)	−0.0482 (−4.10)	0.002420 (1.96)	0.00053 (0.15)	−0.000787 (−2.37)	−0.00266 (−0.47)	40.84	0.0582	2.13	0.895	46.11
	(2B)	1960–78	17.32 (0.85)	−0.6630 (−3.56)	0.072000 (1.08)	0.25400 (1.83)	−0.095700 (−0.15)	−0.00708 (−0.57)	4.30	0.0532	2.09	0.623	32.38
		1952–81	9.61 (0.82)	−0.6450 (−3.68)	0.030100 (1.37)	−0.00733 (−0.06)	−0.613000 (−1.80)	−0.00092 (−0.13)	36.03	0.0615	2.13	0.882	44.44
Ln BR	(3A)	1960–78	19.59 (1.98)	0.0232 (4.10)	0.002720 (2.62)	−0.00520 (−2.43)	−0.000733 (−1.95)	−0.00805 (−1.56)	61.51	0.0224	3.44	0.959	48.80
		1952–81	39.13 (7.54)	0.0191 (3.37)	0.000487 (0.82)	−0.00176 (−0.88)	0.000258 (1.61)	−0.01830 (−6.77)	96.58	0.0281	3.47	0.953	67.96
	(3B)	1960–78	24.20 (2.75)	0.3290 (4.09)	0.068300 (2.37)	−0.15000 (−2.50)	−0.451000 (−1.60)	−0.00933 (−1.74)	58.46	0.0230	3.44	0.957	48.34
		1952–81	37.88 (7.21)	0.2810 (3.58)	0.016900 (1.72)	−0.07630 (−1.43)	0.200000 (1.32)	−0.01840 (−5.75)	100.90	0.0275	3.47	0.955	68.59

Notes: The coefficients of the 'A' equations refer to the independent variables entered in *linear* (non-log) form; those for the 'B' equations refer to the independent variables (except for year t) entered in *logarithmic* form. Year t is entered in *linear* form in *both* the 'A' and the 'B' equations. Thus, the estimated equation (1A) for the time period 1960–78 is:

Ln IMR = 44.54 − 0.0381 HEXP − 0.002900 FEXP + 0.00599 EEXP + 0.000412 PCY − 0.02060 t.

The estimated equation (1B) for the time period 1960–78 is:

Ln IMR = 44.99 − 0.5620 ln HEXP − 0.054400 ln FEXP + 0.20200 ln EEXP + 0.274000 ln PCY − 0.02130 t.

t-statistics are shown in parentheses below the coefficient estimates.

has allowed a *direct* test of this relationship, and is not open to the problems of the cross-section approach (mentioned in Section 2.3(*a*)).

For the full period 1952–81, the results show that HEXP remains significant in reducing IMR: government intervention continues to matter. For this longer period, in contrast, the coefficient on the income term, PCY, becomes significant.

These results shed some light on the role of direct intervention versus an indirect, income-growth strategy in reducing the infant mortality rate. According to our results for the Bhalla–Glewwe period 1960–78, income growth did not matter at all. This is a rather striking finding because not only is it the case that direct intervention has worked—a claim which is at the heart of the Bhalla–Glewwe versus Isenman–Sen controversy—but the estimates suggest that reliance on an income-growth strategy would *not* have worked during 1960–78.

For the full period 1952–81, the estimates do show a significant income effect, but this effect is small. A rupee of government health expenditure diverted to income in the hands of the population would have led to an immediate rise in the infant mortality rate. Comparing the coefficient (−0.0322) on HEXP with that (−0.000982) on PCY in equation (1A), the former is larger than the latter by a factor of 33 in absolute terms. This implies that to redress the effect on IMR of a Rs. 1 decrease in health expenditure would require, *ceteris paribus*, a Rs. 33 increase in equivalent income—a manifestly adverse trade-off for the income-growth strategy.

For both the periods 1960–78 and 1952–81, the results for IMR appear to be well determined and robust with respect to the functional form (various diagnostic tests not reported here support this conclusion). Thus in Table 2.10 the picture for equation (1B) turns out to be very similar to that for equation (1A). When the independent variables are entered in logarithmic instead of linear form, hardly any difference is made to the significance of the coefficients, though obviously their magnitude changes. [12]

In the next set of equations the dependent variable is the logarithm of the death rate, ln DR. For the period 1960–78, the results in equation (2A) are again very striking with real health expenditure per capita being highly significant in reducing the death rate. No other variable is significant. For 1960–78 the results in equation (2B) show the same pattern as in (2A) and, as before, the functional form does not seem to make any qualitative difference to the findings.

[12] For the sample period 1952–81 the absolute value of the coefficient on ln PCY is greater than that on ln HEXP. However, these coefficients, unlike those in the equations in non-log form, are elasticities: they indicate the impact of a *proportionate* change in the independent variable. A 1% decrease in HEXP will only allow an increase of approximately 0.019% in income in the hands of the population, since the average ratio of HEXP to PCY over the sample period is 0.019 (see Table 2.4). Hence the relevant comparison (in terms of 'bang-for-a-buck') is between the coefficient (−0.4300) on ln HEXP and 0.019 times the coefficient (−0.764000) on ln PCY—which implies a factor of 30 for the trade-off.

For the full period 1952–81, the estimates in equations (2A) and (2B) do display a degree of sensitivity to the functional form chosen. In equation (2B) the income variable ln PCY is not significant while in equation (2A) the income variable PCY is indeed significant (but again with very small coefficient). Whereas in equation (2A) the food subsidy variable FEXP is significant (and with positive coefficient), in equation (2B) ln FEXP is not significant. The education expenditure variable EEXP is insignificant in both functional forms. The only robust inference for the 1952–81 ln DR regressions seems to be that health expenditure HEXP has a very significant beneficial impact in reducing the death rate.

The final demographic indicator considered is the birth rate (BR), for which the regression results are shown in equations (3A) and (3B). At the outset, it should be emphasized that this is arguable as a living standard indicator, but we include it here only to correspond to Bhalla and Glewwe's total fertility rate.[13] Over the period 1960–78, the birth rate turns out to be positively related to both health and food expenditure by government, and negatively related to educational expenditure—all significant at the 5 per cent level. In the non-log form, the coefficient on income is negative and (almost) significant; in the log form the income coefficient is insignificant but still negative.

The coefficients on educational expenditure and on average (across-the-board) income are not difficult to rationalize, and may be considered to be of the expected sign. But how are we to interpret the positive coefficients on health and food expenditure? One possibility is that larger health and food subsidies lead to better antenatal care (including nutrition) of mothers, especially at the lower end of the income distribution. This might help more pregnancies to come to term and to avoid miscarriages. To test this hypothesis directly, however, we need more disaggregate data on the composition of health expenditures and on birth rate by income group (*who* is having more children?).

For the full period 1952–81, the relationship seems to be quite different, except in the respect that health expenditure continues to be significant and positive. Otherwise, the coefficients on food expenditure and educational expenditure become insignificant, the coefficient on income turns from negative to positive (but becomes decidedly insignificant), and a strong negative time trend emerges. Our worries about the use of the birth rate as an appropriate living standard indicator are compounded by this non-robustness in the face of sample period variation.

To conclude, then, we note that this first attempt at a time-series analysis of intervention and achievement does provide econometric support for the hypothesis of a link between the two. The results for the infant mortality rate will perhaps bear emphasizing. Over the period 1960–78, and for the full

---

[13] See e.g. Basu (1991: n. 6) who argues that the birth rate should *not* be included as a living standard indicator.

period 1952–81, health expenditure has a very significant effect as an explanatory variable for IMR. Moreover, the estimates for the period 1960–78 indicate that income would have had an insignificant effect on IMR. The estimates for the full period 1952–81 do show a significant effect for income, but this effect is very small. In this context, at least, reliance on income growth alone can be questioned.

We view our results as cautionary rather than definitive. A large and sustained increase in income over a long period might well have an impact on social indicators. Over the short- to medium-run planning horizon, however, developing countries do face real choices between social expenditure and capital investment. Our results would tend to support those who argue for greater benefits at the margin from targeted social expenditure.

2.4. *Conclusion*

The object of this chapter has been to consider Sri Lanka's record of intervention and achievement in some areas of basic needs provision. We have used two methods of analysis. First, we have provided a descriptive account of intervention over the long run of historical developments this century, and have tried to relate this intervention to achievement by an accompanying narrative of the achievement. This discussion is strongly suggestive that purposive and directed intervention has had remarkable effects on health and education standards both in the early part of the century and in the period after independence.

Complementary to the descriptive approach is our second method of econometric analysis. We have reviewed the current literature on establishing and interpreting Sri Lanka's position as an outlier in a cross-section of countries. We argue that in the absence of direct information on intervention for countries in the sample, such cross-section analysis can be problematic. We propose instead that time-series data for Sri Lanka be used to conduct a more direct investigation of the issues. We have presented a first attempt at such an analysis using data for the 1952–81 period. While our results need to be confirmed by further research, they do suggest that income growth alone would not have achieved for Sri Lanka its enviable basic needs record—the role of direct intervention has been significant.

We are not alone in reaching this conclusion. The central finding of Caldwell (1986: 204), who uses a combination of comparative and intertemporal methods, is that 'the provision of health services (and, better still, its accompaniment by the establishment of a nutritional floor and perhaps a family planning program) can markedly reduce mortality'. His findings and ours suggest, therefore, that attention should now shift from the question of *whether* intervention can have a positive impact on basic needs to the more important question of the best patterns and combinations of social welfare expenditure to achieve the *maximum* impact on basic needs.

References

ALAILIMA, P. (1985), 'Evolution of Government Policies and Expenditure on Social Welfare in Sri Lanka during the 20th Century', mimeo (Colombo: Ministry of Finance and Planning).

ANAND, S., and HARRIS, C. J. (1985), 'Living Standards in Sri Lanka, 1973–1981/82: An Analysis of Consumer Finance Survey Data', mimeo (Oxford).

———— (1987), 'Changes in Nutrition in Sri Lanka, 1978/79–1981/82', mimeo (Helsinki: WIDER).

—— and SEN, ABHIJIT (1984), 'The Macroeconomy of Sri Lanka after Liberalization', mimeo (Oxford: St Catherine's College).

BASU, K. (1991), 'The Elimination of Endemic Poverty in South Asia: Some Policy Options', this volume.

BHALLA, S. S. (1988a), 'Is Sri Lanka an Exception? A Comparative Study of Living Standards', in Srinivasan and Bardhan (1988).

—— (1988b), 'Sri Lanka's Achievements: Fact and Fancy', in Srinivasan and Bardhan (1988).

—— and GLEWWE, P. (1986), 'Growth and Equity in Developing Countries: A Reinterpretation of the Sri Lankan Experience', World Bank Economic Review, 1.

CALDWELL, J. C. (1986), 'Routes to Low Mortality in Poor Countries', Population and Development Review, 12.

EDIRISINGHE, N. (1987), The Food Stamp Scheme in Sri Lanka: Costs, Benefits and Options for Modification, Research Report 58 (Washington, DC: IFPRI).

FERNANDO, D. F. S. (1985), 'Health Statistics in Sri Lanka, 1921–80', in Halstead et al. (1985).

GAVAN, J. D., and CHANDRASEKERA, I. S. (1979), The Impact of Public Foodgrain Distribution on Food Consumption and Welfare in Sri Lanka, Research Report 13 (Washington, DC: IFPRI).

GLEWWE, P., and BHALLA, S. S. (1987), 'A Response to Comments by Graham Pyatt and Paul Isenman', World Bank Economic Review, 1.

GUNATILLEKE, G. (ed.) (1984), Intersectoral Linkages and Health Development: Case Studies in India (Kerala State), Jamaica, Norway, Sri Lanka, and Thailand, WHO Offset Publication No. 83 (Geneva: WHO).

—— (1985), 'Health and Development in Sri Lanka: An Overview', in Halstead et al. (1985).

HALSTEAD, S. B., WALSH, J. A., and WARREN, K. S. (eds.) (1985), Good Health at Low Cost, Proceedings of a Conference held at the Bellagio Conference Centre, Bellagio, Italy, 29 Apr.–2 May (New York: Rockefeller Foundation).

ISENMAN, P. (1980), 'Basic Needs: The Case of Sri Lanka', World Development, 8.

—— (1987), 'A Comment on "Growth and Equity in Developing Countries: A Reinterpretation of the Sri Lankan Experience," by Bhalla and Glewwe', World Bank Economic Review, 1.

JAYAWARDENA, L. R., MAASLAND, A., and RADHAKRISHNAN, P. N. (1987), 'Sri Lanka', Country Study 15, WIDER Series on Stabilization and Adjustment Policies and Programmes (Helsinki: WIDER).

KELEGAMA, S. B. (1990), 'The Consequences of Economic Liberalization in Sri Lanka', unpublished D.Phil. thesis, University of Oxford.

Marga Institute (1984), *Intersectoral Action for Health: Sri Lanka Study* (Colombo: Sri Lanka Centre for Development Studies).

Ministry of Plan Implementation (1982), *Evaluation Report on the Food Stamp Scheme*, Publication No. 7 (Colombo: Food and Nutrition Policy Planning Division).

—— (1983?), *Nutritional Status: Its Determinants and Intervention Programmes*, Final Report (Colombo: Food and Nutrition Policy Planning Division).

—— (1984), *Nutrition Strategy* (Colombo).

—— (1985), *Health and Nutrition Sector Report*, National Science and Technology Policy for Sri Lanka, vol. vii (Colombo).

ORDE BROWNE, G. St J. (1943), *Labour Conditions in Ceylon, Mauritius, and Malaya*, Cmd. 6423 (London: HMSO).

PERERA, P. D. A. (1985), 'Health Care Systems of Sri Lanka', in Halstead *et al.* (1985).

PYATT, F. G. (1987), 'A Comment on "Growth and Equity in Developing Countries: A Reinterpretation of the Sri Lankan Experience," by Bhalla and Glewwe', *World Bank Economic Review*, 1.

RASAPUTRA, W. (1986), 'Public Policy: An Assessment of the Sri Lanka Experience', mimeo (Colombo: Central Bank of Ceylon; and Helsinki: WIDER).

RATNAYAKE, R. M. K. (1985), 'A Survey Paper on Nutrition Situation in Sri Lanka', mimeo (Colombo: Food and Nutrition Policy Planning Division, Ministry of Plan Implementation).

RAVALLION, M. S. (1987), 'Growth and Equity in Sri Lanka: A Comment', mimeo (Canberra: Australian National University).

SAHN, D. E. (1987), 'Changes in the Living Standards of the Poor in Sri Lanka during a Period of Macroeconomic Restructuring', *World Development*, 15.

SEN, A. K. (1981), 'Public Action and the Quality of Life in Developing Countries', *Oxford Bulletin of Economics and Statistics*, 43.

—— (1988), 'Sri Lanka's Achievements: How and When?', in Srinivasan and Bardhan (1988).

SRINIVASAN, T. N., and BARDHAN, P. K. (eds.) (1988), *Rural Poverty in South Asia* (New York: Columbia University Press).

TINKER, H. (1974), *A New System of Slavery: The Export of Indian Labour Overseas, 1830–1920* (London: Oxford University Press).

3

Growth and Poverty: Some Lessons from Brazil

Ignacy Sachs

Social development and elimination of poverty are hardly conceivable without sustained economic growth, although a once for ever change in asset distribution may bring about a lasting improvement in the entitlements of the hitherto dispossessed, even in a stationary economy. From the fact that sustainable economic growth is a necessary condition for a socially meaningful development process, it does not follow, however, that social development is subsumed in economic growth. Country after country has learned the hard way that the so-called trickle-down theory is fallacious; that growth can be immiserizing for a sizeable segment of the population; that famines also happen in periods of boom when people's entitlement does not allow them to buy and/or produce the food necessary to keep them alive (Sen 1981); that the anti-inflationary package recommended by the IMF leads to stagflation, with devastating social consequences in countries which cannot afford to stop growing, because of the demographic pressure of new entrants on the labour market and of the backlog of unemployment and underemployment.

If a country is set on the path of *maldevelopment*, observable through the high attendant social and ecological costs, then the higher the rate of growth, the greater the damage done to those who are the victims and not the beneficiaries of such a process. Obviously, no country follows an optimal development path, nor an utterly negative maldevelopment one. Development and maldevelopment are but heuristically useful logical constructs, which help us to ask relevant questions about complex historical configurations (Sachs 1984).

Brazil represents the most extreme case of a very rapid and sustained economic growth—about 7 per cent per year over the forty years 1940–80 —and a spectacular modernization, going hand in hand with persistent poverty, endemic malnutrition, and occasional hunger. The exorbitant social and ecological price paid for this performance is even more surprising, given Brazil's extremely favourable resource and land endowment. The absence of a more generalized trickle-down effect cannot be blamed in this case on adverse natural conditions. Its roots must be sought in the working of the socio-economic system and of the political regimes often described as peripheral, dependent, or retardatory capitalism (see e.g. Furtado 1956; Cardoso 1980; Cardoso de Mello 1982).

3.1. *Growth through inequality and lopsided modernization*

As successive Brazilian governments have sought to derive their legitimacy from the rapid rate of economic growth, the wealth of statistical data and studies on the process of economic expansion contrasts with the dearth of reliable studies on the social condition of the Brazilian people.

Brazilian industrialization took off in the 1930s in a somewhat paradoxical fashion. The country, at that time dependent on exports of coffee and a few other agricultural commodities, was so severely hit by the great depression that imports came to a standstill. But in order to rescue the influential coffee planters, the government continued to buy the coffee surpluses and to burn them. This Keynesian policy *avant la lettre* was instrumental in creating demand for domestically produced industrial goods, as well as in generating private savings eager to invest in manufacturing ventures. São Paulo—the main coffee-producing state—took the lead in the industrialization process, to become the largest industrial centre in Latin America.

The Second World War gave a new momentum to the industrialization drive, but the decisive push came from President Kubitschek's 'fifty years in five' modernization programme (see e.g. Furtado 1956, and Draibe 1984). Then came the so-called 'Brazilian miracle' under the authoritarian regime, which provided ideal conditions for the concentration and accumulation of capital in the hands of multinationals, huge public sector enterprises, private banks, and industrialists by keeping the working-class earnings at abnormally low levels and allowing for a continuous deterioration of income distributions.[1]

Brazil responded to the 1973 oil shock by an overambitious, yet ultimately fairly successful, programme of import-substituting heavy industrialization, stepping up the domestic output of oil, steel, non-ferrous metals, paper, and cellulose as well as expanding the capital goods industry. Without this newly created import-substituting export capacity, the country could never have afforded to service a foreign debt of over $100 billion to the tune of 50 per cent of exports and 4 to 5 per cent of GNP transferred abroad year after year (see Barros de Castro and Pires de Souza 1985).

Quite obviously the burden of servicing the foreign debt and the snowballing internal debt (caused by the need to buy foreign exchange from private exporters) constitutes a severe drain on potential savings that even such a resource-rich country as Brazil cannot tolerate for long. A renegotiation and not mere rescheduling of foreign debt is a *sine qua non* for correcting Brazil's course and taking up the long overdue problems of the substantive 'debts', namely the 'social debt' and the 'ecological debt'.

---

[1] The income distribution among social strata will be discussed in more detail below. Recent years brought about a steady decrease of the share of earnings from labour in the national income and a corresponding increase in the relative share of profits. These passed from 49.7% in 1979 to 51.3% in 1983, out of which 80.8% was interest. No doubt Brazil became a paradise for financial capital, at least till the 1986 monetary reform (data of the Ministry of Labour, quoted by *Folha de São Paulo*, 20 Apr. 1986).

By conventional standards, Brazil has also accomplished a very successful modernization. It has the eighth largest economy in the capitalist world, with a fairly integrated industrial structure capable of operating with a very low import content. About 70 per cent of its population is urbanized (see Figs. 3.1, 3.2).[2] Many of them live in large metropolitan cities, such as São Paulo (14 million), Rio de Janeiro (10 million), Belo Horizonte, Recife, Fortaleza, Salvador, Pôrto Alegre, and Curitiba (all of them with a population above 1.5

Million

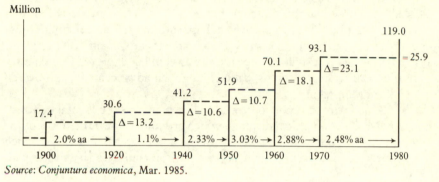

Source: *Conjuntura economica*, Mar. 1985.

Fig. 3.1. Growth of population and annual rates of growth, Brazil, 1940–1980

Million

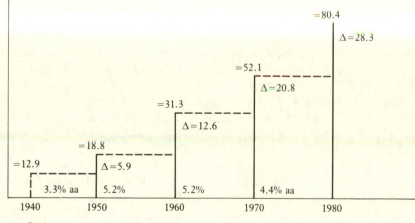

Source: *Conjuntura economica*, Mar. 1985.

Fig. 3.2. Growth of urban population and annual rates of growth, Brazil, 1940–1980

[2] The figures of urbanization are somewhat misleading, to the extent that many smaller towns with a population of less than 20,000 are inhabited by a majority of farmers and casual agricultural workers, the so-called 'boias frias'—landless peasants forced to migrate to the towns. Moreover, these towns have only the rudiments of an urban infrastructure. Thus, at least half of the Brazilian population is still rural and, in many cases, bypassed by the modernization processes (see Dowbor 1986: 46).

million). Brazil indulged in the luxury of building a new capital—Brasilia —famous for the quality of its architecture and design: the first large city in the world planned for cars rather than for people. Brazil's motor car factories—all belonging to large multinationals—produced over one million automobiles in 1986, out of which about one-quarter were exported. Brazil is also the fifth world exporter of weaponry and has been selling planes to the Royal Air Force of the United Kingdom. Brazilian surgeons are renowned for their ability in performing complicated transplants and marvellous plastic operations. Yet, as we shall see subsequently, the country's social indicators are dreadful. In a sense, the situation is the reverse of what happened in Sri Lanka, China, Cuba, or even Kerala (see Gunatilleke *et al.* 1984; Panikar and Soman 1984; Raj *et al.* 1975): Brazil's social profile is much lower than could be expected for a country at this level of technical sophistication, industrial advancement, and overall economic development.

A well-documented report on social policy points to the 'brutal contrast' between Brazil's economic indicators, which give the country the status of the eighth largest economy in the Western world, and its social indicators, which are comparable to those of poor Asian and African countries (Jaguaribe *et al.* 1986).

Beyond short-term immediate relief and welfare measures, the report proposes a fifteen-year reformist blueprint aimed at bringing Brazil to the level of contemporary Greece in terms of basic social indicators. It goes a long way to show that this is a feasible goal, on the condition of correcting the present distortions in the remuneration of factors: the excessive concentration of income in Brazil results from a conjunction of severe underpayment of the labour force, of much too generous rewards for capital—mostly the financial one—and of an insufficient socialization of the economic surplus (Jaguaribe *et al.* 1986: 101).

The report insists on the need to increase sharply the supply of foodstuffs while reducing their prices. In this context, it rightly points to the as yet unexplored potential for better use of available land, postulating a steady increase in agricultural employment at a rate of 2 per cent a year while taking a strong stand in favour of agrarian reform.

It is to be hoped that Brazilian planners will not forget the lessons of the past and will keep in mind that 'some kinds of 10 to 12 per cent growth per annum can lead to an *increase* in poverty rather than to its eradication' (Kurien 1978: 15–16). The temptation of a three-level reductionism must be resisted: development requires more than the steering of the economy; this, in turn, calls for something more than growth alone; lastly growth depends on non-investment factors along with investment.

We turn now to some significant structural aspects of the Brazilian development/maldevelopment process.

(a) Perverse growth and social inequality

As already mentioned, the growth process in Brazil has a built-in bias towards social inequality, or, to put it differently, the state has not imposed up to now any checks against this natural trend in an unbridled capitalist growth. On the contrary, the authoritarian regime, which lasted for over twenty years (1964–84), succeeded in weakening the trade union movement, dismantling the radical left-wing opposition, and slowing down, if not preventing altogether, the emergence of strong peasant organizations. However, Brazilian civil society managed to organize itself in thousands of grassroots action groups, ecclesial communities (supported by the progressive wing of the Catholic Church), neighbourhood associations, women's organizations, black and youth movements, etc. All these were instrumental in progressively changing the political climate and pushing through local demands, but they were unable to influence the income distribution processes in a significant way (see Singer and Brandt 1980 and Cardoso and Sachs 1985). Ultimately, the emergence of these movements, and of what Rajni Kothari calls 'non-party politics', played an important role in the gradual liberalization of the regime (the so-called 'abertura') and the handing back of power to civilians.

In São Paulo independent trade unions, mainly supported by metal workers —by far the best paid in Brazil—succeeded in creating a new left-wing Workers' Party—PT. But before 1986 the recession and mounting unemployment prevented the emergence of a suitable environment for successful bargaining for a greater share of wages in value added. The stabilization plan, implemented since February 1986, theoretically puts a brake on the workers' demands while guaranteeing price stability.[3] In practice, some upward adjustments of wages occurred under the impact of the buoyant conjuncture, to be soon offset once more by the upsurge of inflation. At any rate, they have not significantly affected as yet the extremely skewed income distribution pattern. Industrialists do not object to the co-opting of the workers' aristocracy to middle-class lifestyles, so long as they can rely on the steady inflow of new labour—mainly rural migrants—ready to take unskilled jobs for low pay.

The middle and upper classes account for the bulk of consumption expenditure. Accordingly, the Brazilian industrial structure is biased towards the production of durables, motor cars, and middle- and upper-class housing, in short 'luxuries' (L), as opposed to 'essentials' or 'necessities' (N)—basic goods and housing for low-income people. The L-sector competes successfully with the N-sector for capital and intermediate goods, skills, technical know-how, scarce foreign exchange, and public savings. The U-city (for upper class) absorbs most of the public resources spent on the maintenance, upgrading, and expansion of urban infrastructure (see Fig. 3.3 for a schematic representation of 'development' and 'maldevelopment').

The imbalance between the L-sector and the N-sector is further accentuated

---

[3] The full text of the plan was published by *Gazeta mercantil* on 24 July 1986.

Development: need oriented growth   Maldevelopment: growth through
                                                          the hypertrophy of L

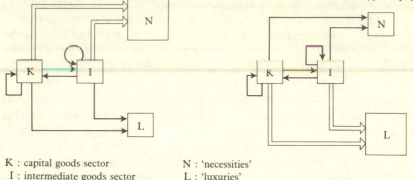

K : capital goods sector   N : 'necessities'
I : intermediate goods sector   L : 'luxuries'

Fig. 3.3. A schematic representation of development and maldevelopment

by the situation prevailing in agriculture. Large landowners get all the incentives to produce commodities for export and, more recently, sugarcane alcohol used as a substitute for petrol (about 90 per cent of all the cars now produced in Brazil are entirely alcohol powered). Food production for the internal market is, however, lagging behind and staple food availability per capita has been dwindling. As was to be expected, food prices had been pushing up inflation, the low-income people being the hardest hit because food takes a larger proportion of their earnings.[4]

The Brazilian growth pattern in the late 1950s, already based on the hypertrophy of the L-sector, was interpreted by this author as a case of 'perverse growth'. Given the shallowness of the market for L-goods, in the absence of land reform opening a market for mass production of consumer goods, industry would soon be faced by a saturated demand and growth led by luxury consumption would come to a standstill.

This prediction proved wrong. Why? Four factors were underestimated:

1. the deepening of the domestic market for L-goods through further deterioration of the income distribution and encouragement of extravagant consumption patterns: 28.3 per cent of Brazilian urban households owned cars in 1980, many of them at the expense of inadequate nutrition; thus the laws of Engel appear to have been distorted by the 'proletarization of durable goods consumption' (Denslow and Tyler 1983);

2. the role played by the opening of the economic frontier and the incor-

[4] This analysis is made on the basis of the Raj–Sen four-sector model, adapted by Sachs (1979) and used for the discussion of the Indian and Brazilian cases at Kalecki's seminar in Warsaw in the 1960s. For the distinction between 'luxuries' and 'necessities' see Kalecki (1976) and, later on, Sau (1985). The industrial structures corresponding to 'development' and 'maldevelopment' are schematized in Fig. 3.2.

poration, often predatory, of new natural resources into the GNP (a process that recalls Rosa Luxemburg's argument on the need for capitalism constantly to appropriate new non capitalist territories in order to grow);

3. the capacity to expand industrial exports. This was due to several factors: the speed at which Brazil absorbed modern technologies, the competitiveness of its products thanks to a combination of cheap natural resources, underpaid labour, and aggressive trade policies on the part of the government, and finally the expansion of world trade;

4. the possibility of raising foreign loans on a massive scale from private banks eager to recycle 'petrodollars'.

Bardhan (1985: 20) is therefore right: 'A home market concentrated in the upper income segments of the population is, of course, not necessarily a constraint on the rate of industrial growth. If exports expand sufficiently, or if the rich get richer at a sufficiently rapid rate and spend their booming income on "luxury" consumption and reinvest their profits, industrial growth may not be broad-based or wholesome, but it can be fast, as the recent history of countries like South Korea or Brazil has shown us.' The other side of the coin is, of course, the exclusion of the poor majority from the benefits of such growth.

(b) Belindia

In order to be able to absorb growing quantities of L-goods, Brazil was transformed into a BELINDIA (the neologism was coined by E. Bacha): a Belgium in the middle of an India, with parts of Nordeste comparable to Bangladesh. Industrialization had the opposite effect to that anticipated by Arthur Lewis. Instead of gradually exhausting the reserve of unskilled labour by drawing it into the modern organized sector, it deepened the process of exclusion and social segregation, creating a huge surplus of underemployed labour in the cities, including the category of 'boias frias', casual agricultural workers expelled from the rural areas by the mechanization of large estates and forced to live in towns while continuing to work in agriculture during the harvest and planting seasons.

Hence the proliferation in the urban economy of all sorts of petty jobs and activities, inadequately described as the 'informal sector'. In reality we are in the presence of a maze of interconnected labour, service, and goods markets, ranging from organized business to organized crime, a non-market household sector, as well as an incipient non-market social sector based on mutual help (*mutirão*). These structures of everyday life are affected by public policies, sometimes in a positive way (e.g. food subsidies), sometimes in a negative way (e.g. policies of eradication of shanty towns or repressive measures against pedlars and hawkers). In Brazil these activities account for much of housing production (in the 'illegal city' to use the terminology of Hardoy and Satterthwaite 1987) and an unknown share of unaccounted income. The existing estimates are utterly unreliable and often based on ideological prejudices.[5]

Little is known about the forms of exploitation to which independent workers are subjected by gangs, middlemen, and money-lenders, their levels of income, the organization of markets, the extent of smuggling (important as far as gold and precious stones are concerned), illegal gambling beside the popular illegal lottery (*jogo do bicho*), etc. The urban economy increasingly takes the form of a 'two gear economy' with a minority of highly productive and well-remunerated people and a majority that struggles for survival. Children and teenagers (0–19 years) account for 47 per cent of the population. Out of their 63 million, 36 million are needy and one-fifth among them, i.e. 7 million, are abandoned and, therefore, forced to live on their own, often in the streets of large cities. The government provides shelter and schooling for 427,000 (data collected by FUNABEM, the agency entrusted with the protection of abandoned children).

Add to this the disparities between the cities and the countryside, between the relatively affluent and industrialized South-East provinces and the depressed Nordeste. As for the prospects, the debate goes on between those who see the Brazilian growth process in terms of continuity and those who see it as dichotomy. Bacha and Klein (1986: i.21) leave the following question unanswered: 'An incomplete or distorted capitalist growth? Do the superior and middle urban classes in São Paulo represent the advanced frontier in direction of which most Brazilians will move? Or else, do they constitute an enclave ever more distant from the rest of Brazil?' In this author's opinion the present growth pattern, if uncorrected, can only lead to further polarization of Brazilian society. This is not to say that some effects of rapid growth do not trickle down to the lower strata of the population. But the real question is, how much more could be achieved for them in the same lapse of time through structural reforms; what kind of social and ecological costs could be avoided while sustaining a reasonable rate of growth; what opportunities for genuine development are being at present forgone in such an exceptionally well-resource-endowed country as Brazil?

(c)   Agricultural expansion: dualism revisited

Brazil is blessed with the largest reserve of arable land in the world. In the 'cerrado' region alone—the savannah-like extensions of central Brazil—there are over 150 million hectares of cultivated land, not to speak of the Amazon

---

[5] Thus Pastore (1986: 45) claims that 4 million people found employment in the informal urban sector between 1981 and 1983, a period of sharp recession and contraction of formal employment. During these two years of sharp recession formal employment in the cities decreased from 18.1 to 17.4 million, while the informal supposedly went up from 14.1 to 18.0 million, the net result being that open unemployment increased only insignificantly from 2 to 2.4 million people, nothing to worry about for people who accept such estimates at face value! The influential conservative newspaper *O jornal da tarde* carried in 1984 a series of articles on the informal sector presented as the last refuge of private initiative persecuted by Leviathan (the state).

region, less amenable to open field cultivation but propitious to well-designed agro-sylvo-pastoral systems.

For many decades, agricultural output has been growing at a rate superior to that of per capita income, i.e. within the range of 4 to 5 per cent a year. Brazil has also become the second largest agricultural exporter in the world. Exports of soybeans, orange juice, and poultry have shown great dynamism in recent years. Yet, the country numbers 7 million landless peasant families while the 100 largest landowners possess 29.6 million hectares. Altogether, private properties cover 569.8 million hectares distributed in 4.1 million holdings, out of which only 80 million are cultivated. The top 1 per cent of holdings controls 231.5 million hectares and the top decile 432.4 million hectares, that is over three-quarters of the whole area. At the other extreme, the 2 million holdings below 50 hectares each account for only 46.5 million hectares (1984 Agrarian Census, IBGE, quoted by *EXAME*, 11 June 1986).

Historically, Brazilian agriculture developed a dualist structure with, on the one hand, large latifundia and, on the other, subsistence-oriented minifundia, both characterized by an extensive pattern of land utilization. The increments in production have been brought about essentially by the addition of cultivated land (see Table 3.1). Technological innovation has been confined to a few exportable and industrial crops.

It has been argued (Oliveira 1972) that the primitive minifundia played an important role in the process of capitalist accumulation by opening for cultivation, at a very low cost, virgin land in frontier areas and by supplying cheap foodstuffs to the urban population; the economic surplus generated through these operations ultimately accrued to urban capitalists. However, a recent survey has shown that the majority of small holdings participate only marginally in the production of traded surpluses. They remain essentially a reserve of a severely underemployed labour force, marginalized by the processes of agricultural modernization and industrialization (see Goodman 1986). At the same time holdings of up to 100 hectares, occupying one-fifth of total cultivated land, account for 80 per cent of the production of cassava, 77 per cent of beans, 68 per cent of corn, 46 per cent of soybeans, and 37 per cent of rice (*EXAME*, 12 Nov. 1986).

By contrast, the last fifteen years have been marked by a process of intensive modernization of an important segment of large holdings, oriented predominantly towards foreign markets and the production of industrial crops, the most

Table 3.1 Brazil: cultivated area, 1950–1980 (m. hectares)

	1950	1960	1970	1980
Total	19.10	28.71	33.98	49.19
Permanent cultures	4.40	7.80	7.98	10.50
Temporary cultures	14.69	20.91	26.00	38.69

Source: FIBGE (1982).

important being sugarcane for the extraction of ethanol used as a substitute for petrol.[6] The emphasis put on the production of sugarcane, together with the priority accorded to exportable cash crops, had a backlash effect on the production of staple foods. Between 1977 and 1984 the per capita production of food crops for the internal market decreased at a compound annual rate of 1.94 per cent, while export crops increased at a rate of 2.5 per cent and sugarcane at 7.8 per cent (Homem de Mello 1985). According to a recent estimate, the per capita supply of staple foods decreased by 8.8 per cent between 1977 and 1986 (*EXAME*, 12 Nov. 1986).

This recent modernization was made possible by an abundant supply of subsidized credits for the purchase of equipment, fertilizer, and pesticides, benefiting mainly the large farms and resulting in a sharp segmentation of the market. Goodman (1986) is right to say that it took the 'Prussian path', as was to be expected under the authoritarian regime committed to an overall project of 'conservative modernization'. 'Industrializing' the processes of agricultural production and encouraging multinational agribusiness companies to set up subsidiaries in Brazil was preferred to undertaking a land reform that would give landless peasants access to land and improve the viability of small family-operated farms.

A socially disruptive consequence of this trend has been the 'emptying of occupied spaces' (Abramovay 1986), i.e. the acceleration of the rural exodus from the most successful agricultural producing areas taken over by large-scale, heavily mechanized production of soybeans and sugarcane. From 1970 to 1980 the rural population of the country decreased for the first time, by 2.4 million in absolute terms. The contrast is striking indeed with the previous trend: from 1940 to 1950 it had increased by 4.8 million, from 1950 to 1960 by 5.6 million, and from 1960 to 1970 by 2.3 million (Goodman 1986). The rural exodus continues through the 1980s at a rate of about 900,000 people per year. Altogether, between 1960 and 1980, some 27 million people migrated from the countryside to urban areas unable to absorb such a huge contingent of additional labour force (Abramovay 1986), not to speak of the prohibitive costs of this massive urbanization.

The situation is therefore paradoxical, especially when compared with densely populated yet predominantly rural countries like China or India. Millions of people could still settle in the Brazilian countryside, both by means of colonization schemes on public land and by redistributing the unproductive latifundia. The theoretical limit of agricultural employment in Brazil, assuming a land–man ratio ten times as high as in Asia and the present level of

---

[6] 11 billion litres of ethanol were produced in 1985, the equivalent of about 150,000 barrels of oil per day. The 'Pro-alcool' is technically a success achieved at a very high economic cost with lavish residues. Though very expensive, it is now irreversible, as already some 3 million cars, out of a fleet of 12 million, are 100% alcohol powered and such cars account for 90% of the output of the Brazilian automotive industry (about one million per year). (For an evaluation, see Sachs *et al.* 1987.)

technology, has been estimated at 66.6 million people, i.e. more than the entire economically active population of the country! However, due to a combination of institutional factors (the tenure system) and of an ill-conceived modernization pattern, millions of 'rural refugees' are unnecessarily pushed to the cities, creating a major problem in terms of urban infrastructure, housing, and jobs.

The urbanization costs thus incurred will end up by taking a sizeable parcel of savings from productive investment, the more so since the maintenance costs of the cities tend to increase as the cities grow older. It may be reasonably assumed that the cost of settling peasants on, say, 25-hectare holdings, and helping them to develop integrated farm systems well adapted to agroclimatic conditions, would be far smaller. Government sources expect to implement the land reform at a cost of $3,000 per family. This appears, however, to be a severe underestimate. Other sources put it at $15,000 (*EXAME*, 12 Nov. 1986). Furthermore, land reform would promote the growth of small towns, as farmers would need their services and could afford to pay for them. By contrast, large estates with few employees usually bypass the local urban centres in their dealings.

Land reform is thus long overdue. It has been on the agenda of Brazilian politics for the last forty years and, in principle, figures prominently among the objectives of the new democratic government. It is hard to conceive how a policy aimed at making a dent in the accumulated poverty could be implemented in Brazil without a redistribution of land assets. The land reform announced in 1985 was supposed to benefit 9.4 million peasant families by 1989, using 71 million hectares of public land and up to 400 million hectares of unproductive private land, expropriated with monetary compensation. The landowners threatened to use weapons. Violence spread and hundreds of people lost their lives, many among them peasant trade unionists. The reform was subsequently watered down. Mainly public land will be used. Meanwhile, only about 7,000 families got their property titles, out of the 150,000 initially contemplated for the first year of the reform. In spite of the strong pressure of the Catholic Church, firmly committed to the reform, the government is taking a cautious attitude to the disappointment of peasant trade unions.

(d) The 'ecological debt'

Growth through inequality breeds environmental disruption at both ends of the social spectrum. Rich people indulge in extremely wasteful patterns of resources use, be it through lavish consumption patterns, extensive and predatory uses of land and forest, or careless technology—the industrial centre of Cubatão near Santos is probably one of the most polluted places in the world due to the excessive concentration of steel mills, oil refineries, and chemical plants, this in a country of 8.5 million square kilometres for a population of 135 million. Poor people living from hand to mouth, in particular the small 'minifundistas' with not enough land and the squatters in the pioneer areas, with no security of tenure whatsoever, end up by overtaxing or plundering their life-support systems by indiscriminately felling the forest, allowing pastures to be overgrazed, and causing widespread erosion by inadequate handling of fragile tropical soils. Thus, the land tenure system is also at the root of the ecological question.

3.2. How many poor?

As already mentioned, data on the social profile of Brazil are scanty and often contradictory. Authors diverge, as would be expected, on the definition of the poverty line. Calsing (1983) proposes five different concepts. Households below the 'poverty line' are those whose income is less than double the cost of the basic food basket. Households below the 'destitution line' have a purchasing power inferior to the cost of the food basket. Households below the 'relative poverty line' have an average income inferior to half the average per capita income of all the households. Families in 'extreme poverty' are those whose per capita monthly income is inferior to 0.25 SM (Salário Mínimo—Minimum Legal Wage). Finally, families in 'relative poverty' are those whose monthly per capita income ranges from 0.25 to 0.5 SM. His results are summarized in Table 3.2.

Jaguaribe's findings, based on the 1984 sample survey conducted by FIBGE, are the following.

Out of an economically active population of 52.4 million, 29.3 per cent of the actually employed earned less than 1 SM per month (the proportion is 42.9 per cent for the rural employed). 22.6 per cent earned between 1 and 2 SM. Another 12.9 per cent did not have any income. Table 3.3 gives the regional distribution.

In the Nordeste 25.4 per cent of the economically active population earns less than 0.5 SM and another 30 per cent earns between 0.5 and 1 SM. The Sen poverty index, calculated by Jaguaribe, assumes the following values for different regions: Brazil 0.516, Nordeste 0.780, Sudeste 0.380, South 0.299.

Turning now to data by families, out of 31,075,602 units, 24.3 per cent had monthly incomes inferior to 1 SM and another 4 per cent no monetary earnings at all. Those with monthly earnings between 1 and 2 SM numbered 24.3 per cent. Altogether, more than half of Brazilian families had incomes below the poverty line and over one-quarter were below the indigency line.

Roughly the same picture emerges from the calculation by Helga Hoffman (1986).

Still another report on the North-East region (Calsing et al. 1985) reached the conclusion that 70 per cent of the families there had a per capita income inferior to 0.5 SM per month, i.e. less than the cost of the basic food ration.

A World Bank Study (Hicks and Vetter) recommended for the cities a poverty line ranging from 3 to 4 SM per family to allow for cost of living differences.

All these studies, imperfect as they may be, and not always comparable as

Table 3.2 Estimates of households and families in a situation of poverty, Brazil, 1970 and 1980

	1970	1980
Percentage of households below the poverty line		
Total	49.0	43.0
Urban	35.0	31.0
Rural	73.0	70.0
Percentage of households below the destitution line		
Total	25.0	21.0
Urban	15.0	12.0
Rural	42.0	41.0
Percentage of households below the relative poverty line		
Total	54.0	42.0
Urban	52.0	28.0
Rural	57.0	68.0
Percentage of families		
In extreme poverty		
Total	43.9	17.7
Urban	22.6	6.5
Rural	61.2	36.0
In relative poverty		
Total	25.2	23.1
Urban	28.1	18.2
Rural	22.8	32.1

Source: Compiled by Calsing (1983).

Table 3.3 Economically active population, Brazil and regions, 1984: relative share of the three lowest earning strata (%)

	Brazil	North	Nordeste	South-East	South	West centre
≤ ½ SM	13.4	7.1	25.4	9.5	8.5	9.3
> ½ ≤ 1 SM	22.8	17.7	29.8	20.5	19.6	21.1
> 1 ≤ 2 SM	25.0	27.0	23.4	24.4	27.7	29.3

Source: FIBGE (1984: 3.16).

they use slightly different concepts of 'households' and 'families', converge to give a staggering picture of deprivation for a country with a GNP per head around $2,000 per year (and probably more in terms of purchasing power parity) which has gone through an intensive industrialization process and managed to create millions of new secondary and tertiary jobs: employment in the secondary sector increased by 2.36 million from 1960 to 1970 and 5.38 million from 1970 to 1980, the corresponding figures for the tertiary sector being 3.64 and 8.84 million (Faria 1983). The relative numbers of the destitute and very poor may have decreased between 1970 and 1980, but the absolute numbers are still very high when contrasted with the economic potential of the country.

It should be noted in this connection that a modest redistribution of income would be sufficient to eliminate abject poverty. According to Helga Hoffman (1986), it would be enough to transfer every year 2 per cent of the total income to the families below the destitution line to push them above this line: 0.8 per cent in the South-East region, but 7.3 per cent in the North-East; 1 per cent in the urban areas, 8 per cent in the countryside. However, the corresponding figures for the poverty line are much higher: 8.8 per cent for the country as a whole, 25.1 per cent in the North-East region, 4.1 per cent in the South-East; 4.9 per cent in urban areas, but not less than 34.5 per cent in the countryside.

Widespread poverty goes hand in hand with an extreme concentration of income. The distribution of income among the economically active population is given in Table 3.4.

Table 3.4 Income distribution (economically active population), Brazil, 1960–1980

Deciles	1960		1970		1980	
	%	% cumulative	%	% cumulative	%	% cumulative
First	1.9	1.9	1.2	1.2	1.1	1.1
Second	2.0	3.9	2.2	3.4	2.1	3.2
Third	3.0	6.9	2.9	6.3	2.9	6.1
Fourth	4.4	11.3	3.7	10.0	3.7	9.8
Fifth	6.1	17.4	4.9	14.9	4.3	14.1
Sixth	7.5	24.9	6.0	20.9	5.5	19.6
Seventh	9.0	33.9	7.3	28.2	7.3	26.9
Eighth	11.3	45.2	9.9	38.1	8.9	36.8
Ninth	15.2	60.4	15.2	53.3	15.5	52.3
Tenth	39.6	100.0	46.7	100.0	47.7	100.0
The richest 5%	28.3	—	34.1	—	34.9	—
The richest 1%	11.9	—	14.7	—	14.9	—

Source: FIBGE (1979: 63–4) and Calsing (1983: 37).

Data presented by Denslow and Tyler (1983) differ slightly from the above table and point to a marginal improvement in the distribution of income between 1970 and 1980. Even so, the pattern is one of extreme concentration. Their data show that the absolute increase in the average income of the highest decile, between 1970 and 1980, represented about 15 times the average total income of the lowest decile in 1980 and, conversely, that the average income of the lowest decile improved by less than 1 per cent of the average income of the highest decile.

It should be noted, furthermore, that data on the distribution of income from dividends, interests, and rents have not been systematically studied; and very little is known about the distribution of wealth with the exception of land assets (Hoffman 1986: 76).

A striking feature of the Brazilian economy has been the gradual erosion of the purchasing power of the Salário Mínimo (minimum wage). According to DIIESE, a trade union think tank, in 1985 the average purchasing power of the SM was less than 50 per cent of its initial value, established in July 1940 (see Fig. 3.4). Accordingly, in São Paulo in December 1985, 77.7 per cent of workers were earning less than the original minimum legal wage adjusted for the increase of prices (UNICAMP 1986).

This reduction in the purchasing power of the SM should be contrasted with a more than threefold increase of average income per head between 1940 and 1983.[7] Singer (1986) calculated the ratios of legal minimum monthly wage to

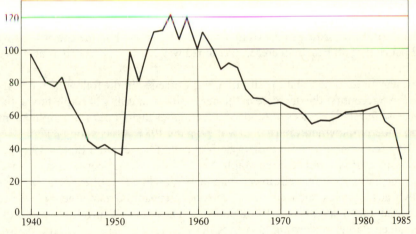

Source: DIIESE, after *Folha de São Paulo*.

Fig. 3.4. Evolution of the purchasing power of the legal minimum wage, Brazil, 1940–1986

[7] The present value of the SM, using the official exchange rate, is about $60. This is, however, a somewhat misleading figure as the purchasing power of the cruzado, when related to the consumption pattern of the low-income population, exceeds what is indicated on the basis of the exchange rate.

average monthly GNP per head. This ratio was 2.1 in 1960, 1.64 in 1969, 1.0 in 1970, 0.41 in 1980, and 0.44 in 1983.

3.3. *Malnutrition and hunger*

Josue de Castro's *A geografia da fome*, published in 1946, opened a new area of studies on the ecology of endemic and epidemic starvation and of partial, specific, and occult nutritional deficiencies. Unfortunately his pioneering efforts were not continued and all recent publications on malnutrition and hunger in Brazil[8] are still based on the ENDEF study conducted in 1975 by the Brazilian authorities with the assistance of the FAO. Lack of more recent data precludes a reliable assessment of the impact of the 1981–4 recession and the shifts that occurred in the consumption patterns of the population (e.g. less rice and beans, compensated by a higher intake of noodles made out of subsidized wheat, and lower consumption of beef).

The ENDEF data, as summarized by Knight and Moran (1981), show that the diets of only 33 per cent of the population in 1975 met the FAO/WHO low calorie requirements, while protein requirements are almost always met in diets composed of the foods normally consumed by the Brazilians (this may have changed in recent years, however, in connection with the shifts suggested above). The diets of 17 per cent of the population were deficient by more than 400 calories. As much as 49 per cent of the urban population in the Nordeste suffered from these serious deficits (see Table 3.5).

ENDEF anthropometric data have been used to estimate the extent of malnutrition according to the Gomez indices. From birth to the age of 17, only 42 per cent of all Brazilian children reached weights normal for their ages (see Table 3.6).

It may be assumed that the situation has worsened in the following ten years on three accounts: the decrease in the per capita availability of staple foods, the increase in relative prices of food, and the higher incidence of unemployment and underemployment, particularly during the 1981–4 recession.

As already mentioned, Homem de Melo (1985) calculated that in 1984 the per capita production of five staple foods (rice, beans, corn, cassava, and potatoes) was 15.1 per cent lower than in 1977, while that of exportable crops (soybeans, oranges, tobacco, cocoa, cotton, and peanuts) increased by 13.3 per cent and that of sugarcane by 74.8 per cent. The per capita production of meat remained stable. According to Ivan Ribeiro (*Gazeta mercantil*, 23 Apr. 1986), the per capita availability of staple foods decreased by 25 per cent between 1965 and 1985.

According to recent estimates, 78 million out of 138 million Brazilians suffer from nutritional deficiencies (*EXAME*, 12 Nov. 1986).

[8] See e.g. Viacava *et al.* (1983) and Minayo (1985).

Table 3.5 Estimates of dietary deficiency in Brazil, 1975

Region and urban or rural location	Total population (000)	Persons whose diets are adequate		Persons having deficits of up to 200 calories		Persons having deficits of 200–400 calories		Total deficits up to 400 calories (m. calories/day)	Deficits of more than 400 calories				Total of all deficits (m. calories/day)
		Thousands	% of total	Thousands	% of total	Thousands	% of total		Persons (000)	% of total	Average deficit (calories/person/day)	Total deficit (m. calories/day)	
North-East													
Rural	17,739.8	5,361.2	30.2	3,775.9	21.3	6,173.8	34.8	1,958.4	2,428.9	13.7	540	1,310.4	3,268.8
Urban	14,291.7	1,217.6	8.5	1,460.6	10.2	4,660.8	32.6	1,473.0	6,952.6	48.7	529	3,678.4	5,151.3
Total	32,031.5	6,578.3	20.5	5,236.5	16.4	10,834.6	33.8	3,431.4	9,381.5	29.3	532	4,988.8	8,420.0
South-East													
Rural	20,046.2	14,010.9	69.9	2,408.2	12.0	3,305.3	16.5	943.1	321.7	1.6	476	153.3	1,096.3
Urban	44,524.8	13,195.1	29.6	10,255.5	23.0	15,603.0	35.1	4,709.9	5,471.1	12.3	527	2,882.6	7,592.5
Total	64,571.0	27,206.1	42.1	12,663.7	19.6	18,908.3	29.3	5,653.0	5,792.8	9.0	524	3,035.9	8,688.8
Frontier													
Rural	5,268.7	678.9	12.9	975.7	18.5	1,850.7	35.1	656.0	1,763.4	33.5	593	1,087.2	1,717.3
Urban	5,274.0	649.8	12.3	1,042.6	19.8	1,943.1	36.9	630.0	1,633.4	31.0	617	968.2	1,624.2
Total	10,542.7	1,328.7	12.6	2,018.3	19.2	3,793.8	36.0	1,286.0	3,396.8	32.2	605	2,055.4	3,341.4
All Brazil													
Rural	43,054.7	20,051.0	46.6	7,226.7	16.8	11,427.2	26.1	3,531.5	4,514.0	10.5	565	2,550.8	6,082.3
Urban	64,090.5	15,062.6	23.5	12,691.8	19.8	22,114.5	34.8	6,858.5	14,057.1	21.9	536	7,529.1	14,367.6
Total	107,145.2	35,113.6	32.8	19,918.5	18.6	33,541.7	31.3	10,370.2	18,571.1	17.3	543	10,079.8	20,450.0

Note: Detail may not add to totals because of rounding.

Sources: Total population by region and urban or rural location from FIBGE (1977). All other estimates were derived from unpublished data of Estudo nacional da despesa familiar (ENDEF).

Table 3.6 Nutritional status of children to the age of 17, by region, Brazil, 1975

Nutritional status	Children (000)				% of the age group			
	All Brazil	North-East	South-East	Frontier	All Brazil	North-East	South-East	Frontier
Adequately nourished	21,723	5,231	14,376	2,116	41.7	31.6	48.3	37.0
First-degree malnutrition	19,349	6,332	10,783	2,234	37.2	38.2	36.2	39.0
Second-degree malnutrition	10,543	4,630	4,581	1,131	20.2	28.0	15.4	23.3
Third-degree malnutrition	447	361	44	42	0.9	2.2	0.2	0.7

Source: Knight *et al.* (1979: Annex 3, Tables 16–19).

3.5. *Unemployment and underemployment*

Definitional problems mar the official surveys of unemployment to the point of making them irrelevant. Underemployment is an even more arbitrary concept. Jaguaribe puts unemployment (including urban underemployment) at 13 million people in 1983, i.e. one-quarter of the economically active population. In the same year, only 60,000 jobs were created in the organized sector; this was, however, an abnormally low figure. During the three years 1981–3 only 700,000 jobs were created, according to estimates of the Ministry of Labour. Another 1.8 million became vacant by death or retirement. The new entrants on the labour market during these years of recession numbered at least 4.5 million. Thus, the number of open unemployed must have increased by about 2 million people (Adriano Lopes de Oliveira, *EXAME*, 12 Dec. 1984). In 1985 employment grew by about 1.5 million. When offset against the figure of new entrants, this figure gives little margin to absorb the backlog of unemployed and underemployed, the more so since many enterprises affected by the recession managed to improve their situation by undertaking labour-displacing rather than capacity-augmenting investment.

The situation is particularly dramatic in the large cities of Nordeste swollen by a massive influx of 'rural refugees' under the combined effect of the recession and of five years of a very severe drought, which affects the region periodically. A 1984 survey conducted in Recife showed that over 9 per cent of the economically active population did not have any income, 13 per cent earned less than 0.5 SM, and another 16 per cent earned between 0.5 and 1 SM (*Senhor*, 22 Apr. 1986). In Fortaleza open unemployment in 1984 was evaluated at 15 per cent of the economically active population and underemployment at 43 per cent. In the organized sector 36 per cent of the workers earned less than 1 SM (personal communication from the mayor's office).

In periods of drought, starvation is not uncommon among rural populations of Nordeste. The emergency public works programmes undertaken by the government have been of little help. Starving peasants move to the nearest towns. Occasionally violence breaks out and food stores are looted. During the last recession, sporadic cases of looting of supermarkets also occurred in São Paulo and Rio de Janeiro.

3.6. *Other social interests*

To complete the description of the social conditions in Brazil we shall briefly review a few other indicators.

Life expectancy at birth in 1976 was 54.8 years for families earning up to 1 SM, and 69.6 years for families earning more than 5 SM (Calsing 1983). The comparison between São Paulo and Nordeste shows, once more, a striking contrast (see Table 3.7).

Table 3.7 Life expectancy, Brazil, 1970 and 1977

	Brazil		North-East		São Paulo state		São Paulo metropolitan region	
	1970	1977	1970	1977	1970	1977	1970	1977
Urban								
Per capita income ≤0.5 SM	52.53	55.43	44.64	49.77	55.77	62.89	58.25	59.91
Per capita income >2 SM	66.58	68.97	62.12	64.68	69.53	69.64	69.32	70.37
Rural								
Per capita income ≤0.5 SM	52.48	—	45.95	—	56.50	—	—	—
Per capita income >2 SM	—	—	—	—	—	—	—	—
Total								
Per capita income ≤0.5 SM	52.53	55.43	44.66	48.63	55.77	62.89	58.25	59.91
Per capita income >2 SM	66.58	68.97	62.12	64.68	69.53	69.64	69.32	70.37

Source: Calsing (1983).

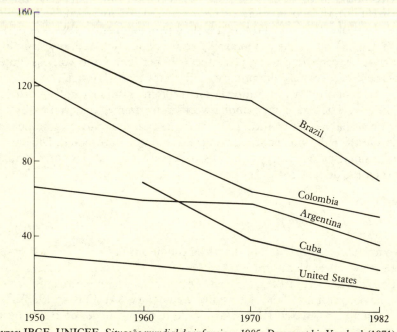

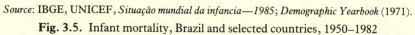
Source: IBGE, UNICEF, *Situação mundial da infancia—1985*; *Demographic Yearbook* (1971).

Fig. 3.5. Infant mortality, Brazil and selected countries, 1950–1982

Table 3.8 Housing conditions, Brazil, 1978

Income category by household	No. of households (000)	Percentage of households with						
		Five amenities[a]	Four amenities	Three amenities	Two amenities	One amenity	No amenities	Unspecified
≤1 SM	1,597.0	11.7	12.3	21.5	27.3	19.1	7.9	0.2
>1 ≤ 2 SM	2,827.6	17.7	16.0	22.1	24.5	14.1	5.5	0.2
>2 ≤ 3 SM	2,267.3	26.6	22.0	20.2	19.9	8.5	2.7	0.1
>3 ≤ 5 SM	3,210.2	37.5	25.4	17.0	14.4	4.4	1.2	0.1
>5 ≤ 7 SM	1,842.9	49.8	27.7	11.5	8.7	2.0	0.3	0.1
>7 ≤ 10 SM	1,453.2	58.9	26.9	8.8	4.4	0.3	0.1	0.0
>10 SM	2,372.8	77.5	17.0	3.8	1.3	0.3	0.1	0.0
Without income	41.8	17.6	14.1	22.5	28.5	12.1	5.2	—
Unspecified	64.2	48.1	19.1	12.1	12.9	4.7	3.1	—
TOTAL	15,676.0	39.2	21.0	15.4	14.8	2.5	7.0	0.1

[a] The five amenities are: water supply, sanitation, density ≤1 person per room, durable construction, and electricity.

Source: Calsing (1983).

Infant mortality in Brazil has been decreasing lately. But it is still about five times as high as in the United States. Cuba and Colombia fare much better (see Fig. 3.5).

The gap is very large between families earning up to 1 SM and those with more than 5 SM. The respective mortality indicators are 118.6 per thousand and 53.0 per thousand for children below 5 years of age (Calsing 1983).

Data on housing illustrate the precarious living conditions of the low-income populations (Table 3.8).

Access to education is still severely limited. Out of a population of 38.4 million in the 10 to 24 years age bracket, only 17.1 million were attending school in 1980, as shown in Table 3.9. Low education goes hand in hand with low pay for the majority of workers (see Table 3.10).

Finally, as far as racial relations are concerned, a survey conducted in 1982 by FIBGE pointed out that 77.5 per cent of the black workers and 70.8 per cent of 'browns' earned less than 2 SM while among the white working population the corresponding figure was 52.3 per cent (Dowbor 1986: 55).[9] An earlier

Table 3.9 School attendance, Brazil, 1980

Age bracket (years)	Population (m.)	School attendance (m.)	% of the population
10–14	13.5	9.6	70
15–19	13.3	5.6	42
20–4	11.6	1.9	16

Source: Data from FIBGE quoted by Dowbor (1986: 25).

Table 3.10 Levels of education and of income, Brazil, 1983

Years of schooling	Working population (m.)	Workers earning less than 2 minimum wages (m.)	% of workers with less than 2 minimum wages
0–1	10.0	7.7	77.1
1–2	6.3	4.3	68.2
3–4	13.9	8.0	57.3
5–8	9.5	5.1	54.5
9–11	5.5	2.1	37.1
12 or more	3.2	0.3	10.0
Unspecified	0.1	0.06	62.7
TOTAL	48.5	27.5	56.8

Source: Data from FIBGE quoted by Dowbow (1986: 25).

[9] Out of a working population of 47.9 million, 27.5 million were 'white', 3.7 million 'black', and 16.2 million 'brown' (coloured).

study, conducted in 1976, but only recently released, indicated that the average wage level of browns was 45 per cent that of whites, while the level of blacks was only 35 per cent that of whites (*The Economist*, 10 May 1986, p. 42).

3.7. *Conclusion*

The continuous deterioration of the economic and political climate underlines the need for the country to face the structural problems exacerbated by twenty years of authoritarian regime: the anachronistic land tenure, the oligopolistic industrial structure, the extremely uneven income distribution, the enormous 'social debt' compounded by environmental disruption, not to speak of the foreign and internal debts. Jaguaribe's recommendations coincide to a considerable extent with the scenario of redistribution with growth put forward by Knight (1981), emphasizing investment in basic public services (through the state sector) and in basic wage goods (through the private sector) and also recommending a land reform, a financial reform, and a fiscal reform.[10]

Emergency social programmes are overdue. As already mentioned, the national plan (1986–9) announced several measures to broaden the schemes of food distribution to expectant mothers and infants, of free school meals, and of subsidized meals for certain categories of workers. The housing policies are to be revised, so as to step up the construction of housing for families earning less than 3 SM per month. However, the BNH (National Housing Bank) has been discontinued as a consequence of a deep financial crisis. Meeting the housing needs of the low-income population would require a drastic departure from previous practices and a resort to substantial subsidization. The deficit of the public budget makes this target unrealistic, so long as a lasting solution is not found to reduce the burden of servicing the external and the internal debts.

In 1985, the outlays for the social programmes did not increase much (UNICAMP 1986). An ambitious social programme should not, however, represent a major financial difficulty, as the outlays involved are not so high and no foreign exchange is required. Right now, organizational problems seem more severe.

In a World Bank report, Knight *et al.* estimated that a virtually full coverage of the population needs in health, nutrition, education, housing, water supply, and sewerage could be achieved between the years 1990 and 2000 by government spending of the order of 5 to 6 per cent of GDP annually between now and then, with maximum additional taxation of approximately 2 per cent of GDP (see Knight and Moran 1981). Another estimate puts at 4 per cent of GDP a year the amount of resources required to lift the whole population to the poverty line (Fava quoted by Homem de Melo). In his report, Jaguaribe

---

[10] Knight recommends *inter alia* the lowering of indirect taxes on basic wage goods along with an increase in the indirect taxation of luxury consumption goods, much as suggested by Kalecki for India in 1959. Jaguaribe *et al.* (1986) advocate a capital tax on apparent signs of wealth, very appropriate in the Brazilian context.

(Jaguaribe *et al.* 1986) puts at 2 per cent of GNP per year the additional outlays on social services required to lift Brazil from the present state of social underdevelopment to the level of Greece by the year 2000. This figure is, however, obtained on a rather shaky basis by comparing Brazil's social expenditure with that of Greece.

Whether the order of magnitude is of 2 or 4 per cent of GDP, these figures ought to be compared with the 4 per cent of GNP drained abroad every year to pay for the interest on the foreign debt alone and another 4 per cent required before the recent monetary reform to service the internal debt.

Brazil, like many other developing countries, could thus afford to build a 'welfare state' without waiting for the levels of affluence of industrialized countries, provided that it makes extensive use of forms of public support that have a high manpower component and a low capital and foreign exchange component (e.g. education, primary health delivery systems, assisted self-help housing construction, etc.).

Brazil has a remarkable 'potential for endogenous development' (see Sachs 1984): the cultural capacity to define a 'national project', the political-administrative capacity to implement it, and a comprehensive and fairly autonomous (but not autarchic) techno-industrial structure to sustain it. Furthermore, many opportunities exist to step up the country's economic growth through 'non-investment sources': by eliminating wasteful patterns of resource use, making better use of existing productive capacities, and decreasing the rate of real depreciation by a better maintenance of equipments and infrastructures. All this provides a solid economic basis for a socially responsive development strategy. Whether political conditions to unfold it really exist remains to be seen.

References

ABRAMOVAY, R. (1986), 'Campo e reforma agrária', in *Nova república, um balanço* (Pôrto Alegre: LPM).

BACHA, E. L., and KLEIN, H. S. (1986), *A transição incompleta: Brasil desde 1945* (Rio de Janeiro: Paz e terra).

BARDHAN, P. (1985), *The Political Economy of Development in India* (Delhi: Oxford University Press).

BARROS DE CASTRO, A., and PIRES DE SOUZA, F. (1985), *A economia brasileira em marcha forçada* (Rio de Janeiro: Paz e terra).

CALSING, E. F. (1983), 'Dimensionamento e caracterização da pobreza no Brazil', mimeo (Brasilia: CNRH/IPEA/UNICEF).

——*et al.* (1985), *Desigualdades sociais no Nordeste* (Brasília: CNRH/IPEA/UNICEF/ SUDENE).

CARDOSO, F. H. (1980), *As ideias em seu lugar: Ensaios sobre as teorias do desenvolvimento* (Petrópolis: Vozes).

CARDOSO, R. L., and SACHS, C. (1985), 'Brésil: La Démocratie venue d'en bas', *Autogestions* (Paris), 22.

CARDOSO DE MELLO, J. M. (1982), *O capitalismo tardio* (São Paulo: Brasiliense).

CHANDLER, W. V. (1986), 'The Changing Role of the Market in National Economies', Worldwatch Paper 72 (Washington, DC).

DENSLOW, D., jun., and TYLER, W. G. (1983), *Perspectives on Poverty and Income Inequality in Brazil*, (Washington, DC: World Bank).

DOWNOR, L. (1986), *Aspectos oconômicos da educação* (São Paulo: Ática).

DRAIBE, S. (1984), *Rumos e metamorfoses: Estado e industrialização no Brasil: 1930–1960* (Rio de Janeiro: Paz e terra).

FARIA, V. E. (1983), 'Desenvolvimento, urbanização e mudanças na estrutura do emprego', in Sorj, B., and Almeida, M. H. (eds.), *Sociedade e política no Brasil pós 64* (São Paulo: Brasiliense).

Fundação instituto brasileiro de geografia e estatística (1977), *Anuário estatístico do Brasil, 1976* (Rio de Janeiro: FIBGE).

——(1979), *Indicadores sociais* (Rio de Janeiro: FIBGE).

——(1982), *Aspectos da evolção da agropecuária brasileira: 1940–1980* (Rio de Janeiro: FIBGE).

——(1984), *Pesquisa nacional por amostra de domicílios* (Rio de Janeiro: FIBGE).

FURTADO, C. (1956), *Formação econômica do Brasil* (São Paulo: Editora nacional).

GOODMAN, D. (1986), 'Economia e sociedade rurais a partir de 1945', in Bacha and Klein (1986).

GUNATILLEKE, G., *et al.* (1984), *Intersectoral Action for Health* (Colombo: Marga Institute).

HARDOY, J. E., and SATTERTHWAITE, D. (1987), 'The Legal and the Illegal City', in Rodwin, L. (ed.), *Shelter, Settlements and Development* (London: Arnold).

HICKS, J. F., and VETTER, M. D. (1983), 'Identifying the Urban Poor in Brazil', World Bank Staff Working Paper No. 565 (Washington, DC: World Bank).

HIRSCHMAN, A. O. (1986), 'Out of Phase Again', *New York Review of Books*, 18 Dec.

HOFFMAN, HELGA (1986), 'Pobreza e prosperidade no Brasil: o quê está mudando?' in Bacha and Klein (1986).

HOMEM DE MELO, F. (1985), *Prioridade agrícola: Sucesso ou fracasso?* (São Paulo: Pioneira).

JAGUARIBE, H., *et al.* (1986), *Brasil, 2000: Para um novo pacto social* (Rio de Janeiro: Paz e terra).

KALECKI, M. (1976), *Essays on Developing Economies* (Hassocks: Harvester Press; Atlantic Highlands, NJ: Humanities Press).

KNIGHT, P. T. (1981), *Brazilian Socialeconomic Development: Issues for the Eighties*, World Bank Reprint Series No. 203 (Washington, DC: World Bank).

——*et al.* (1979), *Brazil: Human Resources Special Report* (Washington, DC: World Bank).

——and MORAN, R. J. (1981), *Brazil* (Washington, DC: World Bank).

KURIEN, C. T. (1978), *Poverty, Planning and Social Transformation* (New Delhi: Allied Publishers).

MINAYO, M. C. DE S. (ed.) (1985), *Raízes da fome* (Petrópolis: Vozes).

OLIVEIRA, F. DE (1972), 'A economia brasileira: Crítica da razão dualista', *Estudos CEBRAP*, 2.

PANIKAR, P. G. K., and SOMAN, C. R. (1984), *Health Status of Kerala: Paradox of Economic Backwardness and Health Development* (Trivandrum: Centre for Development Studies).

PASTORE, J. (1986), 'Desigualdade e mobilidade social: Dez anos depois', in Bacha and Klein (1986).

RAJ, J. N., *et al.* (1975), *Poverty, Unemployment and Development Policy: A Case Study of Selected Issues with Reference to Kerala* (New York: United Nations).

SACHS, I. (1979), *Studies in Political Economy of Development* (Oxford: Pergamon Press).

——(1983), 'Le Potentiel de développement endogène', *Économie et sociétés*, Cahiers de l'ISMEA, Paris, Series F, 29/17/2.

——(1984), *Développer les champs de planification*, Cahiers de l'UCI No. 2 (Paris: Université coopérative internationale).

——MAIMON, D., and TOLMASQUIM, M. T. (1987), 'The Social and Ecological Impacts of Pro-alcool', *IDS Bulletin*, 18.

SAU, R. (1985), 'Expansion of Luxury Goods and Immiserisation of the Poor', *Economic and Political Weekly*, 20.

SEN, A. K. (1981), *Poverty and Famines* (Oxford: Oxford University Press).

——(1986), 'Food, Economics and Entitlements', Working Paper/(Helsinki; WIDER/UNU); and *Lloyds Bank Review*, Apr.

SINGER, P. (1986), *Repartição de renda: Pobres e ricos sob o regime militar* (Rio de Janeiro: Jorge Zahar Ed).

——and BRANDT, V. C. (eds.) (1980), *São Paulo: O povo em movimento* (Petrópolis: Vozes/CEBRAP).

UNICAMP (1986), *Brasil 1985: Relatório sobre a situação social do país* (Campinas: UNICAMP).

Viacava *et al.* (1983), *A desnutrição no Brasil* (Petrópolis: FINEP/Vozes).

4

Malnutrition and Poverty in Latin America

S. M. Ravi Kanbur

4.1. *Introduction and summary*

The object of this chapter is to review the state of malnutrition and poverty in Latin America. We will be particularly interested in quantifying the magnitudes of the problem, and in identifying who the poor and malnourished are. The former provides the reason for policy action while the latter provides the basis for policy strategy. Our focus throughout will be on food-related issues. When we discuss poverty we will be restricting attention to an inability to purchase a minimally nutritious diet, and when we discuss malnutrition we will consider the physical consequences of prolonged dietary deficiency. We will not, therefore, spend much time on the satisfaction of other, non-food, basic needs, although this is clearly an area of great policy interest too.

A recent study, World Bank (1985), estimates that in 1980 almost 13 per cent of the population of 24 Latin American and Caribbean countries had energy-deficient diets falling below 90 per cent of the FAO/WHO (1973) norms. This compared with incidences of food poverty of 44 per cent in sub-Saharan Africa, 50 per cent in South Asia, and 14 per cent in East Asia. According to these figures, therefore, the problem of food poverty in Latin America, while severe, is still not as bad as in most other areas of the developing world. However, as we shall see in section 4.2, there is considerable variation among Latin American countries in terms of food poverty, ranging from lows of 1 per cent to highs of almost 50 per cent. It is the object of section 4.2 to present and evaluate these country-specific estimates of food poverty in Latin America. We will also consider direct measures of the effects of malnourishment, in terms of the growth of children, for example. There are wide variations in the estimates available, since methodologies and measures differ from study to study. However, some patterns do emerge, among which is the uniformly higher incidence of poverty in rural areas when compared to urban areas. Poverty in Latin America is still very much a rural problem. In this the countries of Latin America are indeed rather like their counterparts in Asia and in Africa.

In section 4.3 we move from a discussion of the magnitudes of the problem of malnutrition and poverty to considering who the poor are. In particular, we are interested in obtaining incidences of poverty and malnutrition across different socio-economic groups. But caution must be exercised in inferring continent-wide patterns. At a sufficiently fine level of disaggregation no general inferences can be drawn, important as it is to have such disaggregation for country-specific analysis. However, at a somewhat more general level of aggregation patterns which are not too dissimilar to those found in South Asia are discernible. Within the rural sector, size of landholding is a significant influence on the risk of malnutrition, and agricultural workers and their families are particularly prone to being malnourished or below the food poverty line. Within the urban sector, slum dwellers have higher incidences of food poverty, as do families headed by manual workers. Also, at the national level, large families have a significantly high incidence of poverty, as do children between the ages of 5 and 14. These characterizations of the poor and malnourished prove useful in the policy discussions of section 4.4, to which we now turn.

Section 4.4 takes up two aspects of policy—the efficacy of growth in reducing malnutrition and poverty in Latin America, and the use of targeted redistributive measures. For the growth part of the story we calculate 'cross-over times'—the number of years required for the average poor person to cross the poverty line if income grows at the average rate of growth of per capita GNP of the past twenty years. We find that for many Latin American countries these times are inordinately high—in excess of 30 to 40 years—which may indicate the need for purposive redistribution. Distribution-neutral growth can be seen as one extreme of targeting—the increases in income are not targeted at all. But the other extreme, of 100 per cent targeting where every person below the poverty line gets just enough to bring him up to the poverty line (no more, no less), is not feasible in most LDCs. The question then arises as to whether policy can be directed at broadly defined groups, and whether these groups can be ranked according to targeting priority. A model developed in Kanbur (1986) is used to show that if the object is to minimize the national poverty gap, groups should be ranked according to their incidences of poverty. The empirical findings of section 4.3, on the incidence of poverty and malnutrition by socio-economic groups, thus turn out to be relevant in designing a well-targeted policy for alleviating poverty and malnutrition.

Section 4.5 concludes the chapter with some topics for further research. At the level of Latin America as a whole, there is some payoff to reconciling the different estimates of the magnitudes of poverty to be found in different studies. However, in our view the really high payoff is doing country-specific studies of the pattern of poverty and malnutrition by socio-economic groupings. At the level of disaggregation where these become useful to national policy makers, they will cease to be useful in drawing continent-wide inferences on the pattern of poverty. But that is how it has to be, and we would argue for more detailed country-level research.

4.2. *Magnitudes of the problem*

(a) *Consumption-based measures*

The best-known and most widely referred to measures of poverty for Latin America are those of Altimir (1982). The work on which this paper is based was done in the late 1970s and the data refer to years around 1970. Altimir estimated the incidence of poverty for a number of countries in Latin America based on two poverty lines—one which was constructed as the cost of a diet satisfying minimum nutritional requirements, and another which included non-food considerations as well. We shall start with a discussion of the methodology underlying the estimates, reproduced in Table 4.1.

The food poverty line (or destitution line, as Altimir terms it) is constructed separately for each country. The starting-point is the minimum energy and protein standards recommended by FAO/WHO (1973), for moderate activity and for specified weights (65 kg for males, 55 kg for females). Based on this, per capita calorie and protein requirements were calculated using sex and age composition of each country 'around 1970'. The range of per head calorie requirements so calculated is between 2,260 and 2,350 Kcals per day, while that of protein is between 40.2 and 43.3 grams per day. The *average* requirement is then applied to the intake distribution, but indirectly via the cost of a diet which would supply these requirements in each country. Those households whose per capita income is below the cost of such a minimum requirements diet are then classified as being in 'destitution'.

How is the minimum requirements food basket arrived at? Altimir is concerned to take into account the pattern of consumption in a country, arguing that if minimum requirements can be met with a basket that bears no relation to the foods consumed in that country, it would be unreasonable to choose that as a poverty line. Moreover, in order to be sure that we are within striking distance of the consumption pattern of the poor, it is *their* consumption pattern which has to be chosen as the reference. But how can we know who the

Table 4.1 Estimates of the incidence of poverty in Latin America around 1970

| | % of households below the poverty line | | | % of households below the food poverty line | | |
	Urban	Rural	National	Urban	Rural	National
Argentina	5	19	8	1	1	1
Brazil	35	73	49	15	42	25
Chile	12	25	17	3	11	6
Colombia	38	54	45	14	23	18
Costa Rica	15	30	24	5	7	6
Honduras	40	75	65	15	57	45
Mexico	20	49	34	6	18	12
Peru	28	68	50	8	39	25
Uruguay	10	—	—	4	—	—
Venezuela	20	36	25	6	19	10
Latin America	26	62	40	10	34	19

Source: Reproduced from Altimir (1982: Table 12).

poor are when it is the object of the exercise to identify the poor? Altimir chooses to focus on the food consumption patterns of 'the lower income strata, by which is meant 'the lowest 50% plus one half of the next 30%' (footnote (*a*) to Annex C) as revealed by surveys for Brazil (Rio de Janeiro), Costa Rica, El Salvador, Guatemala, Honduras, Nicaragua, and Peru (Lima). One question that arises immediately is why, if this information was available, it was not converted directly into calorie and protein intake and the numbers of those with intake below FAO/WHO requirements read off the intake distribution. Also, it is not clear how the consumption patterns for the lower strata were estimated for countries not covered in Annex C, although Altimir does note that 'Account was also taken of available nutritional recommendations concerning specific foods in the exceptional case of countries in which such recommendations have been issued and were applicable to present purposes.'

The Altimir method of arriving at minimum food baskets is thus not fully documented, and there appears to be a problem in using low-income consumption patterns to generate poverty lines that are to be used to cut off low incomes. However, accepting these as given there is next the problem of pricing these baskets. This is done mainly for 'the capital cities of the countries under consideration'. Adjustments to construct poverty lines in rural areas are largely *ad hoc*. For example 'it is reasonable to regard the cost of standard minimum food baskets in rural areas as 25 per cent below the budget estimated for the capital city of the particular country'; and 'there would therefore seem to be general justification for assuming minimum food budgets for non-capital urban areas to be five per cent lower than those estimated for the capital city of each country'.

The resulting food poverty lines, converted to 1970 US dollars using purchasing power parities, are shown in Table 4.2. Also shown in Table 4.2 are overall poverty lines, which are obtained by modifying the food poverty lines to take account of non-food needs. Since our focus is on food we will not comment on these lines, except to note that 'urban-area poverty lines [were] taken as corresponding to private consumption budgets amounting to double the corresponding minimum food budget', and that 'the norm adopted in estimating rural-area poverty lines is that expenditure on non-food items represents only 75 per cent of the value of the corresponding minimum food budgets'. In contrast to this way of estimating poverty lines we have the method of Ahluwalia *et al.* (1979), who chose as their reference poverty line the 46th percentile of the Indian income distribution in 1975, and applied this to all countries after adjusting for purchasing power parities. These lines, for Latin American countries, are shown in Table 4.3. Before moving on to our main focus, on food poverty, let us dwell for a moment on a comparison of Tables 4.2 and 4.3. As can be seen the poverty lines used by Ahluwalia *et al.* are on the whole lower than the overall poverty lines used by Altimir. In fact, they are more in keeping with his food poverty lines. Not surprisingly, the incidences of poverty obtained by Ahluwalia *et al.* (1979) are more comparable to the incidences of *food* poverty obtained by Altimir. But even with this comparison there are some big differences. The Ahluwalia *et al.* estimate of the incidence of poverty in Argentina exceeds the Altimir estimate by 4 percentage points while their estimate for Brazil is less than the Altimir estimate by a full 10 percentage points. Now the methods and data underlying these estimates differ greatly so it should not be surprising that estimated incidences of poverty differ (for a

Table 4.2 Poverty and food poverty lines: annual per capita budgets, Latin America (1970 $US)

	Poverty lines				Food poverty lines			
	Metro-politan area	Urban average	Rural average	National average	Metro-politan area	Urban average	Rural average	National average
Argentina	319	319	210	296	160	160	120	151
Brazil	215	215	142	177	107	107	81	93
Chile	269	261	176	226	134	131	101	122
Colombia	302	291	199	252	151	146	113	132
Costa Rica	255	248	167	198	127	124	95	106
Ecuador	301	291	198	237	151	146	113	127
Honduras	217	209	142	162	109	105	81	87
Mexico	261	252	171	221	130	126	98	115
Peru	228	222	150	186	114	111	86	98
Uruguay	287	287	188	263	143	143	108	135
Venezuela	326	315	214	287	163	158	122	147

Source: Reproduced from Altimir (1982).

Table 4.3 Purchasing power parity: poverty lines of individuals in poverty, Latin America, 1975

	Poverty lines ($US)	% in poverty
Argentina	130	5
Brazil	152	15
Chile	141	11
Colombia	165	19
Costa Rica	—	—
Honduras	—	—
Mexico	128	14
Peru	161	18
Uruguay	—	—
Venezuela	121	9

Source: Ahluwalia *et al.* (1979).

critique of the Ahluwalia methodology, see Anand and Kanbur 1986). What is important to realize is that there *are* different methodologies, and widely differing estimates can arise (a sensitivity analysis for the specific case of Brazil is to be found in Hicks and Vetter 1983).

Turning now specifically to food poverty, let us consider Altimir's estimates in Table 4.1. We see here a varied pattern across Latin America, from an incidence of 1 per cent for Argentina to a staggering incidence of 45 per cent in Honduras. For the two largest Latin American countries, the incidences are 25 per cent in Brazil and 12 per cent in Mexico. Comparing the rural and urban sectors, we see that the incidence of food poverty is greater in the rural sector than in the urban sector for every country except for Argentina, where it is equal to the urban incidence of food poverty. This pattern is of course similar to the one found in Asia. However, the much greater degree of urbanization in Latin America means that a greater proportion of the national poor are to be found in urban areas when compared to Asia.

The Altimir estimates of poverty, while widely cited, are not the only ones available. Table 4.4 presents estimates of food poverty for six Central American countries around 1980. In all, CEPAL estimates that in these six countries 13.6 million people, 60.4 per cent of the total population, were in overall poverty, and of these, 8.5 million, or 37.7 per cent of the total population, were in extreme or food poverty. We cannot, of course, directly compare the estimates in Tables 4.1 and 4.4. The time periods differ as do the methodologies. Focusing on Table 4.4, we see that within Central America itself the incidence of food poverty is below 20 per cent only for Costa Rica; for four out of the six countries it exceeds 30 per cent. In keeping with the pattern observed in Table 4.1, the incidence of rural poverty exceeds urban poverty by a large margin. However, as noted earlier, rates of urbanization in Latin America are high by the standards of developing countries in other continents. Central American urbanization rates are lower than for other Latin American countries

Table 4.4 Estimates of households below the food poverty and overall poverty lines in Central America, 1980

	% of households below the poverty line			% of households below the food poverty line		
	Urban	Rural	Total	Urban	Rural	Total
Costa Rica	13.6	34.2	24.8	7.4	18.7	13.6
El Salvador	57.6	76.4	68.1	44.5	55.4	50.6
Guatemala	58.1	66.2	63.4	22.8	36.2	31.6
Honduras	43.9	80.2	68.2	30.6	69.7	56.7
Nicaragua	45.6	80.0	61.5	21.6	50.0	34.7
Panama	42.9	67.3	53.9	11.8	38.3	23.7

Source: CEPAL (1983: Table 2).

(ranging from 39 per cent for Honduras to 56 per cent in Nicaragua, compared to 72 per cent in Brazil and 84 per cent in Argentina, for example—figures for 1984, World Bank 1986*b*), with the result that the majority of the poor do in fact reside in rural areas. In Central America, at any rate, poverty alleviation strategy will have to have a large rural component, and this is taken up later in this chapter.

Following up on the greater degree of urbanization in Latin America when compared to Asia or Africa, it would be interesting to get a more detailed account of the extent of urban poverty in Latin America. The results in Table 4.1 suggest an incidence of urban food poverty in 1970 ranging from 1 per cent for Argentina to 15 per cent in Brazil and Honduras (with Colombia close behind at 14 per cent). In Central America in 1980, Table 4.4 suggests a range of incidence from 7.4 per cent in Costa Rica to 44.5 per cent in El Salvador. However, these are broad aggregates for all urban areas in these countries. An interesting study by Musgrove (1985) focuses on ten cities in Colombia, Chile, Ecuador, Peru, and Venezuela (the cities are: Bogotá, Barranquilla, Cali, Medellín, Santiago, Quito, Guayaquil, Lima, Caracas, and Maracaibo). The study is based on household budget data collected between 1966 and 1969 (see Musgrove 1978). However, its detail makes this a valuable study for us in this section, and in subsequent sections which look more closely at the characteristics of the poor.

Musgrove's (1985) study relies on estimates of the costs of minimum diets in the five countries by Arellano (1975, 1977). Arellano's methodology is similar to that of Altimir (1982). He uses the FAO/WHO guidelines supplemented by recommendations by the Chilean National Health Service (Servicio nacional de salud (Chile) 1974) and calculates minimum costs by using consumption patterns and prices from Salazar-Carillo (1978). Given the cost of the minimum requirements diet, which can be calculated once the family's age and sex composition is known, the distribution of families or individuals according to food expenditure as a percentage of the minimum cost can be constructed. Musgrove's results are reproduced in our Table 4.5. As can be seen, the incidence of food poverty amongst individuals varies from a low of 22.6 per cent in Barranquilla to a high of 65.7 per cent in Quito. The incidence among families is lower in every city—the figures for Barranquilla and Quito are 18.0 per cent and 56.4 per cent. This is related to the fact that families in food deficit tend to be larger (see Musgrove's Table 5). However, the extent of *severe* food deprivation in Latin American cities also stands out from Table 4.5. In every city except Caracas and Lima the percentage of individuals with food expenditure below 65 per cent of the minimum exceeds 10 per cent—in Caracas it is 9.9 per cent and in Lima, the best out of the ten cities, it is 4.5 per cent.

There are some interesting discrepancies between the picture in Table 4.5 and that painted by Altimir's figures in Table 4.1. For example, according to Altimir only 3 per cent of urban households were below the poverty line in Chile. However, Musgrove's calculations show that in Santiago 25.5 per cent

Table 4.5 Distributions of population by food expenditure relative to cost of minimum diet for ten cities in Latin America

	Food expenditure as a percentage cost of minimum diet					Incidence of absolute poverty
	0–64	65–99	100–149	150–499	≥500	
Barranquilla						
Share of population (families)	7.1	10.9	28.2	50.4	3.4	18.0
Share of population (individuals)	10.2	12.4	30.1	44.4	3.0	22.6
Bogotá						
Share of population (families)	11.8	17.0	27.5	39.1	4.6	28.9
Share of population (individuals)	16.0	19.3	27.3	33.8	3.6	35.3
Cali						
Share of population (families)	11.1	19.2	22.7	43.2	3.9	30.3
Share of population (individuals)	14.4	22.9	22.1	37.2	3.3	37.3
Caracas						
Share of population (families)	6.4	11.6	21.8	57.7	2.4	18.1
Share of population (individuals)	9.9	16.6	25.0	47.1	1.4	26.5
Guayaquil						
Share of population (families)	25.8	26.7	23.1	24.0	0.4	52.5
Share of population (individuals)	32.8	29.5	19.5	18.0	0.3	62.3
Lima						
Share of population (families)	3.9	16.2	31.7	46.1	2.2	20.1
Share of population (individuals)	4.5	20.3	34.2	39.5	1.1	24.8
Maracaibo						
Share of population (families)	11.9	19.3	28.9	39.1	0.8	31.1
Share of population (individuals)	13.5	21.9	31.1	33.3	0.2	35.4
Medellín						
Share of population (families)	24.3	21.1	19.7	32.4	2.6	45.4
Share of population (individuals)	32.8	23.0	17.1	25.4	1.6	61.8

Quito						
Share of population (families)	31.0	25.5	20.3	23.0	0.3	56.4
Share of population (individuals)	40.2	25.5	18.5	15.7	0.1	65.7
Santiago						
Share of population (families)	8.9	16.6	24.8	45.4	4.3	25.5
Share of population (individuals)	13.0	20.9	26.6	37.3	2.1	33.9

Source: Reproduced from Musgrove (1985: Table 3).

of all families had an inadequate food intake, i.e. were below the poverty line. Similarly, Altimir's calculations show that only 6 per cent of urban households in Venezuela were below the poverty line, while Musgrove's figures show that in Caracas 18.1 per cent of families were below the poverty line. These are large differences. How can they be resolved? The obvious possibility is that the two sets of poverty lines are different. However, as Musgrove's (1985) Table 2 demonstrates, Arellano's estimates of poverty lines for these two cities at 1968 purchasing power parity are almost identical to the corresponding estimates by Altimir at 1970 purchasing power parity (for metropolitan areas in Chile and for urban areas as a whole in Venezuela). Could Altimir's broader coverage in urban areas account for the difference? This is possible, given that in Chile the percentage of urban population living in the largest city is 44 per cent while in Venezuela it is 26 per cent. However, given that Altimir only makes a 5 per cent adjustment to the poverty line in going from metropolitan to non-metropolitan areas the distribution of income in the two groups would have to be markedly different to generate such large differences. In any case, for Venezuela the other city of Maracaibo shows an incidence of food poverty of 31.1 per cent in Musgrove's figures. In the absence of any obvious reconciling factors, we leave these wide discrepancies as a caution to those seeking to arrive at definitive statements of Latin American poverty on the basis of the current literature —the poverty is undoubtedly severe, but there are some differences in the exact quantitative magnitudes of the estimates.

(b)   The effects of malnourishment

The consequences of prolonged deficiencies in dietary intake are manifold. As well as greater susceptibility to disease, malnutrition affects the normal growth pattern of children, and malnutrition in pregnant women has severe implications for the survival and health of the newborn child. The effects on the growth patterns of children have been discussed extensively in the nutritional literature, and the well-known Gomez (1955) classification is used to distinguish the extent to which children have low weights for age when compared to a reference population. World Bank (1983) provides data on extent of malnourishment for Brazil, based on the 1974/5 Estudo nacional da despesa familiar (ENDEF), or National Household Expenditure Study conducted by Fundação Instituto brasileiro de geografio e estatística (FIBGE). These are reproduced in Table 4.6. As can be seen, over 37 per cent of Brazilian children suffer from first-degree malnutrition (i.e. 76–90 per cent of normal weight for age). The incidence is highest among 5–10-year-olds, with over 43 per cent of this age group being in the first-degree malnourishment category. The lowest incidence of first-degree malnourishment is amongst infants. The picture is reversed for the most extreme form of malnutrition in the Gómez classification (third degree—60 per cent or less of normal weight for age). The highest incidence of this is amongst infants, at 2.5 per cent. Overall, in Brazil 0.9 per cent of children were suffering from the most severe manifestations of malnutrition. If one took an intermediate position between these two extremes and focused on second-degree malnutrition (61–75 per cent of normal weight for age), then around 20 per cent of Brazilian children would be classified as malnourished.

Data on malnourishment of children disaggregated by age are not, unfortunately, available for the whole of Latin America. However, Table 4.7 presents data on incidence of Grades I, II, and III malnourishment in children under the age of 5 for 26 countries in Latin America and the Caribbean. Comparing across Latin America, we see that Guatemala, Dominican Republic, El Salvador, Panama, Nicaragua, Guyana, Costa Rica, Colombia, Brazil, Belize, and Honduras all had incidence of Grade I malnourishment in the under-5s running at over 40 per cent. Guatemala had the highest incidence of extreme malnourishment at 5.9 per cent.

More recent cross-sectional information on the effects of malnourishment among children in Latin America is available from UNICEF (1986), reproduced in Table 4.8. This information is not directly comparable to that in Table 4.7, since it is restricted to children between the ages of 12 and 23 months, and defines the incidence of acute malnourishment *not* according to

Table 4.6 Different degrees of malnourishment in children, Brazil, 1975

Age group	First degree	Second degree	Third degree
Birth–5.99 months	17.4	8.9	2.5
6.00–11.99 months	22.3	11.0	1.4
1.00–1.99 years	32.2	11.1	0.6
2.00–4.99 years	38.1	14.8	0.2
5.00–9.99 years	43.1	25.9	0.4
10.00–14.99 years	36.8	27.5	1.6
15.00–17.99 years	37.1	13.4	0.9
TOTAL	37.2	20.2	0.9

Source: Reproduced from World Bank (1983: vol. ii, Tables 17, 18, and 19).

the Gomez classification but as 'the percentage of children with greater than minus two standard deviations from the 50th percentile of the weight-for-height reference population, i.e. roughly less than 77% of the median weight-for-height of the United States National Center for Health Statistics reference population'. However, the information once again raises the question of the appropriate standard of comparison since not only are the absolute magnitudes of incidence very different (acute malnourishment in Brazil, for example, is reported as being less than 2 per cent on the Gomez classification in Table 4.6 while it is 6 per cent according to the UNICEF standards) but the *relative* rankings of countries can change too.

Table 4.7 Malnutrition in children under 5, Latin America and the Caribbean

Country	Year	Incidence of malnourishment in sample		
		I	II	III
Antigua	1975	35.5	6.8	0.8
Bahamas	1974	14.6	0.6	0.9
Barbados	1969	39.0	11.0	1.2
Belize	1973	40.0	18.0	1.2
Bolivia	1966–9	29.0	10.2	0.7
Brazil	1968	48.4	17.2	2.7
Chile	1975	13.7	3.2	0.9
Colombia	1966	45.6	19.3	1.7
Costa Rica	1966	43.7	12.2	1.5
Dominica	1970	19.7	5.1	3.4
Dominican Republic	1969	49.0	23.0	4.0
Ecuador	1965–9	28.9	9.6	1.2
El Salvador	1965	48.5	22.9	3.1
Guatemala	1965	49.0	26.5	5.9
Guyana	1971	43.0	16.0	1.7
Honduras	1966	43.0	27.2	2.3
Jamaica	1970	39.0	9.4	1.4
Montserrat	1971	28.0	3.5	0.0
Nicaragua	1966	41.8	13.2	1.8
Panama	1967	48.8	10.8	1.1
Paraguay	1973	4.9	2.2	0.7
Peru	1965–71	32.8	10.9	0.8
St Kitts–Nevis and Anguilla	1974	33.3	5.4	0.1
St Lucia	1974	33.0	9.0	1.9
St Vincent	1967	47.0	14.0	1.5
Venezuela	1974	35.3	12.2	1.4

Source: Daza (1979), compiled from Pan American Health Organization data.

Table 4.8 Incidence of acute malnourishment
among children aged 12–23 months, based on
weight for height comparisons, Latin America
and the Caribbean, 1980

Country	Incidence (%)
Bolivia	1
Brazil	6
Chile	11
Colombia	10
Dominican Republic	4
Jamaica	14
Panama	8

Source: Compiled from UNICEF (1986).

So far we have focused on the effects of malnutrition on the growth of
children in Latin America. However, malnutrition can have other effects too.
It can, for example, influence cognitive development (see Berg 1981). Pollitt
(1980) surveys some of the relevant evidence for Latin America. Citing the
work of Brockman and Ricciuti (1971), and Pollitt (1974) in Peru, and
Monckeberg (1968) in Chile, on nutritionally rehabilitated marasmic children,
he argues that their performance on intelligence and developmental tests was
significantly below the average. But for children with kwashiorkor the work of
Barreda Moncada (1963), Birch *et al.* (1971), and Cravioto and Robles (1965),
in Venezuela, Jamaica, and Mexico respectively, did not show up any
permanent effects.

The most extreme form of relationship between malnourishment and its
consequences is the role of malnourishment in infant mortality. Table 4.9
presents World Bank data on infant mortality rates for Latin American
countries. As they stand the data show remarkable declines in infant mortality
rates and child death rates in Latin America over the past 20 years. However,
the death rates are still high compared to industrial market economies (9 per
1,000 live births in 1984 for the infant mortality rate, almost zero for the child
death rate) or some other developing economies in Asia (for Korea the two
figures were 28 and 2 in 1984; for Sri Lanka they were 37 and 2 in the same
year).

Of course, the figures in Table 4.9 establish only the broadest of trends and
comparisons; they cannot, in particular, shed light on the role of malnourishment in child mortality. For this more detailed investigations are needed, and
Table 4.10 summarizes the results of a number of studies from Puffer and
Serrano (1973). They show the uniformly high percentage of total deaths of
children under the age of 5 that can be attributed to nutritional deficiency, the
lowest figure being 20.2 per cent in San Juan city in Argentina, the largest

Table 4.9 Infant mortality rates and child death rates
(age 1–4), Latin America, 1965–1984

Country	Infant mortality rate (aged under 1) (per 1,000 live births)		Child death rate (aged 1–4) (per 1,000 children in the age group)	
	1965	1984	1965	1984
Argentina	59	34	4	1
Bolivia	161	118	37	20
Brazil	104	68	14	6
Chile	110	22	14	1
Colombia	99	48	8	3
Costa Rica	72	19	8	—
Ecuador	113	67	22	5
El Salvador	120	66	20	5
Guatemala	114	66	16	5
Honduras	131	77	24	7
Mexico	84	51	9	3
Nicaragua	123	70	24	6
Panama	59	25	4	1
Paraguay	74	44	7	2
Peru	131	95	24	11
Uruguay	47	29	3	1
Venezuela	67	38	6	2

Source: World Bank (1986a, Table 27).

being 46.9 per cent in rural *municipios* in El Salvador. While open to interpretation because of the exact definition of nutritional deficiency, these figures do suggest that a major requirement in the reduction of child mortality will continue to be the reduction of malnourishment in children.

So much for the effects of malnutrition on children. What about adults? Here too we could compare weights with reference groups, but more interesting are other aspects such as work capacity. Viteri (1971) argued, based on a sample of Guatemalan men, that those who are poorly nourished also have lower working capacity, the latter being measured in terms of the earlier appearance of oxygen debt and of decreased tolerance to oxygen debt, compared to a reference group of well-nourished men. Similarly, he showed that sustained rehabilitation of nutrition in those who had previously been chronically undernourished did in fact increase their work capacity. In a follow-up study in Guatemala, Flores *et al.* (1984) studied 58 sugarcane cutters and 56 coffee pickers. Their results are reproduced in Table 4.11, together with the comparative figures for 22 'well-nourished' men taken from Viteri (1971).

Table 4.10 Nutritional deficiency and immaturity associated with death among children under 5, selected areas in Latin America and the Caribbean

Countries, project sites, and areas studied	Total deaths		% of total deaths		
	No.	Rate per 100,000 of population	Nutritional deficiency	Immaturity	Both causes
Argentina					
Choco Province					
Resistencia	804	2,070	40.0	22.1	62.2
Rural departments	837	2,357	37.6	13.6	51.3
San Juan Province					
San Juan (city)	326	1,291	20.2	33.1	53.4
Suburban departments	780	2,194	27.4	30.4	57.8
Rural departments	1,050	2,403	31.1	23.7	54.9
Bolivia					
La Paz	4,115	2,660	36.0	11.5	47.6
Viacha	161	4,806	30.4	10.6	41.0
Brazil					
Recife	3,635	2,933	46.2	20.2	66.4
Ribeirão Preto					
Ribeirão Preto (city)	464	1,088	34.5	35.3	69.8
Franca	434	1,942	36.4	27.6	64.1
Communities	228	1,300	38.2	28.5	66.7
São Paulo	4,312	1,769	30.4	28.4	58.8
Chile					
Santiago	2,489	1,298	23.7	31.8	55.5
Comunas	225	1,395	35.6	17.8	53.3
Colombia					
Cali	1,627	1,607	36.4	19.7	56.2
Cartagena	1,255	1,459	44.7	20.2	64.9
Medellín	1,348	1,444	42.3	19.7	61.9
El Salvador					
San Salvador	2,738	2,636	37.2	17.1	54.3
Rural *municipios*	1,082	5,049	46.9	7.9	54.8
Mexico					
Monterrey	3,953	1,813	36.1	18.3	54.5

Source: Reproduced from Daza (1979: Table 2); data compiled from studies in Puffer and Serrano (1973).

While these figures, too, have to be treated with care (for one thing the reference group is much younger than the experimental group) they do suggest a relationship between malnutrition (as measured by anthropometric measures such as body weight, height, weight–height, etc.) and maximal work capacity. The economic consequences of this relationship between malnourishment and

Table 4.11 Age, anthropometric measurements, and physical working capacity of two samples of agricultural workers and well-nourished men in Guatemala ($\overline{X} \pm$ SE)

Variable	Sugarcane cutters		Coffee pickers		Well-nourished men	
Age (years)	35.1	±1.2	38.1	±1.4	18.8	±0.4
Body weight (kg)	52.6	±0.7	54.9	±0.8	60.8	±1.1
Height (cm)	159.3	±0.7	163.9	±0.9	166	±1.0
Weight–height (kg/cm)	33.0	±0.4	33.4	±0.4	36.6	±0.6
Mid-upper arm circumference (mm)	251	±2	254	±2	281	±3
Leg circumference (mm)	315	±2	328	±3	352	±3
Triceps skinfold (mm)	4.5	±0.2	4.9	±0.2	8.7	±0.5
Arm muscle circumference (mm)	236	±1.8	238	±1.7	253	±3
Body surface (m²)	1.53	±0.01	1.58	±0.01	1.67	±0.02
Oxygen uptake at 150 beats/min. (ml/min.)	1,761	±38	1,968	±35		
Maximal work capacity (ml/min.)	2,341	±58	2,685	±54	2,800	±124
Maximal work capacity per kg body weight (ml/kg/min.)	44.5	±0.9	49.1	±0.8	46.3	±0.8

Source: Reproduced from Flores *et al.* (1984).

productivity have been explored by Bliss and Stern (1978) and by Dasgupta and Ray (1986). But there is the further question of how malnutrition among men compares with that among women in Latin America. The evidence on this is scanty, but in a study of agricultural migrant workers in southern Brazil, Desai *et al.* (1980) found that low weight for height is less common among women than among men, although in weight, triceps skinfold, and arm circumference women were much below the standard on average. The results are summarized in Hamilton *et al.* (1984), and are reproduced in Table 4.12.

To conclude this section, we note that the problem of malnutrition is severe in Latin America. This is so whether malnutrition is measured by inability to purchase a minimally nutritious diet, or whether it is measured by its consequences in children or in adults. However, a note of caution is needed —while the weight of the evidence does suggest an overall severity in the problem, there are discrepancies between different studies. These arise largely because they adopt different methodologies. Altimir (1982) calculates food poverty lines for each country separately, using the prices and composition patterns in that country, while Ahluwalia *et al.* (1979) simply translate the Indian poverty line to Latin American (and all other) countries. Similarly, while World Bank (1983) uses weight for age to classify malnutrition,

Table 4.12 Anthropometric comparisons: men and women, Brazil

	No. in sample	Mean weight as % of standard	Mean triceps skinfolds as % of standard	Mean arm circumference as % of standard	Mean arm muscle circumference as % of standard	Weight for height relative to standard (% in sample)		
						>90%	81–90%	<80%
Females	85	110	87	97	100	80	14.1	5.9
Males	39	95	40	93	101	66.7	23.1	10.2

Source: Desai *et al.* (1980), summarized in Hamilton *et al.* (1984).

UNICEF (1986) uses weight for height. Thus the rankings of countries within Latin America, as well as comparisons of Latin American countries with other LDCs, may differ from study to study. This is a problem we will have to live with given the literature as it now stands. But it does indicate that care is needed in drawing inferences and that a fruitful direction for further research is to reconcile these differences.

4.3.   *Characteristics of the poor and malnourished*

Who are the poor and malnourished in Latin America? An answer to this question is obviously important in terms both of beginning an analysis of the causes of poverty and malnourishment in Latin America, as well as of designing policy to aid the malnourished. The policy aspects of the question will be taken up in the next section. In what follows we concentrate on the characteristics of malnourished and poor households. We are interested primarily in the incidence of poverty and malnourishment in groups defined by geographical and socio-economic characteristics, since we will use this to derive rankings of groups towards which policy should be targeted.

Let us start with the basic distinction between rural and urban poor which we have already touched on in the previous section. As is clear from Tables 4.1 and 4.4, the incidence of poverty in the rural areas of Latin America is uniformly, and in many cases dramatically, higher than the incidence of poverty in urban areas. However, the extent of urbanization is much higher in Latin America than in comparable LDCs. Thus in Brazil the rate of urbanization was 51 per cent in 1965 and 72 per cent in 1984. In Colombia the figures are 40 per cent and 54 per cent. Hence while it is still true that both in incidence and in absolute numbers poverty is a rural phenomenon in Latin America as a whole, it is much less so than in poor Asian countries, which combine high incidences of rural poverty with low rates of urbanization.

If we were considering policies at the broadest level, designed to raise incomes in rural areas as a whole or urban areas as a whole, then it could be argued that the high incidences of rural poverty indicated a targeting towards policies that benefit rural incomes (see Kanbur 1986). However, most often the policy discussion is at a finer level of disaggregation, and we need to characterize poverty within the urban and the rural sector. Starting with the urban sector, consider Table 4.13, which reports the results of the study of poverty in ten Latin American cities by Musgrove (1985). It will be recalled from the discussion in section 4.2 that poverty is defined in terms of the cost of a minimum diet, so that we are focusing attention on food poverty. Table 4.13 shows incidence of poverty by occupation of family head, and the results are striking though perhaps not surprising. The incidence of poverty is by and large highest among families headed by manual workers. In those cases where this is not true, the leading occupational group in terms of poverty incidence is

Table 4.13 Percentage of families in absolute poverty (food expenditure less than norm) by city and occupation of family head, Latin America

City	Office workers	Vendors	Drivers	Manual workers	Personal services	All families
Barranquilla	0.0	14.6	19.8	18.9	42.8	18.0
Bogota	18.3	24.1	34.5	41.3	46.5	28.9
Cali	9.1	25.2	31.8	39.8	58.1	30.3
Caracas	12.9	12.0	16.4	32.1	34.1	18.1
Guayaquil	41.1	51.5	61.1	69.3	60.9	52.5
Lima	15.0	21.6	16.1	31.4	22.6	20.1
Maracaibo	22.6	23.2	24.5	35.1	36.8	31.1
Medellín	31.7	37.2	47.5	66.9	49.9	45.4
Quito	31.4	46.2	59.6	79.4	70.9	56.4
Santiago	11.1	23.0	21.4	36.6	27.5	25.5

Source: Reproduced from Musgrove (1985: Table 11).

personal services. Office workers have relatively low incidences of poverty. The implications of this structure of incidence for the impact of recession on urban food poverty in Latin America is clear—high unemployment rates will inevitably hit manual workers, and will translate themselves into poverty and malnourishment with maximum effect (see World Bank 1986b). The counteracting policy is the mirror image of this—actions to protect the incomes of manual workers will be the best targeted strategy from the point of view of alleviating poverty. Another striking result from Musgrove's (1985) study (see his Table 6) is that the incidence of poverty is much higher among large families than among small families. From the point of view of targeting, therefore, measures which condition benefits on number of children in a family are likely to be well targeted (see also Ferber and Musgrove (1983) for more detailed analysis for Bogotá, Medellín, and Lima on characteristics of poor households).

A study by Garcia et al. (1981) provides some further information on incidence of poverty and characteristics of the poor in Bogotá and in Cali. While these results are not directly comparable to those of Musgrove since the methodology for identifying households suffering from malnutrition differ —in fact Garcia *et al.* use two different methods—it is interesting to note that the conclusions on incidence of poverty and family size are unchanged. Table 4.14 presents the results and it is seen that for each of two poverty standards (labelled 0.8R and 1.0R) the incidence of malnutrition increases with family size, and dramatically so. Households with 10 members or more have a better than 60 per cent chance of suffering from malnutrition, which has obvious implications for use of observable indicators in targeting expenditures and in policy design (subject of course to the incentive effects of such targeting).

Garcia *et al.* (1981) have some further interesting characterizations of the

Table 4.14 Incidence of malnutrition in Bogotá and Cali by family size, 1978, for two requirement levels (%)

Household size	Bogotá			Cali		
	0.8R	1.0R	% population in category	0.8R	1.0R	% population in category
1	1.8	3.2	1.1	5.4	5.4	1.3
2	3.7	5.7	4.7	4.3	10.3	4.8
3, 4	6.9	13.8	28.2	6.3	14.3	25.3
5, 6	18.2	30.1	31.2	20.0	31.7	31.9
7–9	33.0	49.0	24.8	36.1	58.9	27.2
10+	50.9	73.4	10.0	41.6	63.0	9.6
TOTAL	21.1	33.1	100.0	22.1	36.4	100.0

Source: Reproduced from Garcia *et al.* (1981).

malnourished in urban Colombia. The first concerns the incidence of malnourishment by age. They find that the peak incidence occurs in the age range 5–14 whether they look at Bogotá or Cali, 1973 or 1978, using either one of their two methods for identifying malnourishment, or either one of their two standards for minimal requirements (Garcia *et al.* 1981: Tables 9*a* and 9*b*). This is a very strong result. It matches up with the results on large families, and with the ENDEF results for Brazil (Table 4.6) and confirms the focus that policy must have on children, or at least on households with children.

Turning from the urban sector specifically to the more general national picture, a number of studies exist which give more information on incidence of malnutrition by socio-economic groupings. Table 4.15 reports a disaggregation of incidence of malnutrition in children under 5 by father's occupation, for Guatemala in 1980. The figures in Table 4.15 present a natural ranking of target groups in Guatemala. Overall they reflect the higher incidence of poverty in the rural sector than in the urban sector that we have already commented upon—the agricultural occupations are mostly the high malnutrition incidence categories. Within agriculture, the role of size of landholding is seen very clearly. For children whose father is a farmer with less than one *manzana* the chance of having height below the standard norm is well in excess of a half, while the same chance for those whose fathers have 5 or more *manzanas* is below two-fifths. Policy towards small holdings is clearly indicated, and here the picture is similar to that in Asia (we have deliberately excluded issues of *within* family distribution—see Harbert and Scandizzo 1982).

Agricultural wage-worker households fall somewhere in between small landholdings and larger landholdings in their propensity to contain malnourished children. But differences of 2 or 3 percentage points in incidence should not, perhaps, be significant in determining policy stance given the

Table 4.15 Percentage of children less than 5 years of age below
standard height, by father's occupation, Guatemala, 1980

Father's occupation	% of children less than 5 years of age below standard height
Farmer with less than 1 *manzana*[a]	57.1
Farmer with 1–1.9 *manzanas*[a]	56.5
Agricultural wage worker (coffee and sugar)	54.0
Farmer with 2–4.9 *manzanas*[a]	51.6
Agricultural wage worker (food crops)	51.6
Unpaid family worker	44.8
Unskilled urban wage worker	39.7
Farmer with 5 and more *manzanas*[a]	37.7
Handicraft sales	35.8
Skilled urban worker	34.7
Professional or administrative worker	25.8

[a] 1 *Manzana* = 0.7 ha.

Source: Reproduced from Hintermeister (1984: Table 3.3), compiled from INCAP (1980).

errors inherent in the data. For similar sorts of reasons the fact that incidence of child malnutrition is 2.4 percentage points higher in households where the father is an agricultural wage worker in coffee and sugar than in households where he works in food crops is perhaps not sufficient to dictate a major reorientation of policy towards wages in these two sectors unless further research confirms the differential as being significant and persistent. What *is* clear is that favourable policies towards agricultural wage workers in general *vis-à-vis* their urban counterparts is indicated. Here the poverty incidences differ by 10 percentage points or more (this pattern is also documented for Mexico, see Bergsman 1980). Thus while *within* the urban sector policy should be directed towards raising the incomes of unskilled workers, as between urban and rural workers in general the latter should have priority. These implications for targeting are unlikely to be overturned by further careful research (see also Peek and Raabe 1984).

A similar breakdown of incidence of malnutrition by occupational groups is given in Table 4.16 for Costa Rica. The table is based on a Family and Community Questionnaire of the Ministry of Health, 1980, data from which is reported in UNICEF (1981). While not strictly comparable with Table 4.15 because of different criteria used for identifying malnutrition (Table 4.16 uses the Gomez classification, Grades II and III), it should be clear that what we

Table 4.16 Malnutrition by functional groups, Costa Rica

Functional groups	% with malnutrition Grades II and III
AW vegetables and fruits	9.3
AW unknown products	9.3
AW basic grains	9.1
AW coffee	9.0
Unskilled workers and artisans	8.9
AW beef cattle	8.5
F from 1 to 3 ha	8.1
F from 5 to 10 ha	7.8
F from 3 to 5 ha	7.3
AW cattle not specified	6.7
Workers in the transitory informal economy sector	6.6
Pensioners	6.5
AW sugarcane	6.2
Qualified operators and artisans	6.2
All types of management	6.0
Office employees and salesmen	5.8
F less than 1 ha	5.5
F from 25 to 50 ha	5.0
AW banana and African palm	4.6
Service workers	4.4
F 50 or more ha	4.4
AW dairy cattle	3.5
F from 10 to 25 ha	3.4
Professionals and technicians	1.8
TOTAL	6.6

Note: AW = Agricultural workers; F = Farmers.
Source: Reproduced from Pacey and Payne (1985: Table 6.1).

have is once again a hierarchy with implications for targeting. There are some interesting anomalies, such as the fact that farmers with less than 1 hectare show a lower incidence of poverty than farmers with 1 to 3 hectares—but this is probably because the former group includes some rich urban households. Leaving this aside, a contrasting pattern to that in Guatemala emerges. In Costa Rica agricultural workers by and large have higher incidences of malnutrition than smallholders, although there is of course some overlap. But on the other hand there are similarities—urban workers are less likely to suffer from malnutrition than rural workers, and (after 1 hectare) big farmers are less likely to suffer from malnutrition than small farmers. This seems to be in keeping with the pattern in Asia.

Finally in this discussion of the occupational determinants of the incidence of poverty, we consider the results of Valverde *et al*. (1980). These are based on a broader definition of occupation, grouping together all urban slum households into one category, for example, but they provide a finer breakdown by extent of malnutrition. As can be seen in Table 4.17, so far as first-degree malnutrition is concerned all four groupings are pretty similar in their incidences. The largest difference is one of 5 percentage points (on an average incidence of more than 50 per cent), between workers living on coffee plantations and sugar plantations. The two features that emerge are, firstly, that urban slum dwellers have similar incidences of malnutrition to poor agricultural workers and, secondly, that workers living on coffee plantations have the highest incidence out of the four groups for first-degree malnutrition. The implication of the first feature is that if policies can be targeted towards urban slum dwellers then the choice between those and policies which transfer an equal amount of purchasing power to certain types of agricultural workers will not much affect the overall impact on poverty. However, within El Salvador the wages of coffee plantation workers are clearly a priority if the objective is to reduce poverty.

It has been argued by some that the *regional* divide is more important as a discriminator of poverty incidences than the rural–urban divide. Thomas (1982) recognizes the importance of the rural poor in Brazil, and yet argues for the importance of regional divisions:

The more interesting outcome of the poverty measures undoubtedly points out that considerably more poverty exists in the nation's rural areas than in urban areas. For instance, a poverty index for the nation's rural areas is approximately 20% higher than

Table 4.17 Nutritional status of children 6–59 months (Gomez classification) for four occupational groups, El Salvador, 1976

Regions	No. of cases	% children			
		First degree	Second degree	Third degree	Total
Smallholding, semi-proletariat farmers	1,447	53.8	21.0	1.7	100.0
Workers living on coffee plantations	1,043	54.3	20.4	2.2	100.0
Workers living on coastal cotton and sugar plantations	1,489	48.8	12.5	1.5	100.0
Urban slums	1,369	51.1	14.0	1.3	100.0

Source: Reproduced from Deere and Diskin (1984: Table 5), based on Valverde *et al*. (1980).

the national average, while that of the metropolitan areas is roughly 50% below national averages. Compared to such urban–rural differences, however, some regional differences, particularly between the Northeast and the Southeast, are more striking. The sharpest contrast is provided by a comparison of the state of São Paulo with the Northeast region. While a poverty index for São Paulo state is roughly 2½ times below the national average, that for the Northeast is 1⅔ as high as this average.

The figures on which Thomas bases his argument are reproduced in Table 4.18. While using the same ENDEF survey that we have been relying on for information on Brazil in this paper, they are based on poverty lines which are food poverty lines augmented to take account of non-food needs and are hence not directly comparable to our discussions on malnutrition. However, it is interesting to note that if we take the figures for incidence of malnutrition in children given in Table 4.19, then for the case of Grade III, the national incidence is 4.5 times the incidence in the South-East, while the incidence in the North-East is almost 2.5 times the national incidence. Of course, this happens with much smaller percentages, but Thomas's general point is well taken. Regional variations in the incidence of malnutrition in Mexico are detailed in Table 4.20, and similarly large differences are clear (see also Ferrari 1980, for Peru, and Herrick and Hudson 1981, for Costa Rica).

What, then, do we know about the characteristics of the poor and the malnourished in Latin America? While it is dangerous to generalize from individual country studies, and we have ourselves raised objections to some of the methodologies pursued, some tentative suggestions might perhaps be entertained. Firstly, the incidence of poverty is significantly higher in rural areas than in urban areas. Secondly, while such differences in incidence indicate policy targeting, the differences in incidence between regions can be much larger. Thirdly, the incidence of malnutrition and poverty among large families is very high and, relatedly, children between 5 and 14 are particularly at risk. Fourthly, among rural farmers we have the expected relationship between size of holding and incidence of malnutrition and poverty. Fifthly, agricultural workers show higher incidences of poverty than their urban counterparts. These features of poverty and malnourishment in Latin America have implications for policy, and we have already touched on some of these. The next section continues the analysis in greater detail.

4.4. *Aspects of policy: growth and redistribution*

The magnitude of absolute poverty is a function of both the mean level of income and its distribution. If malnutrition is the specific focus, then its magnitude is a function of mean nutritional intake as well as the distribution of intake. Policies to alleviate poverty and malnutrition can therefore be thought of as either growth oriented or redistribution oriented. Of course in principle there need be no inherent conflict between the two—for example, at low levels

Table 4.18 Regional distribution of poor, Brazil, 1984

Regions	Poverty line (local currency)	% below	No. below (000)
Region I	2,585	16.35	1,419
Metropolitan Rio de Janeiro	2,824	13.88	991
Other urban	2,086	17.78	186
Rural	1,520	31.33	276
Region II	2,663	20.79	4,333
Metropolitan São Paulo	3,374	13.82	1,148
Other urban	2,199	13.28	939
Rural	1,753	20.59	697
Region III	1,885	18.96	3,364
Pôrto Alegre	2,893	14.93	237
Curitiba	2,245	10.54	85
Other urban	2,068	16.73	972
Rural	1,526	18.00	1,607
Region IV	1,631	29.39	3,809
Belo Horizonte	2,282	18.57	340
Other urban	1,775	21.14	1,093
Rural	1,541	40.83	2,431
Region V	1,620	48.01	13,903
Salvador	2,603	27.55	340
Recife	2,152	31.55	612
Fortaleza	1,879	36.24	388
Other urban	1,795	38.13	3,189
Rural	1,377	54.78	8,967
Region VI	2,896	16.00	108
Region VII	1,730	14.35	526
Belém	2,144	20.75	154
Other urban	1,843	27.63	306
Other urban	1,794	12.22	259
Areas			
Metropolitan	2,831	17.38	4,403
Other urban	1,942	22.63	6.944
Rural	1,562	39.36	13,978
National average	1,953	29.36	27,462

Source: Thomas (1982: Table 19).

Table 4.19 Incidence of malnutrition among children below the age of 18 in Brazil, by severity and region (%)

Region	Severity of malnutrition (Gomez classification)		
	I	II	III
North-East	38.2	28.0	2.2
South-East	36.2	15.4	0.2
Frontier	39.0	23.3	0.7
Brazil	37.2	20.2	0.9

Source: World Bank (1983)

Table 4.20 Malnutrition incidence in Mexico, by region (%)

	1st degree	2nd degree	3rd degree
North			
Sonora			
Agua Prieta	31.2	5.5	0.0
Sinaloa			
Concordia	46.8	12.5	0.0
Coahuila			
Finisterre	52.8	20.8	0.0
Nuevo León			
San José de Raices	56.0	24.0	0.0
Central west			
Hidalgo			
Almoloya	41.1	12.8	3.1
Xochiocoatlan	51.5	23.9	1.3
El Nith	30.5	43.9	10.4
Puebla			
San Juan Epatlan	70.5	17.6	5.9
Tlaxcala			
Santa Cruz Aquiahuac	48.4	14.0	1.7
Gulf zone			
Veracruz			
Paso del Toro	50.0	16.7	0.8
Metropolitan Mexico			
Xochinilco			
Santa Cruz Xochitepec	49.8	9.6	0.4
Tlalpan			
San Muguel Xicalco	63.4	8.7	1.3
AVERAGE	49.3	17.5	1.1

Source: Austin (1979: Table 5).

of nutritional intake an improvement in nutrition improves individual productivity and hence the productive capacity of the economy (see Dasgupta and Ray
1990). But in the literature, growth and redistribution are pitted as opposites,
with difficult choices having to be made between the two. In what follows,
therefore, we will divide our discussion of policy into the impact of growth and
the impact of redistribution. In the latter category we will discuss targeting
priorities in the Latin American context.

Consider first the effects of growth on poverty. In doing so we assume that
growth is distribution neutral. It leaves relative inequality unchanged, i.e. all
incomes grow at the same rate. What would be the impact on absolute poverty?
If the poverty line is z and the mean income of the poor is $\bar{y}_p$, then with an
annual growth rate of g it will take:

$$T = \frac{\ln(z/\bar{y}_p)}{\ln(1+g)}$$

years for the average poor person to cross the poverty line. This 'crossover
time' (see Kanbur 1987) gives an indication of the efficacy of growth in
alleviating absolute poverty. Using Altimir's (1982) data, Table 4.21 shows the
crossover time for a selection of Latin American countries on the basis of their
past growth rates in per capita GNP.

Now Altimir's figures for the ratio mean income of the poor to the poverty
line are for the overall poverty line and not the food poverty line. If we can
assume that this ratio is unchanged when using the food poverty line then the
calculations in Table 4.21 are applicable to food poverty alleviation by means of
growth as well. Crude as they are, the figures in Table 4.21 do give an
indication of the magnitude of the problem in Latin America. For Peru and

Table 4.21 Calculations of crossover times, Latin America

Country	$\bar{y}_p/z$ (1)	100g (% per year) (2)	T (years) (3)
Argentina	0.745	0.3	98
Brazil	0.538	4.6	14
Chile	0.567	−0.1	∞
Colombia	0.512	3.0	23
Costa Rica	0.564	1.6	36
Honduras	0.491	0.5	143
Mexico	0.608	2.9	17
Peru	0.448	−0.1	∞
Venezuela	0.625	0.9	52

Sources: (1) calculated from Altimir (1982: Table 14); (2): average annual growth rates
of GNP per capita, 1965–1984, taken from World Bank (1986: Annex Table 1); (3):
calculated from (1) and (2) using formula in the text.

Chile, which have recorded a negative average annual rate of growth over the past 20 years, the crossover time is of course infinite. Obviously these negative growth rates are influenced by the impact of the current recession. But even if this were taken out and a low positive growth rate were substituted, very long crossover times would still result. This is seen for the case of Honduras, where the average annual growth rate of income per head has been only 0.5 per cent. Combining this with the depth of poverty in the country, we get an incredible 143 years for the average poor person to cross the poverty line. Obviously the structure of the data is bound to change over such a long time—the calculation is merely intended to convey the small role that growth at historical rates can play in alleviating poverty. In fact, suppose that the Honduran growth rate of income per head *doubled* to 1 per cent a year as a result of growth-oriented policies. The crossover time would then come down to around 70 years—still a very long time horizon for alleviating the poverty of only the *average* poor person.

However, there are some Latin American countries where, because of a combination of low poverty and/or high growth rates, crossover times are around 15 years. Mexico and Brazil are interesting cases in point. The latter has higher poverty and a higher growth rate, with the result that they have similar crossover times.

There are three major problems with the crossover time calculations. First, the crossover time focuses only on the income of the *average* poor person and says nothing about the numbers of the poor. There have been some attempt to project these numbers in the future, notably the projections by Ahluwalia *et al.* (1979) to the year 2000. These rely on the absolute poverty line discussed in section 4.2, and make an adjustment to the distribution of income based on the Kuznets curve estimates of Ahluwalia (1976). By and large these estimates show significant declines in the incidence of poverty in Latin American countries although (1) they are based on growth projections of the last decade and (2) the methodology underlying them has been criticized by Anand and Kanbur (1986). Secondly, the poverty calculations are not directly nutritionally focused. Thirdly, no account is taken of possible changes in the pattern of consumption as income grows. Of course in order to take into account these criticisms we would have to have detailed survey data and conduct careful simulations for particular countries. One such exercise is that conducted by the World Bank (1983) for Brazil (see also Knight and Moran 1981) and we now turn to those results.

Table 4.22 presents the situation as it was in 1975. We have focused attention on those whose calorie deficits exceed 400 calories (based on standards at the low end of the FAO/WHO guidelines). On the basis of ENDEF data, the table shows that in 1975, 17.3 per cent of Brazilians had a deficit in excess of 400 calories. In contrast to our earlier findings on the incidence of food poverty, we see that the incidence of large deficits is *greater* in urban areas than in rural areas. However, while the incidence is lower in rural areas, the

Table 4.22 Deficits exceeding 400 calories by region, Brazil, 1975

	Total Population (000)	No. in deficit (000)	Incidence (%)	Average deficit (calories/ person/day)	Total deficit (m. calories/day)	Total of all deficits (m. calories/day)
North-East						
Rural	17,739.8	2,428.9	13.7	540	1,310.4	3,268.8
Urban	14,291.7	6,952.6	48.7	529	3,678.4	5,151.3
Total	32,031.5	9,381.5	29.3	532	4,988.8	8,420.0
South-East						
Rural	20,046.2	321.7	1.6	476	153.3	1,096.3
Urban	44,524.8	5,471.1	12.3	527	2,882.6	7,592.5
Total	64,571.0	5,792.8	9.0	524	3,035.9	8,688.8
Frontier						
Rural	5,268.7	1,763.4	33.5	593	1,087.2	1,717.3
Urban	5,274.0	1,633.4	31.0	617	968.2	1,624.2
Total	10,542.7	3,396.8	32.2	605	2,055.4	3,341.4
Brazil						
Rural	43,054.7	4,514.0	10.5	565	2,550.8	6,082.3
Urban	64,090.5	14,057.1	21.9	536	7,529.1	14,367.6
Total	107,145.2	18,571.1	17.3	543	10,079.8	20,450.0

Source: reproduced from World Bank (1983: Table 15).

average deficit of those below the chosen cut-off is greater in the rural areas. Thus although fewer rural people suffer from the extreme of calorie deficit (both in terms of absolute numbers and in relation to the total rural population), those who are poor are, on average, more severely malnourished. Comparing across regions, we see that as before the South-East has the lowest incidence of malnutrition. However, while the North-East and frontier regions are about equal in their incidences, Frontier's incidence is marginally higher, and so is its mean deficit.

From this baseline, the World Bank simulated a pessimistic scenario of 4 per cent per year total income growth and an optimistic scenario of 7 per cent per year total income growth over 1980–2000. The growth is assumed to be distribution neutral and population projections are used to convert total growth into per capita income increases. Estimates of the elasticity of per capita calorie consumption with respect to family per capita expenditure are used to convert income growth into calorie consumption increases. The resulting configurations of extreme malnourishment are shown in Table 4.23. As can be seen, there is a dramatic decline in the incidence of extreme malnourishment for the whole of Brazil. Taking the pessimistic scenario the incidence drops from 17.3 per cent to 4.3 per cent, a factor of 4. However, because of population growth the absolute number of extremely malnourished only drops

Table 4.23 Projected deficits exceeding 400 calories by region in the year 2000, Brazil

	Total Population (000)	Pessimistic (000)	% of total	Optimistic (000)	% of total
North-East					
Rural	24,891.8	—	—	—	—
Urban	31,634.8	4,720.0	14.9	156.0	0.5
Total	56,526.6	4,720.0	8.4	156.0	0.3
South-East					
Rural	25,165.9	—	—	—	—
Urban	96,365.9	664.5	0.7	—	—
Total	121,531.8	664.5	0.5	—	—
Frontier					
Rural	10,061.4	1,522.8	15.1	453.4	4.5
Urban	15,100.5	1,761.3	11.7	416.9	2.8
Total	25,161.9	3,284.1	13.1	870.3	3.4
Brazil					
Rural	60,119.1	1,522.8	2.5	453.4	0.8
Urban	143,101.2	7,145.8	5.0	572.9	0.4
Total	203,220.3	8,668.6	4.3	1,026.3	0.5

Source: Reproduced from World Bank (1983: Table 32).

from 18.6 million in 1975 to 8.7 million in 2000. Extreme malnourishment is eliminated entirely in the South-East under the optimistic scenario, and an incidence of only 0.5 per cent persists over the whole of Brazil.

The above figures do indicate that growth at historically observed rates can make an appreciable dent in *extreme* malnutrition. But this is just a reflection of the very low standard chosen. If we look at the consequences for the population with any degree of deficit at all, then the World Bank (1983) calculations show that under the pessimistic scenario the incidence of calorie deficit drops from 67.2 per cent in 1975 to 46.5 per cent in 2000, but because of population growth the absolute numbers *increase* from 72 million to 94 million. Thus the problem of malnutrition, not of the extreme variety but malnutrition nevertheless, will persist if growth takes place at the assumed rate. Even with the optimistic scenario in the year 2000 there will be over 46 million malnourished Brazilians (22.7 per cent of the total population).

It is with this consideration in mind that the World Bank (1983) analysed the costs of direct distribution of diet supplements to eliminate all calorie deficits, the assumption being of course that the distribution would be targeted 100 per cent efficiently—each individual would get just enough to eliminate his or her own deficit, no more and no less. The cost estimates are thus a lower bound. The estimates obtained, under different assumptions about growth rate, sequencing of implementation, and type of dietary supplements, range between 1 and 2 per cent of GDP in each of the years 1980–2000.

The calculations above indicate once again the importance of targeting. With 100 per cent targeting the burden of eliminating malnutrition is less than 2 per cent of GDP. With untargeted income increases, in the form of distribution-neutral growth, dietary inadequacy would be the norm for almost 50 million Brazilians by the end of the century. Of course, 100 per cent targeting is very rarely available to policy makers, and we turn now to a discussion of the type of redistributive strategies open to them in a Latin American context.

While 100 per cent targeting is a policy maker's pipe dream, information on the poverty characteristics of socio-economic and regional groupings can be used to sharpen the extent to which the benefits of expenditure reach the poor and malnourished (see Mateus 1983). The theory underlying such targeting is discussed in Kanbur (1986, 1987). If y is income, $f(y)$ is the frequency density of income, and z is the poverty line in income space, then Foster *et al.* (1984) have suggested the following poverty index:

$$P_\alpha = \int_0^z \left(\frac{z-y}{z} \right)^\alpha f(y) dy; \ \alpha \geq 0$$

where the parameter α reflects the degree of aversion to the depth of poverty. The poverty measured can be the inability to afford the cost of a minimally nutritious diet (as calculated by Altimir 1982, for example). Or, as Kakwani

(1986) has suggested, if y is calorie intake then P_α could be a direct measure of the extent of malnourishment. Two special cases of P_α are worth noting. When $\alpha = 0$,

$$P_\alpha = P_0 = \int_0^z f(y)dy$$

which is simply the incidence of poverty. When $\alpha = 1$,

$$P_\alpha = P_1 = \int_0^z \left(\frac{z-y}{z}\right) f(y)dy = P_0 \left[1 - \frac{\bar{y}_p}{z}\right]$$

which is simply the incidence of poverty times the average poverty gap as a ratio of the poverty line.

From our point of view the interesting feature of the P_α class of measures is that they are additively decomposable across population subgroups. Thus if x_1 is the fraction of population in group 1 and x_2 is the fraction in group 2 $(x_1 + x_2 = 1)$, then:

$$P_\alpha = x_1 P_{1,\alpha} + x_2 P_{2,\alpha}$$

Where $P_{1,\alpha}$ is the group 1 specific measure and $P_{2,\alpha}$ is the group 2 specific measure (the extension to many mutually exclusive and exhaustive groups is obvious). Consider now a redistribution which takes an amount Δ_2 from every member of group 2 (whether rich or poor) and gives Δ_1 to every member of group 1 (whether rich or poor). Budgetary balance requires:

$$\Delta_1 x_1 = \Delta_2 x_2$$

Should such a redistribution be undertaken? It is shown in Kanbur (1986) that:

$$\frac{dP_\alpha}{d\Delta_1} = -\frac{\alpha x_1}{z}[P_{1,\alpha-1} - P_{2,\alpha-1}]$$

which is negative if:

$$P_{1,\alpha-1} > P_{2,\alpha-1}$$

In other words, if the objective is to minimize P_α budgetary expenditure should be targeted towards groups with high $P_{\alpha-1}$.

This targeting rule has a particularly simple interpretation when $\alpha = 1$. Because then $P_\alpha = P_1$ and $P_{\alpha-1} = P_0$. Thus if the objective is to minimize P_1, groups with high P_0s, i.e. high incidences of poverty, should be the beneficiaries of redistribution. This is natural: if we are concerned to minimize the poverty gap, then we want to maximize the probability that a given (marginal) income transfer will reach a poor person—the extent of his or her own poverty gap is irrelevant. It should now be clear where our characterization of malnutrition and poverty in the previous section comes in. The incidences of poverty in different socio-economic groupings provide a natural ranking for targeting (the identification of 'high risk' groups is recommended as a research strategy by Pinstrup-Andersen 1981). In Latin America, as in Asia, the incidence of poverty in the rural sector is higher than in the urban sector. Redistributive measures which operate at this level of aggregation should therefore he used to raise rural incomes. With more finely tuned instruments, the details of poverty within the rural sector and the urban sector can be used to guide redistributive policy. Within the rural sector, helping smallholders and agricultural workers will be a well-targeted policy. Within the urban sector, manual workers' incomes should be a prime focus of policy. The counterpart to this is the severe effect that recession is bound to have, via manual workers' earnings, on poverty (see ffrench-Davis and Raczynski 1986 and Lustig 1986). In both rural and urban sectors, raising large families' incomes is an extremely well-targeted policy for reducing poverty.

Apart from these general conclusions about regional and occupational groupings at the broadest level, once we get into finer classifications differences do begin to emerge between Latin American countries (cf. the contrasting patterns in Costa Rica and Guatemala in comparing incidences of poverty between smallholders and agricultural workers). But this is not surprising. At a certain level of detail the analysis has to become country specific, and moves beyond the scope of this region-wide survey (for a similar view, see Peek 1984). It is to be hoped, however, that the method of identifying target groups will prove useful in the country analysis as well.

1.5. Further research

To end, we would like to pick out two topics which seem to be high on the research agenda for the analysis and alleviation of malnutrition and poverty in Latin America. Firstly, there is the task of reconciling the many different estimates of the magnitude of the problem. All estimates agree that the problem is severe and, furthermore, the patterns of malnourishment and poverty revealed are fairly consistent. But there are discrepancies in numbers of malnourished and poor as estimated by different authors. The discrepancies can sometimes be attributed to differences in the poverty line chosen, but in many cases the underlying methodologies differ and a systematic attempt at evaluating these methodologies is needed (for a start in this direction see Anand and Kanbur 1986).

However, even more important than resolving the discrepancies in estimates of numbers in poverty at the all Latin America level is the analysis of the patterns of poverty and malnutrition at the detailed, country-specific level. Given the minor role that growth can play in eradicating malnutrition within a generation, there may well be a role for redistribution. But redistribution with 100 per cent targeting towards the poor is not feasible. Rather, we will have to rely on policy instruments which are much coarser, instruments which affect the incomes of broad groups of individuals in the same way. But which of several broadly defined groups should be favoured in a targeted strategy of poverty alleviation? The answer depends on how we measure poverty and what instruments we have at our disposal. Following the arguments in Kanbur (1986), we showed in section 4.4 that if our object was to reduce the national poverty gap (or nutrition gap) then, under a particular model of the effects of policy on income (nutrition), socio-economic groups with a high incidence of poverty (malnutrition) should be high on the list for targeting. If the object of policy is a different index of poverty and malnutrition, or if the effects of policy are modelled in a different way, then of course the targeting rule will be different. Some of these alternative targeting rules are derived in Kanbur (1986), but what is important is to apply them to particular countries.

What is required for such an application is a detailed profile of poverty by policy-relevant socio-economic groupings. It is probably true that the level of disaggregation necessary for policy analysis in each country will mean that no continent-wide inferences can be drawn on the patterns of poverty. But the division of labour we are suggesting is a natural one—the use of broad regional and occupational categories to comment on the pattern in Latin America as a whole, and the use of much more finely disaggregated categories for national policy prescriptions. In our view it is the latter course of research and analysis that will yield the highest payoff.

References

AHLUWALIA, M. S. (1976), 'Inequality, Poverty and Development', *Journal of Development Economics*, 3.
——CARTER, NICHOLAS G., and CHENERY, HOLLIS B. (1979), 'Growth and Poverty in Developing Countries', *Journal of Development Economics*.

ALTIMIR, OSCAR (1982), 'The Extent of Poverty in Latin America', World Bank Staff Working Paper No. 522 (Washington, DC: World Bank).

ANAND, S., and KANBUR, S. M. R. (1986), 'International Poverty Projections', mimeo (Helsinki: WIDER).

ARELLANO, AQUILES (1975), 'Hacia una canasta de consumo mínimo', mimeo (Santiago: Universidad de Chile).
——(1977), 'La pobreza en diez ciudades sud-americanas', mimeo (Rio de Janeiro: ECIEL Program).

AUSTIN, J. (1979), 'The Role of Nutrition in Rural Development: The Mexican Experience', in Inter-American Development Bank (1979).

BARREDA-MONCADA, G. (1963), *Estudios sobre alteraciones del crecimiento y del desarrollo psicológico del sindrome pluricarencial (kwashiorkor)* (Caracas: Editora Grafas).

BERG, ALAN (1981), 'Malnourished People: A Policy View', World Bank Poverty and Basic Need Series (Washington, DC: World Bank).

BERGSMAN, JOEL (1980), 'Income Distribution and Poverty in Mexico', World Bank Staff Working Paper No. 395 (Washington, DC: World Bank).

BIRCH, M. E., PINEIRO, C., ADCALDE, E., TOCA, T., and CRAVIOTO, J. (1971), 'Relation of Kwashiorkor in Early Childhood and Intelligence at School Age', *Pediatric Research*.

BLISS, C., and STERN, N. (1978), 'Productivity, Wages and Nutrition: The Theory', *Journal of Development Economics*.

BROCKMAN, L., and RICCIUTI, H. (1971), 'Severe Protein-Calorie Malnutrition and Cognitive Development in Infancy and Early Childhood', *Developmental Psychology*.

CEPAL (1983), 'Satisfacción de las necesidades básicas de la población del istmo centroamericano', E/CEPAL/MEX/1983/L.32.

CRAVIOTO, J., and ROBLES, B. (1965), 'Evolution of Adaptive and Motor Behavior during Rehabilitation from Kwashiorkor', *American Journal of Orthopsychiatry*.

DASGUPTA, P., and RAY, D. (1990), 'Adapting to Undernourishment', in the first volume of this book.

DAZA, CARLOS H. (1979), 'Formulation and Implementation of Nutrition Policies: PAHO Strategies for Latin American and the Caribbean', in Inter-American Development Bank (1979).

DEERE, CARMEN DIANA, and DISKIN, MARTIN (1984), 'Rural Poverty in El Salvador; Dimensions, Trends and Causes', Working Paper WEP10-6/WP64 (Geneva: World Employment Programme Research, ILO).

DESAI, I., et al. (1980), 'Food Habits and Nutritional Status of Agricultural Migrant Workers in Southern Brazil', *American Journal of Clinical Nutrition*.

FAO/WHO (1973), 'Energy and Protein Requirements', WHO Technical Report Series No. 552, Report No. 52 (Geneva: Report of a Joint FAO/WHO Ad Hoc Expert Committee FAO Nutrition Meetings).

FERBER, ROBERT, and MUSGROVE, PHILIP (1983), 'Identifying the Urban Poor: Characteristics of Poverty Households in Bogotá, Medellín, and Lima', *Latin American Research Review*.

FERRARI, MARCO A. (1980), 'The Urban Bias of Peruvian Food Policy: Consequences and Alternatives', Ph.D. thesis, Cornell University.

FFRENCH-DAVIS, RICARDO, and RACZYNSKI, DAGMAR (1986), 'The Impact of Global Recession on Living Standards: Chile', mimeo (Helsinki: WIDER).

FLORES, R., IMMINK, M. D. C., TORUM, B., DIAZ, E., and VITERI, F. E. (1984), 'Functional Consequences of Marginal Malnutrition among Agricultural Workers in Guatemala', *Food and Nutrition Bulletin*.

FOSTER, J., GREER, J., and THORBECKE, E. (1984), 'On a Class of Decomposable Poverty Measures', *Econometrica*.

GARCIA, JORGE, MOHAN, RAKESH, and WAGNER, M. WILHELM (1981), 'Measuring Urban Malnutrition and Poverty: A Case Study of Bogotá and Cali, Colombia', World Bank Staff Working Paper No. 447 (Washington, DC: World Bank).

GOMEZ, F., *et al.* (1955), 'Malnutrition in Infancy and Childhood with Special Reference to Kwashiorkor', in Levine, S. (ed.), *Advances in Pediatrics* (New York: Yearbook Publisher).

HAMILTON, SAHNI, POPKIN, BARRY, and SPICER, DEBORAH (1984), *Women and Nutrition in Developing Countries* (New York: Praeger).

HARBERT, LLOYD, and SCANDIZZO, PASQUALE L. (1982), 'Food Distribution and Nutrition Intervention: The Case of Chile', World Bank Staff Working Paper No. 512 (Washington, DC: World Bank).

HERRICK, BRUCE H., and HUDSON, BARCLAY (1981), *Urban Poverty and Economic Development: A Case Study of Costa Rica* (Boston, Mass.: St Martins Press).

HICKS, JAMES F., and VETTER, DAVID MICHAEL (1983), 'Identifying the Urban Poor in Brazil', World Bank Staff Working Paper No. 565 (Washington, DC: World Bank).

HINTERMEISTER, ALBERTO (1984), 'Rural Poverty and Export Farming in Guatemala', Working Paper WEP10-6/WP71 (Geneva: World Employment Programme Research, ILO).

INCAP (1980), *Estudio de regionalización de problemas nutricionales en Guatemala* (Guatemala).

Inter-American Development Bank (1979), *Nutrition and Socio-economic Development of Latin America* (Washington, DC).

KAKWANI, N. C. (1986), 'On Measuring Undernutrition', mimeo (Helsinki: WIDER).

KANBUR, S. M. R. (1986), 'Budgetary Rules for Poverty Alleviation', mimeographed (Princeton University).

——(1987), 'Measurement and Alleviation of Poverty', *IMF Staff Papers*.

KNIGHT, PETER T., and MORAN, RICARDO (1981), *Poverty and Basic Needs: Brazil* (Washington, DC: World Bank).

LUSTIG, NORA (1986), 'Economic Crisis and Living Standards in Mexico: 1982–1985', mimeo (Helsinki: WIDER).

MATEUS, ABEL (1983), 'Targeting Food Subsidies for the Needy: The Use of Cost–Benefit Analysis and Institutional Design', World Bank Staff Working Paper No. 617 (Washington, DC: World Bank).

MONCKEBERG, F. (1968), 'Effect of Early Marasmic Malnutrition on Subsequent Physical and Psychological Development', in Scrimshaw, N. S., and Gordon, J. (eds.), *Malnutrition, Learning and Behavior* (Cambridge, Mass.: MIT Press).

MUSGROVE, PHILIP (1978), *Consumer Behavior in Latin America* (Washington, DC: The Brookings Institution).

—— (1985), 'Food Needs and Absolute Poverty in Urban South America', *Review of Income and Wealth*.

PACEY, ARNOLD, and PAYNE, PHILIP (eds.) (1985), *Agricultural Development and Nutrition*, (London: Hutchinson).

PEEK, PETER (1984), 'Rural Poverty in Central America: Dimensions, Causes and Policy Alternatives', Working Paper WEP10-6/WP70 (Geneva: World Employment Programme Research, ILO).

—— and RAABE, CARLOS (1984), 'Rural Equity in Costa Rica: Myth or Reality?' Working Paper WEP10-6/WP67 (Geneva: World Employment Programme Research, ILO).

PINSTRUP-ANDERSEN, PER (1981), 'Nutritional Consequences of Agricultural Projects: Conceptual Relationships and Assessment Approaches', World Bank Staff Working Paper No. 456 (Washington, DC: World Bank).

POLLITT, E. (1974), *Desnutrición, pobreza e inteligencia* (Instituto nacional de investigación y desarrollo de la educación).

—— (1980), *Poverty and Malnutrition in Latin America: Early Childhood Intervention Programs* (New York: Praeger).

PUFFER, R. D., and SERRANO, C. V. (1973), *Patterns of Mortality in Childhood*, Scientific Publication 267 (Washington, DC: Pan American Health Organization).

SALAZAR-CARILLO, JORGE (1978), *Prices and Purchasing Power Parities in Latin America, 1960–1972* (Organization of American States, ECIEL Program).

Servicio nacional de salud, Chile (1974), *Frecuencia y porciones de alimentos según recomendación* (Sección nutrición, Sub-departamento de fomento de salud).

THOMAS, VINOD (1982), 'Difference in Income, Nutrition and Poverty within Brazil', World Bank Staff Working Paper No. 505 (Washington, DC: World Bank).

UNICEF (1981), *Social Statistics Bulletin*, 4/4.

—— (1986), *Statistics on Children in UNICEF Assisted Countries* (New York: UNICEF).

VALVERDE, V., *et al.* (1980), 'Life Styles and Nutritional Status of Children from Different Ecological Areas of El Salvador', *Ecology of Food and Nutrition*.

VITERI, F. E. (1971), 'Considerations of the Effect of Nutrition on the Body Composition and Physical Working Capacity of Young Guatemalan Adults', in Scrimshaw, N. S., and Altschul, A. M. (eds.), *Amino Acid Fortification of Protein Foods* (Cambridge, Mass.: MIT Press).

World Bank (1983), 'Brazil: Human Resources Special Report', vols. i and ii, A World Bank Country Study (Washington, DC: World Bank).

—— (1985), 'Ensuring Food Security in the Developing World: Issues and Options' (Washington, DC: Agriculture and Rural Development Department, World Bank).

—— (1986a), *World Development Report* (Oxford: Oxford University Press).

—— (1986b), 'Poverty in Latin America: The Impact of Depression', (Washington, DC: World Bank).

5

Undernutrition in Sub-Saharan Africa

A Critical Assessment of the Evidence

Peter Svedberg

5.1. *Introduction*

Most of the sub-Saharan African countries have experienced what cannot be labelled anything but an economic and political crisis during the 1970s and 1980s. The annual growth of GDP per capita for the region as a whole went down from 2 per cent in the 1950s and the 1960s to 0.8 per cent during the 1970s; in the 1980s, it was −2.5 per cent. The share of sub-Saharan Africa (SSA) in world exports has declined dramatically and real export earnings of many of the countries in the region have dropped significantly since the early 1970s (Svedberg 1991*a*). In recent years, almost every government in the SSA countries has been faced with the inescapable fact that drastic economic policy changes have to be undertaken during the 1990s. More than a dozen countries with previously highly overvalued exchange rates have already devalued substantially and also initiated, or are in the process of initiating, reform in a large number of areas (see Svedberg 1991*a* and IBRD 1989).

Not only have the overall economic performances of most SSA countries been miserable over the past two decades. The conventional wisdom in the international organizations is that the world's food problems are now concentrated in Africa. According to the FAO, food production per capita has declined over the 1970s and 1980s and the per capita 'availability' of food for human consumption is now only 80 per cent of the FAO/WHO recommended intakes. The FAO further claims, on the basis of estimates of how the food is distributed, that between one-quarter and one-fifth of the population in the region does not have enough food to be able to work or pursue any form of physical activity. Estimates by the World Bank purport that almost half the population in the region is at least moderately undernourished.

The food consumption problems will most certainly continue to be one of the main policy concerns in the SSA during the 1990s. Food will be an issue both in its own right and as a constraint on policy reform in other areas. That food will be a major question of policy concern is self-evident even if the problem is of a less alarming order of magnitude than suggested by the international organizations. Food is after all the most basic of all human needs and the notion that eradicating hunger and undernutrition is a top priority aim for policy is shared almost universally. The nutritional problems will also enter as serious constraints on the structural adjustment programmes that will dominate the African scene during the 1990s. New policies mean shifts in relative prices and redistribution of real incomes. This will affect the food entitlements of different groups. It is, then, of the utmost importance that the nutritional situation is known. If only 5–10 per cent of the population in a country is at risk, there will be many more degrees of freedom in the pursuit of new general economic policies than if it is 30–60 per cent. Moreover, one needs to know who the people at risk are; otherwise it will be impossible to reach them with targeted policies or to see to it that they are compensated if they suffer from side-effects of general policies.

The objectives of this chapter are threefold. The first is to bring together as much as possible of the available evidence on nutritional standards in the SSA (section 5.2). The second objective is to compare the different pictures of the nutritional situation that emerge when different indicators are consulted (section 5.3). The third aim is to try to delineate how much of these differences is explained, on the one hand, by errors and biases in the different estimation methods (sections 5.4–5.7) and, on the other hand, by the fact that the different indicators measure different things, i.e. rest on very different notions of what 'undernutrition' is all about (section 5.8).

5.2. *Indicators of food standards and undernutrition in SSA*

Food consumed by the population in various countries has conventionally been estimated in two different ways. One has been to estimate *food availabilities* from the supply side. This is the approach that has long been favoured by the FAO. The other method is to estimate the *actual intake* of sample populations and extrapolate to more aggregate levels. However, the food 'available' to, or actually consumed by, households, even if accurately estimated, does not say much about the nutritional status of the population as a whole or the prevalence of undernutrition. In order to be able to say something on these issues, the distribution of the food within the population and the (im)balance between the energy intakes and 'desired' expenditures of individuals must be known.

Several different methods have been used to estimate the incidence of undernutrition in different populations. The most aggregate estimates are derived by the FAO and the World Bank. On the basis of the FAO estimates of calories available in various countries and assumptions of how the calories are distributed across households, the FAO and IBRD estimate the share of the population that does not meet the 'desired' calorie expenditures, i.e. that is undernourished. A number of studies have also been conducted at the level of villages, where people's actual intakes have been estimated and related to their assumed energy requirements. A third set of studies has used anthropometric and biochemical and related methods to assess the nutritional status of samples of individuals. A fourth set of assessments focuses on the (presumed) consequences of undernutrition, such as child mortality, without considering the 'underlying' food intake, energy expenditure or the anthropometric status of the population. One can also learn about people's food and nutrition standards by examining their economic expenditures in general and food expenditures in particular. (The latter type of investigation will not be discussed in this paper, but is dealt with in Svedberg 1987, 1991b.)

In the following subsections, we shall describe in more detail how the various estimates of food standards and undernutrition mentioned above are arrived at, and discuss the results that have been obtained for the SSA countries.

(a) The FAO calorie availability estimates

Method The FAO describes its estimation method as follows:

The total quantity of foodstuffs produced in a country added to the total quantity imported and adjusted for any change in stocks that may have occurred since the beginning of the reference period gives the *supply* available during that period. On the *utilization* side, a distinction is made between the quantities exported, fed to livestock, used for seed, put to industrial and other non-food uses, or lost during storage and transportation, and food supplies available for human consumption at the retail level, i.e. in the form food leaves the retail shop or otherwise enters the household. The per-caput supply of each food item available for human consumption is then obtained by dividing the food supplies available for human consumption by the related data on the population actually taking part of it. Data on per caput food supplies are expressed in terms of quantity and also, by applying appropriate food consumption factors, in terms of nutrient elements (calories, protein, etc.). (FAO 1980)

Much of the food production data that underlie the FAO calorie availability estimates have been supplied by national governments in 'the form of replies to annual FAO questionnaires'. Where no official or semi-official figures are available from the countries themselves, the FAO makes its own estimates (FAO, *Production Yearbooks*, introduction).

Estimates The FAO data suggest that in 1961–3, the per capita calorie availability for the region as a whole was 2,014 (Table 5.1). By the mid-1980s, the number had dropped to 1,876, but the year-to-year variations have been too marked for a statistically significant trend to be discernible. In an international comparison, the SSA region comes out the worst. The Near East has seen the per capita availability of calories increase drastically since the early 1960s; in the Far East and Latin America, there have been improvements. Among individual countries, India has experienced a small increase, while for Bangladesh, the FAO estimates suggest a deterioration.

Since 1970, the estimated per capita calorie availability has improved (statistically significantly) in a little more than a third (18) of the 44 sub-Saharan African countries according to the FAO. In some of these, the improvement is substantial, e.g. in Congo, Gabon, Lesotho, Mauritius, Niger, and Tanzania. There are, on the other hand, a dozen countries where there has

Table 5.1 Estimated per capita calorie availability and requirement, by selected countries and regions

	Number of calories				Requirements[a]
	1961–3	1970–2	1980–2	1983–5	
Sub-Saharan					
Africa[b]	2,014	1,896	1,982	1,876	2,340
India	2,038	2,054	2,075	2,161	2,200
Bangladesh	1,938	1,953	1,879	1,859	2,315
Developing					
market economies	2,069	2,187	2,338	2,363	—
Latin America	2,381	2,518	2,692	2,700	2,380
Near East	2,225	2,415	2,879	2,947	2,200
Far East	1,962	2,080	2,186	2,239	2,230
Africa	2,055	2,103	2,200	2,129	2,340

[a] Requirements according to FAO/WHO (1973) standards.
[b] The FAO (1987) tapes provide no separate data for sub-Saharan Africa. The above estimates have been derived by correcting the average for Africa as a whole with the weighted averages of the North African countries (Algeria, Egypt, Libya, Morocco, and Tunisia).
Source: Derived from FAO (1987).

been a statistically significant deterioration; in a few cases (Chad, Ghana, and Mozambique) by more than 1 per cent annually over the 17 years. In 14 countries the year-to-year fluctuations have been very pronounced and there is no statistically significant trend. The FAO data thus suggest a rather varied experience across Africa since the early 1970s (see Svedberg 1991b: Table 5.2).

The most notable development over the 1980s is that the per capita supply of calories has continued to fall in the countries where there has been a secular deterioration since the early 1970s: Chad, Ghana, Guinea, and Sierra Leone. According to the FAO, there is no single country in which there has been a notable increase over the first half of the 1980s. The FAO further suggests that the per capita availability of calories in 1983–85 was lower in 30 of the 44 countries in SSA than in India. In 7 African countries, the situation was worse than in Bangladesh, the FAO claims.

(b) The dietary calorie intake estimates

Methods Three main methods have been used to estimate food consumption at the level of individuals and households in Africa. The most common (and inexpensive) procedure is to collect qualitative information through interviews (recalls). That is, one simply asks people how much of different foods they have consumed over a specific time period, e.g. the past 24 hours, or the last week. The second method is to measure purchases and/or changes in food stocks and convert these into 'consumption' flows. The third (and most expensive) method is to weigh (the equivalent of) the food actually observed to have been consumed by the individual or the household. The nutritional content of the estimated food consumed, whatever the method used, is usually derived from more or less standardized conversion tables.

Estimates   The estimated daily per capita calorie intake in 85 sample studies from African villages lies in the 1,800 to 2,200 range in most cases. There are thus notable intervillage differences and the average fails to meet the FAO/WHO recommended per capita calorie requirement norms, which are about 2,340 calories for the African countries (Schofield 1979: Table 5.5; Hulse and Pearson 1981: Table 5). The estimated (unweighted) average per capita calorie consumption for all the 85 studies together (two studies are covered in both surveys) is 1,950.

(c)   *The prevalence of undernutrition: FAO and IBRD*

Method   The FAO (1985) and the IBRD (1986) use an indirect method to estimate the incidence of undernutrition.[1] The procedure comprises three steps. The first is to estimate the food energy 'available for human consumption' at the country level. The second is to estimate 'desired' energy expenditures. The third is to model how the distribution of the available calories relates to the distribution of calorie 'requirements'. Thus they do not aim to measure people's actual intakes directly (the dietary approach) or the outcome of energy deficiency (clinical and anthropometric approaches).

Model   The main features of the FAO/IBRD model can be described by a simple graph (Fig. 5.1). Let us assume that we have a population of a given number of households (*H*) for which all differences in size, composition (age, sex, etc.), and other factors that affect their calorie 'requirements' have been normalized. All households thus have the same per capita requirements, *R* in Fig. 5.1. It is further assumed that there is a given 'pool' of calories available to this population. On a per capita basis, the availability of calories to the total population is given by *A*. The households are different in one important aspect, however: they have different incomes and the available calories are allocated in proportion to incomes. The households are ranked in ascending order of their per capita calorie intake (PCCI) along the horizontal axis in Fig. 5.1. The household with the lowest income and per capita calorie intake (measured along the vertical axis), is located at the left-hand end of the horizontal axis (at 0). Households with higher per capita calorie intakes are placed successively to the right. The household with the highest income and intake is located at the extreme right of the graph (at *H*). The *DD'* line gives the absolute distribution of the calories across the *H* households; in terms of area, *OAA'H* is equal to *ODD'H*.

---

[1]   The Bank's version of the model is described in some detail in several publications (Reutlinger and Selowsky 1976; Reutlinger and Alderman 1980; IBRD 1986). The FAO version is not as explicitly presented (FAO 1985*a*: 17–30 and Appendix 3), but there are no fundamental differences.

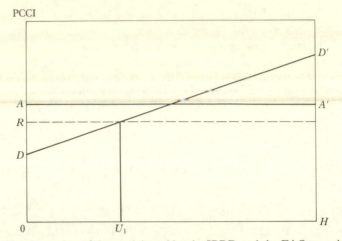

Fig. 5.1. Simple version of the model used by the IBRD and the FAO to estimate the prevalence of undernutrition in developing countries

Out of the H households, U_1 have an estimated per capita intake that fails to meet the per capita calorie requirement norm R. These households are thus undernourished according to the FAO/IBRD estimation procedure. In the particular case depicted in Fig. 5.1, the per capita availability of calories exceeds the per capita calorie requirement ($A > R$), signifying that had the calories been allocated evenly over the population, no one would be under-nourished. It is further notable that the main interest of the FAO and IBRD is in the *share* of the population that falls below R (as defined; see below), not in the *amount* by which the most destitute are short of calories. It is also important to remember that the 'undernourished' households are not identifiable with the FAO/IBRD method; they comprise an anonymous 'poor' section of the population.

Data   Both organizations work with the same aggregate database, i.e. the FAO per capita availability of calorie estimates described above. The 'require-ment' norms are different, however. The FAO uses two cut-off points to define undernutrition. Under the assumption that people have given energy require-ments for internal body functions, i.e. a constant 'basal metabolic rate', BMR, per kilo of body weight, they set the calorie requirement norm at 1.4 times the BMR. This norm allows an individual to exert the minimum of external physical activity needed for the most basic personal undertakings (dressing, washing, etc.) and to maintain cardiovascular and muscular fitness, but no physical activity (such as work) above that. The other cut-off point used by the FAO to estimate the prevalence of undernutrition is 1.2 BMR. This norm is derived on the same assumptions as the higher one, with one exception: the human body is assumed to have a built-in mechanism that ensures that the energy in food is more efficiently metabolized when food is scarce.

The IBRD also uses two alternative calorie requirement norms; not on the basis of different assumptions of the energy requirements human beings have, but rather in order to distinguish between those who are 'moderately' and 'severely' undernourished. The two norms applied by the IBRD are 90 and 80 per cent of the recommended dietary allowances (RDAs) of calories supplied by the FAO/WHO (1973). These cut-off points are higher than those used by the FAO.

The distribution of the available calories across households is assumed by both organizations to be determined by income. The IBRD is explicit in showing what income distribution data and what calorie–income elasticities it has used to map the distribution of calorie consumption from the distribution of incomes. The FAO has undertaken its own distribution and elasticity estimations, but has not published the details. One further difference is that the IBRD works with discrete income groups, such as the 30 per cent poorest, while the FAO uses a continuous income scale.

Estimates The IBRD and FAO estimates for the years 1970 and 1980 are reproduced in Table 5.2. The highest estimate of the incidence of 'moderate and severe' undernutrition in sub-Saharan Africa for the year 1980, 44 per cent of the population, is suggested by the Bank, applying its higher requirement norm. The smallest estimate, 19 per cent, is from the FAO, derived on the assumption that people can 'adapt' to low calorie intakes.

The two organizations did not find a significant change in the relative incidence of undernutrition in the SSA region as a whole between 1970 and 1980, the two points of time examined. In absolute terms, however, the organizations report an increase in the number of undernourished people in the 13–35 million range over this period. Between 1980 and 1986, the FAO estimates of per capita food availability in the SSA show a decline. This implies that had the relative incidence of undernutrition in Africa been assessed by the mid-1980s, using the FAO and IBRD methods, one would have registered an increase (other things being equal). However, preliminary data for more recent years suggest positive growth in per capita domestic food production in some countries, which may have led to increased per capita food consumption as well. It is thus too early to say whether the FAO and IBRD are likely to find that the prevalence of undernutrition has increased or decreased over the 1980s in the SSA.

According to the Bank's estimates, the incidence (in percentage terms) of *severe* undernutrition in the SSA is higher than in South Asia (although the share of the population suffering from *moderate* undernutrition is higher in the latter region). It should further be noted that the Bank provides background tables of estimates for individual countries, which suggest that in 1980 the situation in about a dozen SSA countries was worse than in Bangladesh (Svedberg 1987: Appendix Table 4).

Table 5.2 Prevalence of undernourished people in developing countries, by major regions, as estimated by the IBRD and the FAO

Region	No. of people (m.)			% of population		
	1970	1980	Change	1970	1980	Change
IBRD						
Sub-Saharan Africa						
High estimate	115	150	+35	43	44	+1
Low estimate	60	90	+30	21	25	+4
East Asia and Pacific						
High estimate	93	40	−53	41	14	−27
Low estimate	47	20	−27	21	7	−14
South Asia						
High estimate	341	470	+129	47	50	+3
Low estimate	136	200	+64	19	21	+2
Middle East and North Africa						
High estimate	53	20	−33	35	10	−25
Low estimate	31	10	−21	18	4	−14
Latin America and Caribbean						
High estimate	59	50	−9	20	13	−7
Low estimate	25	20	−5	10	6	−4
Developing countries						
High estimate	664	730	+64	40	34	−6
Low estimate	298	340	+42	18	16	−2
FAO						
Africa[a]						
High estimate	81	99	+18	29	26	−3
Low estimate	57	70	+13	20	19	−1
Far East						
High estimate	303	313	+10	31	25	−6
Low estimate	208	210	+2	21	17	−4
Near East						
High estimate	34	25	−9	22	12	−10
Low estimate	23	16	−7	15	8	−7
Latin America						
High estimate	53	56	+3	19	16	−3
Low estimate	36	38	+2	13	11	−2
Developing countries						
High estimate	472	494	+22	28	23	−5
Low estimate	325	335	+10	19	15	−4

[a] Africa, excluding Egypt, Libya, Sudan, and SAU.

Sources: IBRD (1986: Tables 2–3 and 2–4); FAO (1985a: Table 3–4).

(d)   The prevalence of undernutrition: anthropometric evidence

Method   The basic presumption behind the anthropometric methods is that one need not estimate people's actual calorie intakes and expenditures to assess their nutritional status. Any imbalance between intake and 'desired' expenditure will show up in reduced body weight and retarded growth in stature (for children and adolescents). If weight and/or stature fall below some anthropometric norm, people are defined as undernourished.

The anthropometric studies that have been conducted in Africa have almost exclusively focused on children; very few studies of adults exist. On the other hand, there are a fair amount of height and weight observations for adults, made by anthropologists and human physiologists. Eveleth and Tanner (1976) brought together and made comparable such observations of average height and weight of grown-ups in almost three dozen populations in the SSA. Unfortunately, these data are reported without estimates of variance, so that it is not possible to derive the percentage of the different populations that falls below some anthropometric norm that would define them as undernourished. One can only compare the average height and weight in these populations to the norms. Eveleth and Tanner did not provide such norms, however, which means that we have to construct them ourselves.

The height norm for adults that will be used here (as a first approximation) is established on the presumption that all ethnic groups have roughly the same genetic potential for adult stature. This is what most human biologists claim today. The growth potential is further assumed to have been achieved in the populations that have the *de facto* highest stature. These are found in the Scandinavian countries, where adult males and females reach 180 and 167 cm on the average (in the mid-1980s). For the time being, it is also assumed that inadequate nutrition is the only constraint on achieving the full genetic potential for growth in the SSA populations. The norm is further based on the assumption that the achievement of the full genetic potential has a value in its own right, irrespective of whether modest stunting is linked to dysfunctions or not.

The weight norm is established on the notion that the individual can vary his or her weight within a range without increased health risks and that there is no 'genetic potential' weight. The latest FAO/WHO/UNU (1985: 183) expert committee has endorsed a study suggesting that a weight for height corresponding to a 'body mass index' (BMI) ranging from 20.1 to 25.0 for adult males and from 18.7 to 23.8 for adult females is consistent with health and unimpaired mental and physical capabilities. The weight norms used in the following have been derived from the lower ends of these ranges, with a slight upward revision for females because of the high incidence of pregnancies in the SSA. The weight norms used here are thus derived from a body mass index of 20.1 for men and 19.0 for women.

For small children (below 6), there is a very large number of anthropometric studies. These usually report the proportion of children that fall below the norm for one or more of the three most commonly used anthropometric indicators: weight for height (wasting), height for age (stunting), and weight for age (combined wasting and stunting). The most commonly used weight for height norms are 80 per cent of, or two standard deviations from, the median in the NCHS or Harvard reference populations. The conventional height for age norms are 90 per cent of, or two standard deviations below, the median decile of reference populations.

Estimates: adults   The numbers shown in the first column of Table 5.3 give the average height of the various adult SSA populations as a percentage of the height norm (180 and 167 cm for men and women, respectively). The table reveals that there are enormous differences in actual heights across ethnic groups in the SSA. The 36 populations covered include the Dinkas (southern Sudan), the tallest people measured in the world. Also included are the Bunia pygmies (Zaire), the shortest people measured in the world. The average adult Dinka male, at 181.6 cm, is 25 per cent taller than the average Bunia male (at 145 cm). Contrasted to the Scandinavian norm, the African populations examined have an average height ranging from 82 (Bunia pygmies) to 101 per cent (Dinkas).

The average person in 19 of the 28 populations for which there are weight data in Table 5.3 (second column) is above the weight for height norm. As with height, there are considerable differences in weight for height across the samples. The Dinkas and the Samburies (in Sudan and Kenya, respectively) are the thinnest, at 88 per cent of the norm weight. The well-off from Ibadan in Nigeria are the heaviest.

Estimates: Children   The results of anthropometric examinations of 23 random samples of children in 17 sub-Saharan countries over the 1973–84 period are summarized in Table 5.4. The first criterion, height for age, gives an indication of the incidence of chronic undernutrition. In the seven countries for which these data are available, an estimated 16 to 28 per cent of all children (up to 5 or 6 years old) are stunted by US standards (10 per cent or two standard deviations below these norms). There are notable differences across the countries. Unfortunately, few surveys provide data on the prevalence of severe stunting (i.e. below 80 per cent of the reference median), but the two that do find it low.

When it comes to acute undernutrition, as measured by weight for height, the picture looks unambiguously more favourable. As Table 5.4 shows, the prevalence of mild to modest (between 60 and 80 per cent of weight standard) acute undernutrition among children is only a few per cent in most countries. Not surprisingly, the incidence was significantly higher in the Sahel countries during the famine years 1973 and 1974; in these years also severe acute undernutrition (below 60 per cent of standard references) was found in a small

Table 5.3 Average height and weight of adults in selected African populations (% of height and weight norm)

Country	People/place/group	Ethnic origin[a]	Year	Height[b]	Weight for height[c]
Botswana	Bushmen	(B/P)	1962	89	96
	Bushmen	(B/P)	1970	88[d]	—
Chad	Sara/rural	(N)	1969	97	112
	Sara/urban	(N)	1972	98	—
Ethiopia	Debarech	(N/H)	1969	93	104
	Adi-Arkai	(N/H)	1969	93	100
Gambia	—	—	1952	94	104
Kenya	Students	(B)	1961	91[d]	—
	Samburu	(N)	1969	97[d]	88[d]
Malawi	Lilongwe	(B)	1972	92[d]	—
	Bantu	(B)	1970	92	105
Mozambique	Recruits	(B)	1968	94[d]	105[d]
Namibia	Dama	(B)	1969	93[d]	—
Nigeria	Akufo/Yoruba	(S)	1970	93	107
	Ibadan/well-off	—	—	96	126
	Ibadan/slum	—	—	94	108
	Lagos	—	1970	94	118
Rwanda	Tutsi	(N)	1965	98	99
	Hutu	(B)	1965	93	108
Sudan	Dinka	(N)	1963	101[d]	88[d]
	Shilluk	(N)	1963	99[d]	91[d]
	Nilo Hamites	(N/H)	1961	99[d]	114[e]
Tanzania	Hadra	(B)	1972	90	108
	Bantu	(B)	—	94	—
	Tanganyika	(B)	1961	91[d]	—
	Kasanioja	(N)	1961	99[d]	—
Uganda	Students	(B)	1961	92[d]	—
	Baganda/rural	(B)	1969	92	116
Zaire	Fulero	(B)	1965	88[d]	94[d]
	Tutsi	(N)	1965	96[d]	92[d]
	Congolese	(B)	1970	94	104
	Twa pygmies	(B/P)	1972	89[d]	100[d]
	Mbaiki pygmies	(B/P)	1967	84[d]	100[d]
	Bunia pygmies	(B/P)	1962	82	98
	Kasai	(B)	1964	93[d]	107[d]
	Katanga	(B)	1964	91[d]	105[d]

[a] B/P = Bushmen/Pygmies, B = Bantu, N = Nilotic, N/H = Nilo Hamites, S = Sudanese.
[b] The height norm is based on estimations of adults in the Scandinavian countries (180 cm for males, 167 cm for females).
[c] Based on a body mass index of 20.1 for males, and 19.0 for females.
[d] Observations of males only.
[e] Observations of females only.

Source: Eveleth and Tanner (1976: Appendix tables 44, 45, 77, and 78 (height and weight data)); FAO/WHO/UNU (1985: Appendix table 2.c. (weight norm)).

Table 5.4 Percentage share of undernourished children according to selected anthropometric indicators, Africa, 1973–1984

Country (age or height group)	Year (season)[a]	Category	Size of sample	Height for age below 90% of norm	Weight for height below 80% of norm	Weight for age below 80% of norm	Reference norm used[b]
USAID surveys							
Cameroon (3–59 months)	1978 (Oct.–Apr.)	Rural	3,942	22	1	23	NAS
		Urban	1,733	15	1	12	
		Total	5,675	22	1	21	
		NRG[c]	505	4	—	4	
Lesotho (0–59 months)	1977 (—)	Rural	1,421	24	4	25	NAS
		Urban	285	17	3	17	
		Total	1,706	23	4	22	
		NRG	293	11	5	6	
Liberia (0–59 months)	1975–6 (AH)	Agr.	2,502	20	2	26	NAS
		Non-ag.	977	14	1	20	
		Total	3,479	18	2	24	
		NRG	285	9	3	13	
Sierra Leone (0–71 months)	1978 (—)	Rural	2,937	26	3	32	NAS
		Urban	1,943	14	3	24	
		Total	4,880	24	3	30	
		NRG	361	2	1	5	
Swaziland (3–59 months)	1983–4 (BH)	Rural	3,475	17	0	12	NCHS
		Urban	658	13	0	10	
		Total	4,133	16	0	12	
Togo (6–71 months)	1977 (—)	Rural	—	20	2	16	NS
		Urban	—	11	1	9	
		Total	—	19	2	15	
		NRG	—	—	—	—	
Other surveys							
Benin (0–59 months)	1976 (BH)	Nationwide	127	—	6	—	H

Botswana (0–59 months)	1978–81 (MH)	Nationwide	c.50,000	—	—	27	NS
Burkina (1) (0–9 years)	1973 (BH)	Sedentary	132	—	38	—	H
		Migratory	43	—	49	—	
		Total	175	—	41	—	
Burkina (2) (65–115 cm)	1974 (BH)	Nationwide	875	—	9	—	SM
Burkina (3) (0–71 months)	1978 (BH)	Nationwide	320	—	14	—	H
Chad (65–115 cm)	1974 (BH)	Nationwide	779	—	22	—	SM
Gambia (6–35 months)	1981–2 (DS)	Urban	—	—	6	—	NCHS
Kenya (12–47 months)	1977	Rural	c.3,000	24	—	—	NS
	1979			27	—	—	NS
	1982			28	—	—	NS
Malawi (0–59 months)	1981 (DS)	Rural	—	—	—	32	NS
Mali (1) (65–115 cm)	1974 (BH)	Nationwide	625	—	11	—	SM
Mali (2) (0–59 months)	1976 (BH)	Migratory	208	—	9	—	H
Mali (3) (0–71 months)	1978 (BH)	Rural	122	—	15	—	H
Mali (4) (0–71 months)	1979 (MH)	Rural	249	—	6	—	H
Maurit. (1) (70–120 cm)	1973 (BH)	Sedentary	781	—	8	—	SM
		Migratory	410	—	17	—	
		Total	1,191	—	14	—	
Maurit. (2) (65–115 cm)	1974 (BH)	Nationwide	875	—	10	—	SM
Niger (65–115 cm)	1974 (BH)	Nationwide	774	—	11	—	SM
Senegal (0–71 months)	1979 (AH)	Rural	347	—	9	—	H

[a] The following abbreviations for season have been used: BH (before harvest); AH (after harvest); MH (mid-harvest year); DS (average for different seasons).

[b] The standards applied are: NAS: National Academy of Sciences; NCHS: National Centre for Health Statistics; SM: Stuart Meredith; H: Harvard; NS: Not stated.

[c] National Reference Group.

Sources: USAID (1978a: Tables 21–4) (Cameroon); USAID (1976: Table 50) (Liberia); USAID (1977a: Tables 36, 38, and 40) (Lesotho); USAID (1986: Tables 4.82–4.83) (Sierra Leone, Togo, and Swaziland); Kloth et al. (1976: Table 1) (Chad, Mali (1), Mauritania (2), Burkina Faso (2), and Niger); Greene (1974: Table on p. 1094) (Mauritania (1)); Benefice et al. (1981: Tables 5, 12, and 13 (Mali (2)–(4), Burkina Faso (3), Benin, and Senegal); IDRC (1981: 22) (Burkina Faso (1)); Tomkins et al. (1986: 536) (Gambia); Maribe (1984; Figs. 1 and 2) (Botswana); Chiligo and Msukwe (1984: 25) (Malawi); CNSP (1984: Table 1) (Kenya).

percentage of children. The observations from Malawi and Botswana show relatively high prevalence of combined chronic and acute undernutrition as indicated by weight for age.

5.3. *The conflicting evidence*

In the preceding section, two different sets of estimates of the quantities of food that are consumed in the SSA countries on the average have been presented. First, there were the FAO estimates of the calories 'available' for human consumption on a per capita basis. Second, there were the estimates of the actual calorie intake in 85 different sample populations. If correctly measured, one would expect a reasonable congruence between the two sets of estimates.

In the previous section, two different sets of estimates on the prevalence of undernutrition in the SSA countries were also presented. The first was the estimates arrived at by the FAO and the IBRD at the very aggregate (country) level. The second was a large set of anthropometric studies of sample populations. In this section, the results obtained using the various types of indicators of food standards and the extent of undernutrition will be compared.

(a)   *Calorie availability vs. intake estimates*

For the period 1960 to 1979, the FAO (1987) estimates the average per capita daily availability of calories in sub-Saharan Africa as a whole at 1,964. The average per capita intake in the 85 sample studies consulted from the same period was 1,950. There is thus hardly any discrepancy between the FAO estimate, based on supply side, aggregate data, and the average of the sample estimates derived from demand side, disaggregated consumption survey data. The FAO further claims that if there is a bias in its estimates of the calories available for human consumption in Africa (and elsewhere), it is towards overestimation. This is because some of the available food is 'wasted'. If this is correct, one would expect the FAO 'availability' estimates to be higher than those obtained through direct observation of food consumption in the respective countries.

The little difference there actually is between the FAO and the sample estimates is positive, but small, which may be interpreted to suggest that the 'waste' of the food available at the household level is minuscule. At first sight, one might be inclined to take this almost unbelievably close agreement between estimates obtained in completely different ways as proof of the robustness of the estimation methods. As will be evident in sections 5.4 and 5.5, however, such an interpretation is premature.

(b)   *Average height and weight vs. dietary intake*

The average adult person in most of the samples of Bantu peoples was found to be 7–12 cm shorter than in the Scandinavian populations. This is an indication that as a child, the average Bantu person was deprived of food (although illness can be an alternative explanation). However, the average adult in the SSA populations examined has a weight for height above the lower end of the range that is considered safe for health and physiological capabilities in the Western societies. On average, children in the SSA are also shorter (for their age) than Western children are and, more importantly, than children from well-to-do socio-economic strata in the SSA countries themselves. They have, however, a weight for height that is relatively close to the Western children and well above (on average) what is considered safe for health.

If the current nutritional status is judged by weight for height, it thus seems that the average person in the SSA countries is at least somewhat above the level that is conventionally thought to imply undernutrition. This observation is not readily compatible with the FAO estimate, the dietary sample estimates, that the food 'available for human consumption', or actually consumed, corresponds only to about 80 per cent of the food needed to meet average calorie requirements (the RDAs). That is, if the average person has a weight for height above the safe level, one would expect that, by and large, food consumed is above what is needed to avoid undernutrition.

(c)   Prevalence of undernutrition: FAO/IBRD vs. anthropometrics

Although the FAO and the IBRD use the same basic approach to estimate the prevalence of undernutrition in the SSA region, their models are different in two important respects. They use different cut-off points to delineate the undernourished and they map the distribution of the calorie intakes from the distribution of income across households in different ways. These are also the easily observable explanations for the fact that the two organizations arrive at different estimates of the prevalence of undernutrition (see Beaton 1983). The main difficulty is to reconcile the estimated prevalence of under-nutrition suggested by the FAO/IBRD methods with the anthropometric estimates.

The IBRD (1986) study claims that 44 per cent of the population in the SSA as a whole was at least moderately undernourished in the early 1980s, and that the situation then was no better than in the 1970s (Table 5.1). Dozens of sample studies from these years suggest that only 5 to 10 per cent of children were 'moderately' wasted, indicating acute undernutrition at the time of measurement. Only in a few cases (during years of famine) was the incidence of wasting among children greater.

(d)   Can the conflicting evidence be reconciled?

It has been shown that anything from 5 to 44 per cent of the population in sub-Saharan Africa is undernourished depending on what indicator and source are consulted. This diversity of results is, of course, highly unsatisfactory and, in a policy perspective, a more precise understanding of the underlying reasons is warranted. In the following sections, two hypotheses about the reason are to be tested. The first is that some or all of the indicators are derived on the basis of models/methods and/or from data that are erroneous. It will be investigated whether the highest estimates of the prevalence of undernutrition, derived by the FAO and the IBRD, are built on a biased model and inaccurate data. A parallel investigation of the low estimates, based on anthropometric evidence, will also be conducted. The hypothesis is that after the various biases have been corrected for, the different indicators will show a less diverse picture. The other main hypothesis about why the different indicators, even after correction for 'technical' estimation biases, show different results is that they are derived from different notions of what constitutes undernutrition. To some extent this is simply due to the fact that different indicators aim to capture undernutrition that is more or less 'severe' in a single dimension, but this is not the whole story.

5.4. *The FAO calorie availability estimates: errors and biases*

In assessing the various pieces of evidence on food standards and under-nutrition in the SSA, the FAO calorie availability estimates are central. First, these estimates indicate in themselves that the nutritional situation in the region is very serious. A per capita calorie availability of 1,856 (in the mid-1980s) is only 80 per cent of what the FAO itself, and also the WHO and UNU, deem is required to feed everyone appropriately even if the food were allocated according to needs. Second, the importance of the FAO calorie availability data is enhanced by the fact that they underlie both the FAO and the IBRD estimates of the prevalence of undernutrition in Africa (and elsewhere).

(a) Estimation difficulties

Anyone trying to estimate the food produced and the food available for human consumption in the African countries will face formidable problems and costs. This is for a variety of reasons. Most African countries are large, sparsely populated,[2] and span a multitude of climatological and cropping systems. A high proportion of the population derives its livelihood from agricultural activities and much of the food is produced for subsistence. Many peasants pursue mixed farming, i.e. both crop production and livestock holding. The number of minor crops is usually very large (Eicher and Baker 1982).

The problems with estimating *harvested area* for cereal crops, the dominant food, are much more severe in Africa than in most other parts of the world. First, few of the countries have land records, and the ones that exist only cover the most densely populated regions where cash crops dominate. In other parts of these countries, land is usually owned, not privately, but communally, and production is mostly for subsistence. Furthermore, since slash-and-burn

---

[2] The number of inhabitants per square km in sub-Saharan Africa as a whole was 18 in 1985; the equivalent figure for South and South-East Asia was 145 (UNCTAD 1988).

shifting cultivation is still an important mode of production in many parts of Africa, area harvested is difficult to define even with the best measurement technology. The harvested area also tends to vary significantly from year to year in response to rainfall and other natural vagaries.

The problems involved in estimating harvested area for roots and tubers, the most important food crops in many SSA countries, are especially great. This is because cassava, the major product, is grown in patches and not always harvested annually. Cassava can remain in the ground for up to three years without much loss in nutritional value (although the digestibility of the product deteriorates). The bulk of cassava production is for subsistence and the reason for 'storing' it in the ground is usually to even out yearly fluctuations in household access to food so as to improve food security.

Yields are also more difficult to estimate in the non-commercial agricultural sector in Africa than in most other places. The climatological and soil conditions tend to vary sharply from region to region and the variety of cropping systems is enormous. In some areas, there is mixed cropping, in others multiple or continuous cropping, and also crop rotation (Eicher and Baker 1982). Under such circumstances, very refined and costly measurement methods are needed if reliable yield estimates are to be obtained. The number of sample cuts at each point of time has to be very large and the sampling has to be repeated several times over the year.

With practically no base data on acreages and yields derived with modern, scientific methods, it is, of course, impossible to produce reliable *direct estimates* of staple food production. Consequently, almost everyone who has taken a closer look at the FAO (and other) estimates of food production in the region comes to the obvious conclusion: they cannot be trusted. Lipton (1986: 3–4) goes as far as saying that, even for the main staples in the four largest countries (Nigeria, Zaire, Ethiopia, and Sudan), 'we have no idea of the levels or trends in output or consumption . . . over the past 5–20 years' (see also the other papers contributed to the two recent conferences on food output statistics in Africa: FAO 1985*b* and EEC 1986). According to Lipton's assessment, the available output estimates of main staple crops by small farmers are subject to unknown errors of at least plus/minus 20–40 per cent. When it comes to 'minor' crops, which taken together are important in many parts of Africa, nobody has offered even a guess as to the order of magnitude of the estimation errors that beset the FAO estimates.

In the absence of reliable production data, the FAO derives *indirect* estimates of the 'availability' of main vegetable crops, based mainly on the food that is marketed in each country. At least until recently, this meant a government marketing parastatal (see Ahrin *et al.* 1985). On top of that, a rough allowance is usually made by the national agency or the FAO itself for 'subsistence' production. The problem with this indirect method of estimating food production is that only major cereal crops are usually sold outside the village or district; and of these, often only a small part (20–40 per cent in some samples) is marketed through official channels (Eicher and Baker 1982: 48) and (although imperfectly) measured. In the parts of rural Africa where minor cereal crops and various roots and tubers play an important role in the diet, the measurement problems are especially acute. To estimate accurately the food production that is not marketed (the greater part of total food production) is impossible in Africa as things stand.

(b) Estimation biases

Considering the large margins of error that beset not only the food production data, but almost all the stages in the long chain of estimates from food production to calorie consumption (see Svedberg 1991b: ch. 5), one cannot but conclude that the unreliability of the existing (FAO) calorie availability estimates is great indeed. The FAO itself admits that some of its estimates are incomplete and/or not totally reliable.

When it comes to the possibility of biases, however, the FAO (1984) stresses that 'it is important to note that the quantities of food available relate to the quantities reaching the consumer but not necessarily the amount of food actually consumed, which may be *lower* than the quantity shown, depending on the extent of losses of edible food and nutrients in the household, e.g. during storage, preparation and cooking . . . plate-waste or quantities of food fed to domestic animals and pets, or thrown away' (italics added). That is, if there is a tendency to biases in the availability estimates, the FAO claims that it is towards *overestimation*.

The possibility of household wastage is the only source of bias that is explicitly discussed by the FAO. There is, however, a whole range of other possible biases in their estimates, most of which seem to be towards *under-estimation* rather than overestimation. Given that so little alternative and reliable data can be found, it is difficult to arrive at a firm assessment of the extent of underestimation, but there are some indications. There is also a downward bias (admitted by the FAO if one reads the small print) arising from incomplete coverage of food sources (see below). Let us start, however, by discussing a few a priori reasons why there probably is a net downward bias even in the items actually covered.

Implications If one accepts Lipton's (1986) assessment that the margin of error for main staples produced by smallholders in the SSA is plus/minus 20–40 per cent, is an overestimate of, say, 30 per cent in the production of 'main vegetable food' as likely as an underestimate by the same amount? If the production of main staples (including cassava) is overestimated by 30 per cent, the per capita 'availability' of (all) calories has to be adjusted downwards (*ceteris paribus*) by 15–20 per cent. We are then down to per capita calorie *availability* figures of 1,500 in the 'typical' SSA country. Such a figure implies that between half and three-quarters of the population has an intake below 1.2 BMR (equal to a per capita *intake* of 1,500 calories). (This follows from the FAO/IBRD model that is referred to in section 5.6*e* below.) The implication would be that almost half the African population has an intake which probably no human biologist or nutritionist would say is enough for biological survival, much less economic survival in the African context. We can thus be fairly sure that if there is a bias, it is not towards overestimating production of staple crops by 20–40 per cent. This, however, does not prove that there is a bias in the other direction, i.e. towards underestimation, but there are other indications to that effect.

Incentives   One reason to suspect that the estimates of staple food production in Africa are downward biased is that there are incentives for underreporting at all levels. The smallholder farm sector will certainly gain in a number of ways from giving the official national authorities the information—through whatever channel—that its production is lower than it actually is. First, in many African countries, until recently, trade in main staples has been more or less strictly monopolized by a government trade board, and the prices paid to the farmers have often been below those in the parallel, unofficial market (see Bates 1981; Eicher and Baker 1982; Ahrin *et al*. 1985). The incentives to sell on the unofficial, non-registered, and sometimes illegal markets have thus been strong. Second, to the extent that farmers and pastoralists pay taxes, the taxable incomes are related to what they produce and a way to reduce the tax burden is to underreport production, whether of crops or livestock. Third, in order to qualify for government (input) subsidies of various kinds, it may be advantageous to give downward biased information on productivity.

The national government agencies that supply the FAO with base data also have an incentive to keep food production figures down in order to attract more food aid (and aid in general). The FAO itself has no incentive to overestimate food supplies; the organization's existence is largely based on the notion of severe food problems in the underdeveloped countries. One does not have to go as far as saying that there is a systematic and explicit falsification of data, either at the national or at the FAO level. One need only think that underreporting on behalf of the bureaucracies 'reflects nothing more than the persistence of honourable men attempting to dramatize their case through exaggeration' (Poleman 1977: 387). Considering the unreliability of the base data, there is always scope for choosing 'low' numbers within the confidence intervals without violating conventional practice.

Biased methods   There are reasons to think that the present estimates of acreages in the SSA are based on methods that generate downward biases in the estimated production of 'major vegetable food', the most important food category according to the FAO. In the absence of complete land records, the responsible national government agencies tend to register only the food crop land that is the easiest to identify (e.g. by ocular observation). Small fields in remote and non-accessible areas tend to be incompletely covered. The experience from India in the 1950s and 1960s shows that when complete land records replaced the earlier estimation methods, significant revisions of the cultivated acreage followed (Zarkovich 1962). The experience from India further suggests, however, that the introduction of more sophisticated yield-sampling methods did little to improve the reliability of the production estimates.

Incomplete coverage   A further source of downward bias is that the 'calorie availability' estimates are derived from data on food supplies that are incomplete—in several respects. The data on 'major' food crops from national sources usually cover only part of what is actually produced; mainly the part that is marketed through official channels. Most livestock censuses do not include small domestic animals like pigs, sheep, and goats. The FAO admits that its estimates of some of these items are based on 'incomplete' coverage, which means underestimation. Chicken is underestimated according to the FAO itself. The coverage of various minor roots and tubers is incomplete and so are the data on domesticated fruits, berries, nuts, and honey, as explicitly admitted in the small print of the FAO reports. Food like game meat (especially from small animals), invertebrates, and undomesticated fruit, nuts, berries, roots, green leaves, and other wild flora are not included at all, or very incompletely so.

(c)   The size of the bias

The above assessment of the estimates of calories 'available for human consumption' in Africa, as produced by the FAO, has not permitted us to say exactly by how much the estimates are downward biased. We have mainly been concerned with the domestic food production statistics which are used to estimate, with the help of various conversion techniques, the amount of food available for human consumption. This does not mean that all other links in the long chain of assumptions that the FAO is forced to make to estimate food calories are free from ambiguity (see Svedberg 1991b: ch. 5).

The quantitatively most solid evidence of underestimation stems from the incomplete coverage of 'minor food items'. Adding up the gaps relating to the minor food items for which we have found it possible to say at least something in quantitative terms implies an underestimation of the total supply of calories by about 10 per cent on the average. When it comes to main staple food, the unreliability of the base data is large indeed, but little quantitative evidence on biases exists. There is one such indication, however. The incomplete agricultural land (acreage) enumeration in Africa probably means underestimation of staple food production. Considering the large share of the total supply of calories accounted for by vegetable staple food, an underestimation of acreage and, thus, production, by as little as 10 per cent would imply an additional 3–4 per cent underestimation of total food (calorie) consumption.

5.5.   *The dietary evidence: errors and biases*

In the preceding section, several reasons to expect the FAO calorie availability estimates to be downwards biased were discussed. If this is the case, it must be that the perfectly matching sample estimates of actual calorie intake in the SSA are also downward biased. In the following we shall investigate this issue. The estimation of the habitual food intake in a population entails two general problems. The first is to find a representative sample of households at a representative time. The second is to get a complete and accurate coverage of the food actually consumed.

(*a*)   *Adverse selection*

It is difficult and expensive to obtain a correctly stratified sample in countries where there are large inter- and intra-regional differences in factors affecting household food consumption. It is thus not surprising that the sample populations in most of the dietary studies for the SSA are not representative. This is for several reasons.

First, in most cases, the intention was simply not to obtain a random sample. In a majority of the studies, the focus is on a specific rural population group that was identified as having nutritional problems before the examination; this being the very reason why the investigation was carried out in the first place. The sample population is unambiguously representative for the national population only in four out of the 51 studies covered in Dillon and Lajoie (1981). Schofield (1979: 11) does not discuss the representativeness of the samples in the African studies in her survey in any detail, but she notes that, 'in general . . . investigations are restricted to small, unrepresentative samples'. All this means that the intake estimates derived for these unrepresentative groups must be lower than the national average for the respective country. How much lower cannot be ascertained, but if a population group is at a nutritional disadvantage, one would presume that for this to be detected in the first instance, the 'disadvantage' must correspond to more than a few per cent.

Second, almost all the dietary observations are from rural areas; urban and peri-urban areas are seldom studied. The available anthropometric evidence suggests that food standards in urban areas are significantly higher than in rural ones throughout Africa (Svedberg 1987: Table 4). The sample dietary estimates from rural populations thus probably understate national averages, as between 15 and 50 per cent of the population in the various SSA countries dwell in urban and peri-urban areas.

Third, there is the problem of obtaining estimates that are representative in the time dimension in countries with large intra-year (seasonal) and inter-year variations in food consumption. In 18 of the 51 studies from the Sahel countries surveyed in Dillon and Lajoie (1981), information is given on the time of the year when the investigation was carried out. In 16 of these 18 cases, the study was conducted in the pre-harvest, lean, dry season ('soudure'); in the remaining two, shortly before that period. There is plenty of evidence showing large intra-year variations in per capita calorie consumption in countries with marked seasonality in agriculture (the majority of the countries in the SSA). The difference between the pre- and post-harvest months amounts to several hundred calories according to observations from West Africa (see Schofield 1979: 53–4; Hulse and Pearson 1981: Table 6, 7; Chambers *et al.* 1981: 45–50; Rosetta 1986; Tomkins *et al.* 1986; von Braun 1988). Moreover, it seems that most studies have been carried out in a below average year. It is notable, indeed, that three of the four studies based on otherwise representative samples listed in Dillon and Lajoie (1981) were conducted in the Sahel during the famine in 1972–4, clearly not representative years.

(b)   *Biased estimation methods*

The most reliable dietary estimation method is to survey the individuals continuously (over several days at repeated intervals over the year) and weigh the equivalent of all the different food items they eat. The most reliable estimates of the nutritional content of the (estimated) food intake are obtained through mechanical and chemical decomposition of the (equivalent) food. These methods are very costly, however, and in most instances interviews and standard conversion tables are used.

Less than half of the 68 dietary surveys from the SSA covered by Schofield (1979: Table 4.1) are based on the food 'weighing method'. The majority of these surveys rely on stocktaking, recalls, or qualitative assessment. The main disadvantage with the stocktaking method is that it usually covers only main meals consumed at home; snacks and away-from-home meals are automatically excluded. The recall method entails two main problems. First, when interviewed, people tend to forget minor items consumed and/or snacks in between meals. The second problem is that when people are asked about their food consumption habits, they are inclined to provide the information they think the investigators would like them to give, or what they think would benefit themselves. This may mean that poor people tend to 'talk a good diet', i.e. to exaggerate their food intake, being ashamed of their deprivation. There are thus two conflicting biases in the recall method.

Cross-checking of results obtained by recalls with those obtained through weighing of the food consumed by sample populations in India suggests a net downward bias in the former, however, ranging from 10 to 40 per cent. Only in some recent studies has the underestimation been less.[3] It is notable that the 85 dietary studies from Africa referred to above are all of the not-so-recent type (pre-1979).

There seem to be three reinforcing reasons why many of the sample studies of per capita calorie consumption in Africa show figures that are not representative of the long-term situation for the population of the respective coun-

---

[3] See Harriss (1990) and the references cited there.

tries. In many cases, the sample comprises (1) a rural group that (2) was known a priori to have nutritional problems (3) during the lean season, or in a particularly poor year. Moreover, most of the sample studies have been conducted with (4) methods that have been shown to produce notable under-estimates of food intake. This is a further indication that the FAO per capita calorie 'availability' estimates for sub-Saharan Africa are too low in general, since these estimates are in very close agreement with the ones derived from sample studies of intake.

5.6. *The FAO/IBRD estimates of undernutrition: errors and biases*

The FAO and IBRD estimates of the prevalence of undernutrition rest on three presumptions that can all induce errors and biases in the results. The first is that the 'food available for human consumption' in the region is that claimed by the FAO. As we saw in preceding sections, there are several good reasons to expect these estimates to be downward biased. An underestimation of the food available will unambiguously imply (*ceteris paribus*) that the prevalence of undernutrition in the region is overestimated. However, there is also reason to think that there are biases in the other two exogenous parameters in the IBRD and FAO estimation models: the *calorie requirement norm* and the *function that distributes* the 'available' calories across households.

(a) *Biases in the calorie requirement norms?*

Through the years, the FAO/WHO has constantly been criticized for providing recommended daily allowances (RDAs) of calories that are too high. And over the years, the FAO has repeatedly adjusted its RDAs downwards. Several nutritionists seem to be of the opinion that, if at all useful for identifying undernutrition in a population, the latest RDAs (FAO/WHO 1973)[4] are still biased on the high side (e.g. Mayer 1976; Poleman 1977). However, the notion that they are 'too high' can have at least two very different meanings.

One meaning is that the FAO/WHO estimates of the energy expenditure for specific internal or external activities are too high. The other is that the organizations have derived their estimates on the basis of too high a level of overall external physical activity. The first problem is basically one of deriving appropriate 'technical' coefficients for various types of activities in the human body. The other problem is partly normative and relates to the question of how to conceptualize and define undernutrition. In what follows, we shall be concerned with the first set of 'technical' problems. The normative discussion of the overall level of external physical activity that the requirement norms should allow for is postponed to section 5.8.

---

[4] The FAO/WHO/UNU (1985) expert committee recommended downward adjustments of the RDAs of 1973 on several accounts, but no new RDAs have been published by the FAO. In their annual publication, the *State of Food and Agriculture*, RDAs were formerly presented; in recent issues, this is no longer the case.

Let us first discuss the lowest norm used by the two organizations, i.e. 1.2 times the BMR. This norm is derived by the FAO on the presumption that an individual should (1) cover his or her energy expenditure for internal body processes and (2) the minimum of external activity needed to maintain basic health, (3) after his or her body's metabolic rate has 'adjusted' to a permanently low intake (by becoming more efficient).

Is it possible to claim that the 1.2 BMR norm, which corresponds to only 65 per cent of the RDAs suggested by the FAO/WHO, is too high in any 'technical' sense? The 1.2 BMR norm does not allow for any physical activity beyond the minimal movements involved in sitting up for short moments, to dress and wash, etc. It is presented as a 'baseline biological survival norm'. In one respect, however, this norm may be too high. The FAO/WHO estimate energy expenditure for BMR on the basis of a linear model with a positive intercept and only one independent variable: body weight. Many nutritionists have argued that a quadratic relationship between BMR and body weight has a better theoretical underpinning and fits the data better. With such a model, the estimated requirements for BMR per kilo of body weight will be some 10 per cent lower (with the same data set) for the people with relatively small bodies (Payne 1987).

There is thus one possible reason why the 1.2 BMR norm is 'too high'. It is 'too low', however, for other reasons. First of all, it is based on the assumption that the human body has the ability to adjust its energy needs for basal metabolism and external activity to low intake within a substantial range without any 'costs'. Although an increasing number of nutritionists seem to accept the notion of 'intra-individual adaptation', it is still a controversial issue that has yet to be corroborated by empirical evidence.[5] Second, this requirement norm does not allow for any physical work activity at all; it is a *biological*, 'short-term-survival' requirement norm. In a world where people have to expend energy in work in order to be entitled to food, the *economic* survival requirement must be set higher. Even if the 'true' requirement for BMR is some 10 per cent lower than purported by the FAO, the calories thus 'freed' do not allow for much work activity. On balance, it seems that the FAO lower norm is downward biased in a context where almost every (adult) person is engaged in physical agricultural work with few supplementary factors of production. The higher FAO norm, at 1.4 BMR, differs from the lower one only in so far as it does not allow for intra individual adaptation to low intake.

The calorie requirement norms used by the IBRD in its estimation of the prevalence of undernutrition in the SSA rest on the same assumptions about energy expenditure for BMR as the FAO ones do. However, the IBRD calorie requirement norms differ from the FAO norms in two important respects. The first is that both the IBRD norms are built on the assumption that there is no mechanism in the human body that ensures that the basal metabolism becomes

---

[5] On the general issue of 'adaptation', see Dasgupta and Ray (1990) and Osmani (1990).

more efficient in periods of nutritional stress. The second is that the two IBRD norms allow for various amounts of physical external work activity.

The allowance for external physical activity in the form of work raises the question of how much work should be allowed for; this issue is discussed in section 5.8 below, dealing with the conceptualization and definition of 'under-nutrition'. However, the inclusion of an allowance for work activity, at whatever level, also raises the question of possible biases in the estimated conversions from a specific activity to the energy expenditure (requirement) involved. On that issue there is very little empirical evidence from actual field studies. There are scattered observations, however, suggesting that there has been a tendency for the FAO/WHO to classify many common agricultural tasks as 'too heavy' and, thus, too energy consuming (see Lawrence *et al.* 1985: 759).

(b)   Biases in the calorie distribution estimates?

The third exogenous parameter in the FAO and IBRD estimates of the prevalence of undernutrition in the SSA region is the assumption of how the distribution of the calories within each country is determined. A fundamental fact is that neither the FAO nor the IBRD has any direct empirical knowledge about this. Their mapping of the distribution of the 'available' calories across households from the perceived distribution of incomes is based on a theoretical model that may not be of much relevance (see section 5.6*d*). But even within the confines of this particular model, very strong quantitative assumptions are made on the basis of weak and conflicting stylized facts.

A priori, it is quite clear that even the slightest difference in the assumption about how the available calories are distributed can have huge effects on the estimated proportion of the population that falls below the 'requirement norm'. As an illustration, suppose that we accept the IBRD low cut-off point (at 0.80 RDA = 1.5 BMR), corresponding to a per capita calorie requirement in the SSA as a whole of 1,856. Assume also that the FAO estimate of a per capita availability in the SSA in 1983–6 of 1,876 is correct. It is then theoretically possible that no one in the SSA was undernourished in these years. This would be the case if calorie intake were distributed according to individual expenditure requirement.

With a slight alteration in the assumed distribution, however, 90 per cent of the population in the SSA may turn out to be 'undernourished'. That would be the case if 10 per cent (say the 'urban rich') had a per capita calorie intake of 3,000, and the remaining calories were distributed equally among the rest of the population. The whole of the latter group would then be 'undernourished' (with a per capita intake of 1,750 calories, or 9 per cent below the norm). These are just two out of many conceivable examples, but they underscore the basic point that the FAO/IBRD method is very sensitive to the assumed distribution of calorie intake, especially when per capita 'availability' is close to per capita 'requirement'.

(c)   The FAO/IBRD calorie distribution model

The assumptions made by the FAO and IBRD regarding the distribution of the 'available' calories comply with the conventional wisdom of the mid-1970s. The additional knowledge we have today is not very extensive, but taken together, it clearly suggests a more 'even' distribution of calorie intake in general than assumed by the two organizations. This is so whether or not the basic FAO/IBRD method of estimating the calorie distribution is accepted or not. Within the confines of the FAO/IBRD model, however, three sets of assumptions can be questioned.

The first concerns the assumption about how incomes are distributed in Third World countries. A re-examination of the 'old' studies of income distribution in Africa (on which the IBRD/FAO estimates of the prevalence of undernutrition rest) has shown that these tend to underestimate the income of the poorest groups and, thus, to overestimate the maldistribution of income (van Ginneken and Park 1984). With the techniques used by the FAO and IBRD to estimate the prevalence of undernutrition, starting off with a higher share of income going to the poorest means (ceteris paribus) that calories also become more evenly distributed.

Second, the IBRD and FAO estimates of the prevalence of undernutrition are built on the assumption that the distribution of the available calories across households is a one-to-one transformation of the distribution of income. The general finding today is that income variations explain a very low share of the variation in calorie intake (as measured by the adjusted R^2). This may be for various reasons, including faulty econometric estimation techniques and white noise in the data (see Bouis and Haddad 1988). It is interesting to note, however, that in a recent study, based on the state-of-the-art technique to estimate the conventional 'calorie-as-a-consumption-good' model, the share of the variation in calorie intake that is explained by income is not even statistically significant (Behrman and Deolalikar 1987).

Third, still within the confines of the FAO/IBRD model, there is the question of the size of the income elasticities of calorie intake. The IBRD assumes that the calorie–income elasticity for all African countries is 0.15 at the level of fulfilled requirements. For the lowest income groups, the elasticity is set at 0.55. (The FAO uses a slightly different method to map calories from incomes, but, in effect, the two versions are very similar; see Beaton 1983.) Regarding the first elasticity, we have to ask why it should be at all positive for people with a calorie intake at or above their requirements. If a person's calorie requirements (expenditure) are met, why would he or she indulge in more calories? It has to be recalled that a calorie intake above expenditure (requirement) does not disappear into thin air. By the first law of thermodynamics, or the Atwater formula in the nutrition context, calories consumed over and above those expended in physical activity will accumulate as fat.

The literature aimed at the estimation of calorie–income elasticities in the

poor(est) population segments, where intake supposedly are below requirements, has reached very conflicting results. The elasticity estimates range from
−0.30 to +1.18 (see Bhargava 1988; Bouis and Haddad 1988). It seems,
however, that the IBRD choice of parametric value for the calorie–income
elasticity in the low income range, 0.55, is considerably higher than the
estimates thought to be appropriate today, which are in the 0.10 to 0.15 range
(Bouis and Haddad 1988).

(d)   An alternative model of calorie distribution

So far we have discussed the conventional calorie 'consumption' model that
underlies the FAO/IBRD estimates of the calorie intake distribution. We have
also shown that the predictions of this model have not been easy to reconcile
with empirical evidence. The conventional explanations of the weak results in
the empirical literature are poor estimation techniques and weak data. An
alternative interpretation is that the underlying theoretical model is mis-
specified. In that model, income is the main determinant of the demand for
calories, which is considered an ordinary consumption good that enters the
individual's *utility function*. In an alternative theoretical model (Svedberg 1988),
it is assumed that calories are intermediate goods that enter the individual's
production function.

In the 'production' model, the level at which a person's calorie intake and
expenditure balance is not directly causally related to his or her income. In fact,
both calorie intake–expenditure and income, as well as body weight, are
endogenous variables. The exogenous variables that determine the individual's calorie intake–expenditure are a set of biological (e.g. height and
metabolic efficiency) and economic characteristics (endowment of factors of
production, technology, prices, etc.). These exogenous 'characteristics' tend
to show large variations across individuals of the same sex and age.

The prediction of the production model is thus not that calorie intake is
monotonically and positively associated with income. This model would rather
lead us to expect that the highest-income earners in a Third World population
have a relatively lower calorie intake than the middle-income earners because
they expend less energy in physical work. The richer members of the population are usually not engaged in heavy manual work activities, and they tend to
buy a higher share of the labour-demanding services (such as water and
firewood transportation) than the average person. Still, the individuals in
developing countries that are permanently undernourished (by anthropometric or clinical standards) belong to the poorest income groups almost
without exception. On the other hand, far from all individuals in the lowest-
income decile have an anthropometric status or show medical signs that
indicate undernutrition.

What the production model predicts is that for the population in any one
country, and in the middle- and high-income ranges in particular, other factors
than income determine the level at which calorie intake and expenditure

balance. If we accept that calorie intake does increase monotonically with incomes, the crucial question is to what extent the individual-specific 'desired' expenditure is met by individual-specific intakes. The FAO assumes that, *within each income class*, there is a perfect correlation between individual requirement and intake. Inserting this assumption in our type of model, where there are no 'income classes', while retaining the other assumptions, would lead to the conclusion that there is no undernutrition at all in the SSA by the standards suggested by the FAO.[6]

(e)   Margins of error and biases in the FAO and IBRD estimates

In an important article, Beaton (1983) tried to disentangle the reasons why the FAO and the IBRD, both using the same basic estimation approach, arrive at such different estimates of the prevalence of undernutrition in various parts of the world. Beaton saw two main possible explanations for the divergencies: one was that different 'requirement norms' were used; the second that different assumptions were made about how the available calories are distributed. By combining the different assumptions made either by the FAO or the IBRD on these two accounts into new constellations, Beaton demonstrated that anything between 17 and 80 per cent of the population in a country like Tanzania can be estimated to be undernourished (Beaton 1983: Table II). If, on top of that, one allows the per capita availability of calories to vary by 10 per cent above and below the FAO figure, the range of estimated prevalence of undernutrition becomes even wider (8 to 90 per cent of the population; see Svedberg 1991b: ch. 6).

One major argument advanced above is that the FAO and IBRD estimation models are not only extremely sensitive to small variations in the size of the exogenous parameters; there also seem to be biases in most of the exogenous parameters. The FAO has used per capita requirement norms that are too low, while those used by the IBRD are too high. However, both organizations have based their estimates on the FAO per capita calorie availability data, which are biased on the low side. Moreover, both organizations have assumed that the 'available' calories are more unevenly distributed than predicted by modern theory and empirical investigations. On the whole, both organizations have arrived at figures on incidence of undernutrition that are upward inflated even when 'undernutrition' is defined in the very broad sense of the IBRD and the very narrow sense of the FAO (cf. section 5.8 below).

6 As we have seen, the organization claims that the per capita calorie requirement is 1,747 (1.4 BMR) and that the per capita availability is 1,856. With inter-individual requirements perfectly correlated to actual intake, this would mean that everybody in the region has an intake 6% above requirement (which are too small to allow them to work, but that is another matter). With the IBRD assumption of a 0.70 correlation between personal requirements and intakes, and a higher requirement norm, some households would still be undernourished, but the percentage would be far below that shown in Table 5.2 above.

5.7.   *The anthropometric evidence: errors and biases?*

In the previous section we have shown there are 'technical' measurement errors in the FAO and IBRD aggregate estimates of the prevalence of undernutrition in the SSA which, on balance, tend to overstate the seriousness of the situation. This claim is consistent with the earlier observation that, when anthropometric measures are consulted, the prevalence and severity of undernutrition in the region is considerably lower than purported by the FAO and IBRD. In this section we shall investigate the possibility that the anthropometric indicators themselves are biased in one direction or the other. There are two potential sources for 'technical' biases in the anthropometric estimates reported in section 5.2 above. One is that the sample populations are not representative of the SSA population as a whole. The second is that the anthropometric norms that were used to estimate relative height and weight status are not appropriate in the SSA context.

(a)   Representative samples?

There is the possibility that the samples shown in Tables 5.3 and 5.4 are not representative of the African populations. First, the individuals examined in a given sample are not necessarily representative of the particular ethnic group to which they belong. Second, the 36 samples of ethnic groups may not be representative of the population in the SSA as a whole.

Unrepresentative individuals   That the individuals examined are unrepresentative for the particular population group to which they belong is quite likely in some of the studies of adults. In two of them, from Kenya and Uganda, the samples comprise university students. Since students tend to come from relatively well-off families, their height and weight are probably above those of the average person in their ethnic group. In the study from Mozambique, the sample consists of army recruits. The average height of military personnel is sometimes above that of the base population since recruits with a height below a specific norm are rejected. The recruits' weight for height may also be above average because army personnel is sometimes a priority group in terms of food allocation in Third World countries. In the remaining 33 samples, there is no indication that the individuals are unrepresentative. In the USAID surveys listed in Table 5.4, it is explicitly claimed that the children were selected with random methods; there is little that can be done to check whether random samples were achieved in practice. In some other surveys, there was probably an 'adverse selection' of children, e.g. when the sample comprises children brought to a health clinic.

Unrepresentative samples   According to a recent inventory, there are more than 1,000 ethnic groups in sub-Saharan Africa (Oliver and Crowder 1983).

The question is thus whether the relatively small number of samples in Tables 5.3 and 5.4 are representative for all ethnic groups. Five of the 36 adult samples comprise Bushmen and Pygmy populations. Considering that these make up less than 1 per cent of the total population in SSA, they are clearly overrepresented. Whether the 15 Bantu populations and the 8 samples from Nilotic groups are representative is impossible to say, but there is no reason to believe that the picture is severely distorted. The variance across the Bantu samples is quite small and the same applies to the Nilotic ones. Most of the studies of children have a national coverage that ought to ensure representativeness.

(a) Biased height norms?

The use of Scandinavians as the reference population for height of adults in sub-Saharan Africa poses two main problems. One is concerned with the genetic potential for growth in stature; the other with the existence of other, non-nutritional, constraints on growth.

Differences in genetic potential   The height norm used above was based on the assumption that the genetic potential for growth of Africans is the same as for Caucasians. This is what most contemporary human biologists and geneticists claim (see Eveleth and Tanner 1976 and Roberts 1985). The standard method used to test this notion is to study children from families for which adequate nutrition and health care is not a problem and compare them with 'sound and healthy' children in Caucasian populations. More than a dozen examinations of preschool children from well-to-do families of Bantu stock have been conducted within the past two decades. With few exceptions, these children (0–6 years) are shown to have the same average height (and weight) as those given in the National Centre for Health Statistics (NCHS) height and growth charts (the most commonly used ones).

Since well-to-do Bantu children and adolescents have approximately the same height for age as their Caucasian counterparts, one would expect them to achieve the same final height. However, one cannot be certain because there are variations in the age at which growth terminates. The standard method for checking the genetic potential for final adult height in nutritionally constrained populations is to sample individuals who have lived for a generation or two in places (often abroad) where there are no such constraints. With this method, it has been shown that Blacks living in the US and the UK have the same average stature as the Caucasian population of the respective country (Eveleth and Tanner 1976).

All African ethnic groups are sometimes lumped together into one single 'race', which would be to say that they all have the same potential for growth in stature. At face value, this would imply that the enormous difference in *de facto* average height between individuals from Nilotic and Bantu ethnic groups, respectively, is *phenotypically* explained. That is, the differences have nothing to do with genes; small (or great) stature is solely the outcome of external factors, such as nutrition and the health environment.[7]

No tests of the relative influence of genes and environment on the average height of Nilotic populations have been made, it seems, and only one from a Nilo-Hamitic population. This sample comprises privileged children in Ethiopia, whose height was found to be very similar to Caucasian children (Eksmyr 1970). Therefore we do not know whether the potential for growth in Nilotic peoples is the same as for Bantus and Caucasians. (The ancestors of most of the US Blacks came from West Africa.)

The fact that the actual height of the Nilotic peoples significantly exceeds that of the Bantu peoples, and is at par with the tallest people in Europe, is intriguing. One theoretically conceivable explanation is that they do not face environmental constraints on achieving their full potential for growth. This hypothesis is not altogether convincing, however, considering the fact that the Nilotic peoples often share the environment with significantly shorter Bantu tribes (e.g. the Tutsies and the Hutus in Rwanda). A plausible hypothesis is thus that Nilotic peoples have a larger potential for growth in stature than Bantu peoples and Caucasians (while it is smaller for Bushmen and pygmies).

Nutrition vs. other constraints   The second problem with the Scandinavian height norm is the underlying assumption that an elimination of undernutrition would *ceteris paribus* bring the African populations up to these height standards. This would probably not happen, because there are other external constraints on the African populations' ability to fulfil their potential for growth in stature. Infectious diseases are the most obvious example, but there is a whole range of social and economic factors that correlate with actual height in relatively well-off populations in Europe and America (Floud 1987). The elimination of undernutrition, without doing away with the other constraints would, presumably, raise the average height of the Africans, but not to the Scandinavian standards. (And the elimination of all other constraints than undernutrition would also raise average height but, again, not to the Scandinavian norms.)

In this perspective, the average height of Europeans at a time (1950–70) when undernutrition must have been almost non-existent in Europe, but when large sections of the populations were still not achieving their full potential for growth because of other constraints (Floud 1987), is perhaps a more appropriate norm than the Scandinavian one. The average height of males and females from the various SSA populations reported earlier (male and female average)

---

[7] People with a Nilotic ethnic origin make up about one-quarter of the population in contemporary sub-Saharan Africa (Oliver and Crowder 1983). They dominate in southern Sudan and in the northern parts of the Sahelian countries. They are also found in northern Kenya, Uganda, Tanzania, and in Burundi and Rwanda. The Nilo-Hamites in Ethiopia and Somalia are usually considered a separate race.

have been reproduced together with the average heights at that time of the adult populations in most of the European countries in Fig. 5.2.

When it comes to males (for whom there are more observations than for females), the picture is quite clear. What we see is that the average height of the average man in the Nilotic populations (see Table 5.3 for identification) is the same as for males in the European countries with the tallest people (Scandinavia, the Netherlands, and the UK). In all the seven Nilotic populations, the average male is taller, by 3–4 cm, than the average male in the average European country. However, the average male in the various Bantu populations, at 167 cm (ranging from 164 to 169 cm), is 5–6 cm shorter (3–4 per cent) than the average European male. The picture is roughly the same for females.

(c)   Biased weight norms?

The lower end of the 'safe range' of weight for height that was used as the norm in the above estimates has been derived from observations in developed countries. There are two main reasons to question this approach. One is that there may be genetically determined differences, not only in stature, but also in body build across ethnic lines. The other is that the 'safe' weight range may differ across environments.

Genetic differences   The very tall Nilotic populations are relatively thin and have a body mass index below the norm in half the samples. It would not be wise, however, to conclude that the Nilotic peoples have, on the average, a body weight for height that implies inflated health risk. It may simply be that these people are not only exceptionally tall, but also have a more slender (linear) body build for genetic reasons. Since there is a whole line of genetically determined differences in body composition and shape across ethnic groups (see Eveleth and Tanner 1976), there is no reason why some of these should not show up in the BMI. In examining the 'Nilotic Physique', Roberts and Bainbridge (1963) find at least 20 different body characteristics (from 'thin, fragile-boned face' to 'weak muscling of thighs') of the Nilotic peoples that make them very light for their height.[8]

Environmental differences   For lack of independent knowledge of the safe range in particular African environments, we have relied upon the FAO/WHO/UNU expert committee's general weight for height recommendations. Considering the many different and severe health hazards in the SSA it may also be that a higher weight is warranted in environments with incomplete (credit) markets and high intra- and interseasonal variability in many people's access to food. Under such circumstances, a relatively high body weight

[8] In the words of physical anthropologists, 'the Nilotic group is particularly low in endomorphy and mesomorphy and shows an extreme degree of ectomorphic dominance' (Roberts and Bainbridge 1963: 357).

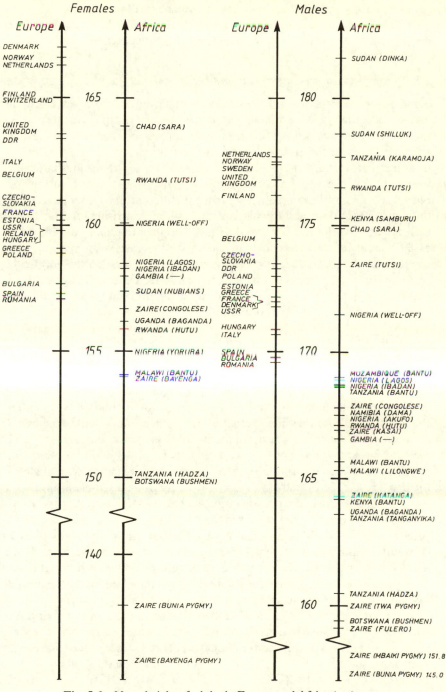

Fig. 5.2. Mean height of adults in Europe and Africa (cm)

provides an energy 'buffer' in times of prolonged illness and/or economic crisis. These issues are not discussed by the FAO/WHO/UNU expert committee, and there seems to be little evidence to be found elsewhere.

5.8. *Different measures: different definitions of undernutrition*

Some of the discrepancies in the extent of undernutrition suggested by the various indicators can be explained, as we have seen in the previous section, by the fact that there are biases in many of the estimation methods and in the data. However, even in the strictly hypothetical situation where we could obtain measurements that are unbiased in the 'technical' sense, the various indicators would still not provide the same picture of nutritional standards in the SSA region. This is for the simple reason that the different indicators are built on different assumptions about what constitutes undernutrition. As mentioned earlier, undernutrition is not a well-defined and unambiguous concept that is easily quantified. In the following, we shall nevertheless attempt to make explicit the different definitions of 'undernutrition' that (often implicitly) underlie the various measurements and indicators. One such explanation is that the various indicators are aimed at capturing undernutrition of different 'severity', but this is only part of the story.

(a) *The FAO/WHO and IBRD dietary norms*

The recommended daily allowances of calories (RDAs) produced by the FAO/WHO (1973), which in scaled-down versions underlie the IBRD (1986) estimates of the prevalence of undernutrition in the world, comprise two main components. The first is the energy requirement for *internal* body functions, the BMR, and other 'baseline' activities. The other component is the calorie requirement for *external* physical activity, such as work and social engagements. The estimation of energy requirements for BMR and other 'baseline' activities is largely a positive problem that can be resolved with scientific methods, at least in principle. In practice, several fundamental empirical and theoretical issues are still highly disputed, as we have seen in previous sections.

When it comes to energy requirements for work, it is a bit unclear on what principle the FAO/WHO norms are based. In their description of what constitutes 'calorie requirements', the organizations say that the norm should allow for the work that is 'economically necessary'. They refrain from any attempt to explain: necessary for what? A priori, there are many conceivable 'what's'. In this very context, however, the most straightforward 'what' is: to avoid undernutrition. Then the obvious next question is: undernutrition, in what sense? If the answer to the latter question is: undernutrition in the sense that the individual's health and functional capabilities are at risk because of his nutritional status (body weight and activity level; cf. below), there are good reasons to think that the RDAs arrived at by the FAO/WHO are too high.

First, the FAO/WHO reference individuals, both adults and children, have a body mass (index) above what these organizations themselves have found to be compatible with unimpaired health and physiological capabilities (FAO/WHO/UNU 1985: 183). This has the implication that the RDAs are derived for a reference person with a weight above what is needed for health and related purposes and, thus, an inflated energy requirement for BMR and all external activities, which are derived as multiples of the BMR. (It may also be that the FAO/WHO/UNU have overestimated the BMR per kilo of body weight, as discussed in a previous section.)

The second and more important 'exaggeration' is in the requirements for work activity. The FAO/WHO assumption is that the reference adult man in the developing countries has to work 2,555 hours per year in moderately heavy physical activities in order to avoid undernutrition in the family. For a 'reference' work load to make sense, it has to be equal to the work load that the *average* man in the population must pursue to avoid undernutrition. The question is then how this reference work load corresponds to the assumed distribution of income and calories in the FAO and IBRD models. The answer is that both organizations assume that there is no correlation between work load (and, thus, calorie expenditures in physical activity) and income. The lack of correlation means (by implication) that the man with the average work load also has the average income.

If one is to trust the income distribution estimates from countries like Kenya, Zambia, and the Ivory Coast reported by the World Bank (IBRD 1987: Appendix table 26), the poorest 20 per cent of households earn less than one-fifth of average income. These households would thus only be able to command less than one-fifth of the calories that the average income household can afford to buy, a household in which the man works 2,555 hours per year and still barely avoids undernutrition.

The poorest households can, of course, adjust their energy expenditure (requirements) downwards to some extent by reducing their body weight and height and lower their non-income-earning external physical activity levels. As an illustration of the scope for such adjustments, consider the standard adult reference male in the developing countries. He is 172 cm tall and weighs 65 kilos (corresponding to a BMI of 22). He works for seven hours per day in 'moderately heavy' physical activities, spends two hours in physically demanding social activities, seven hours in 'residual' (very low-energy-consuming) activities and is at sleep for eight hours (see FAO/WHO/UNU 1985: ch. 6). Altogether, this means that he expends close to 3,000 calories per day (see Table 5.5). Another male adult, who was nutritionally constrained already as a child, at 160 cm and with a body weight of 51 kilos (corresponding to the lower end of the range of BMI that the FAO/WHO/UNU finds acceptable and safe for males) can work the same hours in equally demanding physical activities at three-quarters of the calorie expenditure. This is because his energy demand for BMR is lower as a consequence of his smaller body size and because he has eliminated all social activities that are energy intensive.

Table 5.5 Estimated calorie savings possible for adult males

	FAO standard reference male	Nutritionally constrained reference male
Height (cm)	172	160
Weight (kg)	65	51
BMI	22	20
BMR/kg/day	26	26
Total BMR	1,690	1,326
BMR/hour	70	55
Hours spent in		
Sleep	8; 1.0 BMR	8; 1.0 BMR
Work activity	7; 2.7 BMR	7; 2.7 BMR
Social activity	2; 3.0 BMR	0; 0.0 BMR
Residual activity	7; 1.4 BMR	9; 1.4 BMR
Total calories for external activity	1,303	847
Total calorie expenditure	2,976	2,173
% of FAO reference male	100	73

Source: FAO/WHO/UNU (1985) (FAO 'standard reference male').

However, a reduction of his energy requirements by 27 per cent is not sufficient if his income is 20 per cent of that of his 'average' neighbour, whose earnings are barely enough to avoid undernutrition. The inescapable conclusion is that the IBRD estimation technique implies that one-fifth of the households in the typical African country will be undernourished on a very severe scale. The incidence of anthropometric and clinical signs of undernutrition in these households would be very high. As we have seen, this is not at all what the evidence at hand shows.

The conclusion is that the RDAs are not appropriate norms, even in the scaled-down versions applied by the IBRD, for the identification of undernutrition in any medical or clinical sense. The RDAs may adequately state what is *compatible* with good nourishment, health, and a productive and rich social life, but they include a significant safety margin and overstate what is needed in a more fundamental sense. The RDAs are 'poverty lines' rather than calorie requirement norms.

(b) The 1.2 BMR and 1.4 BMR norms

While the RDAs, which, in the African context, are equivalent to 1.87 BMR, probably grossly overstate the calorie intake that the average person (or per capita equivalent) needs in order to avoid undernutrition in a medical sense, it is equally obvious that this person needs more than 1.2 or 1.4 times the BMR.

These norms are derived from what nutritionists conceive to be the energy requirements for biological baseline activities only; with no allowance at all for work (or any other form of external physical activity). In a world where food entitlements are dependent on the household's own work activities, which in the African region are basically non-mechanized agricultural work, such norms make little sense. The FAO (1985*a*: 24) has stated *en passant* that it has set up the 1.2 and 1.4 BMR norms without any allowances for work because such allowances are impossible to derive accurately and without invoking normative judgements, the very argument used above in more explicit terms against the IBRD norms. However, this, as we have stressed at length, is not a valid reason for ignoring energy needs for physical work altogether. The logical conclusion is that to use standardized calorie norms in order to distinguish the undernourished from the well nourished in a population where there are *de facto* very large variations in calorie expenditure for work is a meaningless exercise.

(*c*)   *The anthropometric norms*

The standard anthropometric norms cannot be used to single out the particular individuals that suffer from undernutrition in a clinical sense, and they cannot be used to provide exact numbers of 'undernourished' people in a population. They can be used, however, to derive a relatively reliable upper limit for the number of those who are at risk. With the anthropometric measures and norms that are used today, the estimated incidence of people at nutritional risk is, in fact, considerably higher than one would find on the basis of clinical observations of actual 'undernutrition'. This is for three reasons.

First, anthropometric measures alone cannot be used to say whether the primary cause of low weight and stunting is lack of food at the household level or whether illness is the basic cause (secondary undernutrition). People who are found to have an anthropometric status below some norm will thus include both those who are primarily undernourished and those who are basically ill.

Second, the health and functional impairment that has been documented in the literature (such as child mortality, reproductive capacity in women, and work ability in adults) is usually only detectable at an anthropometric status below the standard height and weight norms. The latter are derived on the basis of such criteria as 90 per cent of height or weight of reference populations in the Western countries. These norms thus include at least some 'safety margin'.

Third, the anthropometric norms in use are defined on probabilistic grounds. That is, the norm is set above, or at, the level where a low weight or height affects the probability of falling ill or being functionally impaired in one way or the other. This does not mean that all people with a below-the-norm weight will actually become sick; most will not, but all in the risk group will be defined as undernourished. As long as one accepts the paradigm that undernutrition is a state of health and physiological impairment, caused by energy inadequacy, one can thus use the anthropometric measures to estimate the upper limit of the number of people at risk of being undernourished in the clinical sense. However, to live with a constant excess risk of illness is clearly welfare reducing, which is an argument for defining undernutrition in a probabilistic rather than a deterministic (clinical) sense.

5.9. *Summary and conclusions*

The nutritional situation in sub-Saharan Africa looks very different depending on which indicator is consulted. The highest incidence of undernutrition is suggested by the aggregate estimates derived by the FAO and the IBRD. The first important conclusion of the above analysis is that the prevalence of undernutrition in the region is not of the enormous order claimed by the international organizations; not even if undernutrition is defined in the broadest possible sense (the IBRD). The estimates are upward biased because they are built on 'calorie availability' data that understate true food supplies and also because of assumptions of an unduly uneven distribution of calories across households. Moreover, the implied consequences of undernutrition of the magnitude and severity (the very low norms) claimed by the FAO are so far-reaching that they are impossible to reconcile with demographic and anthropometric observations.

The high incidence of moderate stunting among small children, in the 10–30 per cent range, is the only (technically unbiased) indication of a high preval ence of undernutrition in the SSA. Lack of food at the household level may be an important explanation of this phenomenon, but, a priori, there are several other feasible explanations, such as disease, inappropriate weaning food, and intrahousehold discrimination. The fact that only a small proportion of the same children have a subnormal weight for height suggests that food intake is normally adequate. The extra calories needed for growth in stature constitute only a few per cent of a child's total energy requirements after the first year. Moreover, even if primary undernutrition is the reason for moderate stunting, the mortality and dysfunctions that have been observed in relation to short stature usually show up only at what is termed 'severe' stunting (below 80 per cent of reference height for age),[9] which affects a few per cent of children in the samples studied.

On the basis of the studies available today, however, it is not possible to say exactly what share of the population in the various SSA countries suffers from undernutrition in various meanings that are relevant in different contexts and for different policy objectives. The available studies are too few and, above all, in most instances not conducted with appropriate methods (see also Svedberg 1991*b*). The aggregate estimates of the FAO and the IBRD have little meaning.

[9] See Osmani (1990).

The hundreds of dietary and anthropometric sample studies that have been carried out in the SSA, even when representative and unbiased, seldom include supplementary socio-economic data that are required if we are to understand the reason for the undernutrition that exists, irrespective of its severity and prevalence.

Without proper knowledge of which population groups are undernourished there is little hope that these people can be assisted in the near future. Even more important, without such knowledge there are large risks that already vulnerable groups will see their situation deteriorate further as unforeseen consequences of the structural adjustments that almost all the SSA countries will be engaged in during the 1990s.

References

AHRIN, K. (1985), *Marketing Boards in Tropical Africa* (London: KPI Limited).

BATES, R. H. (1981), *Markets and States in Tropical Africa: The Political Basis of Agricultural Policies* (Berkeley, Calif.: University of California Press).

BEATON, G. H. (1983), 'Energy in Human Nutrition: Perspectives and Problems', *Nutrition Reviews*, 41.

BEHRMAN, J. R., and DEOLALIKAR, A. (1987), 'Will Developing Country Nutrition Improve with Income? A Case Study of Rural South India', *Journal of Political Economy*, 95.

BENEFICE, E., *et al.* (1981), 'Surveys of Nutritional Status in Semi-arid Tropical Areas (Sahel 1976–79): Methods and Results', in IDRC (1981).

BHARGAVA, A. (1988), 'Estimating Short and Long Term Elasticities of Food and Nutrients for Rural South India', mimeo (University of Pennsylvania).

BOUIS, H. E., and HADDAD, L. J. (1988), 'Comparing Calorie-Income Elasticities Using Calories Derived from Reported Food Purchases and a Twenty-Four Hour Recall of Food Intakes: An Application Using Philippine Data', mimeo (Washington, DC: IFPRI).

CHAMBERS, R., *et al.* (1981), *Seasonal Dimensions to Rural Poverty* (Exeter: Frances Pinter).

CHILIGO, M. O., and MSUKWE, L. M. (1984), 'Nutritional Surveillance in Malawi', background paper for workshop on Social and Nutritional Surveillance in Eastern and Southern Africa, Cornell Nutritional Surveillance Program.

Cornell Nutritional Surveillance Program (CNSP) (1984), 'Trends in Nutritional Status of Children in Rural Kenya. Review and Policy Implications', Working Paper 30 (Cornell University).

DASGUPTA, P., and RAY, D. (1990), 'Adapting to Undernourishment: The Biological Evidence and its Implications', in the first volume of this book.

DILLON, J. C., and LAJOIE, N. (1981), 'Report on Surveys of the Nutritional Status of the Rural Population in the Sahel from 1960 to 1979', in IDRC (1981).

EICHER, C. K., and BAKER, D. C. (1982), 'Research on Agricultural Development in Sub-Saharan Africa: A Critical Survey', MSU International Development Paper 1 (East Lansing, Mich.: Department of Agricultural Economics, Michigan State University).

EKSMYR, R. (1970), 'Anthropometry in Privileged Ethiopian Pre-school Children', *Acta paediat. scand.* 59.

European Economic Commission (1986), 'Conference Proceedings: Statistics in Support of African Food Strategies and Policies', mimeo (Brussels, 13–16 May).

EVELETH, P. B., and TANNER, J. M. (1976), *Worldwide Variations in Human Growth* (Cambridge: Cambridge University Press).

FAO (1980), *Food Balance Sheets: 1975–1977 Average* (Rome: FAO).

——(1984), *Food Balance Sheets: 1979–1981 Average* (Rome: FAO).

——(1985a), *Fifth World Food Survey* (Rome: FAO).

——(1985b), *FAO Expert Consultation on Production Statistics of Subsistence Food Crops in Africa* (Rome: FAO).

——(1987), 'Daily Per Caput Calories', computer outprint (Rome: FAO).

——(1988), *Production Yearbook* (Rome: FAO).

/WHO (1973), 'Energy and Protein Requirements', WHO Technical Report Series No. 522, Report No. 52 (Geneva: Report of a Joint FAO/WHO Ad Hoc Expert Committee, FAO Nutrition Meetings).

————/UNU (1985), 'Energy and Protein Requirements', Technical Report Series 724 (Geneva: WHO).

FLOUD, R. (1987), 'Anthropometric Measures of Nutritional Status in Industrialized Societies: Europe and North America since 1750', mimeo (Helsinki: WIDER).

GREENE, M. H. (1974), 'Impact of the Sahelian Drought in Mauritania, West Africa', *Lancet*, 1 June.

HARRISS, B. (1990), 'The Intrafamily Distribution of Hunger in South Asia', in the first volume of this book.

HULSE, J. H., and PEARSON, O. (1981), 'The Nutritional Status of the Population of the Semi-arid Tropical Countries', in IDRC (1981).

IBRD (1986), *Poverty and Hunger* (Washington, DC: World Bank).

——(1987), World Development Report (Washington, DC: World Bank).

——(1989), *Progress of Initiatives Benefiting Sub-Saharan Africa* (Washington, DC: World Bank).

International Development Research Centre (IDRC) (1981), *Nutrition Status of the Rural Population of the Sahel* (Ottawa: IDRC).

KLOTH, T. I., *et al.* (1976), 'Sahel Nutrition Survey', *American Journal of Epidemiology*, 103.

LAWRENCE, M., *et al.* (ed.) (1985), 'The Energy Cost of Common Daily Activities in African Women: Increased Expenditure in Pregnancy?', *American Journal of Clinical Nutrition*, 42.

LIPTON, M. (1983), 'Poverty, Undernutrition and Hunger', World Bank Staff Working Paper 597 (Washington, DC: World Bank).

——(1986), 'Improving the Basic Data: Are Present Techniques Satisfactory?', mimeo, European Community.

MARIBE, T. (1984), 'Up-Date of the Nutrition Surveillance in Botswana', background paper for workshop on Social and Nutritional Surveillance in Eastern and Southern Africa, Cornell Nutritional Surveillance Program.

MAYER, J. (1976), 'The Dimensions of Human Hunger', *Scientific American*, 235.

OLIVER, R., and CROWDER, M. (eds.) (1983), *The Cambridge Encyclopedia of Africa* (Cambridge: Cambridge University Press).

OSMANI, S. (1990), 'Nutrition and the Economics of Food: Implications of Some Recent Controversies', in the first volume of this book.

PAYNE, F. (1987), 'Undernutrition: Measurement and Implications', mimeo (Helsinki: WIDER).

POLEMAN, T. T. (1975), 'World Food: A Perspective', *Science*, 188.

——(1977), 'World Food: Myth and Reality', *World Development*, 5.

REUTLINGER, S., and ALDERMAN, H. (1980), 'The Prevalence of Calorie Deficient Diets in Developing Countries', *World Development*, 8.

——and SELOWSKY, M. (1976), 'Malnutrition and Poverty: Magnitude and Policy Options', World Bank Staff Occasional Paper 23 (Washington, DC: World Bank).

ROBERTS, D. F. (1985), 'Genetics and Nutritional Adaptation', in Blaxter, K., and Waterlow, J. C. (eds.), *Nutritional Adaptation in Man* (London: John Libbey).

ROBERTS, D. F., and BAINBRIDGE, D. R. (1963), 'Nilotic Physique', *American Journal of Physical Anthropology*, 21.

ROSETTA, L. (1986), 'Sex Differences in Seasonal Variations of the Nutritional Status of Serere Adults in Senegal', *Ecology of Food and Nutrition*, 18.

SCHOFIELD, S. (1979), *Development and the Problems of Village Nutrition* (London: Croom Helm).

SVEDBERG, P. (1987), 'Undernutrition in Sub-Saharan Africa: A Critical Assessment of the Evidence', Working Paper 15 (Helsinki: WIDER).

——(1988), 'A Model of Nutrition, Health and Economic Productivity', Working Paper 46 (Helsinki: WIDER).

——(1990), 'Undernutrition in Sub-Saharan Africa: Is There a Gender Bias?', *Journal of Development Studies*, 26.

——(1991*a*), 'The Export Performance of Sub-Saharan Africa', *Economic Development and Cultural Change*, 39.

——(1991*b*), *Poverty and Undernutrition in Sub-Saharan Africa: Theory Evidence Policy*, forthcoming.

TOMKINS, A. M., *et al*. (1986), 'Seasonal Variations in the Nutritional Status of Urban Gambian Children', *British Journal of Nutrition*, 56.

UNCTAD (1988), *Handbook of International Trade and Development Statistics* (Geneva).

USAID (1976), 'Liberia National Nutrition Survey', mimeo (Washington, DC).

——(1977*a*), 'Lesotho National Nutrition Survey', mimeo (Washington, DC).

——(1977*b*), 'Togo National Nutrition Survey', mimeo (Washington, DC).

——(1978*a*), 'United Republic of Cameroon National Nutrition Survey', mimeo (Washington, DC).

——(1978*b*), 'Sierra Leone National Nutrition Survey', mimeo (Washington, DC).

——(1986), 'Swaziland National Nutrition Survey 1983: Full Report', mimeo (Washington, DC).

VAN GINNEKEN, W., and PARK, J.-G. (1984), *Generating Internationally Comparable Income Distribution Estimates* (Geneva: International Labour Office).

VON BRAUN, J. (1988), 'Effects of Technological Change in Agriculture on Food Consumption and Nutrition: Rice in a West African Setting', *World Development*, 16.

ZARKOVICH, S. R. (1962), 'Agricultural Statistics and Multisubject Household Surveys', reprinted in FAO, *Studies in Agricultural Economics and Statistics, 1952–77* (Rome: FAO).

6

Policy Options for African Agriculture

Francis Idachaba

6.1. *Introduction*

The dismal performance of African agriculture in the last twenty years has been well documented. This chapter reviews recent trends, examines competing paradigms on the nature of the problem and alternative policy prescriptions, and offers a more balanced agenda of policy options for African agriculture.

Recent trends in African agriculture could be summarized as follows:[1]

First, production growth rates have failed to keep up with population in many countries, resulting in declines in per capita production.

Second, Africa has steadily lost her share of world export trade with, for example, declines from 85.5 to 18.0 per cent for groundnuts, from 79.9 to 69.3 per cent for cocoa, and from 55.0 to 3.0 per cent for palm oil during the period from 1961–3 to 1980–2.

Third, the dependence on food imports has substantially increased. For example, Nigeria moved from being a net exporter of 300 tonnes of maize a year during 1952–5 to being a net importer of 153,246 tonnes a year during 1978–82; from an exporter of 188,234 tonnes of palm oil a year during 1958–60 and 894,455 tonnes of groundnuts a year during 1964/5–1966/7 to a large importer of vegetable oils in the 1970s.

Fourth, declining exports have resulted in worsening trade deficits and balance-of-payments difficulties, especially as increasingly scarce foreign exchange has to be allocated to food imports. The external account situation of sub-Saharan Africa is grim: countries are short of foreign exchange as exports have dwindled; yet, to increase agricultural exports, they urgently need farm input imports such as machinery and farm equipment, inorganic fertilizers, and pesticides.

Fifth, soaring domestic food prices have been a major part of the general domestic inflation because of the heavy weight of food in the consumer price index.

Finally, sub-Saharan Africa has had more than its fair share of droughts, resulting in large-scale famines and starvation.

I thank Glenn L. Johnson and Amartya Sen for encouragement and Jean Drèze for painstaking editiorial work.

[1] For further discussion of some of these trends, see e.g. World Bank (1981, 1986a). See also the contribution by Jean-Philippe Platteau in the second volume of this book.

Falling per capita production translates into declines in food entitlements in economies dominated by subsistence production (Sen 1985). Similarly, widespread drought and pest invasions also translate into food entitlement collapse in the affected areas.

There are competing paradigms as to the root cause of Africa's agricultural and general economic malaise and the policy prescriptions. The World Bank view (World Bank 1981) identifies drought, disorganized production caused by civil wars and strife, inadequate agricultural investments, inefficient input and output marketing systems, and harmful domestic economic policies as the principal causes.

The same document highlights three areas of domestic policy defects: first, foreign exchange rate and pricing policies which have strangulated agricultural exports and overprotected import substituting industries; second, an overstretched and overzealous public bureaucracy that has expanded the role of government in production and distribution beyond available resources; and third, a regime of taxes on agriculture that has drastically reduced Africa's competitiveness in world markets.

While conceding the importance of these factors, critics (IDS 1983, 1985) raise issues as to the completeness, consistency, and direct relevance to specific cases of the World Bank's analysis and conclusions. In fact, the World Bank's agenda has generated rather strong feelings and has been described as 'economic neoliberalism . . . [that] is contentious analytically, disputed empirically and ultimately accepted or rejected on normative, self-interest, and theological rather than pragmatic, public interest, and programmatic grounds' (Allison and Green 1983: 3). There is strong disagreement not only with respect to problem diagnosis but also with respect to the policy prescriptions.[2]

Section 6.2 of this paper discusses the problems and constraints of African agriculture. Section 6.3 deals with the policy options. The chapter is concluded in section 6.4. Much of the empirical material and illustrations relate to Nigeria, though the policy issues discussed in this paper pertain to other sub-Saharan countries as well.

6.2. *Problems and constraints of African agriculture*

Four classes of problems and constraints are identified (in order of priority) as being of crucial relevance to policy prescriptions: rural infrastructures, technology, economic policy (incentives) framework and institutional arrangements. Though of great importance, the problem of economic incentives has

---

[2] The IDS group (IDS 1983) accuses the World Bank position (World Bank 1981) of dressing up ideological neo-liberalism in technical terms. While the World Bank cannot deny a world-view or the fact that authors and reviewers of Bank publications have value systems, the IDS group is guilty of the same offence: they too have a world-view and a thinly veiled ideological position on the role of the state *vis-à-vis* the role of market forces.

recently received such extensive treatment (World Bank 1981, 1984, 1986a) that a more balanced treatment, doing justice to each of these four problem areas, is urgently required. Each of the problem areas is discussed in turn in this section.

(a) Primitive state of rural infrastructures

(i) *Rural roads* Rural roads constitute perhaps the most important single factor in the physical transformation of rural areas. Poor networks of rural feeder roads have resulted in large farmgate-retail price spreads, inflated farmgate prices of farm inputs, and greatly distorted the structure, conduct, and performance of rural markets. Heavy post-harvest losses from ineffective evacuation of farm produce have acted as major production disincentives. Poor rural transportation facilities encourage spatial production inefficiencies as they hamper the emergence of specialized agricultural production patterns. The network of rural feeder roads to service and feed the national road and rail grid remains in a primitive state, with only about 10 per cent of total rural feeder road length being all-season roads. As a result, transportation costs —and retail food prices—remain high on account of high time costs, spoilage, and road user charges, especially vehicle operating costs.[3]

The network of rural markets and market stalls is so poor as to render the implied elasticities of farmgate producer prices with respect to urban retail food prices low. Poor physical infrastructures encourage oligopolistic and oligopsonistic market structures and distributions of marketing margins (returns to risk) that are often derisively described as 'exploitative', 'exorbitant', and, sometimes, 'unpatriotic'.

Poor rural infrastructures seriously constrain the effectiveness of other policies. Guaranteed producer price schemes hardly guarantee anything as available marketable surpluses are bought up by middlemen at discount, with the result that the benefits of the scheme flow to an unintended group of beneficiaries. The benefits of devaluation to export crop growers are seriously limited by poor infrastructures which prevent the farmer from receiving the higher export prices, farmgate. The benefits of farm input subsidies are cornered by unintended beneficiaries who buy up large quantities at subsidized prices only to sell them in fragmented markets at farmgate prices that are sometimes higher than they would have been had there been no subsidy, making farmers worse off than they would have been without government 'assistance'. Attempts at building up national networks of on-farm adaptive research trials are frustrated by inability to attract and retain senior experienced researchers who can put up with the infrastructural inadequacies of remote isolated stations so that achievement in this area does not go beyond the perennial recognition of the need to have such on-farm adaptive research centres. Extension workers are unable to visit most farming communities as

---

[3] For an earlier treatment, see Wharton (1967). For a comprehensive survey of rural infrastructures in Nigeria, see Idachaba (1985).

these remain largely inaccessible by car and quite often by motor-cycle, with the result that even if the village-level extension agent is able to visit villages, however infrequently, the block supervisor or the zonal extension officer hardly visits remote villages to cross-check and monitor the performance of the village-level extension worker. Finally, formal credit institutions have failed to penetrate the grass roots largely because of the poor state of rural infrastructures which result in high operating costs for commercial banks, etc.

(ii) *Irrigation infrastructures*   Near-total dependence on rainfed agriculture has posed the greatest threat to national food security in sub-Saharan Africa. Domestic production has fluctuated widely, thereby hindering access to food at all times (World Bank 1986*b*). Sub-Saharan African countries have not significantly increased the share of irrigated agriculture because programming has concentrated on grandiose, resource-guzzling, large-scale dams which are expensive to build and maintain, are demanding in management, service only a limited area of land below the dam, and benefit only a small fraction of farm families. Large-scale irrigation projects have long gestation periods and high foreign exchange intensity: they get stalled during periods of foreign exchange squeeze. Finally, these projects involve the award of huge contracts especially as politicians (civilian or military) tend to measure achievements by the size of contracts and newsworthiness.

Problems confronting the development of irrigation and flood control infrastructure include: acute shortage of indigenous technical staff (hydrologists, irrigation agronomists, engineers, etc.), poor funding, high foreign exchange content, technical design defects, inadequate monitoring and evaluation of irrigation schemes, the perennial failure to develop a maintenance culture, and sustainability.

In Nigeria, there was the political will to allocate substantial resources to irrigation[4] but the performance has been dismal. Starting with a budgetary allocation of ₦2.060 million to irrigation in 1973/4, the federal government allocated ₦896.900 million to irrigation in 1983, a staggering increase of 43,438 per cent (see Table 6.1). Comprehensive development of river basins started in 1977 when 10 River Basin Development Authorities (RBDAs) were created.[5]

The failure of the River Basin Development Authorities in Nigeria can be traced to five factors. The first was an improper assignment of roles: RBDAs were expected to build irrigation and flood control infrastructures, engage in seed multiplication, direct production of poultry, rice, maize, and other farm produce, distribute fertilizers and other farm products, dabble in rural

---

[4] The policy response to the food entitlement collapse accompanying the Sahelian drought of 1973/4 was to mount a major national effort in national water resources development. Several related policy issues are discussed in Idachaba (1982).

[5] The Niger Delta Basin Development Authority was subsequently created to bring the total number of RBDAs to 11.

Table 6.1 Federal government budgetary allocations to agriculture and irrigation, Nigeria, 1973–1983

Year	Allocations to agriculture (₦m.)	Allocation to irrigation (₦m.)	Allocation to agriculture and irrigation (₦m.)	Allocation to irrigation as % of allocation to all agriculture and irrigation	Indices of allocations to agriculture (1973/4 = 100)	Indices of allocation to irrigation (1973/4 = 100)
1973/4	45.524	2.060[a]	47.584	4.33	100	100
1974/5	56.411	3.986[b]	60.397	6.60	124	193
1975/6	159.351	128.528	287.979	44.67	350	6,244
1976/7	129.950	190.005	319.955	59.38	285	9,224
1977/8	105.493	299.999	405.491	73.98	232	14,563
1978/9	128.402	245.785	374.187	65.69	282	11,931
1979/80	219.673	359.555	573.228	62.07	483	17,454
1980	246.529	538.029	784.558	68.58	542	26,118
1981	412.002	710.516	1,122.518	63.30	905	34,492
1982	531.375	562.263	1,093.638	53.37	1,167	27,294
1983	528.359	896.900	1,425.259	62.93	1,161	43,539

[a] For expansion of South Chad Irrigation Scheme and Sokoto Rima Valley Development Project.
[b] ₦3.986 m. for expansion of South Irrigation Scheme; also ₦11 m. loan to the Sokoto Rima Development Authority for the Bakolori Project. The loan was granted by the Federal Ministry of Finance.

Source: 'Capital and Recurrent Estimates of the Federal Government of Nigeria' (various issues).

institution building, and engage in agricultural extension, to mention a few of their responsibilities. RBDAs were consequently overstretched with respect to their scarce management and technical resources. Since the bulk of the agricultural staff were more at home with rainfed agriculture, they tended to emphasize rainfed agriculture activities to the neglect of their major mandate in irrigation.

Second, strategy focused on large-scale dams, such as the Bakolori and Goronyo dams, which turned out to be too expensive to build and maintain, too complex technically, and too management intensive. Nothing was done with the large amounts of resources allocated to RBDAs to construct small-scale irrigation facilities such as washbores, tubewells, and earth dams that would have had a much greater impact in terms of land area and number of farm families benefiting from the scheme.

The third factor relates to politicization, as manifested not only in organizational changes but also in role assignment. Organizationally, 'the parastatal syndrome' which gripped the nation during the oil boom era resulted in the multiplication of RBDAs from 11 to 18, one per state except Lagos. States came to see the RBDAs as representing their state interests, sowing the seeds of future state conflicts over water rights and the uncoordinated damming of rivers which originate in one state, flow through another, and end up in yet another state (Idachaba 1985). The creation of one RBDA per state roused old feelings about constitutional responsibility to a boiling level in 1981: 6 state governments took the federal government to court for using the RBDAs to engage in agricultural projects at the grassroots level. In a federal system depending on a highly decentralized smallholder agriculture, grassroots implementation of agricultural projects should be devolved to lower tiers of government. The RBDAs were wholly federally owned and, during the civilian political era, they were utilized to compete with mainstream state Ministries of Agriculture in the distribution of farm inputs, bush clearing, and land development. In fertilizer distribution, the RBDAs set up parallel fertilizer distribution programmes to compete with the state agencies especially in those states controlled by parties other than the NPN which controlled the federal government. Such institutional pluralism resulted in extreme forms of institutional ambiguities, with most states complaining that RBDAs were formulating and implementing programmes without proper consultation with the respective state governments.

Fourth, too many RBDAs were created simultaneously, allowing little or no scope for proper programme articulation. Many highly technical staff had to be recruited, leading to heavy management and technical staff import dependency. With no encouragement of a culture of serious programming, the RBDAs soon became a media political event that served as conduit pipes for wasteful public expenditures.

Finally, there was no monitoring mechanism and therefore no checks on RBDA malinvestments.

The programmes of most RBDAs have atrophied in the face of austerity. Nigeria's agricultural landscape is now littered with huge concrete monuments of uncompleted and possibly uncompletable large dam projects caught in the budget squeeze.

The distribution of infrastructures   There is need to go beyond a narrow focus on productive infrastructures to include the question of access of the rural residents to potable water, health care facilities, schools, and electricity. Recent evidence from Nigeria shows not only the gross inadequacies in levels of available rural infrastructures of this kind, but also great rural-urban disparities and regional imbalances (Idachaba 1985).

For example, in Borno State (representing 12.7 per cent of Nigeria's land area) primary school pupils in Kukawa local government area (LGA) must walk an average distance of 7.44 km to get to a primary school compared with 1.42 km for pupils in the Lagos mainland LGA in Lagos State, the seat of the Nigerian federal capital. Many state governments have, in response to the budgetary squeeze, converted boarding schools into day school. In Gongola State, the day secondary school student in Karim Lamido LGA must walk an average of 53.0 km to get to a secondary school, compared with only 9.80 km for his urban counterpart in the state capital (Yola LGA).

Similar rural–urban disparities exist in the distribution of health care facilities (e.g. hospitals, dispensaries, maternity centres), potable water supplies, electricity, and postal and telecommunications facilities. These rural–urban disparities account for an important part of the phenomenal growth in rural–urban migration.

When the comparison is not between rural and urban LGAs, but between different LGAs within a state, great disparities are still revealed. Using the LGA as the unit of observation, component states of the Nigerian federation could conceivably be ranked according to the value of the coefficient of variation of the infrastructural facility. The higher the coefficient of variation, the larger is the degree of regional disparity in available infrastructures among LGAs within a given state (see Tables 6.2 and 6.3 for an example relating to transport infrastructures). These intrastate contrasts explain the observed migration among towns and settlements of various sizes within a state, rather than a unidirectional flow from all the rural areas within a state to the capital city.

(b)   *National agricultural research systems and the generation of new technology*

The shift from low to high productivity inputs holds the key to the transformation of African agriculture. Unfortunately, national agricultural research systems are seriously constrained in their efforts to generate and disseminate new technology (Eicher and Baker 1982; Idachaba 1985).

(i)   *Research funding*   Research funding has been grossly inadequate and unstable. Even where the funding appears reasonable, as was the case in

Table 6.2 The distribution of LGA, state, and federal roads, by states, Nigeria, 1978/9–1980

State	Federal lengths (km)				Measures of dispersion of road lengths across LGAs (coefficient of variation in %)			
	Federal roads	State roads	LGA roads	All roads	Federal roads	State Roads	LGA roads	All roads
Anambra	863.50	1,423.40	810.50	3,097.50	78.91	60.23	156.59	53.94
Bauchi	1,460.20	794.80	3,938.60	6,193.80	56.82	87.97	49.79	42.96
Bendel	1,481.18	3,331.43	7,079.00	11,891.61	110.74	62.40	98.95	73.09
Benue	1,363.40	1,249.00	3,346.20	5,674.00	48.81	53.05	64.08	47.09
Borno	2,963.00	1,086.00	1,172.50	5,221.50	72.70	60.09	29.15	44.50
Cross River	1,380.39	2,747.89	6,504.39	10,632.67	92.67	23.45	53.88	48.55
Gongola	2,587.00	1,338.00	5,479.00	9,404.00	57.11	72.11	59.78	46.96
Imo	890.00	1,189.00	2,552.00	4,641.00	85.41	81.38	63.33	66.35
Kaduna	1,710.00	1,223.00	1,818.00	4,751.00	59.16	94.35	55.97	39.89
Kano	1,212.00	1,606.00	3,988.66	6,806.66	42.47	184.03	78.98	54.82
Kwara	1,896.00	1,123.00	2,306.00	5,325.00	102.85	68.80	54.57	69.95
Lagos	261.30	369.42	1,723.28	2,354.00	100.25	52.81	88.07	70.60
Niger	1,440.00	920.00	3,560.40	5,920.40	52.84	90.98	57.12	50.40
Ogun	782.00	899.00	6,438.00	8,119.00	47.59	40.35	37.22	29.11
Ondo	983.50	2,660.50	3,347.00	7,308.00	113.10	52.35	102.64	70.12
Oyo	1,118.50	928.00	7,821.00	10,002.00	99.21	74.47	123.07	101.70
Plateau	1,777.00	2,214.00	3,497.40	7,488.40	66.54	51.54	47.93	41.77
Rivers	441.80	616.20	n/a	1,058.00	71.36	90.24	n/a	74.87
Sokoto	2,233.00	1,082.00	3,084.00	6,399.00	64.60	113.25	65.64	42.55

Source: Original data from Rural Infrastructures Project Field Survey.

Table 6.3 The distribution of road densities, by states, Nigeria, 1978/9–1980

State	Road densities in metres/km²					Measures of dispersion of road densities across LGAs (coefficient of variation in %)			
	Federal roads	State roads	LGA roads	All roads	LGA median value (all roads)	Federal roads	State roads	LGA roads	All roads
Anambra	50.00	82.00	47.00	179.00	111.50	89.02	215.23	128.65	137.70
Bauchi	22.00	12.00	60.00	95.00	405.00	75.53	75.52	80.80	78.58
Bendel	41.00	92.00	195.00	328.00	600.70	68.68	62.57	121.40	88.00
Benue	27.00	24.00	65.00	111.00	436.60	48.90	78.27	59.84	46.56
Borno	25.00	9.00	10.00	45.00	253.50	98.05	84.64	45.42	61.44
Cross River	48.23	96.01	227.28	371.52	579.40	41.01	58.77	90.66	77.68
Gongola	25.90	13.40	54.80	94.10	522.50	63.66	66.89	92.89	68.66
Imo	70.00	94.00	202.00	366.00	222.00	280.04	210.11	116.21	141.63
Kaduna	25.00	18.00	27.00	70.00	330.00	39.10	83.54	69.91	35.12
Kano	28.00	37.00	93.00	158.00	306.35	47.49	334.92	49.70	121.64
Kwara	31.00	18.00	38.00	88.00	322.00	60.59	103.55	111.19	85.93
Lagos	79.00	111.00	529.00	709.00	220.05	53.75	55.50	151.83	118.37
Niger	32.00	20.00	78.00	130.00	760.00	167.47	138.80	89.29	111.29
Ogun	48.00	55.00	393.00	496.00	842.00	79.19	63.22	60.20	53.55
Ondo	48.00	130.00	183.00	357.00	305.00	83.75	40.48	85.92	57.63
Oyo	25.00	20.00	168.00	215.00	222.00	95.16	83.50	133.50	104.18
Plateau	32.20	40.80	64.50	138.10	500.10	55.23	31.87	60.96	38.51
Rivers	21.00	30.00	n/a	51.00	96.80	157.57	85.97	n/a	97.94
Sokoto	22.00	11.00	31.00	63.00	291.00	54.75	93.59	63.14	32.80

Source: Rural Infrastructures Project Field Survey.

Nigeria until recently, most of the funding is eaten by Africa's bloated salary structure, leaving very little for equipment, consumable supplies, and infrastructures. In general, African countries have no target such as the percentage of agricultural GDP that is annually allocated to research. Many countries have therefore failed to build up the critical mass or threshold for technological breakthrough. Research directors spend too much valuable time worrying about how next month's salaries will be paid and too little time on microresearch management and strategic research planning. In Nigeria where marketing board taxation has been abolished, and with it research funding from marketing board revenues, the research funding situation has become grim (Idachaba 1980, 1986).

Unpredictable and undesirable fluctuations in research funding result in badly formulated and poorly executed projects and the abandonment of uncompleted projects. Funding constraints of this nature compound the underlying serendipity problem in all research, further widening the probability distribution of possible outcomes of research.

(ii) *Resource allocation criteria and research productivity* The resource allocation problem of deciding shares of available resources that go to different research institutions continues to cause distortions in actual allocations relative to research priorities. There are few countries in sub-Saharan Africa, if any, which use explicit sets of allocative criteria to guide resource allocations to research.[6] This has introduced some resource allocation puzzles and four types of research lags: the lag between the emergence of a research problem and its recognition as such, that between recognition and the allocation of research resources for diagnosis, that between problem diagnosis and prescription of solutions, and that between prescription and the allocation of resources to implement prescribed solutions. In addition, there is the time-lag between implementation and impact. These lags appear to be unusually long in sub-Saharan Africa.

There is concern over the appallingly low productivity of reasonably funded African national research systems, measured by the number of technological breakthroughs or standardized published material (Lipton 1985; Boyce and Evenson 1975).

Macro managers of national agricultural research systems have appointed as institute directors many men with little or no known capability for providing research leadership, motivating individual researchers, and liaising effectively with relevant government institutions and functionaries (not only to ensure adequate funding but also to obtain a correct sense of national research priorities from the political leadership).[7] Research directors who fail to master

---

[6] For a statement of some allocative working rules, see Fishel (1971), Arndt *et al.* (1977), and Idachaba (1980, 1981*b*, 1987).

[7] One problem that can only be mentioned here is frequent changes in the macroinstitutional arrangements for managing the national agricultural research system. Nigeria has experimented with virtually all forms: Ministry of Agriculture model, Agricultural Research Council model,

the art of 'research resource canvassing' become ineffective and will continue to bemoan the lack of resources.

Allocation of personnel, money, and materials to different programmes within an institute requires allocative criteria to prevent lopsidedness in funding and ensure consistency with national priorities. Mechanisms within institutes for deriving allocative priorities from the macro guidelines are extremely weak.

Gross inadequacy of qualified and experienced staff remains a critical problem even though a few countries (e.g. Kenya, Nigeria) have made significant progress in this respect. Many systems have not been able to build up the required critical mass and many vacancies exist. This narrow skill base remains crippling because commodity programmes requiring multidisciplinary teams are vulnerable to critical skill gaps, sometimes resulting in valuable research man years being spent on the wrong track.

Staff inadequacy is compounded by great staff instability or turnover (Idachaba 1981a). Institute research staff migrate to the universities, the private sector, and other spheres of the economy either because of higher real incomes and better service conditions or because they have been frustrated by bad research management at the micro- or macrolevel. With high staff instability, research becomes spotty and badly focused as research projects get inherited by successive generations with different research priorities. Part of the problem stems from the identity crisis of the civil servant—scientist whose career is usually a linear function of time but who is at the same time expected to produce technological breakthroughs (see Table 6.4).

There is a complete absence of effective mechanisms to monitor agricultural research that would provide an early warning system on resource use, constraints, and staff performance. Effective monitoring of agricultural research provides research management at the institute level with corrective management information. This requires superior capability in various disciplines and programmes at the macroresearch management level (either in-house or outside) which can readily provide research institutes with needed technical support. Such continuous monitoring can then be fed into the periodic comprehensive evaluations of each institute.

(iii) *Integration of research and extension* Failure to integrate research and extension remains a major problem across countries. Organizationally, the research institutes and extension services of Ministries of Agriculture are not integrated, with the former behaving as if their mandate stopped at placing recommended technologies on the shelf, and the latter behaving as if their responsibility consisted of periodic visits to the shelf to check on available technologies. In most countries, no effective two-way communication flow has developed between farmers and researchers through extension workers and no

Ministry of Science and Technology model, etc. For details on the negative consequences for the national research system, see Idachaba (1987).

Table 6.4 Calculated indices of instability of research staff, Cocoa Research Institute of Nigeria, 1955/6–1977/8 (%)

Discipline	Period				
	1955/6– 1960/1	1958/9– 1963/4	1966/7– 1971/2	1960/1– 1971/2[a]	1966/7– 1976/7
Plant pathology	50.00	100.00	60.00	100.00	70.00
Entomology	0.00	100.00	57.14	100.00	55.71
Soils and chemistry		100.00		100.00	71.43
Plant breeding			42.50	100.00	87.50
Agronomy		100.00[b]	33.33	100.00	50.00
Statistics/economics			50.00		50.00
All research staff	33.33	100.00	50.00	100.00	82.50

[a] By 1961/2, the Ibadan substation of WACRI had only one Nigerian on the research staff (Nwachuku, a plant physiologist). By 1971/2, the entire research staff of 1961/2, including Nwachuku, had left CRIN, the successor to WACRI.
[b] Contains an upward bias because J. F. Longworth who worked as the only agronomist at the Ibadan substation of WACRI in 1958/9 switched to plant pathology by 1963/4.

Source: Idachaba (1981*a*).

national network of adaptive research trials has been effectively inaugurated. Recommended seed varieties for broad ecological zones are unsuited to local environmental stresses; consequently, recorded technological breakthroughs in African agriculture remain few and isolated (Odero-Ogwel *et al*. 1985).[8]

Agricultural extension systems remain weak, ill motivated, overstretched, demoralized, and ineffective. Constraints include long bureaucratic processes, poor funding and infrastructural support (especially transportation logistics), grossly inadequate cadre of subject-matter specialists, and the near-absence of routine programmes in training and visits. Extension systems remain weak not only in their technical mastery of new technologies and how these fit into existing farming systems, but also with respect to their ability to identify and utilize communication techniques that are most effective in a given socio-cultural milieu.

(c)   Harmful pricing policies

Five examples are presented of pricing policies in Africa. First is the regime of marketing board taxes that have choked off production, especially in mono-crop economies where the government depends on a single crop for most of its revenue (e.g. cotton in Mali and groundnuts in Gambia). Gazetted producer prices have remained low relative to world prices, and statutory marketing costs have been high. These have acted as disincentives to mass adoption of innovations.

Second are the adverse terms of trade against agriculture caused by particular patterns of domestic inflation as well as by the primitive state of rural

[8] For an illuminating and comprehensive study, see Johnson *et al*. (1969).

infrastructures. Costs of non-farm consumer goods have risen much faster than farmgate producer prices of farm commodities. Domestic monetary and fiscal policies have inflated production costs at the farm gate and depressed real farmgate producer prices, thus acting as disincentives to increased farm production for given levels of nominal producer prices.

Third is a system of overvalued exchange rates which has encouraged massive imports of cheap food and farm inputs, and at the same time has discouraged exports of farm produce. The adverse effects on export crop production are much more serious where government parastatal monopsonies purchase most of the crop, or where, with multiple market channels, other market channels remain weaker than the export market channel. In Ghana, cocoa production plummeted from 400,000 tons a year in the early 1970s to 158,000 tons in 1983/4, while the production of cotton, tobacco, and rubber dropped from about 11,000 tons, 2,700 tons, and 3,300 tons respectively in the mid-1970s to only about 500 tons each in 1983 (World Bank 1985). The 1984/5 producer price of cocoa at the official exchange rate of ₵53 = $1 was 25 per cent of the f.o.b. price; at a shadow exchange rate of ₵70 = $1, about 19 per cent; and at the black market rate of ₵120 = $1, only about 11 per cent. At the same time, producer prices in neighbouring Ivory Coast and Togo were respectively 3.3 and 2.5 times the producer price in Ghana at the black market exchange rate (World Bank 1985).[9]

In Nigeria, the negative price effects of overvalued exchange rates are slightly ameliorated in those crops with multiple market outlets where the domestic market has been stronger than the export market (e.g. groundnuts, palm oil, palm kernel, maize, sheanuts, etc.). Cotton however provides a classic example of the effect of bad pricing policies. The Cotton Board has the monopoly for purchasing seed cotton for delivery to the ginneries. The producer price of cotton was pegged at ₦330.00 per tonne during 1977–80 within the context of an overvalued exchange rate, at a time when producer prices of competing grains were rising steeply on the domestic market. Cotton output fell and production of competing crops rose in spite of exhortations for farmers to grow cotton.

The fourth example relates to farm input subsidies. These subsidies are useful in the attainment of desired resource-use patterns and factor proportions and in promoting appropriate incentives for the adoption of new technologies. They cushion farmers against the adverse terms of trade and grossly deficient rural infrastructures facing agriculture. Input subsidies could also serve as an instrument of income transfers to the rural sector as its own share of some windfall such as petrodollar earnings.

However, the drawbacks of the fertilizer and cocoa pesticide subsidy schemes in Nigeria in recent decades highlight several problems of farm input subsidies. These include (1) the creation of a 'dependency mentality' where

---

[9] The issue raised by the positive fiscal role of crop taxes will be addressed in section 6.3.

farmers have come to think of input subsidies as a permanent feature of their industry and that successive governments—civilian or military—have an obligation to grant them farm input subsidies, (2) protection of the marginal farmer from the relative price realities of the day, thereby delaying required dynamic adjustments of the agricultural sector, (3) discouragement of private sector participation in retail fertilizer distribution especially where panterritorial pricing policy stipulates uniform retail pricing policy, (4) interstate trafficking in cocoa pesticides from high-subsidy states to low-subsidy states and trafficking across Nigeria's international boundaries in search of foreign exchange, (5) retarded growth of the Nigerian fertilizer market as the quantity of fertilizer on the market tended to be determined by the size of the fertilizer subsidy budget,[10] (6) distribution inefficiencies and contrived input scarcities that are directly caused by bureaucratic bottlenecks, and (7) there have been repeated complaints that a significant proportion of the benefits continues to flow to unintended beneficiaries.

Fifth, the interest rate structure has been unfavourable to agriculture especially when governments impose lending rate ceilings that are not significantly higher than borrowing rates. This has reduced the flow of loanable funds to the agricultural sector, especially from merchant banks and other credit institutions that must borrow from the capital market. The interest rate ceiling has the unintended consequence of limiting the total amount of available loanable funds, which are then rationed using non-price criteria such as personal acquaintance, membership of the same social clubs, etc. As a result the small-scale farmer, the intended beneficiary, fails to get any credit. Those who got credit are the retired civil servants, generals, professors, etc.

These five examples do not exhaust the range of inappropriate pricing policies, and one could also mention, say, inflationary domestic monetary and fiscal policies (especially deficit financing through bank credit) and urban minimum wage laws. These have resulted in high input costs that have rendered the African agricultural system one of the highest production cost economies in the world. The general problem that needs to be addressed is the non-profitability of farming with the present cost–price structure.

(d)   Institutional arrangements

(i)   *Defining the proper role of government*   Increasingly widespread government intervention, particularly in direct agricultural production and distribution, has resulted in considerable administrative inefficiencies and waste of scarce public resources that have high social opportunity costs (World Bank 1981). Critics have argued that African countries do not have significantly higher ratios of public expenditure to GDP than other countries, and that

---

[10] This was because all fertilizer importation and procurement was centralized in the Federal Ministry of Agriculture as from 1976, that is, there was no fertilizer procurement, sale, or distribution through private channels during 1976–86. For further details, see Falusi and Williams (1981).

within the African region, it is not established that countries with low public expenditure to GDP ratios have achieved higher rates of economic growth (Colclough 1985). The issue is not clarified by generalized condemnation of the government's role in agriculture or by the search for correlations between public expenditure—GDP ratios and economic growth rates. The focus should be on the types of public expenditures. More, not less, public spending is needed in small-scale and medium-scale irrigation infrastructures, rural feeder roads, markets, and agricultural research and extension. Less, not more, public funding is required to establish large-scale mechanized farms, produce poultry, dairy products, and engage in routine grain trading in direct competition with private channels (see Table 6.5).

(ii)   *Frequent changes in policy, inconsistencies, and non-response*   A perennial problem of African agriculture is the frequency of policy changes, revisions, modifications, and, quite often, embarrassing reversals. There are three sources for these frequent changes that often produce inconsistencies.

First is the set of changes in policy that are the direct consequence of changes in political regime. In this case, policy instability is the direct result of political instability. Some of the changes in policy introduced by a new regime would be justified in order to correct for bad programming (formulation and/or implementation) and inadequate sense of priorities on the part of preceding regimes. The more stable the political climate, the more stable would be the policy environment.[11] Unless the policy environment is stable, key empirical relationships cannot be established and measured. After all, the issues over which policy analysts and policy makers disagree are mainly empirical, not theoretical, revolving round the signs and magnitudes of estimated coefficients. Since the food and fibre problem is urgent in most African countries, every new incoming regime believes strongly that it has a solution.

Second, policies are changed on purely cosmetic grounds to give a semblance of change when in reality there is none, sometimes to give legitimacy to a regime. Old programmes get dressed in new slogans, new rounds of false expectations are built up, all ending in dashed hopes.

Finally, there is policy change borne out of a 'quick fix' syndrome reflecting an underlying impatience with agricultural programmes which fail to yield results like urban turn-key manufacturing projects.

Unpredictable and confusing policy changes ruin investors' confidence. When expectations on returns from potential farm investments are not stable, investments are smaller than they would otherwise have been. This accounts in part for observed limited new investments and new management entry in those countries that have witnessed frequent changes in food and agricultural policy. Table 6.6 chronicles recent changes in institutional arrangements for managing agricultural research in Nigeria.

---

[11] Tanzania, which witnessed many changes in policy in spite of political stability, is an exception to the general case.

Table 6.5 Government and private sector involvement in farm input distribution, sub-Saharan Africa, 1981

Farm inputs	No. of sub-Saharan countries				
	Low-income semi-arid	Low-income other	Middle-income oil importers	Middle-income oil exporters	All sub-Saharan Africa
Fertilizer supply					
Private	—	—	4 (11.11)	—	4 (11.11)
Government	7 (19.44)	10 (27.7?)	4 (11.11)	2 (5.56)	23 (63.89)
Mixed	—	6 (16.67)	3 (8.33)	—	9 (25.00)
Seed supply					
Private	—	—	4 (11.11)	—	4 (11.11)
Government	6 (16.67)	9 (25.00)	5 (13.89)	2 (5.56)	22 (61.11)
Mixed	1 (2.78)	7 (19.44)	2 (5.56)	—	10 (27.78)
Pesticides					
Private	—	2 (5.56)	4 (11.11)	—	6 (16.67)
Government	6 (16.67)	8 (22.22)	2 (5.56)	1 (2.78)	17 (47.22)
Mixed	1 (2.78)	6 (16.67)	5 (13.89)	1 (2.78)	13 (36.11)
Farm equipment supply					
Private	—	2 (5.56)	6 (16.67)	—	8 (22.22)
Government	6 (16.67)	6 (16.67)	2 (2.56)	1 (2.78)	15 (41.67)
Mixed	1 (2.78)	8 (22.22)	3 (8.33)	1 (2.78)	13 (36.11)

Note: Percentage of all sub-Saharan countries in brackets.

Source: Derived from data in World Bank (1981).

African policy makers have chosen the easier path when confronted with serious food and agricultural problems, which is to create a new parastatal, that ubiquitous tool crafted by civil servants and cherished by their political bosses. Parallel institutions have been created with duplicated roles that quite often overlap with those of existing institutions, creating institutional rivalry and ambiguities that generate enough hostility and resentment to sabotage new programmes, regardless of their intrinsic merit (see Table 6.7 and Appendix 6.1 for recent evidence on Nigeria and Tanzania).

(iii) *Public bureaucracy and implementation indiscipline* Centralized public bureaucracies operating a system of parastatals and ministries strive to manipulate smallholder agriculture through a maze of administrative rules. Implementation indiscipline remains a fundamental problem, especially the inability to follow a rigorous implementation routine without succumbing to conflicting interest groups and preventing avoidable cost overruns. Civil servants are brought up to adhere rigidly to rules and procedures: programmes are expected to adjust to the established bureaucracy and not the other way round. Development programming, as seen through the bureaucrat's eyes, must be within the context of 'workability' within the existing milieu of procedures. Hence the typical, almost instantaneous, response of many civil servants to a new programme is a blunt 'it won't work', backed up by a recital of the administrative procedures and other established norms that irrevocably stand in the way of implementation. Implementation indiscipline has persisted from year to year and from regime to regime largely because there has been no vigorous social articulation to pressurize the agricultural establishment for better performance. Far too many civil servants are concerned with relative positions of institutions and individuals rather than with the programme content of new ideas. Overriding concern with the linear time path of their careers prevents civil servants from venturing into new ideas and implementation procedures.

Far too many programmes get bogged down in bureaucratic snarls, the antithesis of agriculture's requirements of timeliness. Political priorities often fail to get translated into administrative (procedural) priorirites, again suggesting the necessity to reduce some key lags.

(iv) *Political will* There is often a lack of political will to pursue those agricultural programmes that are in the nation's long-term interest, as against short-term political expediency. Political expediency has manifested itself in urban appeasement policies such as urban minimum wage laws and cheap food and input imports maintained by a system of overvalued exchange rates. It requires political will to formulate and implement a programme for the inarticulate rural majority. The problem of political will in sub-Saharan Africa has been compounded by high political instability. Political will, if it is to have an enduring impact, requires a minimum level of political stability.

Table 6.6 Frequent changes in institutional arrangements for managing agricultural research in Nigeria, 1964–1985

Acts and decrees	Year	Provision	Remarks
1. Nigerian Research Institutes Act	1964	Established Cocoa Research Institute of Nigeria, Nigerian Institute for Oil Palm Research, Rubber Institute of Nigeria, and Nigerian Institute for Trypanosomiasis Research	Following dissolution of West African Research Organization in 1962
2. Nigerian Council for Science and Technology Decree	1970	Umbrella organization to co-ordinate research grouped into physical sciences, agriculture, medicine	
3. Agricultural Research Council of Nigeria Decree (ARCN Decree)	1971	Established ARCN to co-ordinate all agricultural research	
4. Agricultural Research Institutes Decree	1973	Vested power to establish institutes to conduct research and training in any field of agriculture, veterinary sciences, fisheries, forestry, agro-meteorology, and water resources in Federal Commissioner for Agriculture; also power to take over any existing state research station	Watershed in state/federal funding of agricultural research. Destroyed all incentive for states to fund agricultural research
5. Research Institutes (Establishment) Order	1975	Established 14 research institutes: NCRI, NRCRI, NIHORT, CRIN, RRIN, NIFOR, FRIN, NVRI, NAPRI, NITR, LRIN, LCRI, KLRI, NIOMR	Clear commodity mandate for each institute

6. National Science and Technology Development Agency Decree	1977	Set up an executive agency to co-ordinate all research in Nigeria, agricultural and non-agricultural. All research institutes established by the 1975 decree were brought under the aegis of the NSTDA	Replaced the 1973 decree but still vested powers to take control of any existing federal or state research establishment in NSTDA Commissioner.
7. Constitution of the Federal Republic of Nigeria	1979		Placed 'industrial and agricultural research' on the concurrent list
8. Federal Ministry of Science & Technology Act	1979	Scrapped the NSTDA, created the Federal Ministry of Science & Technology	
9. Federal Ministry of Education, Science and Technology Decree	1984	Scrapped the Federal Ministry of Science and Technology and merged it with Federal Ministry of Education	Military suspended constitution
10. Federal Ministry of Science and Technology Decree	1985	Created separate Federal Ministry of Science and Technology	

6.3. *Policy options for African agriculture*

This section is divided into six subthemes: sectoral strategy; rural infrastructures; agricultural research and technology; incentives and prices; external aid; and rural institutions and mobilization.

(a) *Sectoral strategy: the role of agriculture in economic development*

Different sectoral strategies have been pursued in Africa, which can be related to different philosophical views of the role of agriculture in economic development.

Agriculture as source of surplus food and fibre When agriculture is viewed primarily as a source of surplus food and fibre to provide needed foreign exchange or food for the urban economy, maximum extraction becomes the strategy. Both the rural sector and agriculture are seen purely in their extraction roles, with rural man or woman, the source of these surpluses, treated merely as a producer of surpluses and not as a household head whose family members need good primary and secondary schools, potable drinking water, housing, electricity, etc. (de Janvry 1981). The World Bank-assisted

Table 6.7 Agricultural parastatals in Tanzania, 1983

Parastatal	Function
(a) *Agricultural Marketing*	
1. National Milling Corporation	Sole rights to buy domestically produced grains and import when necessary
2. Sugar Development Corporation	Sole rights to market, export, and import sugar
3. Tanzania Cotton Authority	Sole rights to purchase and export cotton
4. Coffee Authority of Tanzania	Sole rights to purchase and export coffee
5. Tanzania Pyrethrum Board	Sole rights to purchase and export pyrethrum
6. Tobacco Authority of Tanzania	Sole rights to purchase and export tobacco
7. Tanzania Tea Authority	Sole rights to purchase and export tea
8. Tanzania Sisal Authority	Sole rights to purchase and export sisal
9. Cashewnut Authority of Tanzania	Sole rights to purchase and export cashew
10. General Agricultural Products Corporation	Monopoly rights to purchase and export a range of minor crops
(b) *Agricultural production*	
11. National Agriculture and Food Production	Principally wheat and rice production
12. Rilombero Sugar Corporation	Sugar production
13. Tanganyika Planting Company	Sugar production
14. Mtwimba Sugar Estates	Sugar production
15. Dairy Farming Corporation	Livestock and milk production
16. National Ranching Corporation	
(c) *Agricultural credit*	
17. Tanzania Rural Development Bank	
(d) *Agricultural inputs*	
18. Agricultural and Industrial Supplies Company	Importation of agricultural inputs and equipment
19. State Motor Corporation	Sole rights to import vehicles and spare parts
20. Tanzania Fertilizer Company	Production and marketing of fertilizer
21. Tanzania Seed Company	Production and marketing of seed
(e) *Agricultural research, extension, and education*	
22. Tanzania Agricultural Research Organization	Generation of new technical packages
23. Tanzania Livestock Research Organization	
24. Uyole Agricultural Centre	
25. University of Dar es Salaam	
(f) *Transport and retailing*	
26. Regional Trading Corporation	Food crop retailing
27. Regional Transport Companies	Provision of transport services

Source: World Bank (1983*a*).

Agricultural Development Projects (ADPs) still do not provide the full range of basic social services over and above the integrated supply of farm inputs and physical infrastructural facilities such as rural feeder roads, farm service centres, small earth dams, and market stalls.

Agriculture as foreign exchange earner   Dependence of sub-Saharan Africa on agriculture as a source of foreign exchange earnings measured as a proportion of total export earnings ranges from 0.6 per cent in Gabon to 98.6 per cent in Chad. Pertinent issues to consider are trade-offs between export crops and competing non-exports, especially food crops; the drastic fall in Africa's share of world commodity trade; and the need for diversification of foreign exchange earnings.

But equally important is the question of foreign exchange for what and for whom? Past experience confirms that most countries use the foreign exchange earnings from agriculture to finance five-star hotels, township stadia, breweries, car assembly plants, etc. in the capital cities with little or nothing to show in the rural sector, the source of the original extraction.

Agriculture as source of public revenue   Agriculture's role in most countries is perceived as a major source of public revenue through marketing board taxes. For many countries, this system, which has crippled the agricultural sector, should have been discarded long ago within the framework of deliberate revenue diversification. Extremely resource-poor countries (e.g. Mali) relying on agriculture as the only source of revenue cannot, of course, abolish these taxes overnight. Yet, the production effects of crop taxes can be so adverse that the elasticity of government revenue with respect to the marketing board tax rate can become very small or even negative at sufficiently high tax rates, making taxation ineffective or self-defeating.

Agriculture as generator of employment opportunities   The provision of employment opportunities in agriculture is important not only from the viewpoint of utilizing resources that would have otherwise been idle but also from the viewpoint of reducing the massive rural–urban drift and solving the urban youth unemployment problem. One constraint on this option is the high cost of farm labour, resulting from institutionalized urban minimum wages. In these countries, overvalued exchange rates have in addition made labour substitutes cheaper than they would otherwise have been. Many farm settlement schemes have been tried but have failed. To be a viable option, farm settlement and other related schemes to generate employment opportunities must fulfil certain conditions. First, they must be perceived to go beyond providing the urban élite with a solution to the politically troubling urban unemployment problem. They must aim at developing the rural area with the participants as the centrepiece. Second, such schemes must be designed so that participants see themselves as owners of the farming enterprises and not just as paid government employees only waiting for new off-farm job market opportunities to materialize. Finally, macroeconomic measures (credit, terms of trade between agriculture and non-agriculture, producer price support programmes, domestic inflation and the general price level, etc.) must be supportive of the settlement schemes.

Related to this is the role of agriculture as a source of income that generates demand for rural non-farm goods and services, especially those with income elastic demands at low-income levels. The role of agriculture in providing rural markets for consumer goods and services produced in the non-farm sector should also not be underestimated, emphasizing the linkages between the farm and the rural non-farm industrial sector.

Agriculture and macroeconomic goals   Many countries emphasize self-reliance as a national goal. Agriculture as the dominant sector holds the key to the realization of this goal. Development patterns of the agricultural sector are dictated by the needs of economic nationalism and its specific manifestations in the form of food self-reliance and food self-sufficiency. If agriculture is to be the source of national economic growth, disproportionately large amounts of resources should be allocated to it so that it can carry the 'growth burden' of the other sectors.

(b)   Rural infrastructures

Several general issues arise in the design of appropriate policies for rural infrastructures. First is the choice between consolidation of inherited colonial hinterland–seaport links which service the export economy and the development of a decentralized rural road network to service Africa's food economies. The choice is determined partly by the choice between export crop and food crop production and partly by wider issues of national social cohesion and integration. Second is the allocation of fiscal responsibilities for physical infrastructures (e.g. feeder roads) between government and local communities and between different tiers of government. Appropriate institutional arrangements need to be evolved, involving government and the local communities that are able to tap the creative energies of rural people in the design, construction, and maintenance of rural roads, water pumps, etc. Third, appropriate methodologies need to be evolved for appraising infrastructural projects: should they be assessed as part of an agricultural project package or should they be assessed on their own merits? The significance of this issue lies in the complementarities between the infrastructural programme and the agricultural programme, and in the need for institutional collaboration between the agricultural and infrastructural sectors.

Concerning rural roads, considerations of cost recovery and of the local capacity to finance maintenance costs suggest the priority need to build the first set of rural roads in areas of high agricultural potential as a means of expanding the local fiscal base. The choice between construction of new rural roads and concentration on the rehabilitation of old road networks needs to be based on country-specific circumstances. The failure of many countries to maintain existing roads should not mean an end to all new road construction in all countries.[12] Rather it means that in those countries with clearly demonstrable needs for new roads, safeguards must be built into project design to ensure sustained local maintenance capabilities.

On farm service centres, experience from ongoing projects points to several issues. First is the choice between a strategy of a few primary farm service centres serviced by a network of secondary communal facilities and a strategy in which the project strives to saturate a project area with its own farm service centres. While the ADPs in Liberia adopted the former strategy, Nigeria adopted the latter. The former has the advantage of long-run sustainability because the storage facilities belong to the community. Second is the relationship between commercial sales staff at the farm service centres and extension staff, not only because of recurring conflict but also because of the need for continuous collaboration for farmers to be able to reap the full productivity benefits from the new purchased inputs. Third is the need to reconcile the commercial profitability criterion with the need for equitable development so that backward inaccessible areas are not gradually neglected in the quest to concentrate input sales only in those areas with largest turnover. Fourth is the problem of commercial viability of the farm input account when the government imposes a panterritorial farm input-subsidy pricing policy with no reimbursement to project management for transport and other marketing costs.

Concerning irrigation infrastructures, African countries are confronted with several policy options and dilemmas. First, countries must choose between small-scale, medium-scale, and large-scale irrigation schemes. Capital and foreign exchange intensive colossal irrigation schemes benefiting a limited number of farm households and irrigating a limited area of land represent the one option that most countries have tended to prefer. So much attention is focused on the dazzling engineering aspects of those schemes that primary activities like efficient management and delivery of irrigation water resources and the design of monitoring and evaluation schemes and effective cost-recovery schemes are often relegated to the background. Two trends are expected: first, the share of all irrigation in total resource allocation to agriculture will rise, and second, the share of small-scale irrigation (tubewells, washbores, and small earth dams) in total irrigation will rise. The latter trend must be a deliberate political decision; otherwise, programming for irrigation when left to engineers alone tends to be biased in favour of the big irrigation schemes, almost always to the neglect of the small-scale schemes. Second, some choice is involved at the margin between allocating resources to irrigation

[12] In seven recently launched state-wide World Bank-assisted Agricultural Development Projects (ADPs) in Nigeria, the World Bank was vehemently opposed to the construction of new rural feeder roads.

and allocating resources to breeding work on short-duration seed varieties. What is required is simultaneous programming for breeding work and the development of appropriate irrigation infrastructures. Finally, countries must often choose between accepting foreign technical assistance that is biased in favour of large irrigation schemes (for their high political visibility) and making do with small-scale and medium-scale irrigation projects financed from domestic resources. Such large-scale foreign aid-assisted schemes absorb so much public management input that there is little or no time for national systems endogenously to formulate irrigation policies which emphasize simplicity, replicability, maintenance, and sustainability.

(c) Agricultural research and technology

Agricultural research   The choice must be made between alternative organizational models for managing national research systems: (1) Ministry of Agriculture model, (2) Ministry of Science and Technology model, (3) parastatal model, and (4) an Agricultural Research Council (ARC) Model. The Ministry model, whether Agriculture or Science and Technology, tends to get bogged down in bureaucratic bottlenecks. The fatal flaw of the Science and Technology model is that the national agricultural research system is not keyed into the programming work of the Agriculture Ministry which has portfolio responsibility for executing agricultural programmes. Programme priorities fail to get translated into agricultural research priorities or get translated after unduly long lags. Co-ordination within such a model is obtained through interministerial meetings which are notorious for their operational ineffectiveness. The flexibility of the parastatal or ARC model strongly recommends it for African national research systems, though each country would have to identify the model that works against the background of its historical, constitutional, and cultural legacies.

Attempts at explaining the inadequacies of African agricultural research systems have focused almost exclusively on such supply side factors as inadequate and unstable funding and staffing, institutional ambiguities, etc., to the total neglect of demand side factors. On the demand side, the issue is largely organizational: how to articulate the research needs of widely dispersed small-scale farmers. Research systems must identify new mechanisms to find out why farmers do what they do, their research needs and priorities. The key to this is the active utilization of existing rural institutions to serve as a medium for conveying research needs and priorities to researchers. What is required is a highly decentralized network of rural institutions.

Large-scale farms are becoming important as sources of food and fibre surpluses. So are large-scale poultry farms and fisheries. One option is to allow the research system to respond to issues and problems that have been best articulated, with the socially unacceptable result that big and influential farmers will capture the national agricultural research system and direct it mainly to the issues that concern them. The response of the policy process depends on the linkages between policy makers and the different social classes in the agricultural sector. If policy makers identify mainly with the class interests of the large-scale farmers, then the research system will be motivated to address the research needs of the large-scale and medium-scale farmers. It requires political will and commitment to resist the constant pressures of large- and medium-scale farmers and to get the research system to address the research needs of small-scale farmers.

On research–extension linkages, one option is to continue with the present system of agricultural research institutes which give the worst of both worlds: they are neither Rothamstead nor the land grant system of the USA. The other option is structurally to transform the present system along three possible lines. One is to establish agricultural universities so that state ministry extension services and agricultural research are properly integrated. Second, applied research capabilities within the new World Bank-assisted ADPs could be vastly expanded to form a proper research base linked with the extension arms of these projects. Third, existing research institutes could be merged with university faculties of agriculture in their localities to service their catchment areas. Unless a drastic solution is found, the problem of building up a network of adaptive research centres well suited to local environmental niches will continue to plague these countries.[13]

On institutional arrangements for research at the regional level, two choices are open. One is to rely on the CGIAR system now that most of the panterritorial research organizations have been dismantled. Three issues readily come to mind. First, is the present set of mandates for the CGIAR centres adequate and appropriate for Africa's food crisis? For example, sub-Saharan Africa continues to rely on ICRISAT outposts for breakthroughs in sorghum and millet but recorded success in mass adoption of new varieties is still minimal. Second, are the research priorities of CGIAR of the biological and chemical technology type, though relevant for the land-deficit countries of Asia, appropriate for land-surplus sub-Saharan Africa where the primary need might not be increases in productivity per unit of land area but increases in productivity per man day? In other words, relative factor scarcities and prices in those Asian and Central American countries serviced by the first generation of CGIAR centres are radically different from those of sub-Saharan Africa. Third, African countries must endeavour to promote close collaboration between national research systems and the CGIAR centres especially in the areas of mechanical technology, joint breeding, and release of new varieties.

The other option is to encourage networking among national research systems as a substitute for the erstwhile panterritorial research institutes.

Farm organization, factor proportions and appropriate technology   Dire predictions are being made by informed and uninformed observers about the

---

[13] On this question, see also the contribution by Jean-Philippe Platteau in the second volume of this book.

imminent disappearance of the African small-scale farmer who is to be replaced by the modern large-scale farmer. Policy makers are being called upon to stop wasting resources on a rapidly vanishing species and to concentrate instead on the needs of the large-scale farmer for combine harvesters, tractors, monocropping agronomy, etc.

The modal farm size in Nigeria and many African countries is 1–2 hectares. Most farm families operate holdings within this modal class, and most farm holdings are within this class. Any policy aimed at improving the productive status of the typical farming household or the typical farm holding must therefore focus strongly on the small-scale farm, at least in the short to medium term. Available empirical evidence does not show any inherent superiority of large-scale over small-scale farms in terms of technical efficiency or production elasticity of inputs, net value added, profitability or net farm income per unit area. Since large-scale farmers tend to have the best-quality lands, land quality has to be held constant for any valid comparisons of small-scale and large-scale farmers. Table 6.8 shows that while the ratio of mean output on commercial farms to mean output on communal farms in Zimbabwe is about 4:1, the corresponding ratio of value added is only 2.4:1 because of the high production cost of large-scale commercial farms.

Co-operative and communal farms have been romanticized in popular writings on African agriculture for quite some time, but like most romantic ideas, this one has little or no bearing on reality. Producer co-operatives in Africa, as elsewhere, have largely failed to take off. Communal farms, conceptually and culturally appealing, have little prospect of becoming Africa's future mode of farm organization. What holds out promise is a network of consolidated contiguous farms, individually owned and operated as such, which make for easier and cheaper mechanization.

Table 6.8 Input–output relationships on large- and small-scale farms, Zimbabwe, 1974–1980

Year	Commercial (large-scale)			Communal farm		
	Output	Input	Value added	Output	Input	Value added
1974	369	145	224	108	7	101
1975	385	165	220	106	8	98
1976	415	178	237	107	8	99
1977	404	197	207	108	9	99
1978	430	210	220	75	8	67
1979	452	231	221	104	8	96
1980	687	298	309	147	11	136
MEAN	437	203	234	108	8	99

Source: World Bank (1983*b*).

Africa's ageing farm labour needs to be replaced by more appropriate sources of motive power. Where the tsetse fly permits, oxen technology needs to be intensified. Where this is not possible, appropriate mechanization is needed. Three issues arise. First is the impact of overvalued domestic currencies which have made farm machinery imports cheaper than they would have been otherwise. This has artificially encouraged the substitution of machines for men in countries with severe youth unemployment. Second is the lack of viable 'mechanized land development technological packages' that do minimum damage to Africa's fragile tropical soils. Present destructive patterns by which contracts for bush clearing and land development are awarded to urban-based contractors with little knowledge of tropical soils end up making them increasingly dependent on inorganic fertilizers. The plain fact is that more is known about rainfed crop agronomy than about mechanized clearing and land development. Third is the foreign exchange constraint which greatly limits the mechanization option.[14]

(d)   Incentives and prices

(i)   *Role of government*   Three issues need to be addressed. First, can internal forces be trusted to work endogenously to get governments to disengage from inappropriate roles such as commercial production and sales of poultry, pork, rice, and maize, as well as retail fertilizer distribution? Second, what are the alternatives to government participation in these activities? Third, what are the priorities for appropriate government involvement in agriculture?

Interest groups coalesce into strong opposition of government disengagement. Some of the opposition is ideological, dressed up in technical terms such as market failures, externalities, avoidance of monopoly, and the concentration of economic power in a few hands. Bureaucrats and their political bosses continuously raise expectations about the next round of 'reorganization, revamping, and revitalization' of the parastatals to make them profitable, or at least independent of regular treasury subventions. But periodic changes in top management of agricultural parastatals have not arrested their operating losses. Disengagement has come with the structural adjustment loans of the World Bank and IMF's conditionalities. Some have argued that there are no private sector alternatives when the state retreats (Bienefeld 1983). However, African small-scale farmers have repeatedly demonstrated their ability to respond to economic incentives. Government should concentrate on the provision of a conducive institutional, infrastructural, and policy environment that will elicit maximum response from farmers.

(ii)   *Farm input and output pricing*[15]   Several issues need to be resolved

---

[14]   For a comprehensive analysis, see Pingali *et al.* (1985).

[15]   The omission of marketing and storage programmes in the ADPs is consistent with what appears to be the World Bank's world-view—that these are best left to the private sector (World Bank 1981).

concerning the role of input subsidies. First, criteria must be specified to guide national governments in allocating a given government subsidy budget among different farm subsidies. Relevant considerations include the importance of the resource in total production cost, the 'strategic' importance of the input as it affects the timeliness of farming operations or removes some critical production bottlenecks, and the output elasticity of the input, to name a few. Similarly, criteria need to be explicitly formulated to assign fiscal responsibilities for farm input subsidies between different tiers of government (state and federal). A case can be made, for instance, for relatively higher federal subsidies on inputs used in the production of those commodities that augment and diversify the country's foreign exchange earnings and those inputs that facilitate achievement of national food security and self-reliance objectives (e.g. irrigation water), leaving state governments to focus on inputs used in production of food and fibre of local significance.

On the appropriate levels of input subsidies, what, on a priori grounds, are the determinants of levels of farm input subsidies? In an earlier effort, this author showed that within the analytic framework of the theory of second best with a Cobb–Douglas production function, the required degree of farm input subsidy for given levels of marketing board taxes on crops is related to the input's output elasticity.[16] On producer price support schemes, a critical prerequisite for success is the optimal sequencing of government prices. Countries that have successfully operated price support schemes have also had more advanced networks of rural institutions and rural infrastructures before the implementation of producer price support schemes than currently exist in sub-Saharan Africa. When price support schemes are combined with urban consumer food and industrial price subsidies, the resulting huge budget deficits turn out to be too expensive and inflationary, especially when such deficits are financed through bank credit. The Tanzanian experience with the National Milling Corporation highlights the severe limitations of such pricing schemes.

The relative weights of input subsidies and producer price support schemes in national agricultural pricing policy depend on the objectives to be achieved. If the objective is technological transformation and the promotion of particular resource-use patterns, then farm input subsidies deserve greater weight. Similarly, if the objective is to compensate farmers for taxes on export crops which are taken as institutional realities, then input subsidies are the clear choice in such a second-best situation. If, however, the aim is to cope with the consequences of excess capacity in the presence of price inelastic demands for food, then producer price schemes become instruments for transferring income from the urban to the rural sector (a situation inapplicable to most of Africa).

Using a distributed lag model, this author found that the adjustment lags

---

[16] See Idachaba (1974).

were faster and shorter with input prices than with output prices, suggesting that for the purpose of promoting aggregate input demand, more emphasis should be placed on farm input subsidies than on producer price support schemes.[17] This is eminently plausible as producer price support schemes merely confer generalized purchasing power which ends in buying farm *and* non-farm commodities. Input subsidies are superior in this regard because of their resource specificity. The optimality of subsidies or price support schemes also depends on the concurrent availability of other complementary policy instruments such as rural feeder roads, easily accessible farm credit, and storage facilities, to mention a few.

(iii) *Trade and exchange rate policy options*   Most countries must choose between the demands of efficiency on the one hand, and economic nationalism and self-reliance on the other. In terms of efficiency, resources need to be sharply focused on those commodities in which the country has distinct comparative advantage. For export crops, the clear option is for countries dramatically to raise productivity not only to stop the erosion of Africa's share of world trade but also to reverse it (World Bank 1981). Whether this leads to significant foreign exchange gains or not depends on Africa's relative shares and the price elasticities of demand for its agricultural exports. This calls for diversification of export crop production from 'higher' to 'lower' share exports and from 'low' to 'high' price-elasticity-of-demand crops. Otherwise, Africa could be a victim of the 'fallacy of composition' since what might be true for an individual country need not be true for the entire continent (Godfrey 1983).

The case for departing from the rule of comparative advantage in the direction of greater self-reliance rests on four key considerations. First is the social utility derived by a country's citizens from self-reliance (the reduced dependence on imports). In the case of food, for example, a country's sense of national pride is hurt when it is fed, on the average, by outsiders—hence the desire of many countries for food self-reliance and self-sufficiency. Second is the desire to avoid discontinuities in available food supplies and the attendant entitlement collapse by sudden, unpredictable, and undesirable disruptions in overseas sources of food supply (caused by weather changes and changes in the policy environment) (Sen 1985). Increasing a country's self-sufficiency ratio reduces its exposure to such external exigencies and shocks. Third is the infant industry argument by which protection is offered during the development phase when unit fixed costs remain high relative to market size. Finally, developing countries appeal to 'nth-best' theory, laying stress on certain export subsidies in the developed countries. Imports from developed countries land at African ports at 'border' prices that may not reflect true production costs in the developed countries. The problem arises when multilateral agencies insist on comparing such distorted border prices with domestic prices in African

[17] See Idachaba (1976).

countries as a basis for prescribing what these countries should produce domestically and what they should import based on 'import parity' considerations.

Though second-best arguments are conceptually elegant, there are operational difficulties in evolving consistent and practical policy packages. One option is to compute domestic resource costs (DRCs) of saving or earning one dollar of foreign exchange to determine comparative advantage. Estimates of DRCs for Ghana indicate comparative advantage in cocoa, oil palm, rubber, coconut, tobacco, and cotton, marginal comparative advantage in groundnuts, and a clear disadvantage in sugarcane; food crops have a marginal comparative advantage because of low yields. When the comparative cost analysis meant to determine optimal investment portfolio is examined along with actual incentive schemes, it emerges that the crops with clear comparative advantage (cocoa, rubber, cotton, and tobacco) are also the crops subject to net taxation, while crops with clear comparative disadvantage (rice) have high net protection (World Bank 1985). Many countries have complicated tariff structures and an array of effective protection rates across industries. These need to be rationalized and simplified as an initial step toward trade liberalization, albeit within the context of economic nationalism. Also, if domestic economies are to benefit from the new price relativities, the structural bottlenecks which introduce long response lags in the production of exportables and importables need to be urgently removed.

Countries with overvalued exchange rates should move beyond debating whether or not to adjust exchange rates to considerations of the critical prerequisites for minimizing the pains of exchange rate adjustment. The first prerequisite is an objective assessment of the degree of overvaluation and the initial determination of an operationally effective devaluation strategy: whether the required exchange rate adjustment should be achieved in one large-scale devaluation or whether it should be a series of sequential devaluations.[18] Care must be taken to ensure that a mass psychology of inflationary expectations does not develop. Second, structural bottlenecks with respect to rural infrastructures should be removed to make the agricultural sector flexible and responsive to the new set of relative prices, if the country is to gain on the export side. Third, structural bottlenecks in those sectors that produce import substitutes should be removed to reduce the inflationary impact of devaluation. Fourth, increased government revenues as a result of devaluation need to be consciously spent on the productive sector rather than services on government account to curb the inflationary consequences. Finally, there must be sufficient socio-political discipline to ensure that increases in money income do not wipe out the gains from devaluation; in

---

[18] Several African countries (Nigeria, Zambia, Ghana, etc.) are experimenting with second-tier foreign exchange markets. The same prerequisites for successful devaluation apply.

particular, real effective foreign exchange rates must not be allowed to depreciate after devaluation.

The general inflationary consequences of exchange rate adjustment and the real income effects drastically reduce food entitlements of the poor, given the large weight of food in their consumption baskets. Structural adjustment loans and IMF conditionalities do not adequately consider the distributive impact of exchange rate adjustments, declines in real incomes, elimination of farm input subsidies, and draconian cuts in public expenditures on food entitlements of the poor and vulnerable groups. This is partly due to the changing philosophical position of the World Bank—from the equity and poverty-conscious Bank of the MacNamara days to the market forces posture of the Bank under Clausen. Recipients of loans from the World Bank—IMF system contemplating structural and balance-of-payments adjustments must seriously consider their socio-political consequences.

(e) External aid

Experience in Ethiopia and the Sahel shows that the absorptive capacity of recipient countries needs to be urgently built up so that food entitlements of the genuinely needy do not get bogged down in bureaucratic snarls. This is the lesson from Europe's Marshall Plan: successful technical aid requires technical absorptive capacity. Emphasis must shift from the use of food aid as an emergency tool to its use as a development tool (Singer 1985). Beyond the short-term augmentation of food availability, countries must, in the medium term, utilize available aid to rehabilitate a rural economy that has been battered by prolonged drought and generations of bad government policies.

Part of the problem lies in the inability of some aid recipients to articulate aid needs beyond panic responses to drastically reduced food entitlements of the rural population. Donors quite often dictate the pace with the result that long-term issues and problems are left till another day and another crisis.

World Bank-assisted Agricultural Development Projects raise several issues (Lele 1975). First, are they necessary? As sources of extra resource flows, they are necessary in a region with built-in biases against agriculture and rural development and where the level of political discipline leaves little room for patient programming for a sector with long production lags.

Second, are the designs appropriate? Issues here include programmatic content (rural infrastructures versus agriculture; production versus marketing and storage; physical infrastructures versus social infrastructures such as potable water; strengthening of existing Ministry of Agriculture institutions versus setting up of parallel institutions, etc.). Some of the projects in Nigeria have been criticized for being strong on physical infrastructures and weak on agriculture; this is only a matter of sequencing as the development of rural infrastructures must precede the agricultural package. Though the older generation of ADPs excluded social infrastructures, the newer projects have added these on. Some have argued that rather than encourage new exotic parallel institutions, the World Bank should have concentrated on strengthening mainstream Ministries of Agriculture, especially because of the need for continuity after project completion. State Ministries of Agriculture are part of larger centralized public bureaucracies where possession of or access to bureaucratic power in state organizations has not been translated into a set of moral obligations to the larger society, beyond self, ethnic group, sectoral interest group, or region.[19] Efforts to strengthen Ministries of Agriculture must recognize the total (civil service) institutional milieu; otherwise, such efforts will fail, just like the earlier efforts of USAID to strengthen African faculties of agriculture within the general service conditions of a university.

Third, is there too much World Bank control? The loan agreements typically designate some key positions that must be filled by internationally recruited staff which in the majority of cases also turn out to be expatriates. This is an unsatisfactory position especially in countries with large pools of qualified personnel: when the Project Manager and the Financial Controller are expatriates who play a dominant role in the commitment of millions of dollars of borrowed money, the situation becomes clearly unacceptable.

Finally, have they been successful? By the internal rate of return criterion, the first generation of ADPs in Nigeria were successful. When other benefits such as those from feeder roads, institution building, and the social benefits of the development of a culture of sustained recurrent and capital funding of agriculture by state governments are added, the verdict would be more positive. After the first generation of generalized institutional and infrastructural development, the projects should move to the next phase of industry-wide farm commodity programming and interregional production specialization support cutting across state (administrative) boundaries.

Donor agencies have acquiesced to aid requests in pursuit of policies that have little or no prospect of utilizing a country's resources efficiently. No doubt donor agency officials had good intentions in hoping that they could assist in reforming from the inside but in many cases they have only succeeded in making bad situations worse.

(f) Rural institutions and mobilization

There are at least two options. One is to introduce exogenously from the public bureaucracy particular forms of rural institutions, such as farmers' co-operatives, which will liaise with relevant public and private institutions on matters of interest to members. Results from country experiences are mixed, though there appear to be more failures than successes. Reasons for failure include poor management, financial fraud, loss of confidence, and erosion of membership loyalty. Other reasons include lack of appropriate incentives sufficiently to motivate farmers to want to become and remain members of co-operative societies, inadequate supervisory management from govern-

[19] See the discussion in IDS (1983, 1985).

ments, and a failure on the part of public officials to appreciate why farmers join the institutions that they join. Unless farmers can clearly see the gain from joining co-operarive societies, all efforts of centralized public bureaucracies to round up farmers to join co-operatives will be wasted. A further limitation of the exogenous approach is that farmers are being more or less coerced to join co-operatives and other institutions against the background of an ideological vacuum, the absence of an explicit statement on the type of society that the country seeks to build, and little harmony between these organizations and the overall social milieu.

The second option, the endogenous demand side approach, seeks to utilize the strengths of existing rural institutions. Innovative programming is required to undertake an inventory of existing rural institutions such as age groups, guilds, women's associations, thrift societies; an analysis of the services that they render; their management structure; their conduct and performance; their funding, strengths, weaknesses, problems, and constraints, with a view to identifying ways of utilizing them for dissemination of new technology in production, processing, marketing, and credit, to mention a few. This option reaches the creative energies of rural people, using institutions that they can identify with and have confidence in. The notion that all rural Africa is waiting to be co-operativized must be discarded in favour of rural institutional pluralism. To continue to blame the failure of exogenously introduced institutions (e.g. co-operatives) on financial scandals, poor management, etc. woefully fails to explain why existing rural institutions have not been similarly fatally plagued by such ills but rather have survived from year to year and from one generation to the next. The demand side approach here advocated stresses farmers' demands for the institutional forms they believe will service their interest best, not necessarily those promoted by public bureaucrats. Unless the endogenously inspired network of rural institutions is utilized, the benefits of public programmes will continue to flow to unintended beneficiaries.

6.4.   *Summary and conclusions*

In the attempt to explain the stagnation and decline of sub-Saharan African agriculture, four broad classes of problems and constraints were reviewed (section 6.2). First were those dealing with rural infrastructures. Second were those dealing with the generation and dissemination of new technology. Third were problems relating to harmful economic policies, including agricultural pricing policy. Special attention was paid to the vulnerability of agriculture to overvalued exchange rates. The fourth set of problems related to institutional arrangements and ambiguities which often result in overlapping functions, duplicated roles, and sterile institutional rivalry.

In many countries, there is a 'parastatal syndrome', the perennial desire of policy makers to create a public parastatal almost as soon as a major problem emerges. These parastatals often serve as conduit pipes. Of fundamental importance here is the persistent ambiguity about the proper role of government in African agriculture. In most countries, government has simply assumed the wrong roles, often in competition with the private sector. There is urgent need for a shift of emphasis from these negative and 'interventionist' roles to the 'positive' role of the state in the form of provision of public services, food security, rural credit, productive infrastructure, etc. Other problems reviewed in section 6.2 include agricultural research and extension, rural roads, storage, rural electrification, irrigation, and the problem of centralized public bureaucracies trying to manipulate highly decentralized smallholder production systems.

A review of policy options must necessarily indicate priorities so that policy prescriptions can maintain a sharp focus. Proper sequencing of policy interventions ensures that the full benefits of dynamic—as opposed to static or contemporaneous—complementarities of policy instruments will be realized. A structuralist approach to Africa's food problems begins with the removal of the infrastructural bottlenecks: rural roads, rural markets, marketing infrastructures, rail–road network, potable water, rural health care facilities, primary schools, and rural electricity, to mention a few. The chapter emphasized the needs of the rural household as producer-consumer for physical as well as social infrastructures. Without these, efforts to transform Africa's agriculture will have limited success.

Once the rural infrastructures are in place, Africa's rural economy will be in a position to adopt profitable new agricultural technologies. Sustained adoption of new technology, in turn, requires favourable economic incentives and policies. These include input and output pricing, exchange rates, interest rates, wages, monetary and fiscal policies.

Further, infrastructures, new technology, and a favourable economic environment will not produce the required transformation if the required institutions are not in place and if institutional pluralism leads to role ambiguities. Section 6.3 discussed a range of policy options relating to all these ingredients of a transformation of African agriculture, with sustained focus on the need to promote the food entitlements of the rural population (especially the vulnerable groups).

In maintaining a focus on policy as a main factor in the stagnation and decline of African agriculture, the question that needs to be answered is: why do agricultural policies tend to produce 'unintended consequences' and 'unintended beneficiaries'? Why do observed policy mistakes persist from year to year, from one regime to another, from one development plan to another, and from country to country? The traditional (supply side) approach to perennial policy mistakes focuses on bureaucratic processes, inadequate budgetary allocations, infrastructural bottlenecks, etc. but fails to explain the persistence of these causal factors.

This is what George Stigler, the Nobel Laureate, had to say on the matter:

To believe, year after year, decade after decade, that the protective tariffs or usury laws to be found in most lands are due to confusion rather than purposeful action is singularly obfuscatory. Mistakes are indeed made by the best of men and the best of nations, but after a century are we not entitled to question whether the so-called 'mistakes' produce only unintended results? . . . Alternatively stated, a theory that says that a large set of persistent policies are mistaken is profoundly anti-intellectual unless it is joined to a theory of mistakes. (Stigler 1982: 10)

What is required to understand the policy options facing African agriculture is a demand side approach which seeks to explain why policy makers do what they do. Who are the main policy participants as formulators and implementors? How do they relate to the various interest groups and the recurring class of 'unintended beneficiaries'? Are the people often explicitly labelled as 'unintended beneficiaries' truly unintended? Or are they the 'implicitly intended beneficiaries' of food and agricultural policy? And what is the nature of social relationships between policy makers and the implicitly intended beneficiaries (explicit 'unintended beneficiaries') as opposed to the explicitly intended beneficiaries? These questions take us far into theory of pressure groups, self-interest, altruism, and coalition, an area we cannot develop in this chapter.

Appendix 6.1.   Federal government parastatals in agriculture, Nigeria, 1983

(a) Crop marketing
1. Nigerian Grains Board
2. Nigerian Cocoa Board
3. Nigerian Palm Produce Board
4. Nigerian Rubber Board
5. Nigerian Cotton Board
6. Nigerian Groundnut Board

(b) Agricultural production
7. Nigerian Grains Production Company
8. Nigerian Beverages Production Company
9. Nigerian Rootcrops Production Company
10. Naiwa Mechanized Farms Ltd.
11. Nigerian Dairies Company Ltd.
12. Nigerian Poultry Production
13. Madara Company
14. National Livestock Production Company
15. Nigerian Food Company

16. Bauchi Meat Company

(*c*) *Agricultural credit and input supplies*

17. Nigerian Agricultural and Cooperative Bank
18. National Centre for Agricultural Mechanization
19. National Animal Feeds Company

(*d*) *River Basin Development Authorities*

20. Anambra-Imo River Basin Development Authority
21. Benin-Owena River Basin Development Authority
22. Chad Basin Development Authority
23. Cross River Development Authority
24. Hadejia-Jama'are River Basin Development Authority
25. Lower Benue River Basin Development Authority
26. Niger Delta River Basin Development Authority
27. Niger River Basin Development Authority
28. Ogun-Oshun River Basin Development Authority
29. Sokoto-Rima River Basin Development Authority
30. Upper Benue River Basin Development Authority

(*e*) *Agricultural research institutes*

31. Institute for Agricultural Research, Samaru, Zaria
32. Kainji Lake Research Institute
33. Forestry Lake Research Institute
34. Leather Research Institute
35. National Cereals Research Institute
36. Lake Chad Research Institute
37. National Veterinary Research Institute
38. Nigerian Stored Products Research Institute
39. Rubber Research Institute of Nigeria
40. Nigerian Institute for Oil Palm Research
41. Nigerian Institute for Trypanosomiasis Research
42. Nigerian Institute for Oceanography and Marine Research
43. National Root Crops Research Institute
44. National Horticultural Research Institute
45. Agricultural Research and Extension Liaison Service
46. National Animal Production Research Institute
47. Cocoa Research Institute of Nigeria
48. Institute of Agricultural Research and Training

(*f*) *Agricultural Development Projects (ADPs)*

49. Gongola State Integrated ADP
50. Mambilla Plateau Integrated ADP
51. Lagos State Integrated ADP
52. Accelerated Development Area Project
53. Ayangba ADP
54. Lafia ADP
55. Bida ADP
56. Ilorin ADP
57. Ekiti-Akoko ADP
58. Oyo-North ADP
59. Ogun ADP

60. Kaduna ADP
61. Sokoto ADP
62. Bauchi ADP
63. Kano ADP
64. Anambra ADP
65. Bendel ADP
66. Borno ADP
67. Cross River ADP
68. Imo ADP
69. Rivers ADP

(g) *Others*

70. Nigerian Institute for Water Resources
71. Bendel State World Bank Assisted Third Cocoa Project
72. Ondo State World Bank Assisted Third Cocoa Project
73. Oyo State World Bank Assisted Third Cocoa Project
74. IBRD Assisted Bendel State Nucleus Estate, Small Holder Oil Palm Project
75. IBRD Assisted Oil Palm Project, Imo State
76. IBRD Agricultural Technical Assistance Project

Note: Practically all parastatals in categories (*a*), (*b*), (*c*) (*d*), and (*e*) are wholly owned by the federal government. Most of the parastatals in (*f*) and (*g*) are jointly owned with the states. Parastatals wholly owned by the 19 state governments are excluded from the list.

References

ALLISON, C., and GREEN, R. (1983), 'Stagnation and Decay in Sub-Saharan Africa: Dialogues, Dialectics and Doubts', *IDS Bulletin*, 14.

ANTIIONIO, Q. B. O. (1983), *Recipe for Developing Nigerian Agriculture: Improved Agricultural Marketing for Economic Development in Nigeria* (University Lectures, University of Ibadan, 1983/4).

ARNDT, T. M., DALRYMPLE, D. G., and RUTTAN, V. M. (eds.) (1977), *Resource Allocation and Productivity in National and International Agricultural Research* (Minneapolis, Minn.: University of Minnesota Press).

BIENEFELD, M. (1983), 'Efficiency, NICs and the Accelerated Development Report', *IDS Bulletin*, 14.

BOYCE, J., and EVENSON, R. (1975), *Agricultural Research and Extension Programmes* (New York: Agricultural Development Council).

COLCLOUGH, C. (1985), 'Competing Paradigms in the Debate about Agricultural Pricing Policy', *IDS Bulletin*, 16/3.

DE JANVRY, A. (1981), *The Agrarian Question and Reformism in Latin America* (Baltimore, Md., and London: Johns Hopkins).

EICHER, C. K. (1982), 'Facing up to Africa's Food Crisis', *Foreign Affairs*, Fall.

—— and BAKER, D. C. (1982), 'Research on Agricultural Development in Sub-Saharan Africa: A Critical Survey', MSU International Development Paper 1 (East Lansing, Mich.: Department of Agricultural Economics, Michigan State University).

FALUSI, A. O., and WILLIAMS, L. B. (1981), 'Nigeria Fertilizer Sector: Present Situation and Future Prospects', IFDC Technical Bulletin 18 (International Development Centre).

FELDMAN, D., and IDACHABA, F. S. (eds.) (1984), *Crop Marketing and Input Distribution in Nigeria*, Federal Agricultural Coordinating Unit (Ibadan: Intec Printing).

FISHEL, W. L. (ed.) (1971), *Resource Allocation in Agricultural Research* (Minneapolis, Minn.: University of Minnesota Press).

GODFREY, M. (1983), 'Expert Orientation and Structural Adjustment in Sub-Saharan Africa', *IDS Bulletin*, 14.

IDACHABA, F. S. (1974), 'Policy Distortions, Subsidies and African Rural Employment Creation: A Second Best Approach', *Indian Journal of Agricultural Economics*, 29/2.

—— (1976), 'Econometric Estimation of Input Demand Functions in Developing Agriculture: The Case of Pesticides in Ondo, Oyo and Ogun States of Nigeria', *Indian Journal of Agricultural Economics*, Oct.–Dec.

—— (1977), 'Pesticide Input Subsidies in African Agriculture: The Nigerian Experience', *Canadian Journal of Agricultural Economics*.

—— (1980), 'Agricultural Research Policy in Nigeria', Research Report 17 (Washington, DC: IFPRI).

—— (1981a), 'Agricultural Research Staff Instability: The Nigerian Experience', *Nigerian Journal of Agricultural Sciences*, 3.

—— (1981b), 'Agricultural Research Resource Allocation Priorities: The Nigerian Experience', in Daniels, D., and Nestel, B. (eds.), *Resource Allocation to Agricultural Research* (Ottawa: International Development Research Centre).

—— (1982), 'Water Resources Development and Nigeria's Green Revolution Pro-

gramme', paper presented at a National Symposium on the Role of River Basin
Development Authorities in the Green Revolution, Lagos, 6–7 Dec.

——(1985), 'Priorities for Nigerian Agriculture in the Fifth National Development
Plan 1986–90', Occasional Paper 1 (Ibadan: Federal Agricultural Coordinating
Unit).

——(1987), 'Agricultural Research in Nigeria: Organization and Policy', in Ruttan and
Pray (1987).

Institute of Development Studies (1983, 1985), *IDS Bulletin* (University of Sussex).

JOHNSON, G. L., SCOVILLE, D. J., DIKE, G. K., and EICHER, C. K. (1969), 'Strategies
and Recommendations for Nigerian Rural Development, 1969–1985', Consortium
for the Study of Nigerian Rural Development (CSNRD) 33 (East Lansing, Mich.:
Michigan State University).

LELE, UMA (1975), *The Design of Rural Development: Lessons from Africa* (Baltimore,
MD., and London: Johns Hopkins).

LIPTON, M. (1985), 'The Place of Agricultural Research in the Development of
Sub-Saharan Africa' (Washington, DC: Consultative Group on International
Agricultural Research, World Bank).

MELLOR, J. W. (1966), *The Economics of Agricultural Development* (Ithaca, NY: Cornell
University Press).

ODERO-OGWEL, L. A., *et. al.* (1985), 'Africa's Persistent Food Crisis', mimeo (Addis
Ababa: Food and Agricultural Organization of the United Nations).

OLAYIDE, S. O., *et al.* (1972), *A Quantitative Analysis of Food Requirements, Supplies and
Demands in Nigeria, 1968–1985* (Ibadan: Ibadan University Press).

PINGALI, P. L., BIGOT, Y., and BINSWANGER, H. P. (1985), 'Agricultural Mechaniza-
tion and the Evolution of Farming Systems in Sub-Saharan Africa', Discussion Paper
ARU 40 (Washington, DC: Research Unit, Agriculture and Rural Development
Department, World Bank).

RUTTAN, V. W., and PRAY, C. (eds.) (1987), *Policy for Agricultural Research* (Boulder,
Colo., and London: Westview Press).

SEN, A. K. (1985), 'Food, Economics and Entitlements', Working Paper 1 (Helsinki:
WIDER); published in the first volume of this book.

SINGER, H. (1985), 'Some Problems of Emergency Food Aid for Sub-Saharan Africa',
IDS Bulletin, 16.

STIGLER, G. J. (1982), *The Economist as Preacher and Other Essays* (Chicago, Ill.:
University of Chicago Press).

WHARTON, C. R., jun. (1967), 'The Infrastructure for Agricultural Growth', in
Harman, M. S., and Jonston, B. F. (eds.), *Agricultural Development and Economic
Growth* (Ithaca, NY: Cornell University Press).

World Bank (1981), *Accelerated Development in Sub-Saharan Africa: An Agenda for
Action* (Washington, DC: World Bank).

——(1983*a*), *Tanzania Agricultural Report* (Washington, DC: World Bank).

——(1983*b*), *Zimbabwe Agricultural Sector Study* (Washington, DC: World Bank).

——(1984), *Towards Sustained Development in Sub-Saharan Africa: A Joint Programme
of Action* (Washington, DC: World Bank).

——(1985), *Ghana Agricultural Sector Review* (Washington, DC: World Bank).

——(1986*a*), *World Development Report 1986* (Oxford: Oxford University Press).

——(1986*b*), *Poverty and Hunger* (Washington, DC: World Bank).

7

Poverty and Food Deprivation in Kenya's Smallholder Agricultural Areas

Judith Heyer

7.1. *Introduction*

In this chapter, the nature and extent of food-related poverty in smallholder agricultural areas of Kenya is explored. We look at what makes some areas more successful than others in minimizing poverty and food deprivation. Differences between Kenya's smallholder agricultural areas allow a discussion that is relevant to many other parts of sub-Saharan Africa.

Kenya is one of the minority of sub-Saharan African countries with a relatively impressive record in the 1970s and 1980s, as far as conventional indicators of macroeconomic performance are concerned, although the 1980s has been a more difficult period. Smallholder agriculture has made an important contribution to Kenya's economic performance. Kenya has also done relatively well on basic needs (Ghai 1987). But there is still great poverty in Kenya and this could change for the worse very easily.

The population growth rate is very high in Kenya, at well over 4 per cent a year. Most of the increasing population has to be accommodated in smallholder agricultural areas. The challenge of increasing population densities is met more successfully in some areas than in others, as we will see.

Food is not the only problem and perhaps not even the most important problem faced by the poor in Kenya. The poor in Kenya's smallholder agricultural areas suffer from intermittent food shortages some of which are acute, and their diets can be monotonous, but the grossly inadequate intake of food that is prolonged enough to show up in high incidences of severe malnutrition is rare. There is severe deprivation of other kinds: ill health is still a very major problem, as are drudgery; poor education; inadequate water; limited transport; violence; and inability to participate in the society at large.

It is always difficult to find good indicators of the aspects of poverty in which one is interested. One of the obvious food-related poverty indicators that is available for Kenya's smallholder agricultural areas is child malnutrition, although this appears to be as much an indicator of poor health as of grossly inadequate intake of food. (Svedberg, in Chapter 5 above, comes to a similar conclusion from examining the evidence from a number of sub-Saharan African countries.) There are reasonable figures on child mortality, which is another very serious problem in Kenya's smallholder agricultural areas,

I am grateful to Amartya Sen for inspiration; Carl Eicher and Mahendra Shah for helpful comments; Michael Lipton for helpful discussions; Jean Drèze for his editorial work; and students and colleagues at Oxford for widening my perspectives.

particularly for the poor. It does not appear to be that closely related to malnutrition, though. We discuss the evidence on these and inadequate food expenditure in this chapter.

The chapter starts with an introductory section on the location of poverty in Kenya. Then there is an account of regional differences between Kenya's smallholder agricultural areas based mainly on evidence from the 1970s. The fact that much of the relevant survey evidence is now somewhat dated is a problem, but putting it together with other evidence allows a characterization of different smallholder agricultural areas that continues to be broadly accurate into the 1980s. The next section of the chapter contains evidence on food-related indicators of poverty: food expenditure, food intake, child nutritional status, and child mortality in different smallholder agricultural areas. Finally, in the last section of the chapter there is a discussion of particular factors that might explain why the incidence of poverty and food deprivation differs from one region to another in the way that it does. The discussion centres on processes that produce high incidences of poverty and food deprivation in some smallholder agricultural areas, and much lower incidences in others. Much of the discussion is relevant not only to Kenya. Similar factors are involved in other parts of sub-Saharan Africa as well.

7.2.   *The location of poverty in Kenya*

There has been a good deal of work on the incidence of poverty in Kenya, most of it based on the 1974/5 Integrated Rural Survey and other mid-1970s figures. In this work, households with income or expenditure below certain levels are defined as poor. There has also been work on other aspects of poverty, and some of this is discussed in more detail later in the chapter. But for the broad poverty profile it is the household income and expenditure measures that are used. The estimates are shown in Table 7.1.

Kenya's population is overwhelmingly rural: between 80 and 90 per cent of the population still lived in rural areas in the 1970s. The rural areas can be divided broadly into pastoral, smallholder agricultural, and large farm areas. In the mid-1970s, it was estimated that more than 70 per cent of the total population lived in the smallholder agricultural areas, 7 per cent or more in the pastoral areas (estimates of the pastoral areas' population still vary considerably), and 7–8 per cent in the large farm areas. The urban areas were dominated by Nairobi, responsible for 50 per cent of the urban population, and Mombasa, another 25 per cent or so. There were a number of smaller towns, few of them of any size, and many smaller market centres with a few shops, scattered through the rural areas.

In most of the estimates poverty is defined as income insufficient to ensure that minimum food requirements are met. The definition of minimum food requirements is always problematic. The level of dietary adequacy regarded as critical varies from 2,250 calories per person per day (Crawford and Thorbecke

Table 7.1 Profile of poverty in Kenya, 1974/5

	House-hold poverty line (Kshs p.a.)	Total popu-lation (000)	% of popu-lation	Popu-lation below poverty line (000)	% of class	% of poor
Pure pastoralists	4,285	725	5.0	615	85.0	14.6
Pastoralist farmers	2,700	75	0.5	25	33.3	0.6
Migrant farmers	2,000	200	1.4	110	55.0	2.6
Landless						
Poor occupations	1,900	420	2.9	210	50.0	5.0
Good occupations	n/a	245	1.7	—	—	—
Smallholders (IRS1)	2,000	10,340	72.3	2,990	28.9	71.0
Nairobi	2,150	700	4.9	20	2.9	0.5
Other urban	2,150	700	4.9	40	5.7	1.0
Squatters						
Large farms	2,000	600	4.2	200	33.3	4.8
'Gap' farms[a]	n/a	270	1.9	—	—	—
Large farmers	n/a	20	0.1	—	—	—
All categories		14,295	100.0	4,210	29.5	100.0

[a] Farms in the smallholder areas too large to be included in the smallholder category, but excluded from the large farm census.

Source: Collier and Lal (1980).

1980; Greer and Thorbecke 1986a, 1986b) to 60 per cent of WHO/FAO age- and sex-specific requirements the highest of which is 1,344 (60 per cent of 2,240) calories per adult male (Fischer and Shah 1985). Another of the more serious problems with these estimates of poverty is the lack of reliability of the income and expenditure data.

The figures differ according to whether poverty is estimated at the house-hold or the individual level; whether and how adjustments are made for household size and composition; the level of food requirements regarded as minimal; and the extent to which adjustments are made for regional differences in diet and food prices. Some of the estimates are income based; some are based on expenditure. But as they all use the same data sources, it is perhaps not surprising that the differences are, on the whole, minor.

There are some broad general statements that can be made about poverty in Kenya. (1) Urban incomes are generally so much higher than rural, and the incomes even of the urban poor are so much higher than those of the rural poor, that urban poverty can be regarded as a relatively minor problem. (2) Poverty is widespread in all smallholder agricultural areas, but the incidence is consider-ably higher in some than in others. (3) In common with other parts of sub-Saharan Africa, poverty is most serious of all in arid pastoral areas. (4) Poverty is not as serious a problem among estate labourers as among other groups in Kenya.

From the overall poverty profile, shown in Table 7.1, the severity of poverty among pastoralists and others in arid and very arid areas is evident. The pastoral areas suffer from recurring food shortages sufficiently severe to attract government and other relief measures and from time to time they suffer from famine. The estimates from the mid-1970s suggest that as many as 85 per cent of the pastoral households and 50 per cent of the migrant farmer households in arid and semi-arid areas had incomes below those required to ensure that minimum food requirements were met *on average* over the years. Pastoralists make up 15 per cent of Kenya's poor population and migrant farmers 3 per cent, according to the estimates summarized in Table 7.1. But while the plight of the people living in pastoral areas in Kenya is very serious, the numbers involved are small compared with those in agricultural areas that also suffer from severe poverty and deprivation. It is those in smallholder agricultural areas that are more often ignored and neglected.

Most of the smallholder agricultural areas are in and around the highlands that run from the south-east of Nairobi to the west and north-west. There are also smallholder areas at lower altitudes towards the coast. Plantations and large mixed farms are interspersed with these.

All of the different estimates of poverty in the smallholder agricultural areas suggest that at least 25 per cent of the smallholder agricultural households were poor enough not to be able to afford what were regarded as minimum food requirements in 1974/5. Collier and Lal, estimating the proportion at 29 per cent, conclude that this group represented about 76 per cent of the total poor in Kenya at that time. Although the severity of poverty may not be as great as in arid areas, the numbers affected in smallholder areas make them a dominant part of the poverty problem in Kenya.

The other groups that figure in the overall totals for Kenya are squatter households on large farms, 33 per cent of which were estimated to be poor in the mid-1970s, constituting 5 per cent of the population estimated to be poor at that time; and the poor in urban areas. These latter are possibly underestimated at 2 per cent of the total, but even if the estimates were substantially increased, urban poverty would still be a relatively minor part of the problem.

Food crises, or famines, affecting the arid and semi-arid areas sufficiently seriously to produce a collapse of normal economic relationships, depriving a large proportion of the population of entitlements, and resulting in a significant amount of abnormal migration, have occurred periodically in Kenya. In the past 25 years, there were major food crises in 1962, 1966, 1974/5, 1980/1, and 1982–4. The government prevented the 1982–4 crisis from developing into a major famine (Cohen and Lewis 1987). Continuous relief has been provided in many of the famine-prone areas, but this has by no means always been adequate or well targeted. For pastoralists, recovery from a major drought that significantly reduces the livestock population takes many years. Migrant farmers and others farming semi-arid lands may experience many years of seriously reduced crop production in addition to those officially recognized as years of famine.

The problem of arid areas is now receiving a good deal of attention in Kenya. It is not the main focus of this chapter, which concentrates instead on poverty in the smallholder agricultural areas. We now move on to discussing these in more detail.

7.3. *Kenya's smallholder agricultural areas*

General economic background

The main purpose of this section is to provide a characterization of the different smallholder agricultural areas in Kenya. We start with a brief description of the general economic context within which they operate.

Kenya's economy is heavily agricultural and smallholder agriculture is a major part of the agricultural sector. There is very little mining or mineral production, but tourism has been a significant source of foreign exchange. What has been happening in the manufacturing sector is very important for the smallholder agricultural areas. Manufacturing became increasingly significant in the 1960s and 1970s. Following a period of vigorous import substituting industrialization, it was making a contribution of between 12 and 14 per cent to GDP in the 1970s. Its rate of growth has slowed down considerably since (Sharpley and Lewis 1988). Much of the manufacturing is large scale modern manufacturing, concentrated in and around Nairobi and a few other urban centres. Traditional and smaller-scale manufacturing activity, long discouraged in Kenya, is undoubtedly underenumerated but still relatively less important.

Despite the priority attached to the development of manufacturing, particularly in the 1960s and 1970s, Sharpley estimates that urban bias was mild over that period (Sharpley 1981). Urban growth contributed to agricultural growth as well as vice versa. The bias towards urban areas almost certainly became even less marked in the 1980s.

The contribution of agriculture to GDP in the 1970s varied from 30 to 40 per cent, depending on the world prices of its major exports. These were very high in the mid-1970s. By the 1970s the relative shares of small farms and large farms in the value of gross marketed output stabilized at roughly equal amounts. The share of small farms in value added was higher than their share in marketed output however, so small farms were much more dominant in the agricultural sector in terms of value added and employment than the marketed output figures would suggest.

The overall performance of the Kenya economy was impressive in the 1960s and 1970s, and even in the 1980s, by sub-Saharan African standards (Ghai

1987). GDP growth averaged 6.2 per cent per annum at constant prices from 1964 to 1972, and 4.4 per cent a year from 1972 to 1981 (Republic of Kenya 1984). It slowed down a bit after that. Annual per capita GDP growth averaged 2.7 per cent in the earlier period, but only 0.6 per cent in the later one, and it became negative in the 1980s. Much of the GDP growth was based on agriculture, though manufacturing and services, including tourism, were also important.

Formal sector employment has been growing, though less rapidly than formal sector output, and less rapidly than the labour force. Smallholder agricultural areas still have to accommodate most of the increases in population for which Kenya is notorious.

Smallholder agriculture has been heavily emphasized since the 1950s. Transport is good by sub-Saharan African standards, and marketing is quite well organized. Smallholder agricultural areas in Kenya are all relatively accessible, concentrated along the central axis running from the south-east to the west and north-west of the country. But differences in accessibility are a major part of the explanation of differences in performance. Transport is still a very major consideration in Kenya.

There is a large amount of labour migration, and given the low level of wages it is common for (male) labourers to leave their families in the rural areas so that they may continue to contribute to the family income. There is relatively little migration across international borders, although Uganda was important for western Kenya until the mid 1970s. The loss of migration opportunities there has been an important factor in western Kenya.

The experience of Kenya's smallholder agricultural areas has been mixed. There are many aspects of the Kenya situation that are relatively favourable by sub-Saharan African standards, but high and rapidly growing population densities make the situation much more difficult than it would otherwise be.

Differences in per capita wealth and income are quite large, as are differences in inequality and poverty. This is not only the result of differing access to the opportunities available in the national economy. It is also the result of factors operating within the smallholder agricultural areas themselves. Some are more dependent on agriculture than others, and some more on export crops than on food crops or livestock. Some are more dependent on non-agricultural activities or on income generated outside. Factors such as these help to explain variations in performance with respect to poverty and deprivation, as will be seen later in this chapter.

The 1974/5 Integrated Rural Survey

The 1974/5 Integrated Rural Survey, henceforward IRS1, is one of the main sources of data used in this chapter. It was a relatively small survey, covering 1,668 smallholder agricultural households in the 6 of Kenya's 7 provinces in which there are smallholder agricultural areas, but it was unusually ambitious in scope and coverage for sub-Saharan Africa and the first broad comprehensive rural survey covering smallholder areas throughout Kenya. It was designed for disaggregation to the provincial or agroecological zone, not below. One could certainly do better if there were data at the district level, or below. But although there are *some* comprehensive district-level figures, notably those from the child malnutrition survey of 1982, district-level data are still generally sparse and weak. The major source of district-level economic data is the 1982 Rural Household Budget Survey, results of which are still not available except in very summary form in the 1988 Economic Survey. Given this, there was no real alternative to the use of provincial level figures for the purposes of this paper. Provinces are large and heterogeneous, but there is some sense in which regional economies are contained broadly within provincial boundaries. There are substantial barriers to movement across the ethnic boundaries with which many of the provincial boundaries coincide. There are also a number of other distinctive features characterizing the different provinces' interaction with the larger economy.

Map 7.1 shows the provincial distribution of smallholder agricultural areas. The 6 provinces in which smallholder agriculture is important are: Central, Eastern, Nyanza, Western, Rift Valley, and Coast. The smallholder agricultural areas are relatively compact. It is only in Rift Valley and Central Province that large farm areas are at all widely interspersed with smallholder agricultural areas. The smallholder agricultural areas contain small towns and market centres, not covered by the rural survey data. There are no real villages. Patterns of settlement have always been dispersed.

Table 7.2 shows total area, population, and population density in the 6 Kenya provinces in which smallholder agriculture is important. Table 7.2 also shows the smallholder agricultural populations, household sizes, and household expenditure and income levels derived from IRS1 for 1974/5. The IRS sample is too small for accurate total population estimates. It overestimates the smallholder agricultural population considerably, as the table shows.

There are well-known problems in using statistics based on households. Problems of data omission resulting from recording at the household level are probably the most serious for our purposes. Variations in household size and composition are less of a problem as much of what follows focuses only on the relative importance of different components of household income and expenditure.

The IRS1 sample did not include landless households in the smallholder agricultural areas. Their numbers were estimated in the 1976/7, 1977/8, and 1978/9 surveys (IRS2–4) as shown in Table 7.3. The estimates vary considerably from survey to survey, the total for all provinces from 14 per cent to 22 per cent. The landless include rich as well as poor households. In Kenya the incidence of poverty among landless households is not dissimilar to the incidence among landed households (Livingstone 1986).

The other main group excluded from IRS1 was households with farms of 20 hectares and over. Their numbers were estimated in IRS4 in 1978/9 at 53,000,

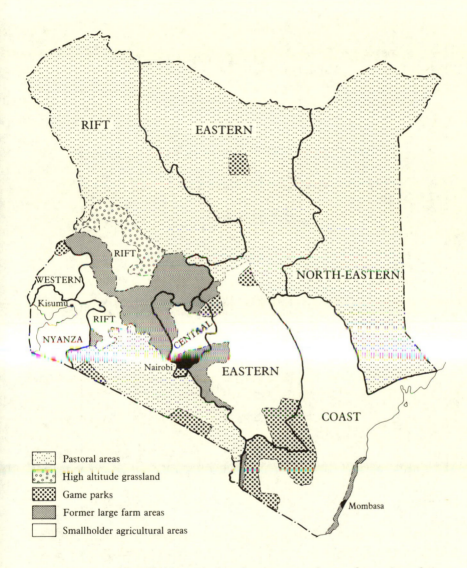

RIFT

EASTERN

RIFT

WESTERN

Kisumu

RIFT

NORTH-EASTERN

NYANZA

CENTRAL

Nairobi

EASTERN

COAST

Mombasa

Pastoral areas

High altitude grassland

Game parks

Former large farm areas

Smallholder agricultural areas

Map 7.1. Kenya smallholder agricultural areas, pastoral areas, former large farm areas, and game parks

Table 7.2 Land area, population, and population density in 1969 and 1979 and smallholder population, mean expenditure, and mean income in 1974/5, in different provinces, Kenya

	Hectares (000)	Hectares HPLE[a] (000)	Population (000)		Persons/ha		Persons/ha HPLE[a]		Smallholder agricultural population 1974/5						
									Persons (000)	Households (000)	Mean household size		Mean expenditure (Kshs p.a. 1974/5)		Mean income per household (Kshs p.a. 1974/5)
			1969	1979	1969	1979	1969	1979			Persons	Adult-equivalents	Per household	Per capita	
Central	1,317 (3)	912 (14)	1,676 (17)	2,346 (18)	1.27	1.78	1.34	2.57	2,290 (22)	330 (22)	6.95	4.94	4,473	644	4,241
Eastern	15,576 (36)	955 (15)	1,826 (19)	2,578 (19)	0.12	0.17	1.91	2.70	2,380 (23)	353 (24)	6.74	4.84	4,020	596	3,486
Rift	16,388 (38)	2,151 (33)	1,958 (20)	2,948 (22)	0.12	0.18	0.91	1.37	674 (7)	90 (6)	7.51	5.35	3,426	456	4,577
Coast	8,304 (19)	568 (9)	698 (7)	977 (8)	0.08	0.12	1.23	1.76	562 (5)	70 (5)	8.04	5.89	3,139	390	3,325
Western	820 (2)	741 (11)	1,328 (14)	1,833 (14)	1.62	2.23	1.79	2.48	1,893 (18)	255 (17)	7.44	5.42	2,808	377	2,494
Nyanza	1,253 (3)	1,225 (19)	2,122 (22)	2,644 (20)	1.69	2.11	1.73	2.16	2,542 (25)	386 (26)	6.58	4.95	2,546	387	3,911
All provinces	43,658 (101)	6,552 (101)	9,608 (99)	13,346 (101)	0.22	0.31	1.47	2.04	10,341 (100)	1,486 (100)	6.97	5.06	3,450	495	3,652

[a] Percentages in brackets.

Note: HPLE: High potential land equivalents.

Sources: Livingstone (1986); Republic of Kenya (1977a).

Table 7.3 Percentages of households landless in different provinces in Kenya, 1976/7, 1977/8, 1978/9

	Central	Eastern	Rift	Coast	Western	Nyanza	All
IRS2 (1976/7)	10.3	8.9	17.6	27.0	8.2	16.6	13.7
IRS3 (1977/8)	16.6	19.2	28.0	20.3	6.6	16.6	17.9
IRS4 (1978/9)	21.8	19.7	36.8	29.0	8.7	15.8	21.6

Source: Republic of Kenya (1981).

and they were mostly located in Rift, Eastern, and Nyanza Provinces (Republic of Kenya 1981).

Central Province

Central Province is the rich, fertile, highland area bordering on the northern edge of Nairobi, that dominates people's thinking on Kenya's smallholder agricultural areas. It is typical of a relatively well-endowed agricultural area serving a large urban area nearby. Important also are its neighbouring large farms and estates. It benefits from the urban and estate markets for agricultural produce, the commuting possibilities, and many of the advantages offered by access to the centre of power and influence. It has long had a relatively large share of government expenditure. It is *the* success story among Kenya's smallholder agricultural areas from the mid-1950s to the 1980s.

In Central Province, the interaction between the national and the local economy has enabled per capita incomes to rise in a situation of rapidly increasing population densities. But Central Province is not that far ahead of other provinces, and average income is only about twice the income associated with the poverty line. Furthermore, success has been accompanied by a continuing high incidence of poverty as will be seen in the next section.

Central Province shares with the smallholder agricultural areas in most other provinces in Kenya high levels of labour migration (Table 7.4). It also has the unusual advantage of high levels of relatively lucrative employment for commuters from smallholder agricultural areas.

Table 7.5 shows the proportion of household income derived from different sources in different provinces. There are some problems with the figures here. A later set of figures from the 1982 Household Budget Survey is available in the Economic Survey 1988, and this is a helpful check on the plausibility of the figures in Table 7.5. The figures for Rift Valley, Central, Eastern, and Western Provinces look fairly robust, set against those of the 1982 Household Budget Survey, but those for Coast and Nyanza look much less so. More generally, it has been suggested (ILO 1982), from a comparison with national income figures, that IRS1 underestimates income from agriculture. Kongstad and Monsted (1980) have suggested that it underestimates income from non-farm business activities too. It is important to bear these points in mind in using the

Table 7.4 1979 province of enumeration by province of origin, Kenya (%)

Province of enumeration	Province of origin						
	Central	Eastern	Rift	Coast	Western	Nyanza	All
Nairobi	6	4	1	2	5	4	5
Central	82	2	2	1	1	1	15
Eastern	1	91	0	1	0	0	18
Rift	9	1	95	1	8	5	21
Coast	1	2	0	96	1	2	9
Western	0	0	1	0	82	1	12
Nyanza	0	0	1	0	2	87	17
North-Eastern	0	0	0	0	0	0	2
Total	99	100	100	101	99	100	99
Total no. (m.)	2.6	2.9	2.8	1.2	2.1	2.9	15.3
Net migration as % 1979 population	−11.7	−6.4	+14.8	+13.0	−15.7	−10.1	

Source: Republic of Kenya (n.d.).

figures as a framework for the discussion of the structure of income in smallholder agricultural areas in the different provinces.

Remittances and regular employment earnings together provided Central Province smallholder agricultural households with an estimated 31 per cent of their income in 1974/5 (Table 7.5), a figure that seems plausible. A substantial amount of outside employment income is invested in the smallholder agricultural areas, mainly in agriculture which contributed 50–60 per cent to income in 1974/5. Central Province has good agricultural resources that provide the basis for the production of high-value export crops, and also for relatively high-value food crops for the nearby markets in Nairobi, smaller Central Province towns, and estates. Central Province is one of the most 'export' or 'cash-crop'[1] oriented of the smallholder agricultural areas in Kenya (Table 7.6). The fact that there was a high level of government expenditure on roads, starting in the 1950s, helps to make the agricultural produce markets more lucrative. The relatively good transport and distribution system also helps in making inputs widely and relatively cheaply available. Smallholder agriculture is relatively commercialized in Central Province which has high

---

[1] The terms 'export' and 'cash crop' are problematic, as is the term 'food crop'. 'Food crop' is used here to refer to basic foods, mainly staple foods consumed in large quantities by large numbers of people in Kenya. 'Export' is used to refer to 'non-food' products exported from the smallholder agricultural areas to the wider economy or beyond. It includes beverages (tea, coffee), pyrethrum, cotton, sugar and other products. 'Cash crop' also includes basic food products sold in significant quantities on the national or international market. The most important 'cash crops' not included in 'exports' are maize and dairy products.

Table 7.5 Sources of income per smallholder household in different provinces, Kenya, 1974/5

	Farm operating surplus		Non-farm operating surplus		Regular employment		Casual employment		Remittances		Other gifts		Total	
	Kshs	%	Kshs	%	Kshs	%	Kshs	%	Kshs	%	Kshs	%	Kshs	%
Central	2,120	50	326	8	921	22	365	9	393	9	117	3	4,241	101
Eastern	1,911	55	491	14	368	11	353	10	300	9	62	2	3,486	101
Rift	3,086	67	303	6	796	17	135	3	163	4	94	2	4,577	99
Coast	828	25	626	19	449	14	474	14	829	25	117	4	3,325	101
Western	1,186	47	126	5	559	22	165	7	407	16	50	2	2,494	99
Nyanza	2,789	71	365	9	415	11	108	3	178	5	57	1	3,911	100
All	2,081	57	354	10	566	16	252	7	324	9	75	2	3,652	101

Source: Republic of Kenya (1977a).

Table 7.6 Composition of sales of agricultural output per household in different provinces, Kenya, 1974/5

	Food crops		Export crops		Cattle (net)		Other livestock (net)		Milk		Total		Sales as % of total output
	Kshs	%	Kshs	%	Kshs	%	Kshs	%	Kshs	%	Kshs	%	
Central	369	24.7	411	27.6	218	14.6	122	8.2	371	24.9	1,491	100.0	47.5
Eastern	421	31.6	337	25.3	299	22.4	134	10.0	143	10.7	1,334	100.0	53.6
Rift	475	24.9	115	6.0	577	30.3	260	13.6	479	25.1	1,906	99.9	47.2
Coast	168	30.6	2	—	154	28.1	99	18.0	126	23.0	549	99.7	45.0
Western	291	52.9	20	3.6	136	24.7	42	7.6	61	11.1	550	99.9	36.2
Nyanza	994	84.0	192	16.2	−161	−13.6	10	0.8	149	12.6	1,184	100.0	38.2
All	528	44.3	231	19.4	143	12.0	88	7.4	201	16.9	1,192	100.0	44.8

Source: Republic of Kenya (1978).

levels of expenditure on purchased inputs compared with other smallholder agricultural areas in Kenya (Table 7.7).

Investment in Central Province agriculture has been cumulating significantly particularly since the Swynnerton Plan was introduced in the 1950s. Central Province now has a relatively good stock of agricultural capital in the form of tree crops (coffee and tea), high-quality livestock, etc. What is perhaps surprising is that mean farm operating surplus is not higher as compared with that of other provinces. This is partly a reflection of the alternative opportunities available to Central Province people, but it also reflects the density of population on agricultural resources.

IRS1 suggests that there is relatively less non-agricultural business activity in Central Province than in other smallholder agricultural areas. Although this may in part be a statistical artefact (the figures from the 1982 Household Budget Survey suggest that Central Province is much more like other areas in this respect), it would not be surprising if a large proportion of consumer goods needs were met from outside Central Province smallholder agricultural areas because of the relatively good agricultural opportunities, and the relatively well-developed transport and distribution system. Another factor could be the degree of urbanization within Central Province itself.

The proximity of outside employment opportunities makes an important contribution to Central Province smallholder agricultural areas. This makes it possible for wage and salary earners, and businessmen, to maintain an involvement in their smallholdings, providing the opportunity to oversee investments and increasing the incentive to invest in them. Whether, or for how long, this will continue is an interesting question. It is possible that Central Province people involved in employment or self-employment outside the rural areas may get more detached from the rural areas over time, and that

Table 7.7 Expenditure per household on purchased inputs and wage labour in different provinces, Kenya, 1974/5

	Crop inputs (Kshs)	Livestock expenses (Kshs)	Wages (Kshs)	% of farm operating surplus			
				Crop inputs	Livestock expenses	Wages	Total
Central	271	156	227	13	7	11	31
Eastern	202	34	149	11	2	8	20
Rift	391	162	284	13	5	9	27
Coast	31	2	242	4	—	29	33
Western	96	16	119	8	1	10	20
Nyanza	137	3	99	5	—	4	9
All	185	56	161	9	3	8	20

Source: Republic of Kenya (1977a).

they may gradually relocate their families in the process. But as of the late 1980s, there is little to suggest that this is happening. There are strong incentives to keep families in the rural areas maintaining family smallholdings, and making substantial contributions to family income in the process. Schools, housing, and access to health services are better in Central Province small-holder agricultural areas than those to which most of these families would have access in Nairobi or elsewhere. Further, retirement in Central Province rural areas still provides a more attractive alternative for many than retirement outside. This makes it likely that there will be a continuation of reasonable prosperity in Central Province smallholder agricultural areas, as they continue to provide homes for families of those involved in the wider economy, places of retirement for outside income earners, and a basis for productive activities that continue to feed on the proximity of the urban and estate economy and to some extent also the local prosperity with which this is associated. The continuing prosperity of the urban and estate economy is crucial. If it is not maintained, then Central Province will become more congested in relation to the resources that have been built up there. There are some signs that this is happening in the 1980s already.

Despite all this, however, average incomes in Central Province do not appear to be as high as those in Rift Valley smallholder areas, nor do they appear to be much higher than in smallholder agricultural areas in other parts of the country. A lot of wealth has been going out as well as coming in: people are using Central Province as a base from which to make investments elsewhere too.

There are parallels all over sub-Saharan Africa in the relatively well-endowed agricultural areas near major centres of economic activity. Each has its own particular features, but the benefits to a relatively well-endowed agricultural area of a growing urban population nearby, bringing market opportunities, employment opportunities, and other opportunities of a less tangible kind, enabling the rural areas to sustain increasing populations at higher standards of living, are something that is repeated throughout sub-Saharan Africa. There are many examples, and one always has to remember that they are by no means typical of smallholder areas in general: only of those particularly well located and often also particularly visible.

Eastern Province

Eastern Province is much more diverse ecologically than Central Province and combines rich, fertile, hill areas with extensive drier lowland areas, east and north-east of Nairobi. It has nearly as high smallholder agricultural incomes as Central Province if we are to believe IRS1 (and the 1982 HHBS figures published in the Economic Survey in 1988), despite the fact that it has less favourable agricultural resources. Its population is more dispersed. It is considerably further away from Nairobi than much of Central Province which greatly reduces its commuting possibilities. However it has more links with

Mombasa and with the tourist industry, and it has a long tradition of trade and business activity. This is an area with rather mixed agricultural resources, supplemented by substantial trade and business incomes, and substantial income from migration. Furthermore, it is reasonably commercialized. It does not have the commuter incomes of Central Province, nor the very nearby urban markets, but it does have reasonably good access to markets a little further away.

Remittances were responsible for a similar percentage of the income of smallholders in Eastern Province smallholder agricultural areas to that in Central Province in 1974/5, but the absolute amounts were lower. Outside employment income was considerably lower. Remittances and outside employment earnings together amounted to little over 20 per cent of Eastern Province income in 1974/5 (Table 7.5).

Agriculture was responsible for 55–65 per cent of income. It is perhaps surprising that, despite a considerable proportion of lower-potential land, agricultural incomes were as high as they were, but population densities are not as high in Eastern Province as in Central. Eastern Province smallholders have invested a large amount in coffee and tea: this is reflected in relatively high incomes from export crops in 1974/5 (Table 7.6). There are more low-quality cattle, and there is more 'food' production in Eastern Province than in Central. Further, Eastern Province smallholder agriculture is considerably less commercialized than that of Central Province. Its use of purchased inputs is relatively low (Table 7.7).

Non-agricultural activity was bringing in a substantial amount of Eastern Province smallholder income in 1974/5. This was partly serving the local market (Table 7.8). It was also serving national and international markets. Eastern Province produces craft products, mainly baskets and woodcarvings, that sell well to tourists and as direct exports. It also has a long tradition of trade with other parts of Kenya, in tobacco among other things. Table 7.8 suggests a high degree of involvement in internal as well as external trade and business.

In many ways Eastern Province appears to be in a much less favourable position than Central Province. It is hardly surprising that its income per household is lower. It has generally poorer agricultural resources, less good transport and infrastructure, and less easy access to Nairobi. Within its constraints, however, it seems to do quite well, on average. Yet it still has relatively high levels of poverty, as will be seen in the next section. Conditions vary enormously from one part of the province to another: parts of Eastern Province still suffer from severe food shortages and even famine in some years.

Western Province

Western Province is one of the poorest of the smallholder agricultural areas, and it was, until the late 1970s at least, a classic labour reserve. It is a highland area adjacent to the Uganda border and rather far from Nairobi or other major centres of economic activity except the former large farm areas to the north and

Table 7.8 Percentage of smallholdings engaged in different types of non-agricultural activity in different provinces, Kenya, 1976/7

	Central	Eastern	Rift	Coast	Western	Nyanza	All
Services	14.0	26.2	10.9	25.0	21.4	14.7	17.8
of which							
Transport	4.3	6.5	2.3	—	4.2	.8	3.3
Hotels, etc.	3.9	10.0	1.7	—	2.1	4.7	4.5
Trade	7.3	8.0	5.9	6.4	12.1	13.7	9.3
of which							
Shops	3.4	4.0	3.2	0.8	5.0	3.8	3.7
Butchers	1.1	1.9	2.0	0.8	2.5	2.1	1.9
Petty trade	0.3	0.2	0.4	1.6	2.8	1.6	1.0
Repairs	3.1	8.2	2.5	3.2	6.2	8.9	5.4
of which							
Clothing	1.4	1.5	0.9	—	0.9	2.5	1.4
Bicycle	—	1.3	0.4	1.6	0.3	1.2	0.8
Furniture	0.8	1.9	0.4	—	0.9	2.1	1.2
Shoes	—	1.9	0.2	0.8	1.5	1.2	1.0
Building	0.8	9.4	0.8	2.4	4.6	6.9	4.7
Pottery	—	1.0	0.2	0.8	0.9	5.4	1.7
Metal products	1.7	1.0	0.7	0.8	1.2	1.6	1.2
Food, beverages, tobacco manufacture	5.9	18.3	20.5	24.2	25.1	36.5	22.3
of which							
Beer brewing	3.4	5.9	15.0	2.4	17.6	26.0	13.4
Resource extraction	2.5	14.5	10.0	9.7	14.0	17.5	12.1
of which							
Wood cutting	1.1	3.4	5.9	—	4.0	4.5	3.7
Fishing	0.3	—	0.2	4.0	4.6	5.4	2.2
Wood products	11.8	17.0	11.2	6.4	14.0	16.9	14.0
of which							
Charcoal	6.7	7.2	7.3	1.6	4.0	6.0	6.1
Furniture	2.0	1.3	0.9	0.8	2.5	1.4	1.5
Calabashes	0.3	3.0	1.6	—	2.8	5.8	2.7
Saw mills	1.7	0.2	0.4	—	0.3	0.8	0.6
Plant, animal fibre products	4.2	19.6	13.2	21.0	6.8	12.2	12.4
of which							
Mats, bags, clothes	1.9	12.1	0.2	16.6	2.4	6.6	5.7
Textile and clothes	2.0	6.3	5.0	4.0	3.4	4.2	4.3
Hides and skins	—	0.4	5.9	—	0.3	0.6	1.4
TOTALS	41.4	123.0	74.9	99.9	106.3	134.3	100.9

Note: many households recorded more than one activity each, or none, so percentages do not add to 100.

Source: Republic of Kenya (1977c).

west. There has been a high level of labour migration (Table 7.4). Remittance income formed a very important component of total income in 1974/5 (Table 7.5). Regular employment, much of it in the nearby large farm sector, contributed an income that was higher than in Nyanza, Coast, or Eastern, but not as high as in Rift or Central Provinces. Remittance and regular employment income together made up 38 per cent of total income in 1974/5 according to IRS1.

The relatively large remittance and employment earnings from outside appeared to be financing consumption as much as investment in Western Province in the mid-1970s. In this sense Western Province appeared to be a classic example of a labour reserve, providing a place for migrant labourers' families to reside and contribute, relatively modestly, to family income. But the investment, and/or sufficient growth in outside income, that was needed to enable it to accommodate its increasing population was missing. This appears to have changed somewhat since, as suggested below.

The agricultural resource base in Western Province is not strong: population densities are high and markets are a problem. Western Province agriculture was based on rather low-value products in 1974/5: only 4 per cent of the smallholders grew coffee and only 5 per cent tea (Table 7.9), and only 4 per cent of the value of marketed agricultural output came from high-value export crops. Food crops contributed 53 per cent and livestock 43 per cent (Table 7.6). Western Province smallholders also used relatively little purchased inputs and hired labour (Table 7.7).

Non-agricultural activity in Western Province was providing very little income in 1974/5. Western Province appeared to be too far from markets for other products that might have been exported from the area; and there was too

Table 7.9 Percentage of smallholders growing selected crops in different provinces, Kenya, 1974/5

	Central	Eastern	Rift	Coast	Western	Nyanza	All
Tea	18	11	15	—	4	n/a	12
Coffee	45	44	5	1	5	21	27
Pyrethrum	8	7	16	—	—	18	9
Cotton	—	2	5	5	20	17	9
English potatoes	86	52	8	2	—	1	32
Local Maize	95	99	59	94	74	80	86
Hybrid Maize	67	30	92	19	73	36	50
Beans	98	86	22	28	79	39	69
Sorghum	1	16	1	2	37	75	30
Millet	—	19	51	—	45	33	24

Note: n/a = not available.

Source: Casley and Marchant (1978), derived from IRS1, reprinted in Livingstone (1986: Table 9.19).

low an income level within the area to support much activity serving local markets. In the mid-1970s the non-agricultural sector had the characteristics of a residual sector. It occupied a high percentage of the population (Table 7.8), but brought in only a very small proportion (5 per cent) of the income (Table 7.5). Much of this appears to have been changing recently.

It is not surprising to find signs of really high levels of poverty in Western Province in the 1970s, as will be seen in the next section, but this too may have been changing.

The distance of Western Province from centres of economic activity was an important factor, both from the point of view of markets and in making it less easy for people employed outside to keep an active and continuous involvement in their home areas. This appears to have been changing since the mid-1970s though: there has been substantial investment in the area, including a huge paper mill and a large sugar factory; there has been a general increase in development expenditure in the area; and there has been a real boom in the neighbouring area to the north and north-west in which Western Province people have played a major part. The Uganda situation which has made it possible for Western Province people to profit from black marketeering and smuggling may also have been a factor.

Nyanza Province

Nyanza Province, also in western Kenya, had one of the lowest recorded 1974/5 mean smallholder household expenditures according to IRS1, but by no means the lowest mean income. The IRS1 figures seem particularly problematic for Nyanza, but something can be said using other evidence as well.

In Nyanza agricultural income dominates, and the economy is relatively uncommercialized still. Nyanza has long been recognized as neglected in terms of government development expenditure (Table 7.10). This shows up in things like transport but extends to the whole range of government services crucial to agriculture and other economic activity. There are high levels of labour migration.

Agriculture contributed a large proportion of income—over 70 per cent of total household income in 1974/5 if IRS1 is to be believed on this count (Table 7.5). It is dominated by food crops. Nyanza has long been a major source of food for other parts of Kenya. Livestock are important too, but relatively low quality only. Export crops were estimated to have contributed 16 per cent to total agricultural sales in 1974/5. They are concentrated in a few areas. Expenditures on purchased inputs and hired labour are both far lower than in any other smallholder agricultural area (Table 7.7).

Remittance income is almost certainly higher than the IRS1 figures suggest. The proportions of migrants are quite high and other estimates of remittances, including that of the 1982 Household Budget Survey, are much higher.

The fact that regular employment income is low is not surprising. There are

Table 7.10 Selected statistics on government expenditure and services in different provinces, Kenya

| | Expenditure per capita, 1973/4 (Kshs) | | | | Health centres per m. population, 1975 (no.) | Dry-season drinking water within 1 mile 1976 (% above + /below − national av.) | Adult literacy, 1982 (%) | |
| | Total recurrent | Development | | | | | Male | Female |
		Roads	Curative health	Secondary education				
Central	9.7	9.7	0.50	0.53	15	+15	72	57
Eastern	6.4	4.9	0.64	0.20	9	−16	62	39
Rift	8.8	5.5	0.34	0.19	23	−3	53	30
Coast	13.1	6.3	0.97	0.25	6	−40	58	35
Western	4.1	4.7	0.18	0.23	19	+20	62	38
Nyanza	3.3	1.9	0.58	0.15	10	−4	54	29

Sources: Republic of Kenya (1977a, 1977d); Hazlewood (1979); Bigsten (1980).

relatively few commuting possibilities within reach of people living in Nyanza smallholder agricultural areas. Total earnings from remittances and regular employment income taken together were almost certainly responsible for a relatively low proportion of total income in 1974/5, though not as low as IRS1 suggests.

Income from non-agricultural activity appears to be reasonable, supporting the local economy as much as anything (Table 7.8).

Nyanza is a relatively well-endowed, still rather traditional economy, not integrated as much as others with the outside economy (although sales of food and export crops are important), and not very developed within.

It has rather high levels of poverty, and appalling levels of child mortality and child malnutrition as will be seen. These are not just the result of low income.

Rift Valley Province

Rift Valley smallholder agricultural areas are the richest of all, according to IRS1 which is almost certainly correct on this count. They are relatively far from Nairobi, but they border on the heart of the large farm area and benefit from its employment opportunities, its markets, and the proximity of its well-developed infrastructure. Agricultural resources are exceptionally favourable by Kenya smallholder agricultural standards, and population densities are still relatively low, as is total population (Table 7.2). Rift Valley smallholder agricultural areas have benefited disproportionately from the opportunities for outmigration provided in the subdivision of the former large farm sector into small farm areas not included in IRS1 data. There is a fair amount of inmigration. Remittances are very low, but outside employment earnings are high. Contrary to those of Central Province, the outside employment earnings of Rift Valley smallholders nearly all come from employment on nearby large mixed farms. There are relatively few Rift Valley people working far from home (Table 7.4).

Some of the relatively plentiful outside income is invested in agriculture, less in export crops than in maize and livestock. Livestock contributed 69 per cent and food crops 25 per cent of the value of smallholder agricultural sales in 1974/5. Export crops only contributed 6 per cent (Table 7.6). Agricultural income per household is higher than in any other smallholder agricultural area and it completely dominates total income. Rift Valley smallholder agriculture is relatively commercialized. Smallholders use comparable levels of purchased inputs and hired labour to those in Central Province, and considerably more than those in any other province (Table 7.7). Here too, the Rift Valley smallholder agricultural economy benefits enormously from the proximity of the large farm sector.

Non-agricultural activities appear to be rather unimportant among Rift Valley smallholders, although these may be underestimated (Kongstad and Monsted 1980). There appear to be higher proportions of the population involved in beer brewing, wood cutting, and hides and skins production than in other areas, as one might expect in an area so rich in natural resources (Table 7.8).

Rift Valley smallholder agricultural areas are a good example of well-endowed and reasonably well-supported rural areas, if rather backward in some respects. These areas are accommodating their populations at reasonable income levels, but, as will be seen, poverty, malnutrition, and child mortality still appear to be quite serious.

Coast Province

Coast Province also has a relatively small smallholder agricultural population (Table 7.2). It extends over the large hinterland stretching inland from the area around Mombasa. It has decidedly poor agricultural resources, but benefits from its proximity to Mombasa and (with its beaches and its proximity to some of the more popular game parks) more generally from the tourist industry.

Remittances were almost certainly overestimated in the IRS1 survey, at 25 per cent of smallholder income (the much lower 1982 Household Budget Survey figure looks much more plausible). The high regular employment income figure was probably nearer the truth though. Agriculture appeared to contribute only 25–40 per cent of total income according to IRS1, depending on how much casual employment income is attributed to smallholder agriculture. This may be an underestimate, but there is very little export production and Coast smallholder agricultural products are generally low valued. There was relatively little government development expenditure in Coast smallholder agricultural areas until recently. Extremely low levels of purchased inputs are used in agriculture. There is a large amount of wage employment, however. Much of this seems to be associated with traditional production relations rather than modern commercialization (Parkin 1972).

Coast Province smallholders appeared to have relatively high non-agricultural business incomes. This is partly due to the relatively poor agricultural opportunities, and partly to tourist and other local outlets for non-agricultural business activities (Table 7.8).

Despite the relatively high incomes from employment and from non-agricultural activities, Coast Province smallholders have average total incomes that are certainly much lower than those of smallholders in Central and Rift Valley Provinces, and probably lower than others as well. Coast malnutrition and child mortality figures are appalling as will be seen shortly.

Overall summary

The extent to which areas are dependent on agriculture, and within agriculture on exports; the extent to which non-agricultural activities supplement agricultural ones, and what sorts of non-agricultural activities; the extent to which members of smallholder households are involved in outside employment, locally or further afield; all contribute to differences in the levels of income and expenditure attained in smallholder agricultural areas, as well as in the prospects for their future growth. They also make a difference to the inequality of wealth and incomes, and the incidence of poverty.

Central Province's ability to accommodate its rapidly increasing population is very closely related to the success of the national economy and also to conditions in the international markets for coffee and tea; the success of Rift Valley smallholder agricultural areas is much more closely related to the success of the large farm sector, and also to conditions in the national markets particularly for maize and livestock. Eastern Province and Coast Province are heavily dependent on tourism as well as other aspects of the national economy. Nyanza depends on its ability to continue to sell food, and to a lesser extent export crops. Western Province used to be critically dependent on outside employment opportunities but there are signs of more internal development now. Thus, it is partly a question of how well the national and international economy are doing, and the terms on which rural areas relate to these. It is also a question of what is going on internally. Government development expenditure is an important part of this.

Although mean smallholder agricultural household incomes and expenditures are higher in some provinces than in others, in all provinces they are rather low. The highest provincial mean household expenditure of smallholder households covered by IRS1 in 1974/5 was less than twice the lowest. Furthermore, the highest provincial mean household expenditure was only a little over twice that associated with the poverty line that has been defined for Kenya. This does not suggest that smallholder agricultural households in any area were doing well. It is not surprising that in all areas poverty is still a serious problem.

7.4.   Food-related poverty indicators for Kenya's smallholder agricultural areas in the 1970s

The links between different indicators

There are many different aspects of poverty that could be considered here. In this paper, the emphasis is on those for which evidence is available that are in some sense food-related. These include poverty, food poverty, food intake, child malnutrition, and child mortality. The interrelationships between them are complex as Fig. 7.1 suggests.

Fig. 7.1 shows the connections between different food-related poverty indicators, some linked as much with public as with private expenditure. There are substantial 'leakages' and 'injections' at different stages. Starting near the top of Fig. 7.1, the relationship between household expenditure and household food expenditure depends on the relative priority attached to non-food expenditure in the household. Food may be the most important component of expenditure in poor households, but expenditures on such

Kenya Indicators

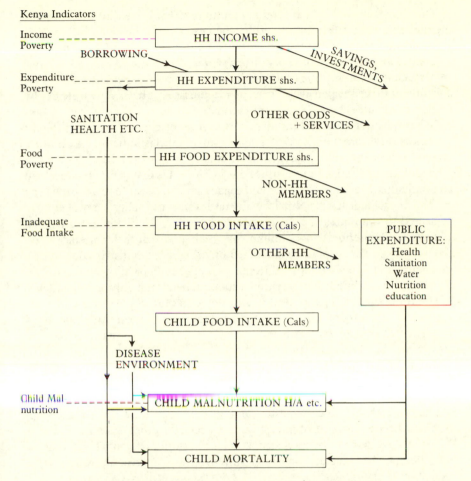

Fig. 7.1. The links between food-related poverty indicators

things as shelter, clothing, and health-related goods and services are also vital, and there are many other claims on expenditure in poor households as well. Some of the non-food elements of household expenditure may have as important an influence on nutritional status and mortality as food. In 1974/5, 75 per cent of the mean expenditure of Kenya's smallholder agricultural households was on food. (This may be an overestimate as non-food subsistence does not appear to have been included in the expenditure total.) As has been found elsewhere, the percentage of expenditure on food varied surprisingly little between different income groups, although the absolute amounts varied substantially. Thus 25 per cent or more of the total expenditure of poor households went on non-food items that compete strongly even at very low levels of income.

The efficiency with which food expenditure is converted into food intake measured in calories is represented by the next link in the chain in Fig. 7.1. Low-income groups spend higher proportions of their food budget on low-cost calories. The proportion of expenditure represented by food may not change very much between income groups in Kenya, but more expensive calories are substituted for less expensive calories as income rises. This is shown clearly by Greer and Thorbecke (1986a) who estimate the relevant elasticities. Their estimates of calorie elasticities at poverty levels of expenditure in different provinces vary from 0.63 to 0.70. Their estimates of elasticities of expenditure on food at the same levels of expenditure vary from 0.88 to 1.17.

One of the more important distinctions in Fig. 7.1 is that between household and individual measures. Poverty and inadequate intake of food are measured at the household level. Nutritional status and mortality, however, are measured for individuals. Poor correlations between (individual) nutritional status and (household) food intake, or (individual) nutritional status and (household) poverty, could be explained by differences in distribution within the household. Likewise the differences between mortality and poverty. Furthermore, we know that nutritional status depends not only on food intake, but also on such things as health and demographic status, activity rates, feeding and cooking practices, and health care. Public expenditure may be as important as private expenditure, and public expenditure may not be very closely correlated with private expenditure.

The final link in Fig. 7.1 might be between malnutrition and mortality. Mortality is not very closely related to nutritional status however. Somewhat different health variables seem to be involved in each case.

Factors such as those suggested in Fig. 7.1 complicate the relationships between different aspects of poverty and between different estimates of these. Many of them have to be seen against a background of seasonal and year-to-year fluctuations that are poorly captured by available data. Kenya is no exception here.

Expenditure and income poverty

Tables 7.11, 7.12, and 7.13 show the different estimates of inadequate food intake, child malnutrition, and child mortality for the different provinces. The estimated incidences of income (and expenditure) poverty are also shown in Table 7.11. The most widely used estimates of poverty in Kenya are the income poverty estimates, despite the fact that income includes many transient elements in any particular year. In IRS1, nearly 7 per cent of the households were recorded as having negative incomes in 1974/5. These reflect such things as losses from the death of livestock and poor crop yields, events that can easily affect particular households in any one year. The households with negative income in IRS1 were not on the whole poor: they had a relatively high expenditure profile. They are not therefore counted as poor for the purpose of estimating income poverty. The other major problem with the income poverty

Table 7.11 Incidence of poverty and food poverty among smallholders in different provinces, Kenya, 1974/5 (% households)

	Poverty		Food poverty (Greer and Thorbecke 1986a)	Severity of poverty index (Greer and Thorbecke 1986a)	Inadequate food intake (Fischer and Shah 1985)
	Household income <Kshs 2,000	Household expenditure <Kshs 400/AE[a]			
Central	22	10	33	0.028	14
Eastern	35	22	32	0.026	18
Rift	19	37	45	0.039	33
Coast	31	36	42	0.046	26
Western	50	34	46	0.037	36
Nyanza	38	37	41	0.039	32
All	34	29	39	0.034	27

[a]: AE = Adult Equivalent
Sources: Republic of Kenya (1977a); Greer and Thorbecke (1986a); Fischer and Shah (1985).

Table 7.12 Children[a] less than 90% height for age, smallholder agricultural areas in different provinces, Kenya, 1977, 1978/9, 1982

	Nutrition Survey 1 (1977)		Nutrition Survey 2 (1978/9)		Nutrition Survey 3 (1982)	
	%	Mean	%	Mean	%	Mean
Central	26	93.6	21	94.5	24	94.0
Eastern	34	92.8	24	94.6	27	93.3
Rift	25	94.0	24	94.2	22	94.9
Coast	(14)	(96.3)	40	92.9	39	92.2
Western	16	95.0	24	94.0	29	92.9
Nyanza	21	94.7	34	93.6	33	93.4
All	24	94.1	27	94.5	28	93.6

[a] 1977: 12–48 months; 1978/9: 6–60 months; 1982: 3–60 months.
Source: Republic of Kenya (1983).

Table 7.13 Estimates of child survival, life expectancy, and child mortality in different provinces, Kenya, 1969 and 1979

	1969		1979: no. dying in 1st 5 years per 1,000 live births
	% of births surviving to age 3 years	Life expectancy at birth (years)	
Central	89	60.1	85
Eastern	84	49.8	128
Rift	87	54.1	132
Coast	80	43.4	206
Western	80	43.5	187
Nyanza	75	38.6	220
Nairobi	89	56.8	104

Sources: Anker and Knowles (1977); Republic of Kenya (n.d.).

estimates is that they are not adjusted for household size and composition. This means that they underestimate poverty in Coast, Rift, and Western Provinces relative to Nyanza, Central, and Eastern where household sizes are smaller.

Greer and Thorbecke (1986a) estimated expenditure poverty using an adult-equivalent standard. This is also shown in Table 7.11. The trouble with this measure, as also with the income measure, is that it does not allow for differences in costs of living between provinces. These are quite large, particularly where food is concerned.

'Food poverty'

Greer and Thorbecke's estimates of 'food poverty' are also shown in Table 7.11. A household is deemed to be 'food-poor' if its total food expenditure is less than that required to purchase what is defined as 'an adequate diet' for its members. The 'adequate diet' is defined as the normal diet around the poverty level in each case. This is thus a measure of the willingness of a household to allocate enough of its budget to food, and its *capability*, given its total food budget, to be adequately fed, rather than whether it is actually adequately fed. It does not take account of the possibility that food expenditure is more inefficient in some households than in others, or that it may be poorly distributed among the members of the household.

Greer and Thorbecke (1986a), in a very careful exercise, used observed regional diets around the poverty line for their estimates. The diets that were normal around the levels consistent with the consumption of the relevant number of calories varied considerably in cost between provinces. This reflected differences in prices but also differences in the quality of the diet regarded as normal around the poverty level. Greer and Thorbecke did a number of estimates based on slightly different assumptions in these and other respects. These showed their provincial rankings of food poverty, reproduced in Table 7.11, to be robust.

Greer and Thorbecke also provided an estimate of the *severity* of food poverty which is reproduced in Table 7.11. They defined this as the sum of the squared deviations of the food expenditure of the food-poor from the poverty level, normalized over the number of households concerned. This is equivalent to a weighted sum of the food expenditure gaps of food-poor households, the weights being equal to the expenditure gaps in each case. Thus, households with large deficits have a significantly greater influence on the index than households whose deficits are small. The absolute numbers are difficult to interpret, but the rankings are just as interesting for our purposes as the rankings of the incidence of food poverty. Central and Eastern Provinces have the lowest proportions of households suffering food poverty, and also the lowest extent of shortfall suffered by food-poor households. Rift and Western Provinces may have the highest proportions of food-poor households, but they rank similarly to Nyanza where the severity of food poverty is concerned. It is Coast Province which has the most severe shortfall in total, although it does not rank quite so low on the proportion suffering from food poverty. Coast Province must be regarded as the most seriously affected by food poverty on this count.

The food poverty ranking is different from the income and expenditure poverty ranking, in that Central Province does not seem much better off than Eastern Province as far as food poverty is concerned; Rift, Western, and Nyanza all seem fairly similar, although in Nyanza a smaller proportion of households is affected; and Coast looks very much the worst off if the severity of poverty is taken to be the more significant measure. A comparison between expenditure poverty and food poverty figures makes it look as if non-food expenditure is a particularly high priority in Central and Coast Provinces, and a particularly low priority in Western Province, compared with other provinces. It might be dangerous to make too much of this, however, without investigating it further.

Food intake

Fischer and Shah (1985) estimated the adequacy of household food intake. In their measure the efficiency of the conversion of food expenditure into calories is taken into account (but not the efficiency of the distribution between household members). They took IRS1 household food intake figures and compared them with FAO/WHO 1973 age- and sex-specific requirements for a moderately active population, the highest adult male requirement for which was 2,440, and female 1,840, calories per day. Households with intakes less than 60 per cent of their total requirements, given their age- and sex-specific composition, were defined as poor.

The provincial rankings of poverty obtained by Fischer and Shah are similar to those obtained by Greer and Thorbecke. The differences are that Rift appears on a par with Nyanza, but Western much worse; that Coast appears considerably better than Western, Nyanza, and Rift; and that Central appears considerably better than Eastern at the other extreme. It is quite difficult to accept Fischer and Shah's rankings, however. They try to capture variations in the efficiency with which food expenditure is converted into calories among households around the food poverty level, but in doing so they have to accept food intake figures which are unreliable (Fischer and Shah 1985).

Child malnutrition

We next consider the estimates of the incidence of child malnutrition in 1977, 1978/9, and 1982. Malnutrition estimates are only available for children in the 0 to 5 years age group, not for adults or for children of other ages. The percentage of children aged 1 to 4 years who were less than 90 per cent of the height for age of the reference population, shown in Table 7.12 for the different provinces, is the measure that is most relevant here. Estimates of height for age, weight for age, and weight for height are all available. However, wasting is less of a problem than stunting in Kenya. Furthermore, stunting reflects relatively longer-term problems of undernourishment which are more relevant to our concerns in this chapter. This justifies a concentration on height for age indicators.

    There were serious problems with sampling at the Coast in the 1977 survey, so the Coast figure for that year should be ignored. Drought biased the 1977 Eastern Province figure downwards, but drought is a reality that needs to be taken seriously in discussions of malnutrition. The Western Province figure that appears high in 1977 is significant. Preliminary investigations of relevant cohorts of children suggest that there was a real increase in child malnutrition in Western Province between 1977 and 1982 (Test *et al*. n.d.).

    It is difficult to make serious comparisons between provinces when the estimates from the different surveys range so widely for each province: indeed the differences between surveys are often greater than the differences between provinces. The figures do suggest, however, that the nutritional status of children is relatively better in smallholder areas of Central, Rift, and Western Provinces, and relatively worse in Nyanza, Coast, and Eastern. These rankings are different from the poverty and food poverty rankings.

    One would not expect the estimated incidence of child malnutrition to correlate well with household poverty or food poverty measures partly because intrahousehold distribution varies between areas. Cultural traditions concerning the care of children, the priority attached to their well-being, and the well-being of their mothers, can vary enormously. This is an important subject, beyond the scope of this paper. As important may be other factors that influence malnutrition more generally, in particular health and disease. It is striking in Kenya that the incidence of child malnutrition is so much higher in Coast and in Nyanza than in other provinces. These are the two provinces in which the underlying health environment is particularly bad: malaria is endemic and water-borne gastro-intestinal and other diseases are widespread. The poor quality and availability of health services and water supplies are important contributory factors. Female education may also be important. In Coast Province this has been particularly neglected, although this is not the case in Nyanza. Eastern Province also has a high incidence of child malnutrition. This may reflect its poor health record, but in this case there may also be a closer connection with intermittent food deprivation not reflected in the 1974/5 food poverty estimates.

A comparison of the estimated incidences of child malnutrition with the estimated incidences of household poverty and food poverty, in the different provinces, shows that Western Province has a much better record on child malnutrition than one would expect judging from its poverty record (although not so much better than its food poverty record would suggest). Rift looks as good as Central Province on child malnutrition, much better than its food poverty record (and substantially better also than its poverty record) would lead one to expect. Nyanza's record is perhaps not quite as bad on poverty and food poverty as on malnutrition, but it is not good on any. Coast Province, on the other hand, looks as bad on malnutrition as the worst of its poverty and food poverty estimates suggest. Eastern Province looks much worse on malnutrition than its poverty and food poverty estimates might suggest, but this is primarily because its 1977 malnutrition figure is so bad. Central Province, which is ahead on so many of the poverty indicators, does not stand out where child malnutrition is concerned. Indeed, child malnutrition appears surprisingly high in Central Province. Child malnutrition is not at all closely linked with income poverty, expenditure poverty, or even food intake estimates. This is consistent with micro-level evidence on the role of health and other factors.

Child mortality and life expectancy

Some life expectancy and child mortality figures based on the 1969 and 1979 Population Censuses are shown in Table 7.12. These apply to provinces as a whole, not just their smallholder agricultural areas. Although substantial additional populations are involved, and in Rift and Eastern Provinces these include some of the poorest populations in Kenya, the additional populations are not large enough for the rankings of the different provinces to be affected. Central, Eastern, and Rift Valley Provinces all appear considerably better off, as far as child mortality is concerned, than Western, Coast, or Nyanza. The biggest surprise here is perhaps Western Province. Although Western Province had a relatively better record on child malnutrition, its child mortality incidence is relatively high. The health factors associated with a high incidence of child mortality are different from those associated with high levels of child malnutrition. This must be particularly important in Western Province. The high incidences of child mortality evident in Nyanza and Coast Provinces are not so surprising, although the ranking between the two is the opposite of that which one would have expected, suggesting again that somewhat different factors are responsible for high incidences of child mortality on the one hand and high incidences of child malnutrition on the other.

The ranking of the different provinces on these different indicators of deprivation is summarized in Table 7.14.

Central Province is clearly ahead of all other provinces taking all the indicators together. Eastern Province comes a close second to Central Province except on child malnutrition, which is greatly influenced by the high 1977 figure. At the other extreme, Western Province comes out clearly worst on most indicators, although good on child malnutrition and not as bad as Nyanza or Coast on child mortality. It does not look so bad on severity of poverty either. Nyanza comes out quite badly on most indicators, particularly badly on child mortality and child malnutrition, but also badly on expenditure poverty and the severity of food poverty. Coast comes out similarly to Nyanza. It does not appear to have quite such a bad record on expenditure poverty, but Nyanza's high figure is suspect here. Rift Valley looks above average, with particularly good income and child nutrition figures.

Thus, to the extent that an overall ranking might be legitimate, it would put provinces in the following order: (1) Central, (2) Eastern, (3) Rift, (4) Coast, (5) Nyanza, (6) Western. Western might however have a claim to be placed above Coast and Nyanza on the basis of its better child malnutrition and mortality figures.

It would clearly be valuable to consider these interrelationships further. Food may be less important than health, in the Kenyan context. Likewise private expenditure may not be as important as public. Some of the worst aspects of poverty in Kenya may be more easily eliminated through public expenditure programmes than through programmes designed to increase the individual or household incomes of those below the poverty line. But the inadequacy of household income is an important problem and one that must contribute significantly to acute deprivation. The question pursued in the next section is what makes Central and Eastern Provinces better off on these food-related indicators than Western, Nyanza, and the Coast, and what puts Rift in an intermediate position?

7.5. *The relative positions of smallholder agricultural areas*

The questions addressed here are: in what conditions can population pressure be accommodated without increasing poverty? In what conditions might a decrease in subsistence production be associated with an increase in poverty? In what conditions does export cropping lead to a decrease in poverty? And what is the role of non-agricultural incomes in smallholder agricultural areas?

Table 7.14 Summary of provincial rankings on some food-related poverty and deprivation indicators in Kenya

Rank	Mean household income (Kshs p.a.)	Mean household expenditure (Kshs p.a.)	Income poverty (% households)	Expenditure poverty (% households)	Incidence of food poverty (% households)	Severity of food poverty index	Inadequate food intake (% households)	Child malnutrition, 1977–82 av. (% households)	Child mortality, 1979 (0–5 years 1,000)
1	Rift 4,577	Central 4,473	Rift 19	Central 10	Eastern 32	Eastern 0.026	Central 14	Western 23	Central 85
2	Central 4,241	Eastern 4,020	Central 22	Eastern 22	Central 33	Central 0.028	Eastern 18	Central 24	Eastern 128
3	Nyanza 3,911	Rift 3,426	Coast 31	Western 34	Nyanza 41	Western 0.037	Coast 26	Rift 24	Rift 132
4	Eastern 3,486	Coast 3,139	Eastern 35	Coast 36	Coast 42	Rift 0.039	Nyanza 32	Eastern 28	Western 187
5	Coast 3,325	Western 2,808	Nyanza 38	Rift 37	Rift 45	Nyanza 0.039	Rift 33	Nyanza 29	Coast 206
6	Western 2,494	Nyanza 2,546	Western 50	Nyanza 37	Western 46	Coast 0.046	Western 36	Coast 40	Nyanza 220

Population pressure

There is a marked diversity in Kenya in rural areas' relative success or failure in accommodating increased population pressure. The intensification of agricultural production is (obviously) often a key to success. This may come about through improved market opportunities which raise the value of agricultural products as much as through technical change. Rural non-agricultural activities can also be crucial: what is important is their ability to compete successfully with outside supplies of goods and services in meeting local demand, and/or to form the basis for successful exports. Then there are the opportunities for rural people to earn income outside the rural areas. There has been some debate in the literature on remittances as to whether outside employment has a positive or negative effect on the areas of origin of employees (Rempel and Lobdell 1978). It obviously depends on the circumstances. When there are profitable opportunities in the rural areas for the investment of remittances or other earnings from outside employment, outside employment can play a very positive role. The use of the earnings from migration to supplement consumption in the home areas can also help to enhance investment opportunities, but it is important that earnings finance investment as well as consumption. Outside employment can be a drain on the area of origin if too much of the labour force migrates and not enough earnings are ploughed back into the area of origin. When the circumstances are right, then, outside employment can contribute greatly in getting income to increase faster than population, even in areas that are already densely populated. Its role is not always so positive, however.

In Kenya, smallholder agricultural areas in Central and Eastern Provinces appear to have been able to accommodate high and increasing population pressures relatively successfully by increasing agricultural production for the market, by developing non-agricultural activities, and by putting to profitable use substantial incomes from outside employment almost to the point of generating an internal dynamic that is self-reinforcing. Western Province, in contrast, at least until recently, has had great difficulty in accommodating its high population pressure: its people have been successful in obtaining employment outside the province, but they were not able at least in the 1970s to raise the income earning potential within the province's smallholder agricultural areas at all significantly. In the case of Eastern and Central Provinces, it is not just the additional outside opportunities that have been important: the ability to attract outside earnings into investments in the smallholder areas has also been crucial.

There are a number of channels through which increased population pressure can affect the poor adversely by increasing inequality, even if the area as a whole is doing well. The first is land concentration and/or landlessness.

High degrees of land concentration among those with land may distinguish provinces with high population pressure. They do not, however, distinguish provinces with high incidences of poverty. In a comparison between Western,

Nyanza, and Central Province smallholder agricultural areas, Collier and Lal (1986) demonstrate that poverty is closely correlated with size of holding in Western, and quite closely in Nyanza, but not at all closely in Central Province. As Collier and Lal point out, the size of landholding is obviously less important where technical change has involved intensification in the use of the land, as is the case in Central Province, and more important where it has not, as in Western, and to some extent Nyanza, Province. The extent to which the size of holding is correlated with poverty also depends, obviously, on the importance of non-agricultural sources of income and whether these are correlated with the size of landholding.

There is a surprisingly high degree of landlessness in Kenya's smallholder agricultural areas. Different estimates were shown in Table 7.3. Landlessness is not at all clearly associated with population pressure in Kenya, however. The incidence of landlessness is higher, if anything, in the less densely populated areas. Nor is landlessness particularly associated with poverty. Being without land is often associated with the availability of other sources of income, from regular employment, or non-farm business (Livingstone 1986). The high degree of landlessness in Rift Valley smallholder agricultural areas, for example, clearly reflects the availability of plentiful large-farm employment opportunities in the area. In Coast Province, it reflects the relatively less important role of agriculture in the local economy, and the availability of employment and income generating activities of other kinds. In Western Province, subsisting without land is more difficult. It is not surprising that people have been less willing to give up land in this province, where the proportion of landless is much lower.

Population pressure may lead to a reduction in local food production, but this is only a problem if reasonably priced food supplies are not forthcoming from elsewhere. Population pressure is often associated with shifts into the production of non-food agricultural products with higher per hectare yields than food, and/or with shifts away from agricultural production altogether. This only causes particular problems for the poor however, if as a result they have to purchase food at higher prices, and/or if they do not get sufficient access to increased income earning opportunities to compensate for increases in the price of food (or other goods and services) that occur. The distribution of food through the market is not as serious a problem in Kenya as in some sub-Saharan African countries. This is a very important factor, further discussed below in connection with decreasing subsistence production and increasing export crop production.

Another question is whether population pressure is associated with an increasing labour surplus or not, and how a labour surplus or shortage is reflected in wages and incomes. A labour *shortage* actually accompanied strongly increasing population pressure in Central Province in the 1960s and early 1970s. In that period, the growth of employment opportunities for Central Province people was so rapid that smallholder agriculture suffered from a labour shortage. This meant that the considerable intensification of smallholder agriculture, which involved shifts into higher value per hectare products, was accompanied by decreasing inputs of labour both per activity and per hectare (Collier and Lal 1986). The Central Province labour shortage does not appear to have lasted, however. By the 1980s, Central Province was showing signs of a labour surplus again (Livingstone 1986).

One has to look beyond the labour market to see what determines the wages and incomes of the poor. Conditions in the markets for land and other factors of production are also important, as is the whole political and institutional framework within which these markets operate. Collier (1983) has argued that in Kenya 'malfunctioning factor markets' have resulted in output being less than it would otherwise be, and inequality being worse. Whether or not this is so, it is clear that the wages and incomes of the poor are affected by the way in which all factor and product markets operate, and these in turn are a matter of state policy among other things.

Population pressure may also affect distribution within the household and thus affect vulnerable groups within households adversely. There are direct and obvious factors operating at the demographic level within the household. Increased population pressure may also lead to more commercialized production relationships in which more income is used for investment, less for food and other items of consumption particularly affecting women and children. Population pressure may make food production more difficult, affecting women adversely in societies in which women bear the main responsibility for food production. There are no general rules (as Ann Whitehead emphasizes in her contribution to the first volume of this book), but the effect of increased population pressure on distribution within the household is seldom neutral as far as the vulnerable are concerned.

To summarize, it is not surprising that there is no evidence of a direct association between population pressure and poverty at the regional level in Kenya. The means of accommodating higher population densities are more open to people in some areas than in others. Central Province and Eastern Province may be able to accommodate their increasing populations by a combination of strategies involving taking advantage of opportunities provided by Nairobi and elsewhere and of conditions favouring investment within the provinces' smallholder agricultural areas themselves. But it is easy to get into the opposite syndrome, as Western Province smallholder agricultural areas appeared to have done, in the 1970s at least. Increasing population pressure can easily be associated with increasing poverty because the outside opportunities are neither plentiful nor lucrative and the economic base within the area itself is also weak. The absence of acute population pressure has not made other provinces' smallholder agricultural areas obviously more successful in Kenya. On the contrary, their problems are for the most part more serious than those of the more densely populated provinces.

Decreasing 'subsistence' production

Increased market involvements have almost certainly been associated with increased average incomes in Kenya's smallholder agricultural areas, at least in recent decades, more so in some than in others. Interprovincial comparisons suggest that market involvement is associated in some cases with high and in other cases with low average incomes. The *terms* of market involvement vary considerably from product to product and from area to area. This may be most obvious in comparisons between different export crops but it also applies to the production for sale of food and other goods and services.

Differences in the role of 'subsistence' production show up clearly in IRS1 figures. IRS1 data on own consumption as a proportion of total food, and own consumption as a proportion of all consumption including non-food items, are shown in Table 7.15. Production for own consumption is proportionately higher in Rift, Eastern, and Nyanza Province smallholder agricultural areas, and proportionately lower in Western, Central, and Coast. The evidence from IRS1 suggests that subsistence production may be something of a luxury: it represents a higher proportion of total production among higher-income groups than among lower-income groups of households. But this is not the only consideration as far as poverty is concerned. If production for own consumption is widespread in any area, food may be less expensive for those who have to purchase much of their own food.

Western Province is a good example of low levels of subsistence production being associated with high incidences of poverty. But Central Province provides the opposite example. Rift appears to be a good example of relatively high levels of subsistence production being associated with a relatively low incidence of poverty. Nyanza Province provides an opposite example again. There is obviously no straightforward relationship between subsistence production and poverty. Subsistence production may be associated with low per capita incomes unless natural resources are plentiful. However even where resources are plentiful, there is a distinct limit to the income levels attainable in communities heavily dependent on production for own consumption within the household.

Increasing 'export' cropping

Another aspect of increasing market involvement is increased involvement in production for export. Whether or not this undermines the ability of rural smallholders to meet their food needs depends on many things (Longhurst 1988). One of the reasons that export crops are thought to be particularly problematic is because they displace food production. Whether or not food then becomes more expensive in real terms depends on many factors.

Government policy can be crucial here. In most sub-Saharan African countries governments are heavily involved in agricultural product markets. How much smallholder agricultural areas benefit from their involvement in

Table 7.15 Own consumption, food consumption, and total consumption per smallholding in different provinces, Kenya, 1974/5

	Total food		Own consumption			Purchased food			Other consumption		Total consumption	
	Kshs	% total	Kshs	% food	% total	Kshs	% food	% total	Kshs	% total	Kshs	% total
Central	3,118	70	1,530	49	34	1,588	51	36	1,365	31	4,473	100
Eastern	3,068	76	1,667	54	41	1,401	46	35	952	24	4,020	100
Rift	2,564	75	1,686	66	49	878	34	26	862	25	3,426	100
Coast	2,613	83	670	26	21	1,943	74	62	526	17	3,139	100
Western	2,108	75	896	43	32	1,212	57	43	700	25	2,808	100
Nyanza	2,039	80	1,047	51	41	992	49	39	507	20	2,546	100
All	2,594	75	1,297	50	38	1,297	50	38	856	25	3,450	100

Source: Republic of Kenya (1977*a*).

export production depends at least partly on government policy concerning the marketing and pricing of export crops, and the marketing and pricing of food. It also depends on a whole lot of other government policies relating to the provision of credit, input subsidies, and such things as agricultural research, fiscal and exchange rate policy and the trade regime. Sharpley (1986) and Jabara (1985) contain recent discussions of Kenyan evidence on these.

Some smallholder agricultural areas in Kenya heavily involved in coffee, tea, and pyrethrum production for export have benefited overwhelmingly both from the point of view of increased average incomes and from the point of view of reduced poverty. There is evidence in support of this from Keller *et al.* (1969) on Central Province tea and coffee, Fleuret and Fleuret (1983) on Taita coffee and vegetables, Rabaneck (1982) on coffee, and Hitchings (1982) on tea and coffee, both the latter more generally in Kenya. Not all export crops have been as successful though. Cotton, for example, has always generated much lower incomes than tea or coffee. Some cotton-producing areas have high incidences of poverty. In a comparison of poverty in different agroecological zones, Smith (1978) shows incidences of poverty to be much higher in western Kenya coffee and tea zones than in eastern Kenya, but eastern Kenya cotton zones have similar incidences of poverty to those more generally obtained in the west. Smith's figures are presented in Table 7.16. The contrast between the different areas is partly a reflection of contrasts in the extent to which they are involved in export production, but it is also a reflection of contrasts between the different export crops. Cotton is not a very attractive crop to produce in Kenya conditions. This means that the proportions of smallholders in the cotton zones involved in cotton production are relatively small, but it also means that those involved are not obtaining very high incomes from it.

Specialization in export production by some creates opportunities for

Table 7.16 Composition of agricultural output by agroecological zone, Kenya, 1974/5

	Total (m. Kshs)	Av. per holding (000 Kshs)	Food crops (%)	Export crops (%)	Livestock and milk (%)
Tea east of Rift	622	3.7	51.0	16.5	32.5
Coffee east of Rift	994	2.9	58.0	12.5	29.5
Tea west of Rift	430	3.1	34.2	14.6	51.2
Coffee west of Rift	897	3.6	74.4	1.1	24.4
Coast composite	84	1.2	65.2	0.6	34.2
Cotton east of Rift	153	1.1	95.8	0.8	3.4
Cotton west of Rift	542	1.6	51.6	2.1	46.3
TOTAL	3,722	2.6	58.8	8.4	32.8

Source: Smith (1978).

specialization in food production by others. There have obviously been gains for food producers in Central and Eastern Province as a result of the expansion of export production in those provinces. There have been even more substantial gains for food producers in other provinces. Smallholder food producers in Nyanza Province have gained substantially from opportunities for increased specialization in food production created by specialization in export crop production in other provinces.

When domestic food supplies have run short, the government has usually been prepared to import food. The marketing system has on the whole worked well enough to avoid localized food shortages in smallholder areas specializing in high-value exports. This has not been difficult as most of the major smallholder exporting areas are well served with transport, and centrally located, geographically as well as politically. They have had the purchasing power to attract food through normal market processes. But while food policy and food marketing have been fairly effective as far as the areas of high-value exports are concerned, there have been problems in areas specializing in low-value exports and other non-food products.

The extent to which poor people have lost out relatively in areas with high degrees of market involvement is an important question. Kenya sugar schemes have been cited as examples of increased inequality of incomes leading to increased poverty despite the increase in average incomes that is associated with the sugar schemes (Hitchings 1982 among others). An examination of district-level evidence from the Child Nutrition Survey of 1982 concluded that there was no evidence linking child malnutrition with export cropping in Kenya in general (Test et al. n.d.), but Haaga et al. (1986) did find it a problem in the case of Eastern Province coffee.

There are all sorts of factors involved in the relationship between export cropping and poverty, none of them clearly dominant except in particular cases, and all of them making it possible for the relationship to go either way. The development of smallholder agricultural areas in which exports play a prominent role can be associated with an increase in income and a reduction in poverty if the terms on which the exports are produced and traded are favourable, and if the distribution of benefits from exports is not too unequal. Overall, the evidence in Kenya suggests a positive relationship between export cropping and the reduction of poverty, at least in recent decades.

Non-agricultural incomes

It is not only a question of subsistence versus market production, or export production, in agriculture. The ability of smallholder agricultural areas to draw on sources of income outside agriculture may also be crucial to their success in reducing poverty, particularly as population pressure increases. The key distinction is not between areas that are more, and areas that are less, dependent on agriculture. Smallholder agricultural income makes up a relatively small proportion of total income in Coast smallholder areas which fare badly on poverty. But the areas that are most heavily dependent on agricultural income, Rift Valley and Nyanza, are not strikingly more successful as far as poverty-related indicators are concerned. Central, Eastern, and Western Provinces all share relatively heavy dependence on agriculture, but they have very different records on poverty.

The extent and profitability of non-agricultural income generating opportunities varies substantially from area to area as we have seen. The most important supplement to smallholder agricultural income is income from regular employment. This is a key factor in Central Province where smallholders get more per household from regular employment than do smallholders in any other province; it is very important in Rift Valley smallholder agricultural areas and in Western Province; and quite important in the other smallholder agricultural areas also. Most regular employment is outside smallholder agriculture, some in government and private sector activities in the smallholder agricultural areas themselves, some in small towns in the neighbourhood, some in larger towns, and some in the large farm sector. All must be within commuting distance of the smallholdings to which it accrues. Location within reach of sources of regular employment is thus one of the important factors helping to determine how successful any particular smallholder agricultural area is (Rempel and Lobdell 1978 also make this point strongly in their article on remittances).

Remittances from more distant employment can also be crucial. Remittances are a major factor for Central, Western, Nyanza, and Coast Provinces, but less important for Rift and even Eastern. It is worth noting that remittances are high in provinces in which problems of poverty are most severe, Coast, Nyanza, and Western, but high also in Central for quite different reasons. The burdens imposed on people working away from home can be serious. In the case of Central Province, however, the relatively large burden probably reflects a positive involvement in investment in smallholder agricultural areas, rather than a heavy burden of dependency.

7.6. *Conclusion*

This chapter has attempted to bring out some aspects of the nature and incidence of deprivation in different smallholder agricultural areas of Kenya, and to relate the observed patterns to the economic characteristics of the corresponding regions. In this concluding section, rather than attempting to summarize the complex picture emerging from this investigation, we should take note of a few general lessons arising from this case-study.

A consistent finding is that the economy of smallholder agricultural areas in Kenya cannot be seen in isolation. Access to earning opportunities outside the sector makes a great deal of difference, especially as natural resources begin to come under pressure. Employment opportunities in the urban and large-farm sectors, in particular, have a major effect on what is possible within small-holder agricultural areas. Opportunities for exporting non-agricultural products overseas can also be crucial, as population pressures increase.

This is not to deny the importance of smallholder agricultural development; rather to stress that smallholder agriculture is not enough, even with all the supplementary activities supporting it. It may be possible for a predominantly agricultural economy to support its population without excessive poverty and deprivation when natural resources are plentiful, people are satisfied with generally limited standards of living, and there are no irresistible pressures from outside to extract the surpluses. But in countries like Kenya, with its high and rapidly growing density of population, greater interaction between agricultural and non-agricultural activities is essential if endemic poverty is not to increase.

Thus, Kenya can accommodate a large population and rapid population growth in smallholder agricultural areas if it can continue to develop the urban, industrial, and large-farm areas as well as smallholder agriculture. The failure to develop the whole economy may cause as much trouble in smallholder agricultural areas as within these areas themselves.

This case-study of Kenya brings out several observations of more general relevance for research and action. First, and in line with the preceding discussion, economic diversification can be of great importance, not only for the urban but also for the rural population. This point, which also emerges from the contributions by Jean-Philippe Platteau, Francis Idachaba, and Samuel Wangwe elsewhere in this book, needs to be given greater recognition in discussions of the 'food crisis' in Africa. Second, deprivation has many aspects which are not always closely related, and this together with the limited reliability of relevant statistics makes it difficult to interpret the evidence. In particular, regional, occupational, and temporal patterns in the incidence of different kinds of deprivation are often hard to ascertain, even when the underlying contrasts are quite significant. Third, the heterogeneity of African economies and agriculture, which is even greater than this chapter suggests if one includes pastoral and large farm areas, is of crucial importance for the study of hunger and deprivation. Probing regional diversities, as has been attempted in this chapter with reference to Kenya, is a major challenge for empirical research on poverty in Africa. Finally, and relatedly, it is a waste of time to try to establish universal relationships between deprivation on the one hand and population pressure, or 'commercialization', or export crops, or 'cash crops', or sectoral balances, on the other. The economic and social relations that come into play in the causation of poverty are too diverse to produce stereotypical links of this type.

References

ANDERSON, D., and LEISERSON, M. (1980), 'Rural Non-farm Employment in Developing Countries', *Economic Development and Cultural Change*, 28.

ANKER, R., and KNOWLES, J. C. (1977), 'An Empirical Analysis of Mortality Differentials in Kenya at the Macro and Micro Levels', Population and Employment Working Paper No. 60 (Geneva: ILO).

BIGSTEN, A. (1980), *Regional Inequality and Development: A Case Study of Kenya* (Farnborough: Gower).

BISWAS, M., and PINSTRUP-ANDERSEN, P. (eds.) (1985), *Nutrition and Development* (Oxford, New York, Tokyo: Oxford University Press).

CARLSEN, J. (1980), *Economic and Social Transformation in Rural Kenya* (Uppsala: Scandinavian Institute of African Studies).

CASLEY, D., and MARCHANT, T. J. (1978), 'Smallholder Marketing in Kenya', FAO Marketing Development Project (Nairobi: Ministry of Agriculture).

CHAMBERS, R. (1983), *Rural Development: Putting the Last First* (London, Lagos, New York: Longman).

——LONGHURST, R., and PACEY, A. (eds.) (1981), *Seasonal Dimensions to Rural Poverty* (London: Frances Pinter).

COHEN, J. M., and LEWIS, D. B. (1987), 'The Role of Government in Combatting Food Shortages: Lessons from Kenya 1984–5', in Glantz (1987).

COLLIER, P. (1983), 'Malfunctioning of African Rural Factor Markets: Theory and a Kenyan Example', *Oxford Bulletin of Economics and Statistics*, 2.

——and LAL, D. (1980), 'Poverty and Growth in Kenya', World Bank Staff Working Paper No. 389 (Washington, DC. World Bank).

————(1984), 'Why Poor People Get Rich: Kenya 1960–79', *World Development*, 12.

————(1986), *Labour and Poverty in Kenya 1900–1980* (Oxford: Oxford University Press).

COMMINS, S. K., LOFCHIE, M. F., and PAYNE, R. (eds.) (1986), *Africa's Agrarian Crisis: The Roots of Famine* (Boulder, Colo.: Lynne Rienner Publishers Inc.).

COWEN, M. (1981), 'Commodity Production in Kenya's Central Province', in Heyer, J., Roberts, P., and Williams, G. (eds.), *Rural Development in Tropical Africa* (London: Macmillan).

CRAWFORD, E., and THORBECKE, E. (1980), 'Analysis of Food Poverty: An Illustration from Kenya', *Pakistan Development Review*, 19.

FISCHER, G., and SHAH, M. M. (1985), 'Food Consumption and Nutrition Level (Kenya Case Study)' (IIASA, Collaborative Paper).

FLEURET, P., and FLEURET, A. (1980), 'Nutrition, Consumption and Agricultural Change', *Human Organization*, 39.

————(1983), 'Socio-economic Determinants of Child Nutrition in Taita, Kenya: A Call for Discussion', *Readers Forum*, 8.

GHAI, D. (1987), 'Successes and Failures in African Development: 1960–82', paper prepared for the seminar on 'Alternative Development Strategies', OECD Development Centre, Paris.

GHAI, D., GODFREY, M., and LISK, F. (1979), *Planning for Basic Needs in Kenya* (Geneva: ILO).

——and RADWAN, S. (eds.) (1983), *Agrarian Policies and Rural Poverty in Africa* (London: Macmillan).

GLANTZ, M. H. (ed.) (1987), *Drought and Hunger in Africa: Denying Famine a Future* (Cambridge: Cambridge University Press).

GREER, J., and THORBECKE, E. (1986*a*), *Food Poverty and Consumption Patterns in Kenya* (Geneva: ILO).

—— ——(1986*b*), 'Food Poverty Profile Applied to Kenyan Smallholders', *Economic Development and Cultural Change*, 35.

HAAGA, J., MASON, J., OMORO, F., QUINN, V., RAFFERTY, A., TEST, K., and WASONGA, L. (1986), 'Child Malnutrition in Rural Kenya: A Geographical and Agricultural Classification', *Ecology of Food and Nutrition*, 18.

HAZLEWOOD, A. (1979), *The Economy of Kenya: The Kenyatta Era* (Oxford: Oxford University Press).

HITCHINGS, J. (1982), 'Agricultural Determinants of Nutritional Status among Kenyan Children with Models of Anthropometric and Growth Indicators', unpublished Ph.D. thesis, Stanford University.

HOUSE, W., and KILLICK, T. (1983), 'Social Justice and Development Policy in Kenya's Rural Economy', in Ghai and Radwan (1983).

HUNT, D. (1984), *The Impending Crisis in Kenya: The Case for Land Reform* (Farnborough: Gower).

ILO (1972), *Employment, Incomes and Equality: A Strategy for Increasing Productive Employment in Kenya* (Geneva: ILO).

ILO Jobs and Skills Programme for Africa (1982), *Rural–Urban Gap and Income Distribution: The Case of Kenya* (Addis Ababa. ILO).

JABARA, C. L. (1985), 'Agricultural Pricing Policy in Kenya', *World Development*, 13.

JAMAL, V., and WEEKS, J. (1988), 'The Vanishing Rural–Urban Gap in Sub-Saharan Africa', *International Labour Review*, 127.

JOHNSON, G. E., and WHITELAW, W. E. (1974), 'Urban–Rural Income Transfers in Kenya: An Estimated Remittances Function', *Economic Development and Cultural Change*, 22.

KELLER, W., MUSCAT, E., and VALDER, E. (1969), 'Some Observations Regarding Economy, Diet and Nutritional Status of Kikuyu Farmers in Kenya', in Kraut, H., and Cremer, H.-D. (eds.) *Investigations into Health and Nutrition in East Africa* (Munich: IFO-Institut für Wirtschaftsforschung).

KENNEDY, E., and COGHILL, B. (1987), 'Income and Nutritional Effects of the Commercialization of Agriculture in Southwestern Kenya', Research Report 63 (Washington, DC: IFPRI).

KILLICK, T. (ed.) (1981), *Papers on the Kenyan Economy* (Nairobi, London, Ibadan: Heinemann Educational Books).

——(ed.) (1984*a*), *The IMF and Stabilisation; Developing Country Experiences* (London: Heinemann Educational Books).

——(1984*b*), 'Kenya 1975–81', in Killick (1984*a*).

KITCHING, G. (1980), *Class and Economic Change in Kenya: The Making of an African Petite Bourgeoisie, 1905–70* (New Haven, Conn., and London: Yale University Press).

KLEIST, T. (1985), 'Regional and Seasonal Food Problems in Kenya' (Food and

Nutrition Studies Programme, Kenya Ministry of Finance and Planning, and Africa Studies Centre, Leiden).

KNOWLES, J. C., and ANKER, R. (1981), 'An Analysis of Income Transfers in a Developing Country: The Case of Kenya', *Journal of Development Economics*, 8.

KONGSTAD, P., and MONSTED, M. (1980), *Family, Labour and Trade in Western Kenya* (Uppsala: Scandinavian Institute of Development Studies).

LIPTON, M. (1983), 'Poverty, Undernutrition and Hunger', World Bank Staff Working Paper No. 597 (Washington, DC: World Bank).

LIVINGSTONE, I. (1986), *Rural Development, Employment and Incomes in Kenya* (Farnborough: Gower).

LONGHURST, R. (1988), 'Cash Crops, Household Food Security and Nutrition', in Maxwell (1988).

MAXWELL, S. (ed.) (1988), *Cash Crops in Developing Countries*, Special Issue of *IDS Bulletin*, 19.

MBITHI, P., and BARNES, C. (1975), *The Spontaneous Settlement Problem in Kenya* (Kampala, Nairobi, Dar es Salaam: East African Literature Bureau).

MIGOT-ADHOLLA, S. E. (1975), 'Migration and Rural Differentiation in Kenya', unpublished Ph.D. thesis, University of California, Los Angeles.

NORCLIFFE, G. (1983), 'Operating Characteristics of Rural Non-farm Enterprises in Central Province, Kenya', *World Development*, 11.

NYANGIRA, N. (1975), *Relative Modernisation and Public Resource Allocation in Kenya* (Kampala, Nairobi, Dar es Salaam: East African Literature Bureau).

PACEY, A., and PAYNE, P. (eds.) (1985), *Agricultural Development and Nutrition* (London, Melbourne, Sydney, Auckland, Johannesburg: Hutchinson).

PARKIN, D. (1972), *Palms, Wine and Witnesses: Public Spirit and Private Gain in an African Farming Community* (London: Intertext Books).

PINSTRUP-ANDERSEN, P. (1985), 'The Impact of Export Crop Production on Human Nutrition', in Biswas and Pinstrup-Andersen (1985).

POLEMAN, T. J. (1981), 'Quantifying the Nutrition Situation in Developing Countries', *Food Research Institute Studies*, 18.

RABANECK, S. (1982), 'The Determinants of Protein-Energy Malnutrition among Preschool Children in Kenya with respect to Cash Cropping and Self Sufficiency in Staple Food Production', unpublished Ph.D. thesis, Cornell University, Ithaca.

REMPEL, H., and LOBDELL, R. (1978), 'The Role of Urban-to-Rural Remittances in Rural Development', *Journal of Development Studies*, 14.

Republic of Kenya (1968), *Economic Survey of Central Province 1963/4* (Nairobi: Republic of Kenya).

——(1977a), *Integrated Rural Survey 1974/5, Basic Report* (Nairobi: Republic of Kenya).

——(1977b), *Rural Household Survey of Nyanza Province 1970/71* (Nairobi: Republic of Kenya).

——(1977c), *Social Perspectives*, 2/2 (Nairobi: Republic of Kenya).

——(1977d), *Social Perspectives*, 2/3 (Nairobi: Republic of Kenya).

——(1978), *Economic Survey 1978* (Nairobi: Republic of Kenya).

——(1979), *Development Plan 1979–83* (Nairobi: Republic of Kenya).

——(1981), *The Integrated Rural Surveys 1976–79: Basic Report* (Nairobi: Republic of Kenya).

——(1983), *Third Rural Child Nutrition Survey 1982* (Nairobi: Republic of Kenya).

——(1984), *Development Plan 1984–88* (Nairobi: Republic of Kenya).

——(1986), *Economic Management for Renewed Growth* (Nairobi: Republic of Kenya).

——(1988), *Economic Survey 1988* (Nairobi: Republic of Kenya).

——(n.d.), *1979 Population Census*, ii: *Analytical Analysis* (Nairobi: Republic of Kenya).

——and UNICEF (1984), *Situation Analysis of Children and Women in Kenya* (Nairobi: Republic of Kenya/UNICEF).

SHARPLEY, J. (1981), 'Resource Transfers between the Agricultural and Nonagricultural Sectors: 1964–77', in Killick (1981).

——(1986), 'Economic Policies and Agricultural Performance: The Case of Kenya' (Paris: OECD Development Centre).

——and LEWIS, S. R. (1988), 'Kenya's Industrialisation, 1964–84', Discussion Paper 242 (Institute of Development Studies, University of Sussex).

SMITH, L. D. (1978), 'Low Income Smallholder Marketing and Consumption Patterns: Analysis and Improvement Policies and Programmes', FAO Marketing Development Project (Nairobi: Ministry of Agriculture).

SVEDBERG, P. (1988), 'Undernutrition in Sub-Saharan Africa: A Critical Assessment of the Evidence', Working Paper 15 (Helsinki: WIDER); published in this volume.

SWAINSON, N. (1980), *The Development of Corporate Capitalism in Kenya 1918–1977* (London, Ibadan, Nairobi: Heinemann).

TEST, K., *et al.* (n.d.), 'Trends in Child Nutritional Status in Rural Kenya 1977–82', mimeo (Cornell Nutritional Surveillance Programme, Cornell University).

VANDERMOORTELE, J., and VAN DER HOEVEN, R. (1982), 'Income Distribution and Consumption Patterns in Urban and Rural Kenya by Socio-economic Groups', World Employment Programme Research Working Paper (Geneva: ILO).

VON BRAUN, J., and KENNEDY, E. (1986), 'Commercialization of Subsistence Agriculture. Income and Nutritional Effects in Developing Countries', Working Papers on Commercialization of Agriculture and Nutrition, No. 1 (Washington, DC: IFPRI).

WHITEHEAD, A. (1988), 'Women in Rural Food Production in Sub-Saharan Africa: Some Implications for Food Strategies', mimeo; published in volume 1 of this book as 'Rural Women and Food Production in Sub-Saharan Africa'.

World Bank (1982), *Growth and Structural Change in Kenya* (Washington, DC: World Bank).

8

The Contribution of Industry to Solving the Food Problem in Africa

Samuel Wangwe

8.1. *Introduction*

Recent studies on the economic conditions in Africa have portrayed a deepening crisis. An important aspect of this crisis is the food problem, visible not only in recurrent famines but also in high and possibly increasing levels of endemic undernutrition. Addressing the interrelated problems of poverty and hunger in an effective manner is one of the most urgent policy challenges facing African countries today.

In 1980 the share of the labour force engaged in agriculture in sub-Saharan Africa was estimated at 72 per cent. For the 23 low-income countries of sub-Saharan Africa this share was even higher, averaging 78 per cent (World Bank 1984). In analysing the problem of hunger and poverty, the focus must be on the agricultural sector, but not in isolation from sectors related to it (e.g. industry). While rightly focusing on the problems of the agricultural sector, many recent studies of the food crisis in Africa have tended to analyse the problems of this sector in isolation.

A closer examination of agriculture and the food problem in Africa reveals that intersectoral relationships are pervasive and important. The purpose of this chapter is to investigate some of these interrelationships, with a view to bringing out the positive contribution of industry to alleviating the problem of hunger and poverty. The contribution of industry is basically twofold. First, industry plays an important role in raising productivity in agriculture. Second, it enhances access to food by creating incomes outside agriculture.

In analysing the problem of hunger and poverty, some scholars have focused on aggregate food supply, taking its distribution as given. Other scholars, led by Sen (1981), have focused on the issue of entitlement, suggesting that changes in the conditions of acquisition of food can have a considerable effect on the extent of hunger even for a given level of aggregate food supply. The issues of food supply and food access are obviously not unrelated. Given a particular distributional pattern, a decline in food supply per capita would

I am grateful for useful comments made on an earlier draft by a number of colleagues. Specifically I would like personally to acknowledge the insightful comments of Paul Streeten who kindly accepted to be a discussant of the first draft of this paper at the WIDER Conference. Comments made by Amartya Sen, Carl Eicher, Barbara Harriss, Judith Heyer, and Nanak Kakwani have contributed considerably to the improvements made in this chapter. However, as usual I take responsibility for the views expressed in it.

result in reduced entitlements for vulnerable groups and exacerbate hunger. Ultimately, entitlement analysis must pay due attention both to the mechanism through which the aggregate supply of food is distributed, and to the determination of aggregate supply itself. This chapter examines the positive contribution of industry to enhancing the entitlements of vulnerable groups, keeping in mind both the aggregative and the distributional elements of the determination of entitlements.

The plan of the chapter is as follows. Section 8.2 reviews some recent trends of the food situation in Africa. Section 8.3 discusses the major determinants of entitlements in sub-Saharan Africa, and the role that industry can play in protecting and promoting them. Section 8.4 is devoted to a case-study of agricultural equipment as a source of intersectoral linkages. Section 8.5 discusses the role of industry in agricultural processing. Section 8.6 offers some concluding comments.

8.2. *Aggregate trends in the food situation*

The deepening food crisis in Africa is partly evident in terms of aggregate indices from the declining growth rates of food production, declining food output per capita, increasing growth rates of food imports and food aid, and declining food self-sufficiency ratios. These trends are shown briefly in this section.[1]

(*a*) *Growth rates of food production*

While food output increased at an annual rate of 2.5 per cent during 1960–70, it increased by only 1.7 per cent per annum during 1970–82 (World Bank 1984). As shown in Table 8.1, Africa performed below the world aggregate trends after 1970.

The growth of population (about 3 per cent a year) considerably outstripped the growth of food output during 1970–82. Thus annual growth of food output per capita declined from 0.2 per cent during 1960–70 to only −0.9 per cent during 1970–82 (World Bank 1984).

The index of food production per capita in Africa (1969–71 = 100) was 93.9 in 1975, falling further to 88.3 in 1980 and 83.1 in 1983 (World Bank Tables). The index was above 100 in only 6 countries in 1980–2 (World Bank 1984).

These trends are alarming, not only because food production is an important source of food supply in Africa, but also because the production of food is a crucial source of income for much of its rural population.

(*b*) *Food self-sufficiency*

During the 1970s, 39 out of 44 countries had lost in food self-sufficiency (Burki 1985), while the food self-sufficiency ratio fell from 98 per cent in the 1960s to

---

[1] The evidence is discussed in greater detail in Jean-Philippe Platteau's contribution to the second volume of this book.

Table 8.1 Growth in agricultural production 1961–1980 (% p.a.)

	1961–5 to 1970	1971–80	1961–5 to 1980
Africa	2.8	1.4	1.8
World	2.6	2.2	2.4

Source: FAO (1981: 5).

86 per cent in 1980 (Burki 1985 citing World Food Council 1984). According to FAO (1981), in Africa self-sufficiency ratios in cereals have fallen from 95 per cent in the early 1960s to 83 per cent in the late 1970s. By the year 2000 Africa's self-sufficiency ratio (on the basis of present trends) could drop to 56 per cent.[2] In FAO's view an annual food production growth rate of at least 4.3 per cent in the 1980–2000 period is required to reverse these declining trends.

During 1974–83 food imports (in cereals) increased at the rate of 9 per cent a year while food aid (in cereals) increased at 13.3 per cent per year. Food aid (in metric tons of grain equivalent) increased from 1,237,200 tons in 1978 to 2,168,600 tons in 1982 (i.e. about 5 per cent of total cereals production) (World Bank 1984). The aggregate food inflow (in cereals) from outside the region increased at 9.6 per cent a year during this period. When this trend is juxtaposed with worsening balance-of-payments problems and the increasing reluctance of donors to provide food aid, it would appear that entitlement to food at the national level (i.e. the ability of the nation as an entity to establish command over an adequate amount of food) is at stake.

Even when food imports and/or food aid are available, the logistics of distributing food to the hunger-stricken areas have often been problematic, as demonstrated by the recent experiences of Sudan and Ethiopia (Prattley 1986, several African Emergency Reports). This suggests that a reasonable level of self-sufficiency, and related food security arrangements, are necessary, especially in areas which are difficult to reach with food coming through ports. Food imports and food aid cannot be a reliable way of preventing loss of entitlements to food.

This poses at least two challenges. First, the need to increase domestic food production. Second, the need to revamp the export sector so that the expanded export revenues can be used to import food or to improve production and processing technology in the food-producing sectors.

The options here will reflect country-specific situations and the pertaining long-term comparative advantages. On the food production side, care should be taken against trying to achieve food self-sufficiency at any cost, e.g. by growing crops which are not appropriate for climatic conditions in Africa. For example, Andrae and Beckman (1985) have indicated that in Nigeria the

[2] The concept of self-sufficiency as used by these sources (e.g. FAO, World Food Council) only captures the relationship between domestic food supply and food imports (including food aid) and does not reflect the adequacy of food supply (e.g. in terms of nutrition).

illusion of food import substitution has sustained a massive waste of national resources on large-scale, technologically advanced, import intensive wheat production which can do little to solve Nigeria's food crisis and dependence on imports. On the side of exports, the predominance of traditional exports and their deteriorating terms of trade point to the need to examine possibilities of developing non-traditional exports if export revenues have to increase substantially in future. Decisions as to what exports to promote can only be country specific but the principle of avoiding expansion of the output of traditional exports which are characterized by a low income elasticity of demand seems to be worth adopting in the formulation of export strategies in Africa.

8.3.   Challenges of the entitlement problem

This section discusses the major determinants of entitlements in sub-Saharan Africa, and the possible causes of loss of entitlements. An attempt is also made to bring out the positive contribution of industry to solving the hunger problem, both by raising productivity in agriculture and by enhancing the entitlements of those who derive their incomes from non-agricultural activities. Considering the limitations of data on sub-Saharan Africa as a whole, this study will be based on a sample of case-studies from selected countries in sub-Saharan Africa.

(a)   Loss of harvest

Those groups in society who acquire food by producing it (either as owner-cultivators or as cultivating tenants) usually lose their command over food in the event of loss of harvest. For these groups, preventing crop failures is important for safeguarding their command over food. In this context, it has been pointed out that various risk-reducing practices, such as mixed cropping, combination of upland and valley plots, or cultivation of drought-resistant crops, can contribute to the security of farmers in spite of reducing average yields because they reduce the variation of total farm output (Berry 1984, Richards 1983, Norman et al. 1979). These practices reduce the risk of entitlement failures for farmers. Industry can further enhance the entitlements of this group by generating employment and incomes in non-agricultural activities, or through food preservation and processing of foodstuffs. These issues are taken up in the appropriate sections of this paper.

(b)   Marketable surplus

Food-producing groups often produce a surplus over and above their food requirements. If this happens, then food can be made available to the other groups. As the size of groups which rely on purchasing food increases (e.g. due to urbanization), the need to increase marketable surplus from the food-producing groups increases. The response to this demand should take the form of expanding production while at the same time enhancing or at least safeguarding the consumption levels of farmers. The other alternative of obtaining food through imports is feasible only if a viable export sector can be developed.

Marketable surplus can partly be stimulated by increased supply of relevant industrial goods for peasants to purchase. There are at least two important categories of such goods. First, the supply of farm inputs from the industrial sector can play the role of enhancing the capacity of the food-producing groups to produce more food (e.g. by employing more productive agricultural inputs and implements produced in the industrial sector). In section 8.4 it is shown that much of industry in Africa has not been geared to supply agriculture with the equipment and inputs it requires. Second, the supply of 'incentive goods', especially manufactured consumer goods, can enhance the willingness of the food-producing groups to produce food for sale in the market. For instance, studies on Tanzania and Mozambique have revealed that the non-availability of incentive goods in rural areas has had a negative effect on the size of marketed output. Such experiences suggest that the availability of incentive goods (mainly industrial) is an important component of the policy package for increasing marketable surplus.

The role of food prices in this policy package has been controversial. If food prices are kept low, efforts to increase food output may be reduced but the ability of vulnerable groups to acquire food may be enhanced. If prices are kept high, food producers' efforts may be stepped up but the poor groups in society may not have access to the more expensive food. The solution of subsidizing food often runs out of steam in the face of budget deficits. However, Mellor (1986) has argued that rising food prices are usually indicators of supply problems arising from sluggish technological change, while declining food prices indicate success in inducing rapid technological change. This suggests that helping food producers to increase output and marketable surplus requires not only price incentives but also agricultural inputs, innovations (e.g. new seeds, new technology), information (e.g. extension services), infrastructure (e.g. roads, irrigation), and effective institutions (e.g. marketing, credit, land reform). Industry can make an important contribution to increasing marketable surplus at reasonable prices by promoting the availability of some of these factors.

(c) Allocation of investment resources

The share of agriculture in development resources has been low in Africa, and within the agricultural sector the resources have been allocated in such a way that small farmers have hardly benefited from them.

On the allocation of resources to agriculture, Lipton (1985) citing FAO (1983) and UN (1983) has presented some data on the share of gross fixed investment to agriculture in 10 sub-Saharan countries. The results, given in Table 8.2, indicate that this share was below 10 per cent in seven countries. In four countries the share of investment allocated to agriculture was not more than 3 per cent.

Table 8.2 The share of gross fixed investment allocated
to agriculture

Country	% of gross fixed investment allocated to agriculture	% of the workforce engaged in agriculture
Botswana	1–3	80
Burundi	1–3	80
Togo	1–3	70
Zambia	1–3	65
Mauritius	6	28
Tanzania	6–7	80
Kenya	8	75
Lesotho	12	82
Zimbabwe	12	57
Rwanda	16	90

Source: Lipton (1985).

Within the agricultural sector, governments have tended to allocate resources so as to support the production of marketable agricultural surplus. The
question is whether and to what extent this policy has assisted small farmers in
consolidating their entitlements to food.

This question is approached here by considering the agricultural sector in
terms of two subsectors. One is the traditional sector (hereafter sector T),
dominated by small-scale farming peasants employing a low level of technology (usually based on hand-tools and to some extent on animal-drawn
equipment). The other is the modern farming sector (hereafter sector M),
dominated by large-scale private or state farms employing a high level of
technology (usually based on imported or high import content motorized
machinery) and providing the bulk of the agricultural sector wage employment. Fig. 8.1 depicts the two subsectors.

As capital accumulation takes place in sector M, line AC shifts to the right,
but OL_t also shifts to the right towards L_{t+i}. Since the proportion of the labour
force in sector T is 70–80 per cent of the total labour force in Africa, 'dualism'
(in the sense of a marked difference in labour productivity in the two sectors) is
likely to be perpetuated. In economies where capital accumulation in sector M
is accompanied by a fast expansion of employment in other sectors of the
economy (e.g. industry, services), the absorption of labour in these sectors may
be rapid enough to prevent a shift of OL_t to the right towards L_{t+i}. L_t may even
shift to the left. This is what happened in the now developed countries in
Europe and North America. In the context of Africa, however, the relative size
of CL_t is high (70–80 per cent of the total labour force and about 98 per cent of
the labour force in agriculture), and the rate at which non-agricultural sectors
are absorbing labour is very low.

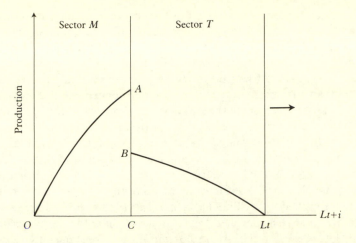

Note: *Lt*: total labour force in agriculture; sector *M*: modern farming sector; sector *T*: traditional farming sector.

Fig. 8.1. Production and productivity in two subsectors

Under these conditions, investment in sector *T* to upgrade the level of technology and raise labour productivity is likely to be a more appropriate strategy than further investment in sector *M* for two reasons. First, the degree to which investments in sector *M* are increasing employment is far below the degree to which the population in sector *T* is increasing. This partly explains the high rate of urbanization which has outpaced even the growth of employment in the non-agricultural sectors. Further investments in sector *M* would increase agricultural output and labour productivity in this sector but would not increase output, productivity, and incomes in sector *T* where 70–80 per cent of the labour force is employed. In other words, that kind of investment decision would not necessarily enhance entitlements to food for 70–80 per cent of the population. In fact, in some cases investments in sector *M* have resulted in loss of entitlement on the part of some groups in sector *T*. For instance, in the case of Nigeria, Andrae and Beckman (1985) have shown that, as a result of the Bakolori project (sector *M*), some groups (in sector *T*) lost their land, were prevented from cultivating their farms for two or three consecutive seasons, and in some cases even had their crops destroyed by contractors. Second, investments in sector *T* are likely to affect the majority of the low-income earners more directly by increasing their productivity.

In practice, however, the allocation of resources in Africa has usually favoured sector *M*. A number of studies have shown how the modern sector bias of resource allocation by governments, while creating entitlements for some wage-earning groups in agriculture, has led to the neglect of large groups of small-scale farmers. It has also been suggested that post-colonial governments have demonstrated a common inclination to allocate resources to state farms, parastatal enterprises, and joint government–private ventures in large-scale farming, often providing generous loans, subsidies, infrastructure, and technical assistance to a small number of large modern farms (Berry 1984; Heyer *et al*. 1981; Hill 1977; Samoff 1980; Bates 1981). For instance, it has been estimated that of the little public expenditure allocated to agriculture (often less than 10 per cent of the total) about 90 per cent has been allocated to the modern farming sector. In the area of research, very little has been directed to the food crops which are usually grown by the majority of small farmers. For instance, Eicher (1986) has cited Spencer (1986) on the point that less than 2 per cent of total sorghum, millet, and upland rice area in West Africa is sown to cultivars developed through modern genetic research. Although maize is more promising in East and Southern Africa, improved seeds have not been adequately supplied to smallholder farms. In the case of fertilizer consumption, IFPRI (1986) has indicated that although smallholder farms account for 75 per cent of Kenya's total agricultural output they consume only 42 per cent of total fertilizer supply. Similarly, about 80 per cent of agricultural equipment imports are destined for the modern farming sector (state farms, plantations, and agro-food complexes). The majority of peasants (70–80 per cent of population) receive direct benefit from less than 5 per cent of agricultural equipment imported (UNIDO 1983*a*: 81).

Moreover, the efficiency with which the resources allocated to sector M are used is not always impressive. The levels of utilization of modern equipment has been low, even though its importation consumes scarce foreign exchange. For instance, according to UNIDO (1983*a*), a report from the Kenyan Ministry of Agriculture shows that the level of productive utilization of tractors from Kenya's Tractor Hire Service was only 7 per cent. Similarly low rates have been recorded in many countries of sub-Saharan Africa.

Attempts to combine high-level mechanization with the peasant economy have not been very successful either. The contradictions pointed out by Andrae and Beckman (1985) in the case of wheat production in Nigeria, between the social organization implicit in a high level of mechanization and that of the peasant economy, are quite instructive. For instance, they have pointed out that mobile combine harvesters were turned to stationary combine harvesters which had to be fed manually by farmers who cut their wheat with sickles. The high-capacity combines are made to perform the work of a simple stationary thresher partly because the farmers' plots are too small to be harvested by a combine if each peasant is to receive his own crop.

In this section it has been shown that only a very small proportion of total investment is channelled into agriculture. Out of this small investment only a small proportion is channelled into the smallholder farming community in spite of this community's high share of the total labour force. In order to enhance the productivity of smallholder farmers and enhance their entitlement to food there is a strong case for channelling more resources into the small-holder farm sector. In the light of interaction of household decisions as both producer and consumer as demonstrated, for instance, by Singh *et al.* (1986) the numerous linkages between agriculture and other sectors (e.g. through investments, consumption, production, foreign trade, and employment) must be taken into consideration. Support towards raising productivity and incomes of the smallholder farmers will consist of a broader policy package than direct investments in agriculture. In this context investments in rural industry, in rural workshops for manufacturing and repairing farm tools and equipment, rural-based agricultural processing activities, rural transport systems, and investment in employment intensive and local resource-using activities producing incentive goods would result in the growth of productivity, incomes, and employment in the bulk of the rural areas in Africa.

(d) Wage employment in agriculture

Agricultural wage earners are usually employed on large farms (private or public). For some of them the wage earned is all the entitlement they have to exchange for food while for others this is supplementary income. This group is a product of the process of agrarian change over time in many ways. In some cases rural poverty compelled people to seek off-farm employment (Hill 1972). Such rural poverty may be due to loss of access to an adequate amount of land (or to any at all) or to the loss of harvest due to drought as in the case of parts of Ethiopia (Burki 1985; Sen 1981). In many cases, however, this group consists of members of the family who migrate to work on the large farms and leave behind the rest of their family members on the small farm. This has been a way of ensuring that resources generated from the land are supplemented by wage income in a way which reduces risk of loss of entitlement in case of crop failure. In some cases this additional income has been used to help finance purchases of rural land or to increase the peasant production for the market (Collier and Lal 1980; Berry 1984).

There are, thus, diverse reasons for the expansion of wage employment in African agriculture. While some of these reasons relate to the impoverishment of some sections of the rural population, it is also important to recognize the positive contribution of wage employment to the diversification of rural incomes. The development of non-agricultural or off-farm employment in rural areas, e.g. by relocation of some industries in these areas, can play a similarly positive role.

(e) Off-farm activities

In order to safeguard their entitlements in the event of crop failure, some peasants engage in off-farm economic activities for extra income. Other groups who were formerly peasants and lost their entitlement to land have no choice but to seek alternative employment. Since wage employment opportunities in other sectors are limited, these groups are often forced to turn to non-farm activities to earn a living.

As regards the first group (i.e. peasants who seek to supplement their farm incomes), their entitlements to food have tended to be enhanced by their non-farm activities. For instance, a study of smallholding households in central Kenya has shown that on average nearly half of their annual cash incomes were derived from off-farm sources (Njonjo 1981). In fact, one of the main observations made in the predominantly smallholder zone in Kenya is the growth of private services, a trend which brings out the linkages between agricultural production and non-agricultural employment (IFPRI 1986; Heyer in Chapter 7 above). Berry (1984) has pointed out that income from off-farm employment is a kind of windfall gain for rural households whose members seek a vent for their surplus labour in the dry season by migrating (Prothero 1975). For instance, Byerlee *et al.* (1983) found that adults in rural areas in Sierra Leone worked an average of 70 hours per month in the dry season, mainly on small-scale manufacturing which was for them an important source of dry-season employment.

The tendency to diversify sources of income has been noted even among the surplus earning farmers who tend to diversify their portfolios using the proceeds of their farms to invest in trade and urban real estate rather than in expanded agricultural production (Berry 1984; Boesen and Mohele 1979; Cliffe 1978). This may be a reflection of greater profit-making opportunities in the tertiary sector, as suggested by Berry (1984), but it may also be an expression of the importance of spreading the sources of income for purposes of reducing the risk of loss of entitlements. Thus, there are also important linkages between agriculture and other sectors through the processes of saving and investment. The tendency of surplus-earning farmers to diversify their portfolios into non-agricultural activities suggests that, if conditions were favourable, these investments could be channelled into the industrial activities which are complementary to agriculture. But as shown in sections 8.4 and 8.5 this has largely not been the case in practice.

(f) Employment in industry

In the African context, industrial employment has remained quite small. Industrial sector employment constitutes only 3–5 per cent of the labour force in sub-Saharan Africa. Moreover, the rate of growth of industrial employment has lagged behind that of industrial output. The increasing use of capital intensive techniques of production is one of the reasons why the contribution of industry to enhancing entitlements through employment has been limited.

A more important observation in our context is the nature of the relationship between the development of large-scale industry on the one hand, and rural small-scale and cottage industries on the other. The relationship between them has been more competitive than complementary, with large-scale industry developing at the expense of, rather than in support of, rural industries. In Tanzania, for instance, Muller (1978) has indicated that rural-based metal-working skills degenerated when large-scale farm implements came into use, while in Kenya, Kongstad (1980) has pointed out that mechanical workshops in non-urban areas are degenerating partly because of the influx of products from the large Nairobi-based factory. In the case of Ethiopia, Mohammed (1980) has referred to the same phenomenon in the textile sector. This particular tendency has resulted in a loss of incomes for those who were engaged in such small-scale industrial activities. To the extent that individuals in the food production sector were partially engaged in these small industrial activities, this loss makes them more vulnerable to loss of entitlements in the event of crop failure and/or depresses their purchasing power (e.g. for agricultural inputs and consumer goods).

Two policy implications arise from these observations. First, there is a need to make rural industries and large-scale industries complementary, e.g. through contracting. Second, the linkage between industry and food production activities in agriculture needs to be developed.

8.4. *Agricultural equipment and inputs*

The agricultural sectors of most African countries have experienced shortages of agricultural equipment and inputs. One report (World Bank 1981) has suggested that this shortage is caused by weaknesses in distribution. It has argued that the distribution of these equipments and inputs has been in the hands of state organizations and that these state organizations have not carried out this function effectively and efficiently. The problem of shortage of agricultural equipment and inputs in Africa, however, goes beyond the sphere of distribution. The experience of most African countries suggests that in analysing this problem the otherwise well-known relationship between industry and agriculture has been neglected. This has largely inhibited industry from contributing to the alleviation of hunger and poverty through increased productivity in agriculture and in food production in particular.

In order to bring out this phenomenon, this section will examine one case-study, namely production of agricultural equipment. The choice of study of agricultural equipment is not necessarily a reflection of its importance relative to other agricultural inputs. The findings on the manufacture of agricultural equipment will provide useful lessons on the role of industry in developing agricultural technology, a role with three distinct benefits: first, increasing productivity in agriculture, thereby increasing the supply of food among other things; second, increasing the productivity of the low-income small farmers; third, creating incomes for those who are engaged in the industries which manufacture and repair agricultural equipment. The findings from this case-study are largely applicable for other types of agricultural inputs too.

(a) *Level and structure of production*

The experience of most countries in Africa suggests that the inadequate supply of equipment to agriculture reflects sectoral imbalances. The industrial sectors, even in countries where industry is relatively well developed (e.g. Nigeria) have not been linked to the agricultural sectors in terms of supplying the latter with equipment. The domestic industrial sector produces a very small share of all equipment actually used in agriculture. Africa's own agricultural machinery sector employs less than 1 per cent of the total industrial labour force. Its output accounts for less than 10 per cent of the total market for agricultural machinery (UNIDO 1983a). In fact, the study of UNIDO (1983a)[3] suggests that the present indigenous agricultural machinery industry in most African countries is not only small but also in such poor shape financially and technologically that its very survival is in doubt.

As far as the problems faced by manufacturers of agricultural equipment in Africa are concerned, experience has shown that:

1. even though a demand often exists, local producers take only a small share of it and have so far been unable to contribute anything more;
2. they lack the ability to compete with imports and they are often not protected from these imports,
3. they lack the knowledge to supply the market with what it really needs.

As a consequence, some firms underutilize their capacity while others diversify into other lines of business.

Links between the existing basic industrial installations and agricultural machinery companies are very limited. This is in spite of the fact that nearly all the industrial units studied by UNIDO (1983a) in the sector were set up during the 1950–72 period. They benefit from long experience but in many cases they operate almost in isolation of other engineering activities in the local industrial sector.

In recent years only a few units have been established, while many have either disappeared, or been merged with others, or have abandoned production of agricultural equipment in their manufacturing programme. Only about one-third of the companies exclusively produce agricultural equipment. The others have diversified production into other product lines or are producers coming from outside the sector.

Via their subsidiaries and agents it is the Trans National Corporations that supply most of the imported equipment. TNCs' local production takes place in response to government pressure and is usually limited to final assembly of imported pre-assembled units. Because of the importance of the size of the market these are found in the larger African countries. Their emphasis in local production is always on tractors and heavy equipment for land improvement.

---

[3] The study by UNIDO (1983a) is based on a major data-gathering exercise which was undertaken in 16 countries of Africa in 1981. Each case-study focused on the ability of the country to produce agricultural hand-tools, machinery, and equipment locally and on the demand for such goods at the beginning of the 1980s. The 16 countries represent different development levels and agroecological conditions in the four geographical subregions of Africa. In this sample agriculture contributes 35% of the GDP and employs 74% of the active population.

The local producers' share (the rate of self-sufficiency) is thus 15 per cent based on final value and only 5 per cent based on added value (UNIDO 1983*a*).

The level of development of the agricultural equipment manufacturing sector is low both in relation to total industrial output and in relation to total demand. The structure of the sector is biased in favour of assembly of equipment for sector M with weak, if any, links with the rest of the domestic industrial sector.

(b)   Imports of agricultural equipment

To the extent that the domestic industrial sector is not geared to the production of agricultural equipment, most of the demand for this has had to be met by imports. Thus imported agricultural equipment constitutes about 90 per cent of total supplies. As shown in Table 8.3, tractors constitute 60–70 per cent of all imports of agricultural machinery. In world terms, Africa shows a greater than average emphasis on tractors.[4] Import data show a rapid increase in agricultural machinery up to 1975 followed by a series of erratic moves in the second half of the 1970s.

Another characteristic of imports of agricultural equipment is the proliferation of the importing channels in most countries in Africa. There is a tendency to allow too many import companies to operate, resulting in numerous models irrespective of the size of the market. For instance, UNIDO (1983*a*) has reported that in Sudan there are 20 companies importing tractors for a market of 575 units (1980), while in Zambia there are 17 companies from 15 different countries importing a total of less than 800 units. In many countries in Africa this tendency exacerbates the problems of maintenance and supplies of spare parts. The situation is further aggravated by the weak link between the activities of these importing channels and the local engineering activities. These factors play an important part in the observed low levels of tractor utilization.

These observations point to the need to formulate import policies which (1) encourage selective agricultural equipment imports with a view to supporting local industry and maintenance (possibly by stimulating demand through local manufacture of parts and components as well as maintenance and repair workshops), and (2) protect infant industries which are engaged in the production of various types of agricultural equipment.

(c)   The link with research and development

It has been observed that most local manufactures of agricultural equipment in Africa have been assemblies of imported components. To the extent that this is the case, these manufactures need not coincide with the real needs of the agricultural sector in Africa. One way of linking local manufacture of agricultural equipment to the needs of farmers in sector M, and even more

---

[4] The world average is 55% compared to 60–70% for Africa.

Table 8.3 Africa's imports of agricultural machinery, 1973–1979 ($000)

Year	Group	Hand-tools[a]	Tractors[b]	Other[c]	Total
1973	All developing Africa[d] of which:	14,366	142,092	77,595	234,053
	Sub-Saharan Africa	11,189	93,389	36,171	140,749
	LDCs	3,472	25,609	14,168	43,249
1974	All developing Africa[d] of which:	20,016	227,215	102,724	349,955
	Sub-Saharan Africa	16,310	129,389	50,506	196,205
	LDCs	5,193	36,133	19,183	60,909
1975	All developing Africa[d] of which:	28,934	366,026	166,723	561,683
	Sub-Saharan Africa	25,644	244,632	83,983	344,259
	LDCs	10,113	50,354	32,026	92,493
1976	All developing Africa[d] of which:	28,859	349,012	134,477	512,348
	Sub-Saharan Africa	25,482	235,268	73,785	334,259
	LDCs	9,018	41,480	26,301	76,799
1977	All developing Africa[d] of which:	34,682	441,983	167,338	664,003
	Sub-Saharan Africa	28,912	296,793	107,169	432,874
	LDCs	10,079	50,113	30,040	90,232
1978	All developing Africa[d] of which:	42,274	535,126	213,613	781,013
	Sub-Saharan Africa	37,095	270,975	135,635	443,705
	LDCs	14,831	46,084	41,328	102,243
1979	All developing Africa[d] of which:	32,004	293,481	193,623	519,108
	Sub-Saharan Africa	35,504	171,195	101,450	298,149
	LDCs	8,166	60,115	44,282	112,563

[a] Standard International Trade Classification 695.1.
[b] Standard International Trade Classification 712.5.
[c] Standard International Trade Classification 712 less 712.5.
[d] Excludes only South Africa.

Note: LDCs = Least developed countries in sub-Saharan Africa.

Source: United Nations Statistical Office, New York.

importantly sector T, is through local research and development. A strong link between local research and development units and the farmers on the one hand and the local manufacturers of this equipment on the other is necessary. In this context UNIDO (1983a) examined the status of R. & D. activities and observed that there is little R. & D. capability at the producer level, which constitutes a major barrier to technological progress and prevents design and adaptation of machinery to local needs. Furthermore, it has been noted that there are no subregional or regional organizations (or associations of national organizations) devoted to designing, testing, and manufacturing agricultural machinery (whereas in, say, Southern Asia there is a Regional Network for Agricultural Machinery).

Most of the activities of the agriculture-oriented research and development centres principally concern testing of imported equipment. Efforts are often duplicated (intra- and inter-country), there is little exchange of prototypes, little co-ordination of programmes, and most prototypes remain as prototypes (because of the weak link with manufacturing or lack of financing). Weak R. & D. facilities combined with a weak base of local production of agricultural equipment make it very difficult to respond to the needs of the majority of small farmers in sector T.

The results of the interaction between weak R. & D. and a weak manufacturing base have been demonstrated in a number of studies. For instance, the report of the Commonwealth Secretariat (1979a) found that even where locally developed implements were being tested the absence of local workshop/manufacturing capacity inhibited production of the recommended modifications and adaptations. On the limited manufacturing capacity, the workshop[5] noted *inter alia* that although the technique of manufacturing mouldboard ploughs is not sophisticated there are few workshops where these are being assembled or manufactured in Africa. Kaul (1979) has further indicated that, according to research carried out by the Institute of Agricultural Research at Zaria, implements introduced to Nigeria (e.g. Ariana, Unibar) have a potential use but have not been widely adopted due to lack of availability and inadequate users' training. An earlier Report of the Rural Technology Meet (Commonwealth Secretariat 1977) indicated that in response to the growing realization of the need for low-cost, locally made, and easily managed implements, R. & D. institutions in many countries of Africa have developed new models of animal-drawn ploughs and planters, water pumps, windmills, carts, and other types of simple equipment. However, the report goes further to indicate that with few exceptions the designs have not been manufactured on a large scale and have not yet been widely accepted by farmers. This is in spite of the benefits of using this equipment. In his study of the economics of animal traction in Burkina Faso, Jaeger (1985) observed acreage increases of 30 per cent where the weeding implements were used, and yield increases were found where the ox-plough was dominant. A further study by Kjaerby (1983) found that in Tanzania users of ploughs have higher earnings than users of hoes, while in addition he cites studies from other countries which show that the plough made the work load for women relatively lighter in The Gambia

---

[5] The workshop was organized by the Commonwealth Secretariat in Zaria (Nigeria) in 1979.

(Mettrick 1978) and Senegal (Venema 1980). These studies demonstrate that the adoption of appropriate agricultural equipment is capable of increasing the earnings of the small farmer. What seems to be lacking, as was mentioned earlier, is a strong link between R. & D. and the farmers (especially the small farmers) on the one hand and the local manufacturing units on the other.

In examining the process involved between perceiving specific needs of target groups in society and actually meeting these needs through local production of agricultural equipment, the six stages suggested by Wright (1977) are useful in locating the obstacles in this process. These stages are as follows:

1. analysis of needs, resources, and constraints;
2. search for suitable existing equipment;
3. design, construction, and testing of experimental prototypes;
4. field testing of production prototypes;
5. limited adoption;
6. widespread adoption.

While numerous programmes in Africa have reached stages (3) or (4), few have gone beyond. Wright examined those cases which had failed to go beyond stages (3) or (4) and those few which had gone through all the stages with a view to identifying reasons for success or failure in this context. He found that cases which have not gone beyond stages (3) or (4) were characterized by failure to prove their economic viability in the hands of local farmers, or were inhibited by limited local manufacturing facilities. The successful cases were both economically viable and enjoyed the support of the available local manufacturing facilities.

The co-ordination of inputs, Wright (1977) observes, has proved to be another stumbling block in moving through the six stages. Citing the experience of Tanzania, Wright indicates that while testing and development of agricultural equipment was carried out by TAMTU (Tanzania Agricultural Machinery Testing Unit), nobody seemed to be willing and able to manufacture the items the unit had successfully developed. The large factory (UFI) was already utilizing all its capacity to meet demands for standard hand-tools and the mould plough. TAMTU therefore set up a limited number of pilot rural craft workshops in several regions of the country. These, however, being run as government departments could not be operated commercially and often ran into financial difficulties. Beeney (1975) has evaluated the performance of these rural craft workshops and has observed that they suffered from lack of financial support and positive direction. Some had too little physical space (100 square metres) and their machine tools were too small for batch production of the ox-carts that they were required to produce. Instead of providing facilities required to strengthen these workshops, the government was going ahead through SIDO (Small Industries Development Organization) to set up common facility workshops for industrial estates in various regions. The link between R. & D. and manufacturing activities remained rather weak, making it difficult for programmes initiated by TAMTU to proceed beyond stage (3) or (4).

From the above observations, it appears that the link between the needs of the farmers (especially the small farmers) and the local manufacture of the kind of agricultural equipment they need has been inhibited by both weak R. & D. and weak base of local industry.

(d) Demand for agricultural equipment

The interaction between R. & D. activities and the local manufacturing capacity does not imply that there are no problems on the demand side. In fact there are considerable problems on the demand side, such as small size of national markets, an absence of subregional trading, general insolvency of the rural population (aggravated by inadequate agricultural credit, low producer prices, and restricted subsidies for equipment purchases), market instability resulting from policy and climatic changes, and competition from imports.

In most countries of Africa there is no clear agro-mechanization policy (Commonwealth Secretariat 1977). This contributes to making it difficult to marshal such support measures within the overall development plans of these countries.

There is a need to stimulate demand for equipment in order to facilitate widespread adoption and expanded local manufacture of the equipment. However, credit and servicing facilities have been a constraint in some countries. For example, the Commonwealth Secretariat (1979b) has reported that in Swaziland the Tinkabi (a small locally developed tractor) is selling in very small numbers (only 23 units were sold within the country in 1977 compared to the production capacity of 2,500 units a year and imports of about 200 tractors per year) because of lack of market promotion and credit facilities. It is reported that it is easier for a Swaziland farmer to get a bank loan of E7,000 for an imported Massey-Ferguson tractor with no implements than a loan of E2,700 for a Tinkabi with a full set of implements (plough, planter, harrow, ridger, and trailer) built in. This is in spite of the fact that services for Tinkabi are well developed in the country and that farmers are keen to buy the machine, using it as a mobile maize mill and irrigation pump as well as for transportation, in addition to land preparation and planting. In his study of the development of ox-cultivation in Tanzania, Kjaerby (1983) found that government actions tended to support tractorization via credit and allocation to villages and state farms. For instance, during 1981/2 TRDB (Tanzania Rural Development Bank),[6] which is the main institution providing credit facilities for the rural areas, approved shs 7 million for tractors compared to shs 1 million for ploughs. Although oxen and ploughs are complementary there was no credit

---

[6] It has changed its name to CRDB (Cooperative and Rural Development Bank).

facility for oxen. Kjaerby further observed that although donor reports by FAO (1975) and World Bank (1977) endorsed the superiority of the plough over the tractor, in practice they continued to channel their support facilities into tractorization.

On credit, the UNIDO (1983*a*) study found that when Senegal halted distribution of credit to the co-operatives there was a major collapse of demand for agricultural machinery. In contrast, Togo introduced credit for purchasing draught cattle resulting in increase in demand for animal-drawn equipment.

As regards the competition from imports, the case-studies (UNIDO 1983*a*) have indicated that local production of agricultural tools in Kenya and Nigeria declined as a result of this competition. This suggests that there is a case for pursuing import policies which complement rather than inhibit local production.

These observations suggest that there is need to stimulate demand through

1. improving credit facilities especially to the small farmers;
2. improving service facilities for agricultural equipment, probably by establishing rural workshops in the areas where such equipment is used;
3. formulating mechanization policies which incorporate the interests and ability of the low-income small farmers;
4. formulating and implementing import policies which enhance the complementarity between imports and local industry, especially in the field of production of agricultural equipment.

8.5.   *The role of industry in agricultural processing*

Agricultural processing can play the role of stabilizing the incomes of peasants, preparing products for exports, facilitating inter-regional and intra-regional trade, stabilizing prices of food products between seasons, inducing an increase in marketable surplus and productivity by reducing wastage of seasonal surpluses and by extending the marketability of the farmers' crops nationally or internationally, and integrating agricultural and industrial operations. The share of Africa in world manufacturing value added (MVA) declined from 1.9 per cent in 1970 to 1.7 per cent in 1981 for food products, while for beverages and tobacco it increased respectively from 1.8 per cent to 3.1 per cent and from 2.9 per cent to 3.5 per cent (UNCTAD 1985: 4).

The state of the agro-food sector in Africa reflects the relatively low levels of industrialization and the slow progress of agricultural production. In sub-Saharan Africa the best results seem to occur in countries which have a diversified agricultural sector (e.g. Ivory Coast, Kenya, Zimbabwe, Cameroon, Nigeria). At the top of the scale are a few export industries operated mainly by foreign firms, usually TNCs. This extensive involvement of TNCs in processing activities in Africa is influenced by factors such as the size of the domestic market and the development of export markets. Overall, however, the performance of the export agro-industrial sector has not been impressive in spite of the good market networks that foreign firms are expected to have.

The developed market-economy countries have tended to divert their imports of agro-industrial products away from sub-Saharan Africa, contributing to the decline of the share of imports from Africa from 8.7 per cent in 1974 to 4.3 per cent in 1984. The most sharply declining shares were those of food products (from 14.6 per cent to 8.2 per cent), processed vegetable and animal oils (from 21.7 per cent to 6.3 per cent), and wood products (from 13 per cent to 6.4 per cent) (UNCTAD 1985). Another factor which has contributed to this decline is the fact that developed countries that were previously major importers of agro-industrial products have become self-sufficient (or even surplus producers). Demand problems (e.g. low-income elasticity of demand, utilization of synthetic substitutes) and protectionism (with tariffs escalating with the stage of processing) have contributed to the unfavourable trend. For instance, during 1970–80 industrialized countries almost doubled production of sugar even though beet sugar cannot compete with tropical sugar without protection. Yet in spite of the bleak prospects of sugar exports some African countries have invested heavily in sugar complexes (e.g. Ivory Coast, Cameroon, Sudan).

The dependence of agro-industries on the agricultural sector for the supply of raw materials meant that they could not perform well when agricultural sector performance was low. For instance, in Somalia the low capacity utilization problem in the food-processing sector has been attributed to the bottlenecks in agricultural production (UNIDO 1983b). In contrast, Malawi has been pursuing a strategy of resource-based industrial development where about 51 per cent of manufacturing value added (MVA) originates from agro-processing. During 1973–9 about 70 per cent of the increase in MVA was in agro-processing, reflecting the expansion of agriculture (UNIDO 1983c).

From the technological point of view, the bulk of agricultural processing activity has taken place in large-scale centralized production capacities. These technologies have been employed by foreign firms or state enterprises and have been associated with the modern farming sector rather than the small farmers who are in the majority. The logistics involved in having to supply raw materials to a few centralized large plants (e.g. in terms of infrastructure and maintenance requirements) have tended to erode the expected superiority of these enterprises. However, the local manufacture of equipment for the agro-processing industry has remained virtually non-existent. The bulk of agro-processing activities have had a weak link with agricultural activities of small farmers on the one hand and with local industrial and technological activities on the other.

The positive contribution of local industry food processing has been inhibited by the choice of technologies which make use of imported capital intensive plants, sometimes not based on the use of locally available resources. In addition, the organization of production is so centralized that the links between processing plants and the rural areas have tended to remain weak. For instance, Jones (1986) has argued that many of the decisions on food technology in Tanzania have not taken into account the balance of resources available locally. He has cited the case of National Milling Corporation's (NMC) large-scale bakery which involved high capital cost in foreign exchange to process a product which is not adequately produced locally, hence not promoting food security based on local agriculture. On the latter point Andrae and Beckman (1985) have made at least two further observations in the case of Nigeria. First, they observe that the bread industry almost entirely depends on imports. Second, the presence of wheat flour mills obstructs any attempt to scale down wheat imports, and dependence on imported food is built into the industrial structure of the economy.

Jones (1986) has cited another NMC project, the Silo project, which is high capital cost, import intensive, and centralized. He argues that the same storage capacity could have been created at about one-quarter of the cost (hardly involving any foreign exchange) by constructing 120 go-downs spread throughout the country. In addition this would have improved food security in the regions, employment, the use of locally available construction materials, and would have economized on transport requirements. The decision to adopt this project was partly influenced by the already established large-scale grain mills. Similar issues arise in the case of fruit canning, milk preservation, oilseed extraction, sugar production, and grain milling. In many cases, in practice, it is not a matter of choice between large- and small-scale or centralized and decentralized plants, but of an appropriate combination of these reflecting different levels from village and district levels to regional, national, and subregional levels. What is rather conspicuous here is the very rare occurrence of decentralized organization of production at village and district levels.

It has also been observed that the existence of advanced technology for processing imported foodstuffs like wheat and barley has inhibited the development of technologies for processing locally grown food products. This has been demonstrated quite well by Andrae and Beckman (1985) in their study of wheat in Nigeria.

The observations made above suggest that in order to enhance the positive contribution of industry to the availability of and access to food, there is a need to pay greater attention to the decisions on food technology with a view to spreading the processing units to the countryside, to stimulating the local machine-building industry, to economizing on infrastructural requirements (e.g. transport, complex management systems), and to stimulating employment and incomes in the economy particularly in the countryside.

8.6. *Conclusion*

This chapter has examined the positive contribution of industry in alleviating the food problem in sub-Saharan Africa. It has been pointed out that the declining rate of growth of food production and falling food output per capita in Africa represent a threat of increasing hunger. The declining food self-sufficiency ratios raise concern but it has been argued that food self-sufficiency objectives must take into account country-specific long-term comparative advantages. The role of industry has been examined in terms of its contribution both to raising productivity in agriculture and to generating incomes in non-agricultural activities.

It has been shown that only a small proportion of total investment is allocated to agriculture, the bulk of which goes to the large-scale and usually capital intensive farms. The majority of the small-scale farmers are bypassed by investments made in agriculture. It is suggested that in order to enhance productivity and entitlements of the majority of the low-income small farmers, investments should be channelled to the smallholders' farm sector not only directly in agriculture but also in related activities like rural industry, rural workshops, and rural transport.

The chapter has indicated that non-agricultural activities in the rural areas are important in making use of surplus labour (all the time or during the dry season when there are no farming activities), supplementing rural incomes, and reducing the risk of loss of entitlements on the part of the low-income small farmers.

The chapter proceeded to observe that direct industrial employment has been limited largely to undertaking capital intensive investments. The relationship between large-scale industry and rural small industry has tended to be competitive rather than complementary. This competitive relationship has resulted in loss of entitlements on the part of income earners in small-scale industries. This suggests that there is need to make rural small-scale industries and large-scale industries complementary and create linkages between industry and food production activities in agriculture.

In respect of agricultural technology, an investigation of the case of agricultural equipment has indicated that the industrial sector in Africa produces a very small share of all equipment actually used in agriculture. Links between the existing basic industrial installations and agricultural machinery companies are very limited. The bulk of agricultural equipment is imported and there is a proliferation of the importing channels. In addition, there is little R. & D. capability at the producer level and this inhibits technological progress, and design and adaptation of equipment to local needs. The link between the needs of farmers (especially the small farmers) and the local manufacture of the needed agricultural equipment has been inhibited by weak R. & D. and a low base of local manufacturing industry. These findings suggest that there is a need to strengthen the link between R. & D. and small farmers on the one hand

and R. & D. and local manufacture on the other. Considering that the incomes of most small farmers are low, the role of credit is of considerable importance in generating an adequate demand for agricultural equipment. As regards imports, it will be appropriate to design import policies which are supportive of the local production of agricultural equipment.

The level of development of food-processing industries in Africa is relatively low, reflecting low levels of industrialization and the slow progress of agricultural production. The bulk of food processing has taken place in large-scale centralized production capacities mainly associated with the large-scale farming sector. These activities have exhibited a weak link with agricultural activities of small farmers on the one hand and a weak link with the local industrial and technological activities on the other. This suggests that there is a need to pay greater attention to the development of local food-processing technology, decentralize food-processing units to the food-producing countryside, stimulate the local machine-building industry, and economize on infrastructural requirements.

References

African Emergency Report No. 7, Apr.–May 1986, 'A Periodic Report on the Crisis'.

AMANI, H. K. R. (1986), 'Food Problem: The Role of the National Food Strategy', paper presented at the International Conference on the Arusha Declaration, Arusha, 16–19 Dec.

ANDRAE, G., and BECKMAN, B. (1985), *The Wheat Trap: Bread and Underdevelopment in Nigeria* (London: Zed).

BATES, R. (1981), *Markets and States in Tropical Africa* (Berkeley, Calif.: University of California Press).

BEENEY, J. M. (1975), 'Agricultural Mechanization Study', UNDP Report to the United Republic of Tanzania (Rome: FAO).

BERRY, S. S. (1984), 'The Food Crisis and Agrarian Change in Africa: A Review Essay', *African Studies Review*, 27.

BOESEN, J., and MOHELE, T. (1979), *The 'Success Story' of Peasant Tobacco Production in Tanzania* (Uppsala: SIAS).

BRAUN, J. VON, and KENNEDY, E. (1986), 'Commercialization of Subsistance Agriculture: Income and Nutritional Effects of Developing Countries', Working Paper (Washington, DC: IFPRI).

BURKI, S. J. (1985), 'The African Food Crisis: Looking Beyond the Emergency', paper presented at a Conference on South–South Cooperation, 11–14 Nov., Harare.

BYERLEE, D., *et al.* (1983), 'Employment Output Conflicts, Factor-Price Distortions and Choice of Technique: Empirical Results from Sierra Leone', *Economic Development and Cultural Change*, 31.

CLIFFE, L. (1978), 'Labour Migration and Peasant Differentiation: The Zambia Case', *Journal of Peasant Studies*, 5.

COLLIER, P., and LAL, D. (1980), 'Poverty and Growth in Kenya', World Bank Staff Paper No. 389 (Washington, DC: World Bank).

Commonwealth Secretariat (1977), Report of the Rural Technology Meet for East, Central and Southern Africa, Arusha, Tanzania, 29 Aug.–9 Sept.

——(1979a), Proceedings of the Appropriate Tillage Workshop, IAR, Zaria, Nigeria, 16–20 Jan.

——(1979b), Proceedings of the Appropriate Technology Coordinators Meeting, Lusaka, Zambia, 9–25 June.

EICHER, C. K. (1986), 'Transforming African Agriculture', *Hunger Project Papers*, 4 (Washington, DC).

ELLMAN, A., MACKAY, B., and MOODY, T. (1981), *Guide to Technology Transfer in East, Central and Southern Africa* (London: Commonwealth Secretariat).

FAO (1975), 'Assistance to Agricultural Mechanization: Tanzania, Mission Report' (Rome: FAO).

——(1981), 'Agriculture: Toward 2000', Economic and Social Development Series No. 23 (Rome: FAO).

——(1983), *Production Year Book 1981* (Rome: FAO).

GEOFREY, M. (1985), 'Trade and Exchange Rate Policy? A Further Contribution to the Debate', in Rose (1985).

GOODY, J. (1980), 'Rice Burning and the Green Revolution in Northern Ghana', *Journal of Development Studies*, 16.

HEYER, J., et al. (1981), *Rural Development in Tropical Africa* (New York).

HILL, F. (1977), 'Experiments with a Public Sector Peasantry', *African Studies Review*, 20.

HILL, P. (1972), *Rural Hausa* (Cambridge: Cambridge University Press).

International Food Policy Research Institute (1986), International Food Policy Research Institute Report 8 (Washington, DC: IFPRI).

ISHIKAWA, S. (1964), *Conditions for Agricultural Development in Developing Asian Countries* (Tokyo: Committee for the Translation of Economic Studies).

JAEGER, W. K. (1985), 'Agricultural Mechanization: The Economics of Animal Traction in Burkina Faso', unpublished Ph.D. dissertation, Stanford University.

JOHNSTON, B. (1951), 'Agricultural Productivity and Economic Development in Japan', *Journal of Political Economy*, 59.

—— and KILBY, P. (1975), *Agriculture and Transformation* (Oxford).

—— and MELLOR, J. W. (eds.) (1966), *The Economics of Agricultural Development* (Ithaca, NY: Cornell University Press).

JONES, J. V. S. (1986), 'Food Security and Economic Development in Tanzania? Past Problems and Proposals for a New Strategy', paper presented to the International Conference on the Arusha Declaration held in Arusha, 16–19 Dec.

KAUL, R. N. (1979), 'Some Considerations for Tillage Research', in Commonwealth Secretariat (1979a).

KIGODA, M. A. (1984), 'Incentives for Food Crop Production in Tanzania with Special Reference to the Mbeya Region', unpublished Ph.D. dissertation, Columbia, University of Missouri.

KJAERBY, F. (1983), 'Problems and Contradictions in the Development of Ox-Cultivation in Tanzania', Research Report No. 66 (Uppsala: Scandinavian Institute for African Studies).

KONGSTAD, P. (1980), 'Kenya: Industrial Growth or Industrial Development', in Rweyemamu (1980).

LEMMA, H. (1985), 'The Politics of Famine in Ethiopia', *Review of African Political Economy*, Aug.

LEWIS, W. A. (1954), 'Economic Development with Unlimited Supplies of Labour', *Manchester School*, 2, May.

LIPTON, M. (1985), 'Research and the Design of a Policy Frame for Agriculture' in Rose (1985).

MELLOR, J. W. (1986), 'Agriculture on the Road to Industrialization' in Lewis, J. P., and Kallab, V. (eds.), *Development Strategies Reconsidered*, US–Third World Policy Perspectives No. 5 (Washington, DC).

—— and LELE, U. (1973), 'Growth Linkages of the New Food Grain Technologies', *Indian Journal of Agricultural Economics*, 1.

METTRICK, H. (1978), 'Oxenization in the Gambia: An Evaluation' (London: Ministry of Overseas Development).

MOHAMMED, D. (1980), 'Industrialization and Income Distribution in Ethiopia' in Rweyemamu (1980).

MORRISSON, C. (1985), 'Agricultural Production and Government Policy in Burkina Faso and Mali', in Rose (1985).

MULLER, J. (1978), 'Promotion of Manufactures of Rural Implements in the United Republic of Tanzania', in UNIDO, *Industrialization and Rural Development* (New York: United Nations).

NJONJO, A. V. (1981), 'The Kenya Peasantry: A Reassessment', *Review of African Political Economy*, 20.

NORMAN, D., *et al.* (1979), *Technical Change and the Small Farmer in Hausaland, N. Nigeria* (Department of Economics, Michigan State University).

O'BRIEN, J. (1985), 'Sowing the Seeds of Famine: The Political Economy of Food Deficits in Sudan', *Review of African Political Economy*, Aug.

OHKAWA, K. (1972), *Differential Structure and Agriculture: Essays on Dualistic Growth* (Tokyo: Hitotsubashi University).

PEARSON, S., *et al.* (1981), *Rice in West Africa: Policy and Economics* (SUP).

PRATTLEY, W. (1986), the special representative of the UN Secretary General in the Sudan quoted in Africa Emergency Report No. 7, Apr.–May.

PROTHERO, R. (1975), *Migrant Labour from Sokoto Province, Northern Nigeria* (Liverpool: Department of Geography).

RANGER, T. (1971), *Agricultural History of Zambia* (RLI).

RICHARDS, P. (1983), 'Farming System and Agrarian Change in West Africa', *Progress in Human Geography*, 7.

ROSE, TORE (ed.) (1985), *Crisis and Recovery in Sub-Saharan Africa* (Paris: OECD).

RWEYEMAMU, J. F. (1980) (ed.), *Industrialization and Income Distribution in Africa* (Dakar: CODESRIA Book Series).

SAMOFF, J. (1980), 'Underdevelopment and its Grass Roots in Africa', *Canadian Journal of African Studies*, 14.

SCHOEPF, B. G. (1985), 'Food Crisis and Class Formation in Shaba', *Review of African Political Economy*, Aug.

SEN, A. K. (1981), *Poverty and Famines* (Oxford: Oxford University Press).

——(1986), 'Food, Economics and Entitlements', Working Paper 1 (Helsinki. WIDER).

SHEPHERD, A. (1981), 'Agrarian Change in Northern Ghana', in Heyer *et al.* (1981).

SINGH, I., SQUIRE, L., and STRAUSS, J. (1986), 'A Survey of Agricultural Household Models: Recent Findings and Policy Implications', *World Bank Economic Review*, 1.

SPENCER, D. S. R. (1986), 'Agricultural Research in Sub-Saharan Africa: Using the Lessons of the Past to Develop a Strategy for the Future' in Berg, R. J., and Whitaker, J. S. (eds.), *Strategies for African Development* (Berkeley, Calif.: University of California Press).

United Nations (1983), *Year Book on National Accounts Statistics 1981* (New York: UN).

UNCTAD (1985), 'Protectionism and Structural Adjustment: Problems of Agro-industrial Production and Trade', TD/B/1086, 23 Dec., Geneva.

UNIDO (1983a), 'Agricultural Machinery and Rural Equipment in Africa: A New Approach to the Growing Crisis', Sectoral Studies No. 1 UNIDO/IS.377, 25 Mar., Vienna.

——(1983b), 'The Potential for Resource Based Industrial Development in Least Development Countries', No. 6 Somalia UNIDO/IS426, 16 Dec., Vienna.

——(1983c), 'The Potential for RBID in LDCs', No. 5 Malawi UNIDO/IS 389, 15 June, Vienna.

——(1985), Industrial Development Review Series, Nigeria, UNIDO/IS 557, 9 Sept., Vienna.

VENEMA, L. B. (1980), 'Male and Female Farming Systems and Agricultural Intensification in West Africa: The Case of the Wolof, Senegal', in Presvelon, U., and

Spijkers-Zwart, S. (eds.), *The Household, Women and Agricultural Development*, Miscellaneous Papers 17 (Wagemingen: Land-Labour Hogeschool).

World Bank (1977), 'Rural Development Sector Policy Paper (Tanzania)' (Washington, DC: World Bank).

——(1981), 'Accelerated Development in Sub-Saharan Africa' (Washington, DC: World Bank).

——(1984), 'Toward Sustained Development in Sub-Saharan Africa: A Joint Programme of Action' (Washington, DC: World Bank).

World Food Council (1984), 'Food Strategies in Africa', *Progress and Critical Issues*, June.

WRIGHT, D. (1977), 'Integrated Programme for Technical Change', in Commonwealth Secretariat (1977).

9

The Food Problems of Bangladesh

S. R. Osmani

9.1. *Introduction*

When hunger is as pervasive and as persistently so as in Bangladesh, the food problem ceases to be just one aspect of the economic problem. It becomes indistinguishable from the totality of the development problem itself. While an analysis of this totality is beyond the scope of a single paper, we shall at least try to highlight the major forces impinging on the problem of hunger—both in the past and in the future. Moreover, in an attempt to bring some kind of order to the diversity of the issues involved, we shall organize the discussion around two themes.

The first theme relates to the long-term process of the genesis of hunger and its persistence. We shall attempt to identify the structural forces determining the long-term trend of hunger and the changes therein. An interesting issue in this context is the relationship between persistent hunger and famine. It has been observed, and rightly so, that while famine has of late become a recurrent feature in some parts of Africa, Bangladesh has successfully avoided a recurrence of famine since 1974, despite a couple of close calls. Does this success indicate an improvement in the underlying trend of persistent hunger? If not, how does one explain the avoidance of famine, particularly in the years 1979 and 1984 when crop damage was comparable to that of 1974? In trying to answer these questions, we hope to be able to shed some light not only on the question of what is happening to persistent hunger in Bangladesh, but also on whether the country is becoming increasingly or decreasingly susceptible to famine.

The second theme relates to the future—how is the future likely to be shaped by the policies being implemented at present. Of particular interest here is a decisive shift that has occurred in the recent past in the orientation of food policy in particular and development strategy in general—away from government control and towards a greater reliance on market forces. We shall critically examine the implications of this shift in strategy *vis-à-vis* alternative policy options.

But we begin by giving a brief account of the incidence of hunger in Bangladesh.

I am grateful to Iftikhar Hossain and two anonymous referees for extremely helpful comments on an earlier draft, and to Matiur Rahman for his generous permission to use unpublished material from his Ph.D. dissertation.

9.2. *Magnitude and distribution of hunger in Bangladesh*

The most common method of estimating the magnitude of hunger is to calculate the percentage of people with a calorie-deficient diet. Using this method and taking FAO recommendations as the standard of calorie requirement, a recent Nutrition Survey has found that 76 per cent of the rural population of Bangladesh are unable to consume enough calories (INFS 1981/2). This survey was based on actual measurement of food consumed within a household. Another survey, using the same FAO norms but based on information on household expenditure on food, has estimated that 79 per cent of the rural households did not have enough income in 1981 to afford a calorie-adequate diet (Table 9.1).

Since rural population constitutes over 90 per cent of the total population, the above figures clearly indicate the pervasiveness of hunger in Bangladesh. But it is by no means confined to rural areas only. An occupation-wise breakdown of per capita calorie intake in 1976/7 shows that the urban informal sector, which constitutes 60 per cent of urban population, has a per capita calorie intake 15 per cent below the FAO norm (Table 9.2). Even the urban formal sector is not free from hunger, although per capita calorie intake of this group is above the FAO norm. As the Nutrition Survey of 1981/2 has found, the average calorie intake of industrial workers, who constitute a sizeable part of the urban formal sector, was only 74 per cent of requirement.

Table 9.1 Distribution of hunger by occupation in rural Bangladesh, 1981

Occupation group	% of households with inadequate food	Share of the group in total rural households (%)	Share of the group in inadequately fed rural households (%)
	(1)	(2)	(3)
Farming	72.5	40.7	37.2
Service	77.4	6.3	6.2
Business	60.9	16.6	12.7
Agricultural wage labour	96.6	25.6	31.3
Non-agricultural wage labour	95.5	9.3	11.2
Others	71.7	1.5	1.4
ALL	79.3	100.0	100.0

Source: This table has been drawn from the first draft of an ongoing Ph.D. dissertation by M. Rahman (forthcoming). It is based on an expenditure survey of over 4,000 rural households drawn from different parts of Bangladesh.

Table 9.2 Foodgrains and calorie intake by socio-economic class, Bangladesh, 1976/7

Class	% of population	Average income per month (Tk)	Calories (day/capita)	% of calories from foodgrain
Landless farm workers	21	897	1,519	92
Small farmers	12	894	1,638	92
Medium farmers (mainly tenants)	12	1,119	1,764	91
Medium farmers (mainly owners)	13	1,285	1,956	90
Large farmers	10	1,659	2,150	89
Very large farmers	4	2,789	2,087	87
Rural informal non-farmers	11	850	1,482	91
Rural formal non-farmers	7	1,840	2,118	88
Urban informal	6	1,039	1,708	90
Urban formal	4	2,612	2,080	82
Average for all classes	100	1,281	1,782	90

Note: Calorie requirement (day/capita): 2,020

Source: World Bank (1985a: Table 1, p. 4).

Before proceeding further, however, several limitations of these estimates need to be pointed out.

First, the estimates depend crucially on the norm of calorie requirement. The difficulties of determining this norm are well known and the traditional approach (as embodied in the FAO recommendations) has come under severe criticism recently. But unfortunately the debate has not yet resolved any of the difficult issues and it seems that the use of a cut-off norm is bound to involve some amount of ambiguity.[1] Definitive estimates of hunger are thus difficult to provide, even leaving aside the problem of data reliability. Nevertheless, one may note that the qualitative conclusion regarding the severity of hunger in Bangladesh is not substantially changed under alternative methodologies, such as taking a cut-off point at 80 per cent of average requirement, a popular way of correcting for the criticism that the average norm does not allow for inter-personal and intrapersonal variation in requirement. It may be seen from Table 9.2 that landless agricultural workers, small farmers, and rural informal workers in the non-farm sector, who together constitute nearly 50 per cent of

[1] A review of this debate can be found, *inter alia*, in Osmani (1984) and Srinivasan (1983).

rural population, have an average calorie intake which is either below or close to the lower cut-off point (i.e. 80 per cent of average requirement).

Secondly, while the estimation of calorie deficit implies measurement of hunger from the input side, it may be argued that measuring the outcome directly in terms of physical undernutrition may be more appropriate. Not only will this help to avoid the troublesome issue of specifying requirement; but conceptually the more important point is that the food problem, in so far as it is a problem, consists after all in the harm it does to the 'functioning' and 'capabilities' of a person; and the measures of undernutrition can be taken as a measure of such 'functioning'.[2] Unfortunately, however, the scientific status of the traditional (anthropometric) measures of undernutrition as an index of 'functioning' is no less in doubt today than the concept of calorie requirement itself.[3] Yet, for whatever they are worth, these traditional measures too confirm the pervasiveness of the food problem in Bangladesh. Food deficit has a most immediate and visible impact on the nutritional status of children; and the Nutrition Survey of 1981/2 shows that over 60 per cent of rural children in the under-5 age group suffer from second- or third-degree malnutrition (INFS 1981/2).[4] Mortality is also very high in this age group; it is estimated that nearly 50 per cent of all mortality in Bangladesh occurs in this cohort. The severity of malnutrition (in terms of weight for height measures) subsides in the age group of 5–14 years; but the prevalence of stunting persists among three-quarters of these children due to the cumulative effects of long-term nutritional deprivation.[5]

Thirdly, even as an input-based measure, calorie deficit is an incomplete guide to the severity of the food problem. At best, calorie deficit indicates the 'quantity' of the food problem; but no less important is 'quality', i.e. the ability of the diets to provide all nutrients in the right amounts. It has been estimated that of all the occupational groups enumerated in Table 9.2, only the urban formal group, comprising a tiny 4 per cent of the population of the country, consume diets which are adequate in both quantity and quality. This they are able to achieve by virtue of their relatively diversified diet which consists of both cereals and non-cereals in the right proportion. On the other hand, large farmers and other rich people in the rural areas who on the average consume adequate calories in terms of quantity tend to derive an excessive proportion of

[2] For a welfare-theoretic justification of the 'capabilities' approach, see Sen (1985).

[3] See Beaton (1983) for a critical view of excessive reliance on anthropometry as a measure of undernutrition.

[4] A similar incidence of malnutrition is reported by UNICEF/FREPD (1981).

[5] It is of course well recognized that inadequate intake of calories is not the only and sometimes not even the most important cause of physical undernutrition. Diseases related to environmental health conditions such as sanitation and the quality of drinking water are also a major determining factor of malnutrition in the developing countries. But it is also true that lack of food accentuates the effects of such disease-induced malnutrition. As a result, those with a poorer entitlement to food are more vulnerable to physical malnutrition. See World Bank (1985a) for a review of studies showing positive association between malnutrition and economic status in Bangladesh.

their calories from cereals which are poor in micronutrients and minerals. As a result, their diet tends to be qualitatively inadequate (World Bank 1985a) However, it has also been noted that, given the dietary pattern in Bangladesh, those who consume adequate calories also in general consume adequate protein (Osmani 1982). Thus a focus on quantity serves at least to cover the two most important nutrients.[6]

One other aspect of the food problem, which is of great importance but cannot be covered in this chapter, is the problem of intrafamily distribution of food. There is some evidence of systematic bias against females in the distribution of food within the family (Chen *et al*. 1981). The effect of this bias is also reflected in the outcome, i.e. in the relative nutritional status of males and females. The Nutrition Survey of 1981/2 has noted for example that in both the preschool and school-age cohorts, female children suffer from a greater degree of chronic and acute malnutrition than male children (INFS 1981/2). Limitation of space prevents us from exploring the socio-economic basis of this sex bias in the distribution of food.

We shall however have a good deal more to say on another kind of distribution—the occupational distribution of hunger. One can see from Tables 9.1 and 9.2 that rural wage labourers, both in farm and non-farm sectors, are the most severely deprived among all socio-economic groups. But food deprivation is not confined to these groups only; it is widely distributed among both wage labourers and the self-employed, and similarly among both producers and non-producers of food.

The phenomenon of food deprivation thus encompasses different segments of the labour force who have very different modes of acquiring entitlement on food. As column 3 of Table 9.1 shows, just over one-third of all those who cannot afford an adequate diet in the rural areas comprises direct producers of food, i.e. the farmers. Another one-third, though being involved in the production of food as agricultural labourers, do not acquire food through the production process, but from the market. The other one-third, who are primarily engaged in the non-farm sector, also have to rely mainly on the market to realize their food entitlement. Thus market exchange plays a crucial role in determining the food entitlement of nearly two-thirds of the underfed people in the rural areas.

It may be noted that even the farmers among the underfed are not entirely independent of the market. It has been estimated that as many as 50 per cent of the farmers have a net deficit even in a normal crop year (Ahmed 1981). They are perforce compelled to buy food from the market in the lean season. Part of the money to buy this food comes from wage labour which is known to account for almost half the family income of small farmers. Thus both the wage rate and the price of food turn out to be crucial market variables in determining the food entitlement of the farmers as well.

[6] For a discussion of the issues and evidence related to the deficiency of other nutrients in Bangladesh, see World Bank (1985a).

This simple analysis already reveals the great complexity of the problem of food entitlement in Bangladesh. Three rural groups—small farmers, wage labourers, and a large part of the non-farm sector—are severely afflicted by food deprivation, but each has a different acquisition problem. As a result, the structural forces as well as various policies and programmes operating in the economy may affect them differently through different channels. Identification of these channels and their operation over time is of crucial importance in understanding the long-term process of persistent hunger, to which we now turn.

9.3. *Trend of persistent hunger: the long-term process of entitlement contraction*

The statistics of persistent hunger

We may begin by looking at the aggregate picture of foodgrain production and its availability. It may be seen from Table 9.3 that between 1960/1 and 1983/4 total production of cereals expanded at the rate of 2.3 per cent, while population grew in the same period at the somewhat higher rate of 2.7 per cent. Per capita production has thus declined over time. However, when production is combined with imports (and adjusted for changes in government stocks), per capita *availability* is seen to be not very different in the early 1980s (if anything, slightly higher) compared to what it was two decades ago (Table 9.4).

Table 9.3 Comparative rates of growth of cereal production and population, Bangladesh (% p.a.)

Period	Foodgrain	Population
1960/1–1983/4	2.3	2.7
1960/1–1969/70	3.7	3.1
1975/6–1983/4	3.0	2.4

Notes: Cereal includes both rice and wheat.
   Rate of growth of foodgrain production refers to trend rate of growth.

Source: Statistical Yearbook of Bangladesh, various years.

Table 9.4 Production and availability of cereals in Bangladesh (yearly average for different time periods)

Period	Production (m. tons)	Availability (lbs/capita/day)
1960/1–1964/5	8.76	0.984
1965/6–1969/70	9.72	0.958
1972/3–1977/8	10.38	0.948
1977/8–1980/1	12.22	0.958
1981/2–1984/5	13.70	1.008

Source: MOF (1986: Tables A2.1 and A2.2).

Cereals of course give only a part of the picture, albeit by far the major part (around 90 per cent of total calorie intake at present). The other part, relating to non-cereal food crops, presents a particularly grim picture. While per capita availability of cereals has not changed much, taking the last two decades as a whole, per capita production and availability of the major non-cereal food crops (such as pulses, oilseeds, and sugar) has declined drastically over this period (Hossain 1985c). The result, as revealed by the Nutrition Surveys, is an overall decline in per capita calorie intake in the rural areas—from 2,251 calories per day in 1962/4 to 1,943 calories in 1981/2 (INFS 1981/2).

The trend for the overall period, however, gives a somewhat misleading picture of the race between food and mouth. The race was lost only during the years immediately following the War of Liberation in 1971 when production was seriously disrupted by the accumulated effect of political turmoil and a series of natural disasters. In order to get a better appreciation of the underlying trend, it is therefore necessary to exclude these turbulent years and look separately at the 1960s and the period since the mid-1970s. This is done for cereals in Table 9.3, and it may be seen that the production of cereals has been able to keep ahead of population growth in both the subperiods. Not just production; per capita availability too has been moving on a rising trend in the 1970s (Table 9.4). As for non-cereal food crops, one finds a somewhat mixed picture—with the per capita availability of pulses continuing to decline but that of potato and sugar either rising or stagnating (Hossain 1984b).

What then is the overall trend of per capita calorie availability in the recent subperiod, i.e. during the period since the mid-1970s? On this there is a bit of conflicting evidence. According to two Nutrition Surveys, per capita calorie intake in rural Bangladesh has declined from 2,094 calories per day in 1975/6 to 1,943 calories in 1981/2 (INFS 1981/2). However, the picture is reversed if instead of using the Nutrition Survey of 1975/6 one uses the Household Expenditure Survey of 1976/7 as the base, which shows rural per capita calorie intake to be only 1,768 calories per day (World Bank 1985a: Table 1). There is of course a problem of comparability between the two kinds of surveys;[7] yet the main reason behind the difference between the figures for 1975/6 and 1976/7 would appear to lie in random fluctuations in agricultural production—1975/6 was a year of bumper crop, while 1976/7 was a below average year when viewed against the overall trend. If, as a rough compromise, one takes the average of the estimates for the two years as representing the picture in the mid-1970s, one finds very little change in per capita calorie intake between then (1,931 calories) and 1981/2 (1,943 calories).

When this finding is combined with the evidence presented earlier on the rising trend of per capita cereal availability and mixed performance of non-

---

[7] The Household Expenditure Surveys are much bigger in scale and are hence subject to a lower sampling error. But the Nutrition Surveys probably contain fewer measurement errors, as they estimate calorie intake from direct measurement of food consumed within a household, whereas the Expenditure Surveys rely on memory recall by the respondents.

cereal food crops, one feels inclined to take the view that per capita calorie availability has probably not declined in the post-Liberation period. Whether it has improved, one cannot say for sure given the available data.

If these statistics of aggregate availability appear a bit shaky, they are at least on firmer grounds than those on the long-term trend of hunger. The latter requires quite detailed information on the distribution of food intake, which is available only for a few points in time. Analysis of changes in hunger and poverty has usually involved comparison between pairs of some of these points in time. One may of course try to deduce the long-term trend by piecing together these point-to-point comparisons. But there are two difficulties here that one must guard against.

First, the data sets of different studies are not always comparable. For instance, for the 1960s and up to the mid-1970s one could use nationally representative large-scale surveys of household income and expenditure. The last such survey for which results are available in sufficient detail relates to 1976/7. For the period since then, one has to rely on much smaller surveys such as the Nutrition Survey of 1981/2 or some village survey, of which there are plenty but most of which are too small to represent the national picture (we have used one of the largest of such surveys in constructing Table 9.1). The second difficulty is that the various point-to-point comparisons often use different methodologies, including different requirement norms. As a consequence of such discrepancies in data sets as well as methodology, the numbers thrown up by different studies are not often comparable.

However, one can still make some progress by piecing together information on the direction in which the level of hunger has changed. In other words, we are assuming that the findings about the *direction* of change are much more robust than the *numbers* themselves. As a result, if hunger is seen to have increased between time periods A and B according to one study, and increased again between B and C according to another, we hope to be able to say that hunger has increased between A and C, although we shall not know by how much.

Following this procedure, it is possible to conclude that the long-term trend of hunger in Bangladesh is one of persistent deterioration. According to a comparative study of the time periods 1963/4 and 1973/4, the magnitude of food deprivation (as measured by the Sen index of poverty) increased over time in rural Bangladesh (Osmani 1982). A subsequent study on income distribution showed that rural inequality had worsened between 1973/4 and 1976/7 while per capita income had also declined a little, indicating that the poorer segments faced an absolute decline in their living standards (Osmani and Rahman 1984). In fact, taking the longer period from 1963/4 to 1976/7, the same study also noted that while per capita income in real terms actually declined over this period, the richest 10 to 15 per cent of the population enjoyed an increase in their absolute real income. It implies that the poorest 85 per cent of the population not only bore the entire brunt of the overall reduction of per capita income, they were also forced into a perverse redistribution of income towards the rich. Although this study did not go on to estimate the magnitude of hunger, it is easy to infer from the above findings that absolute hunger increased over this period. One other study which did go into this estimation confirms this inference (Ahmad and Hossain 1985).

The picture since the mid-1970s is rather sketchy, mainly because results of large-scale household surveys have not been available in sufficient detail since then. However, as our subsequent analysis of structural changes will show, all the pointers are strongly towards further deterioration. For the moment we may note that two Nutrition Surveys in 1975/6 and 1981/2 found the food consumption of the rural poor to have declined over this period (INFS 1975/6 and INFS 1981/2). Although these surveys did not find a corresponding decline in the physical nutritional status of the poor, yet another Nutritional Survey of 1981 (UNICEF/FREPD 1981) shows marked deterioration in the nutritional status of children when compared with the findings of INFS (1975/6). Finally, the Nutrition Survey of 1981/2 found that when compared with the findings of an earlier survey of comparable methodology (USDH 1962–6), the proportion of rural households with inadequate food seemed to have increased substantially (from 59 to 76 per cent) from the early 1960s to the early 1980s.

The forces of entitlement contraction

The preceding evidence of course relates to overall hunger and does not say anything about how the different occupational groups have been doing over time. There is unfortunately no concrete information on the trend of occupational or any other distribution of hunger. We shall however try to deduce the picture by examining the structural forces operating on the economic environment facing each of the major food-deprived groups (namely the small farmers, rural wage labourers, and the poorer segment of the rural non-farm sector).

In order to choose an appropriate analytical framework for such a structural analysis, it is first necessary to have an understanding of the relationship between production and entitlement of food. One obvious linkage between production and entitlement is of course through the price of food and hence the exchange entitlement of those who rely heavily on market purchase to meet their food requirement. But there are also other, no less important, linkages whose significance emanates from the fact that food occupies a pre-eminent position in the production structure of Bangladesh agriculture. Production of food crops (cereals and non-cereals together) accounted for over 90 per cent of the total value of crop production in the 1980s, rising from about 83 per cent in the middle of this century. The share of cereals (rice and wheat) alone has risen from 73 per cent to 85 per cent during the same period (Hossain 1985c).

Given this overwhelming importance of food in the production structure, it is natural that food production should have a decisive impact on the level of economic activity in general and hence on the incomes and entitlements of almost all groups of people.

In the first place, food production has an immediate relevance for the entitlement of farmers who try to acquire as much food as possible from the production process itself, i.e. by growing food on their own land.

Secondly, because of its pre-eminence, food production exerts a preponderant influence on the demand for wage labour in agriculture. The consequent impacts on wage and employment are crucial factors in determining the entitlement of agricultural wage labourers.

The same pre-eminence of food also ensures that, through the linkages between farm and non-farm sectors, the ripples of its production effect will spread strongly to the non-farm sector as well. One such linkage is the trading in food crops. A recent evaluation of a credit programme for the poor in the non-farm sector has shown that trading is the most popular non-farm activity among the poor and that loans for trading in crops and vegetables account for nearly half the loans taken for trading purposes (Hossain 1984c). Obviously, then, food production has a lot to do with the trading income of a lot of non-farm poor. But perhaps the most significant linkage operates on the demand side—the line of causation running from food production to farm income to the demand for non-farm products. At the current low levels of income, a huge proportion of a rural household's budget is spent on basic food items, produced mostly in the farm sector, leaving very little room for non-farm products. For instance, a recent survey of rural expenditure pattern has found that an average rural household spends around 80 per cent of its budget on food alone (Osmani and Deb 1984). Of course some of the food items are produced or processed in the rural industrial sector; but even the combined food and non-food products of rural industry account for only 13 per cent of the average budget. While the total size of the market is thus severely limited by existing levels of income, it can however expand quite rapidly with the rise in rural income, since the income elasticity of demand for most of these products happens to lie above or close to unity (Osmani and Deb 1984). The same is true also about most kinds of non-farm products in general (Hossain 1984c). These estimates of budget-shares and elasticities clearly indicate that the growth of demand for non-farm products depends crucially on the growth in rural income. But the bulk of rural income is generated by the production, processing, and trading of agricultural products in general and food crops in particular; hence the importance of food production for the expansion of the non-farm sector, and for the incomes and entitlements of those engaged in this sector.

There is thus ample reason to believe that all three major rural groups afflicted by severe hunger have much at stake in the growth of food production. This point is perhaps worth emphasizing a little. Although production and entitlement are conceptually distinct categories and it has been rightly demonstrated that changes in one do not necessarily correlate with changes in the other (Sen 1981), the causal nexus between them seems strong enough in rural Bangladesh to entail a close positive association between the two. This closeness of association derives simply from the overwhelming importance of foodcrops in agriculture and from the importance of agriculture in turn in the rural economy of Bangladesh. It is of course possible that even in the case of Bangladesh, the nexus may not appear to be a strong one in the event of a sudden collapse of entitlement, as has indeed been shown to have been the case during the famine of 1974 (Sen 1981). But as far as the long-term evolution of entitlement is concerned, development on the front of food production can certainly be expected to play a decisive role in an economy with a food-dominated production structure.

Yet, as we have noted, the growth of food production, despite surpassing the rate of population growth in the post-Liberation era, does not seem to have been able to reduce the incidence of hunger. An understanding of the reason for this discordance between growth and hunger is crucial for identifying the structural forces of persistent hunger.

One can think of three alternative hypotheses to explain this observed discordance: (1) hunger expanded 'regardless of' growth, because the benefits of growth did not reach the poor, (2) hunger increased 'because of' growth, since the very process of growth created or strengthened the forces of hunger, and (3) hunger expanded 'in spite of' growth, because growth was inadequate to overcome some underlying force of hunger.

We shall argue that the particular empirical reality of Bangladesh suggests the third hypothesis to be the most plausible one.

The first hypothesis is valid when growth takes place in a lopsided manner, confining all the productivity gains to the lands of the large farmers and bypassing the smaller ones. This is indeed believed to be a characteristic of the so-called 'Green Revolution' in many parts of the world. It is well known that the seed-fertilizer-water technology of modern agriculture raises the working capital requirement well beyond the level obtaining in traditional agriculture. Unless special measures are taken to meet this enhanced requirement for working capital the small farmers are likely to remain outside the orbit of new technology, and the large farmers will reap all the gains. While this explanation is internally consistent,[8] it does not square with the actual observations on the pattern of growth in Bangladesh. Numerous field surveys have shown that the diffusion of modern technology has not remained disproportionately confined to the large farmers. For example, the results of a fairly large-scale survey of this kind are shown in Table 9.5.[9] The small farmers are seen to have

[8] But note that the argument, as presented, is not quite complete. If productivity gains are concentrated on the lands of the larger farmers, it only explains why relative inequality will increase over time; it does not explain why absolute hunger should deteriorate for those not blessed with improved productivity. It can nevertheless be shown that absolute hunger will increase, by bringing in the notion of an underlying immiserizing force which we discuss in the context of the third hypothesis.

[9] Evidence from several other studies is discussed in Osmani and Rahman (1984).

Table 9.5 Shares of different farm-size groups in the consumption of modern inputs, Bangladesh, 1981/2

Size of farm (acres)	% of farms	% of land operated	Share of fertilizer (%)	Share of irrigated land (%)	Share of institutional credit (%)
Up to 1.00	31.5	12.6	15.6	16.7	3.2
1.01–2.50	32.8	22.0	23.2	25.1	21.9
2.51–5.00	21.9	27.5	28.8	27.9	35.7
Above 5.00	13.8	37.9	32.4	30.2	39.2

Source: Abdullah (1985).

participated equally in the adoption of modern seed-fertilizer-water technology, if anything slightly more than in proportion to their share of land. This pattern, we believe, is owed mainly to the policy of heavy subsidization of agricultural inputs which the government has pursued until recently, thus enabling the small farmers to overcome the working capital constraint.[10]

Turning now to the second hypothesis, one can think of several ways in which hunger can expand 'because of' growth, i.e. through the process of growth itself. For instance, the growth-augmenting technology may be a labour-displacing one, as it is the case when mechanization spreads along with the seed-fertilizer-water technology. By reducing demand for labour, such growth can indeed accentuate the hunger of agricultural labourers. Even the small farmers can be harmed. This will happen if the profitability of new technology induces the landowners to bring back land from the share-croppers for cultivation under their own management. There are also other possibilities. While the share-croppers receive only half of the increased yield, they typically have to bear the entire burden of the increased cost of cultivation. This may conceivably lead to a situation where the net return to share-croppers' labour actually goes down with the adoption of new technology.

While all these are theoretical possibilities and some of these tendencies have actually been observed in different parts of the world where a Green Revolution has occurred, they do not seem to have a great deal of empirical relevance for Bangladesh agriculture. In the first place, mechanization of Bangladesh agriculture is still of a very minuscule order of magnitude—less than 1 per cent of farms use tractors or power tillers, according to the Agricultural Census of 1977. On the eviction of share-croppers, it is well known that this does happen at times, but there is no quantitative estimate of its degree of occurrence. However, from what is known about the size of the tenancy market and its changes over time, it does not appear that eviction could have been a

---

[10] The question of subsidies and credit constraint is discussed further in the final section of the chapter.

quantitatively significant phenomenon; according to the Agricultural Censuses of 1960 and 1977, the proportion of tenant farmers among all farm households rose from 39 per cent to 42 per cent during the intercensal period and the proportion of total land under tenancy fell marginally from 18 per cent to 17 per cent during the same period. Finally, it is also well known that the share-croppers in Bangladesh do typically incur all the increased cost of new technology; yet empirical estimates show that net return to their labour from the cultivation of HYV crops is considerably higher than what the traditional crops typically offer.[11] Thus none of the channels through which the process of growth can plausibly lead to a squeeze of the entitlement of the poor seems to fit the empirical reality of Bangladesh.[12]

We are thus left with the hypothesis of 'inadequate growth' to explain the observed discordance between growth and hunger. Before going into the empirics of this explanation, let us first spell out the logic of the hypothesis. The essence of the argument is that the combination of private property relations and intense demographic pressure obtaining in rural Bangladesh is constantly generating an 'immiserizing' force which growth will have to overcome before it can begin to reduce the incidence of hunger. The way this force works can be seen most simply by assuming a 'no growth' scenario. It is also convenient to begin the story with the case of small farmers.

A high rate of population growth from an already high base of population density combines with the Muslim law of inheritance to lead to a progressive reduction in the average size of farm over the years. It has indeed declined from 3.5 acres in 1960 to 2.4 acres in 1982. With reduced landholding, the small and marginal farmers can only maintain their standard of living if corresponding gains can be made in land productivity. In the absence of such productivity growth, demographic pressure leads inevitably to a continual increase in the number of economically unviable holdings. The resulting marginalization of the peasantry is the beginning of the process of overall impoverishment. Under constant economic pressure, the marginalized peasantry eventually becomes alienated from land and swells the rank of landless labourers whose own stock

[11] It has been estimated for instance that whereas the return to share-croppers' labour in the cultivation of traditional crops is often less than the agricultural wage rate, in the case of high-yielding varieties it is clearly higher, although not as much as in the case of owner-farmers. See the discussion in Hossain (1981: 77).

[12] There is one other channel which is sometimes mentioned, but not with enough theoretical justification in our view. It is suggested that by increasing the income of large farmers, Green Revolution enhances their ability to buy the land of marginal farmers, thus accentuating the process of rural landlessness. This argument ignores the point that since most land sales by the poor are in the nature of 'distress sale' intended to meet some given cash needs, they will tend to sell less if the price of land goes up (because the same cash needs can now be met by selling a smaller piece of land). Therefore, higher income of the rural rich, by raising the demand price of land, should if anything reduce the volume of distress sales, other things remaining the same. If landlessness is nevertheless seen to have gone up, as it indeed has in Bangladesh, then obviously the other things did not remain the same, and this is where the analysis should turn. We take up this analysis in the context of the third hypothesis.

has also been growing at a rapid pace due to the same demographic pressure. While the supply of wage labour is thus being doubly augmented, demand for labour cannot obviously rise in the absence of productivity growth. The consequent decline in real wage and employment leads to persistent contraction in the entitlement of the wage-labour class. Many of them pour into the non-farm sector in search of alternative employment. But this only adds to the misery of the non-farm population whose real income cannot expand (because the demand for their products does not expand) in the absence of agricultural growth.

This tendency towards pervasive impoverishment can be overcome if the growth in productivity is strong enough to arrest the marginalization of the peasantry, to raise the demand for wage labour ahead of expanding supply, and to strengthen the demand for non-farm products. It is thus apparent how growth can occur and hunger can spread at the same time because growth is inadequate to outweigh the underlying force of immiserization.[13]

Turning now to the actual record of growth, it has to be first noted that, given very limited possibility of augmenting the size of cultivable land, growth in Bangladesh agriculture must occur mainly through the diffusion of yield-augmenting technology. It is of course true that the use of high-yielding variety (HYV) seeds has expanded rapidly in the 1970s starting from a meagre 2.5 per cent of total cereal acreage in 1969/70; but even by 1983/4, nearly three-quarters of all cereal acreage remained under the low-yielding traditional seeds. Irrigation facilities, which are crucial for the adoption of HYVs, have also expanded rapidly; yet by 1982/3, four-fifths of all cultivated land remained outside the ambit of controlled irrigation. Chemical fertilisers, which are most productive when used with HYVs but can also improve the yield of traditional seeds, have achieved the fastest rate of expansion; yet field surveys indicate that over 40 per cent of all cereal lands are not treated with fertilizer at all. Even when fertilizer is applied, the rate of application is well below the recommended dose. Moreover, almost half the fertilizer is applied on rainfed land where its return is both low and insecure.[14]

Thus although modern technology has made a significant inroad and the small farmers too seem to have participated in this process, Bangladesh agriculture still remains dominated by the moribund technology of yester-year. It is in the light of this inadequate technological diffusion, and hence inadequate growth, that we shall now analyse the available empirical evidence on the structural forces operating on the entitlement of the rural poor.

---

[13] This argument assumes that the existing system of private property relations and the associated system of entitlements remain intact. Under a more egalitarian system of ownership and entitlements, the 'warranted' rate of growth, i.e. the rate of growth required to neutralize the underlying immiserizing force, would be lower, and could conceivably be even lower than the observed rate of growth.

[14] For more detailed information on the diffusion of modern technology in Bangladesh agriculture, see Hossain (1984b) and Osmani and Quasem (1985: ch. II).

We shall begin with the situation of the small farmers. Table 9.6 shows the change in the distribution of landholding that has taken place over the last two decades. It shows how demographic forces have exerted a downward pressure on the overall distribution of landholding, reducing the proportion of large farms and increasing the proportion of smaller ones. This downward pressure has pushed many small farms out of the farming occupation altogether by making their subdivided plots too small to be economic. This is evidenced by the fact that the total number of farms increased at the rate of only 1.3 per cent a year, while population increased at the rate of 2.7 per cent. Assuming that the number of households grew at the same rate as population, the number of farms should also have grown at the same rate if all the farms created through subdivision remained in business.[15] This obviously did not happen; the number of farms grew only at half the rate, which means a great many farms were thrown out of business, the small plots of land being sold or leased out to the larger farmers. Whatever technological improvement has occurred has not obviously been able to prevent many small farms from becoming uneconomic. The resulting process of land alienation has been confirmed by a number of field surveys.[16] A general finding of these studies is that the sale of land occurs predominantly at the bottom end of the scale and it is the medium farmers who buy up most of the land on offer. Supportive evidence of this phenomenon at the national level is offered by Table 9.6 which shows that the medium farmers (2.5 to 7.5 acres) hold an increasing share of land, despite going down in numbers in both relative and absolute terms.[17]

The long term effect of this process of land transfer is reflected in generational transition from one occupation group to another. Table 9.7, which shows the occupation of predecessors of a cross-section of the rural population, tells the story poignantly. Nearly 75 per cent of the landless labourers are seen to have come from families which as recently as their father's or grandfather's time had farming as the principal occupation.

By all accounts, the process of land transfer has continued unabated leading to an increase in the proportion of landless rural people. Combining information from various censuses and surveys, Hossain (1985a) has estimated that between 1960 and 1982 the number of landless households grew much faster

---

[15] This argument is premissed on the prevailing law of inheritance which entitles every son (and to a lesser extent every daughter) to a piece of his father's land.

[16] The relevant evidence has been collated by Khan (1976) and Osmani and Rahman (1984), among others.

[17] Note that the small farmers' share of total holdings has also gone up, but this is to be expected because, unlike in the case of medium farmers, the proportion of small farmers has gone up too. It is true that their share of land has gone up at a faster rate than their share of farm households; but it does not mean that the small farmers are actually gaining land! All it means is probably that those erstwhile small farmers who have now become landless and do not therefore figure in Table 9.6 under the column of the year 1982 had a smaller average size of land than that which the new entrants to the category of small farmers have brought from their erstwhile status of medium–large farmers through the process of land subdivision.

Table 9.6 Changes in the distribution of landholdings, Bangladesh, 1960–1982

Size of farm (acres)	% of farms		% share of holding	
	1960	1982	1960	1982
Up to 1.00	24.3	34.0	3.2	7.1
1.01–2.50	27.3	33.5	12.9	22.3
2.51–7.50	37.7	27.6	45.7	47.0
Above 7.50	10.7	4.9	38.1	23.6
All farms	100.0	100.0	100.0	100.0

Notes: Number of farms: 1960: 6,139,000; 1982: 8,124,000.
Average size of farm: 1960: 3.5 acres; 1982: 2.4 acres.

Source: Compiled from Agriculture Census of 1960 and the Pilot Agriculture Census of 1982.

Table 9.7 Transition towards impoverishment through generations in rural Bangladesh

Occupation of predecessors	Owner-farmers	Share-croppers	Landless labourers	Beggars
Grandfather: farmer / Father: farmer	95.1	84.8	60.2	59.8
Grandfather: farmer / Father: labourer	0.4	1.6	12.7	9.9
Grandfather: labourer / Father: farmer	0.4	2.5	1.5	0.9
Grandfather: labourer / Father: labourer	0.3	2.2	16.6	12.3
Others	3.8	8.9	9.0	17.1
ALL	100.0	100.0	100.0	100.0

Source: Quoted from Muqtada and Alam (1983). The findings are based on *IRDP Benchmark Survey of Rural Bangladesh*, 1973/4.

than both rural households in general and farm households in particular. It is however worth pointing out that such estimates based on census of rural areas at two points in time are likely to underestimate the growth in landlessness, since many landless choose over time to migrate to the urban areas rather than stay in the village.

Despite such underestimation, Hossain found that the proportion of completely landless households increased from 33 per cent in 1960 to 37 per cent in 1982, and the proportion of functionally landless households (with less than 0.5 acres of land) rose from 42 per cent to 47 per cent.

Alienation from land is of course the last desperate act of an impoverished farmer who likes to cling to his land for as long as he can. Growing landlessness thus clearly implies growing impoverishment of the peasantry. As we have argued, the principal reason for this is the slow rate of technological improvement and the resulting slow growth in production.

The long-term evolution in the entitlement of wage labourers can be explained in terms of the same set of forces. It is possible to argue that inadequate growth of production has adversely affected their wage and employment, by augmenting an already existing imbalance between supply and demand for wage labour. How this imbalance has developed can be seen most clearly by tracing the effect of slow growth on both supply and demand sides of the labour market and relating the growth of supply and demand to the rate of population growth as a common reference for comparison.

On the supply side, slow growth has augmented the natural increase in labour force by helping to create a marginalized peasantry who would seek employment in the labour market not only when they became landless, but even as they remained peasants. As the Pilot Agricultural Census of 1982 shows, 33 per cent of all farm households and 60 per cent of all households with less than one acre of land depend upon wage labour in agriculture as their *main* source of income. Because of this forced augmentation of the labour market, the supply of wage labour has naturally grown faster than the rate of population growth.

On the other hand, there is reason to believe that the demand for wage labour has grown at a slower rate than that of population growth. Once again inadequate growth of food production has played its part. While production itself has grown at about the same rate as the rural labour force (around 3 per cent), employment opportunities have grown a lot slower, since the employment elasticity of productivity growth is known to be substantially less than unity in Bangladesh agriculture.[18] Moreover, a part of the increased employment must have been taken up by the hitherto underemployed family labour. The residual increase in the demand for wage labour must therefore have been less than the growth of employment opportunities and hence less than the rate of population growth.

Since demand for wage labour is thus seen to have grown slower than population, while supply is seen to have grown faster, there obviously developed a growing imbalance between supply and demand for labour. The resulting depression of real wages of agricultural labourers has been well documented for the period of the 1960s and early 1970s (Khan 1976). The picture since the mid-1970s is given in Table 9.8. Although there is no clear trend for this period, the rice exchange rate of wages is seen to have remained generally below the pre-Liberation level. Of course to the extent that the rural labour market does not completely clear, as is generally believed to be the case, the fall in real wage may not fully reflect the magnitude of excess supply. In that case a part of excess supply will be resolved through employment rationing,

[18] Clay and Khan (1977) conclude after a careful review of available evidence that the yield elasticity of employment would vary between 0.2 and 0.5 for various types of yield-increasing operations, including the shift from traditional varieties to the HYVs.

Table 9.8 Rice exchange rate of agricultural wages in Bangladesh,
1969/70–1982/3

Year	Index of nominal wage	Index of retail price of rice	Index of rice exchange rate of wages
1969/70	100	100	100
1976/7	301	293	103
1977/8	317	360	88
1978/9	366	407	90
1979/80	421	548	77
1980/1	473	471	100
1981/2	520	583	89
1982/3	576	628	92

Source: Constructed from World Bank (1984: Tables 9.5, 9.7, 9.10).

which will imply a reduction in per capita employment. It is difficult to tell exactly in what proportion the excess supply has in fact been resolved through the two channels. But it does not really matter for the present analysis, since whichever channel it takes, the effect is to contract the entitlement of wage labourers.

Turning now to the non-farm sector of the rural population, we find precious little that can be presented by way of concrete evidence on the long-term trend of their entitlement. Some inference however can still be drawn by putting together indirect evidence of various kinds.

The first point to note is the growing size of the non-farm sector. According to census data, the labour force engaged primarily in non-farm activities has expanded from 19 per cent in 1974 to 39 per cent in 1981.[19] The rise in the relative share of the non-farm labour force is not surprising in view of the evidence presented earlier that employment opportunities in the farm sector have grown more slowly than the rural labour force. Unable to find sustained employment in the farm sector, many among the landless people must have turned to the non-farm sector. From the findings of some recent surveys of occupational distribution in rural Bangladesh, it can be roughly estimated that not less than 60 per cent of the functionally landless people (owning less than 0.5 acres of land) are primarily engaged in the non-farm sector, while no more than one-third have agricultural wage labour as their primary occupation.[20]

Does this preponderance of non-farm activities among the poor indicate a dynamism in the non-farm sector which attracts the labour force, or does it merely imply that this sector acts as a residual absorber of those impoverished

[19] Several other studies also confirm that the present size of the non-farm labour force would be about 40–5% of the total. See BIDS (1981), Hossain (1984c).

[20] Findings of these surveys are discussed in Hossain (1984c, 1984d).

agricultural workers who cannot make a living out of agriculture any more? The answer to this question will provide at least some indirect evidence on what has been happening to the income and entitlement of the non-farm population.

Unfortunately, it is not possible to give a very definitive answer to this question. But there is some evidence to suggest that the returns from non-farm activities, especially where the poor are mainly involved, are simply not attractive enough to divert labour away from agriculture. For instance, a recent study has found that nearly one-third of the rural industrial workforce, usually the poorer ones, are engaged in industries where return to family labour is lower than the agricultural wage rate. Average labour productivity in rural industries in general is of course higher than agricultural wages. But productivity is found to depend mostly on capital intensity; and the poorer among the workforce cannot afford to undertake the relatively high-yielding capital intensive activities. As a result, the landless and near landless families are found to be engaged mostly in the low-yielding activities (Hossain 1984a). This is not a characteristic of rural industries alone, but of non-farm activities in general. For instance, Muqtada and Alam (1983) have found in a survey of the rural labour market that income from non-farm activities is positively correlated with the amount of land owned. Obviously, those with more land have greater access to resources in general and hence can afford to take up those activities which yield higher returns through the use of more capital. The landless and the near-landless can use little more than their physical labour and, when they do that, return is usually lower than the agricultural wage. For instance, in 10 out of 14 major cottage industries, the wage rate for hired labour was found to be less than the wage rate for unskilled labour in agriculture (Hossain 1984e).

Non-farm activities do not therefore seem to provide a haven where the poor in the farm sector would have found a more rewarding employment.[21] One cannot thus explain the growth of the non-farm sector as a 'pull-effect' of its attractiveness *vis-à-vis* the farm sector.[22] The explanation must rather lie in the 'push-effect' of entitlement contraction that has occurred in the farm sector.

[21] This is not to deny that more rewarding employment can be found in the non-farm sector if opportunities are created. The crucial factor is to help the poor with credit so that they can avail themselves of the opportunities which remain otherwise open to the richer stratum only. The celebrated Grameen Bank experiment in Bangladesh has shown that a well-executed credit programme for the poor in the non-farm sector can indeed raise their earnings well above the agricultural wage rate, especially in trading and livestock activities and some types of cottage industries (Hossain 1984c). But this experiment is very recent and by now it has covered only about 15% of all villages in the country. Its effects are therefore unlikely to have been significant enough to invalidate the broad historical generalization we have made about the relative unattractiveness of the non-farm sector from the point of view of the poor.

[22] This argument is based on the premise that the labour market does not clear in the farm sector and excess supply is taken care of by some form of employment rationing, so that many among the farm sector labour force come over to the non-farm sector despite the prospect of a lower rate of return on their labour.

The most probable consequence of this scenario is an increasing degree of work and income sharing in the non-farm sector, hence a contraction in per capita entitlement, especially among the poorer group.

The preceding analysis thus suggests that all three rural groups with severe problems of hunger have probably been experiencing a secular contraction in their entitlement to food. As is to be expected, their fates are closely related to each other. Impoverishment of the small farmers has a spill-over effect on the income of agricultural wage labourers. These two classes in turn tend to drag the non-farm poor along with them, when they are themselves sliding down the slippery road to hunger. It is therefore not surprising that the same set of forces can explain their common predicament. As argued before, these forces consist of an underlying immiserizing tendency emanating from intense demographic pressure and private property relations, a tendency that can in theory be neutralized by strong enough growth (in food production in particular and agricultural production in general); but what growth has actually occurred has obviously not been strong enough to neutralize this tendency. It is important to realize that a rate of growth that is arithmetically higher than the rate of population growth may still be qualitatively weaker than the immiserizing force of demographic pressure.

This brings us to the fundamental question of why production has not been able to grow any faster. The reason certainly does not lie in the limiting constraint of known technology. It has been estimated, for instance, that only about a third of the suitable land is currently being planted with HYV crops, and not more than half of the potentially irrigable land is actually being irrigated. Capacity utilization of the existing irrigation facility is also well below the true potential. The technologically feasible maximal growth rate is therefore considerably higher than what has been achieved so far.[23]

However, a more rapid diffusion of technology would have called for increased investment in water control in the rainy season and irrigation in the dry season. Investment would thus appear to have been the limiting factor. The reason however does not lie in the lack of investible resources, for there are reasons to believe that both private and public investment in agriculture have remained well below the potential. A number of field surveys have shown for instance that the large farmers devote only a small proportion of their surplus (over essential consumption) to agricultural investment.[24] Also a rather negligible proportion of this surplus is siphoned off by the state machinery through its fiscal system (Hossain et al. 1985), which is a crucial factor in limiting the size of public investment. Even within the limits of total resources

[23] For further details on the gap between potential and realized technological achievement, see Osmani and Quasem (1985: ch. II).

[24] Rahman (1979) reports from a field survey that the large farmers devote only 15–20% of their savings to agricultural investment. Yet another survey found the ratio to vary from 10 to 16% (CSS 1980). Note that these figures are expressed as proportions of savings: as proportions of surplus (income minus essential consumption), the figures would be even lower.

available for public investment it cannot be said that agriculture has received resources commensurate with its importance. The importance of agriculture does not consist simply in the fact that it generates more than half the national income; we have demonstrated that the entitlement of all the rural poor depends directly or indirectly on the progress of agricultural production in general and food production in particular. Yet agriculture has historically received no more than a third of public investment funds; and the share is showing an ominously declining trend in recent years.

Why has the bulk of private surplus shied away from agricultural invest-ment, why has so little of the surplus been siphoned into public investment, and why has resource allocation in the public sector failed to give agriculture its due? These are some of the crucial questions that must be answered in order to understand why food production has remained well below the technological frontier and thus failed to make a dent into the problem of persistent hunger. This enquiry would however lead to all the complex issues of the political economy of underdevelopment in Bangladesh, a task that cannot obviously be attempted, let alone be accomplished, in this short chapter. The limited objective of this section was merely to demonstrate that lack of growth rather than the nature of growth has historically been responsible for persistent contraction of food entitlement in rural Bangladesh. How the future is likely to emerge in view of recent policy changes is the subject matter for the final part of the chapter. But before that, we turn briefly to the issue of famines and their relationship, if any, with the trend of persistent hunger.

9.4. *Persistent hunger* vis-à-vis *famine*

The grip of persistent hunger may be tightening in rural Bangladesh, but at least there has been no famine since 1974. There were however famine scares on two occasions—once in 1979 and again in 1984. On both occasions the scare arose from genuine enough reasons. In 1979 successive crops were damaged by severe drought. Actual loss was less than feared, but the crop was still down by 4.8 per cent from the previous year. More significantly, per capita systemic availability (production plus imports) was in fact lower than in the famine year of 1974. In 1984, there were several rounds of severe flooding causing extensive crop damage. In the event, production was only 1 per cent less than in the previous year; but the important point is that the floods were even more severe than those of 1974 and production declined, while in 1974 production had actually risen despite the flood.

In spite of all this and in spite of the fact that, according to our analysis, endemic hunger has worsened over time, famine did not occur in either year. This observation raises a number of interesting issues. Does it imply that just as aggregate food availability has no necessary correlation with the occurrence of famine, so the secular contraction of food entitlement does not imply greater susceptibility to catastrophic breakdown in entitlement? Or does it raise doubts about the thesis of worsening hunger itself? Or does it merely mean that the authorities have learnt some secret trick of averting famine, which they did not know in 1974? We shall try to answer these questions by comparing the situations obtaining in each of the three years 1974, 1979, and 1984.[25]

As several analyses of the 1974 famine have shown, the most vulnerable groups are those who sell their labour for wages and buy food from the market (Alamgir 1980; Sen 1981). What happens to their employment and to the rice exchange equivalent of their wage are the two crucial variables that determine whether there is going to be a famine or not.

Loss of employment due to flooding clearly played its part in the 1974 famine. Especially significant was the damage to the jute crop, whose production declined by a massive 42 per cent. Jute is one of the most labour intensive crops of Bangladesh agriculture and wage income from its production provides the principal cushion for surviving through the lean season of July–October in the jute-growing areas. Loss of this cushion was no doubt a crucial factor in precipitating the famine that struck in the lean season.[26]

In contrast, the 1979 jute output suffered a relatively modest decline of only 8 per cent. But one must set against this the fact that foodgrain production in this year fell by 4.8 per cent due to severe drought, whereas 1974 saw an increase in output. As a result, loss of employment in the foodgrain sector must have been much more extensive in 1979. In view of the fact that foodgrain acreage was more than twelve times that of jute (in 1979), it is not altogether improbable that overall loss of employment was no less severe in 1979 than in 1974, although it is difficult to be very precise about this.

In 1984, the damage to the jute crop (18 per cent decline) was much more extensive than in 1979, though not quite as bad as in 1974. On the foodgrain front, however, output declined by about 1 per cent, as against an increase in 1974. Moreover, as in 1974, there was extensive inundation of the acreage devoted to the winter crop whose output becomes available in the following year but whose employment effects are felt here and now.

Thus, on the whole, employment does not seem to have been the crucial difference in the three years in question. The difference in fact lies in the contrasting movements in the purchasing power of labour. In the crucial famine months (August–November) of 1974, the rice exchange rate of the agricultural wage fell by almost 40 per cent compared to the same period in the preceding year, as against a 30 per cent decline in 1979. But more importantly, while the exchange rate continuously fell during the famine period of 1974, it improved steadily throughout August–November of 1979. Finally, the exchange rate in this period remained 50 per cent higher in 1979 than in 1974.

[25] The comparative analysis for the years 1974 and 1979 draws heavily on Ahmad (1985). The chief source of data for 1984 is World Bank (1985b). For 1974, heavy use has also been made of the information and analyses contained in Sobhan (1979), Alamgir (1980), Sen (1981).

[26] It is significant that two of the three worst famine-hit districts (namely Mymemsingh and Rangpur) are also the two most important jute-growing areas of Bangladesh.

The key of this difference is the movement in the price of rice. While the price of rice in the famine months of 1974 was about 250 per cent higher than in the same period of the preceding year, the corresponding increase was only 54 per cent in 1979 and a meagre 11 per cent in 1984. Moreover, while the price kept on rising throughout the famine period of 1974 at the rate of 20 per cent a month, it had a declining trend during the corresponding lean months of 1979 and rose at the modest rate of only 1 per cent a month in 1984. On the whole, the price of foodgrain rose by more than 100 per cent in 1974 over the preceding year, whereas the average rise in 1979 was only about 35 per cent. In 1984, the price increase was even more modest—just about 10 per cent, nothing more than the normal rate of inflation.

What explains such disparate movements in the price of foodgrain? Certainly not the size of its availability. As mentioned before, per capita systemic availability was in fact lower in 1979 than in 1974. While it was somewhat higher in 1984, that alone cannot explain the difference between a 100 per cent and a 10 per cent increase in price. Nor can it be explained by general inflationary forces such as expansion of money supply, as has been demonstrated in the case of the 1974 famine by Ravallion (1985) and Ahmad (1985). Ravallion (1985) has also shown that the dramatic price increase of 1974 can be neatly explained by the speculative behaviour of rice traders. Exaggerated reports of crop damage led the traders to overestimate future scarcity. The resulting overshooting of future price expectations caused 'excessive hoarding' and hence the abnormal increase in current price.

While this story fits very well with the experience of 1974, it runs into some difficulty in 1979 and 1984. Exaggerated fear of crop loss was also a characteristic of both these years. At the peak of drought in 1978, the Bangladesh Ministry of Agriculture had estimated that the 1979 *aman* crop (the main rice crop) would be 20–5 per cent below normal. In reality, output turned out to be marginally higher than that of the preceding *aman* crop. But the important point is that the fears persisted until the harvests actually came in. Meanwhile, however, the drought continued and threatened to damage the two subsequent crops, which it partly did. As a result of this prolonged drought a famine scare persisted throughout the year. Yet, as we have noted, there was no extraordinary rise in the price of rice. In 1984, the scare was even greater, with several rounds of flooding damaging and threatening to damage four successive crops, an unprecedented mishap in the recent history of the country. In the end, loss of output turned out to be quite modest, thanks largely to an unexpected improvement in yield (World Bank 1985b). But this was an *ex post* achievement which could do nothing to diminish the *ex ante* scare. Yet the price of rice rose very modestly.

Obviously, something more than mere overestimation of crop damage is involved. Ravallion (1985) seems to be aware of the missing link and speculates correctly in his concluding observation, 'The most plausible conclusion is that the stock-holders' over-optimistic price expectations and/or anticipations of future rationing during the 1974 famine were premised on a belief that the Government would be unable to implement a suitable stabilising response to the reported damage to the future crop' (p. 28). Belief in the ability of the government's public food distribution system (PFDS) to deal with an emerging crisis seems indeed to be crucial. An analysis of PFDS in the famine *vis-à-vis* non-famine years brings out the point quite clearly.

It has been well documented that the public stock of foodgrain was very low in 1974 and the government's capacity to import was also very limited due to an unfavourable aid climate on the one hand and dwindling foreign exchange reserves on the other (Alamgir 1980; Sen 1981; Ahmad 1985). This was no secret and the speculators were obviously aware of the predicament. They were quite right in thinking that PFDS was in no position to redress the emerging crisis. But this was not the case in 1979 or 1984. As soon as the crisis bell rang in 1979, the government lined up imports on both aid and commercial bases. The same happened in 1984 and foodgrain import in that year reached an all-time peak. In each of these two later years, monthly stock and distribution were substantially higher than in 1974.[27] What this distribution did to bolster aggregate availability is not the important part of the story. What is important is the effect it seems to have had on the speculators. By pursuing a vigorous import and distribution policy, the authorities succeeded in softening future price expectations. The resulting containment of current price level was an additional and by far the more important effect of PFDS on top of whatever it did to affect the current balance of supply and demand.

It is of course true that apart from containing the speculative price spiral, the PFDS in 1979 and 1984 also achieved much more than in 1974 by way of directly relieving the distress of the immediate victims of drought and flood. The quantity of foodgrain supplied to the rural poor through rationing, food-for-work, and relief in 1979/80 was higher than in any other year during 1973/4–1980/1. Also, during the crucial months of May to November 1984, the amount of relief distributed per month was three times the typical levels of the preceding years. These measures undoubtedly helped in alleviating human misery in the worst affected areas. But they do not by themselves explain why localized crisis did not turn into generalized disaster through a spiralling price increase, as it did in 1974; for, as we have already noted, despite a much higher level of public distribution, total (systemic) availability of foodgrain was no higher in 1979 than in 1974 and was only marginally higher in 1984. This is

[27] Average monthly distribution of foodgrain during the famine months of 1974 was 170,000 tons, as against 250,000 and 230,000 tons in the corresponding months of 1979 and 1984 respectively. More striking is the difference in the level of stocks: the average month-end stock of foodgrains in government stores was only about 140,000 tons in the famine months of 1974, as against 700,000 and 650,000 tons in 1979 and 1984 (corresponding months) respectively. Thus although the difference in terms of offtake is not all that dramatic, the difference in stock would indicate that the government's ability to tackle a crisis was much higher in 1979 and 1984 than in 1974. It also has to be remembered that the level of offtake improved in 1974 only towards the end of the famine. In the earlier period, when speculative pressure was gradually building up, both stock and offtake were much lower than during the famine months.

where the role of PFDS in containing speculative price increase comes in. The price spiral of 1974 was a direct consequence of speculative market withdrawal encouraged by a perceived inability of the PFDS to deal with future scarcity. In contrast, the health of PFDS in 1979 and 1984 in all its aspects (namely import, stocks, and distribution) signalled the futility of speculating on future scarcity. This had an obvious softening effect on market withdrawal and the consequent rise in the current price of foodgrain. The limitations of PFDS in 1974 and its vitality in the two later years should therefore constitute the key explanation of why famine occurred in one case and not in the others.[28]

The time has now come to answer the questions posed at the beginning of this section. Note first that while the authorities were highly successful in checking speculative price increase in both 1979 and 1984, they were also helped in this effort by a couple of fortunate circumstances. On both occasions, the government found itself blessed with a healthy foreign exchange reserve, a rare phenomenon in a country with a chronic balance-of-payments problem. The situation in 1984 was particularly fortuitous, as the reserves actually represented the 'unwelcome' consequence of a recession in the preceding years which had depressed imports to disconcertingly low levels. But it turned out to be a boon in disguise when the floods came, and helped to procure a record level of imports on a commercial basis. In fact, in both 1979 and 1984, commercial imports accounted for over half of total imports, while usually food aid accounts for more than two-thirds of imports in normal years. Commercial imports on such a scale were a dream in 1974, as foreign exchange reserves had already been drawn down to precariously low levels when the real crunch came.

The second fortunate circumstance was the highly favourable aid climate obtaining at the time, particularly in 1979. Not only were the donors generous and prompt in their response, even the IMF was very understanding! The country was under a stand-by agreement with the IMF in that year and there was, inevitably, an agreed ceiling on government borrowing. That ceiling was breached as the government borrowed heavily from the Central Bank in order to finance its commercial imports, but the IMF did not raise any fuss.[29] The donors were somewhat less forthcoming in 1984, but nowhere near as niggardly as in 1974.[30]

---

[28] It would appear that Sen (1981) has underestimated the role of a weakened public food distribution system in precipitating the famine of 1974. He recognizes its importance in constraining the relief operations of the government once the famine had struck, but does not attach any *causal* significance to it. This he does by ignoring the effect of PFDS on speculative price increase and concentrating merely on its effect on the current availability of foodgrains.

[29] However the very next year, in 1980, when the government broke its credit ceiling again, this time to replenish its depleted food stock through a massive drive for domestic procurement out of a bumper harvest, the IMF responded by cancelling a newly contracted Extended Fund Facility programme. For a critical review of these incidents see Matin (1986).

[30] For information on donors' response in 1984, see World Bank (1985*b*). The story of 1974 is told most vividly by McHenry and Bird (1977).

Thus the episodes of 1979 and 1984 do not really testify to any systemic improvement on the front of short-term food security. Aid climate, one of the favourable factors, is essentially an exogenous variable. The other factor, namely a healthy foreign exchange reserve, is in principle a control variable, and there has been a lot of discussion about holding such reserves in lieu of or as a supplement to a buffer stock of food. But the government has not been able to pursue any consistent policy in this regard, hard-pressed as it is to provide foreign exchange for much-needed imports. Accumulation of reserves has always been a consequence of unforeseen shortfall in the import programme. The two years in question were no exception. Therefore, the hypothesis that the government has acquired a greater capability of dealing with famine threats remains untested, at best, and in considerable doubt, to be more realistic.

The fortuitous manner in which famine was averted in 1979 and 1984 also gives no comfort to the thought that the structure of Bangladesh economy has acquired a greater resilience over time against threats of dramatic entitlement failures. Nor does it negate the thesis of secular deterioration in the trend of endemic hunger.

Finally, what can one say about the relationship between 'persistent entitlement contraction' and 'sudden entitlement failures'? The experience of the recent years of course shows that, despite entitlement contraction, catastrophic failures of entitlement can be avoided if fortune smiles. But that is not saying much. One would suspect on a priori grounds that the probability of 'failure' would increase with the intensification of 'contraction'. Indeed it is possible to argue that entitlement failure in 1974 turned out to be as precipitous as it was mainly because of severe entitlement contraction that had occurred in the preceding years, partly through natural calamities and partly through the destructions and dislocations caused by a prolonged war of liberation. The destruction of assets (houses, cattle, etc.) caused by these events was a direct dent in the 'endowment set', especially for the rural people. Endowment contractions of this kind must have accentuated the gravity of the famine. These contractions of entitlement of course occurred under exceptional circumstances, in a relatively rapid manner. But persistent contractions can also produce qualitatively similar results. There is therefore hardly any ground for feeling confident that the Bangladesh economy has acquired a greater immunity from famine in recent years.[31]

---

[31] It ought to be recognized, however, that the production structure of Bangladesh agriculture has probably acquired a somewhat greater degree of resilience against the destructive effects of natural disasters such as flooding. But for the recent advances in dry-season cultivation through modern irrigation and spread of HYVs in the rainfed winter crop, the effect of the 1984 floods would have been much more devastating, making it harder to contain a potentially dangerous price spiral. On this, see World Bank (1985b). It should also be noted that the necessary physical infrastructure for the storage and distribution of foodgrains is much better now than it was in 1974. It means that, if the necessary foodgrains can somehow be acquired at the right time, the authorities can now deal with a crisis more effectively than before. But the crucial 'acquisition' problem remains as uncertain as ever.

9.5. *Elements of food strategy*

We have analysed the structural forces governing the evolution of entitlement over time and also tried to judge the prospect of dramatic failures in entitlement. The analysis reveals a rather grim picture. It is now necessary to move on to the level of policy, to see if the policies being pursued have the potential to change the course of structural evolution.

While policies with long-term structural effects are our primary interest here, it should also be recognized that a comprehensive food strategy ought to incorporate short-term elements as well. These short-term policies can be broadly classified into two groups—those in the nature of 'palliatives' and those meant for 'crisis management'. The two are often merged under the common rubric of short-term 'food security'; but they perform two separate functions and it seems analytically more helpful to recognize the distinction. Since hunger is going to persist for some time yet no matter what long-term measures are adopted, 'palliatives' are required to redress the more extreme cases of misery. Policies of 'crisis management' on the other hand are meant to prevent calamitous failures of entitlement and to minimize the effect of such failures, if they occur. Although conceptually distinct, the two objectives can often be pursued through the same set of policies. This is indeed the case in Bangladesh: The Public Foodgrain Distribution System (PFDS) is meant to provide both the palliatives and the instruments of crisis management. We shall have a brief look at it before turning to the long-term issues.

Foodgrain distributed through PFDS has expanded over time both in absolute terms and in relation to total availability.[32] The offtake–availability ratio has risen from an average of 8 per cent in the 1960s to about 14 per cent in the decade and a half since Liberation. There has also occurred a significant shift in the relative shares of different channels of distribution. Modified rationing (MR), which distributes subsidized foodgrain to the rural poor, used to account for about 55 per cent of total offtake in the 1960s. In the early years of the 1970s, its share came down to 30–40 per cent, dropping further to only 18 per cent in the 1980s. Statutory urban rationing (SR), which supplies subsidized foodgrain to the residents of certain important urban areas, has also faced a relative decline, but not to the same extent as MR. Its share remained at around 23 per cent throughout the 1960s and 1970s, but fell rather sharply to 15 per cent in the 1980s. The channels which have gained in relative share are mainly three: (1) other priorities (OP), which supplies subsidized foodgrain to certain priority groups (mainly urban), (2) food-for-work programme (FFW), which serves the rural labourers by paying them in kind in return for work, and (3) open market sales (OMS) plus marketing operations (MO), both of which are designed to augment market supply for the general benefit of all consumers rather than for any particular target group.

---

[32] For a recent in-depth study of the operation and effectiveness of PFDS, see MOF (1986). The following statistics are derived from this source.

Among all the shifts that have taken place, the most remarkable one is the dramatic decline in the share of MR from the 1960s to the 1980s. It is also apparently the most perverse one, when viewed in the light of our earlier analysis of widening rural hunger. Recent policy disposition appears to be one of going further ahead in the direction of phasing out MR, and replacing it by market augmentation in the rural area. It is not at all obvious, however, how the strategy of leaving the poor entirely at the mercy of the market is going to improve their food security. To the extent that market augmentation helps to stabilize prices, the cause of food security will indeed be served to some extent. But it is not clear that the resulting 'price security' will be more effective than the assured 'quantity security' for those living at the edge of subsistence.

When the foodgrain distributed through the food-for-work programme is added to MR, the share of rural poor does not appear quite as bad, but it is still less than used to be the case in the 1960s. The expansion of the FFW programme is on the whole a welcome phenomenon, as recent studies of its impact appear to indicate.[33] But equally unwelcome is the contraction of modified rationing. A recent survey of MR beneficiaries has shown that about 95 per cent of them actually belong to the target group (MOF 1986). Many of the eligible households are of course left out and even those who receive the ration only gain a small increase in real income (2 per cent); but that is a consequence of the small size of the whole operation. It has at least the potential to make a bigger contribution to the real income of rural poor if the scale of operation is expanded.[34]

There are however serious problems with urban statutory rationing (SR) as it is currently practised. It has been found that the average income of SR beneficiaries is considerably higher than that of an average urban household, and per capita calorie intake comfortably above the national average (MOF 1986). Thus, unlike in the case of modified rationing, the contraction of statutory rationing did not imply a great loss for the urban poor, since they did not receive much benefit from it anyway. This does not however mean that urban rationing should therefore be abandoned, though that again is the current trend of policy. But it does mean that a method has to be found for reaching the urban poor.

On the whole, then, with the exception of its FFW component, PFDS in its

---

[33] The short-run impacts of the FFW programme are analysed in Osmani and Chowdhury (1983). The long-term effects are studied in BIDS/IFPRI (1985).

[34] In so far as both MR and FFW are 'targeted' to the rural poor, there may be an inclination to treat them as substitutes and to take a lenient view of the contraction of MR in view of the fact that FFW has expanded so rapidly. But it will be wrong to take such a view in our judgement. The two should really be treated as complements rather than substitutes because, first, MR can reach those who are not capable of the physical rigour demanded by FFW, and, secondly, MR can operate throughout the year while FFW is necessarily constrained to the short intersection between the dry season and the lean period of agricultural operations. However, in so far as FFW has the additional benefit of creating potentially useful rural infrastructure, there is indeed a case for giving it preference when seasonality permits.

present shape does not appear to be particularly effective as a short-term palliative for persistent hunger. However, as we have noted earlier in the context of the events of 1979 and 1984, it has been a good deal more effective as an instrument of crisis management.

9.6. *The long-range strategy*

While the importance of a properly targeted public food distribution system can hardly be questioned, especially as a short-term palliative for extreme cases of poverty, its limitations as a strategy for solving the long-term problem of hunger are also pretty obvious. The sheer magnitude of the problem of food deprivation rules out public distribution as an effective long-term strategy. The administrative problem of targeting food distribution to nearly three-quarters of the total population is one of the reasons for doubting its effectiveness, but by no means the most important one. An even bigger problem is the limited amount of food available for distribution. Of course, if the total available food were to be distributed according to one's requirement, the currently available calories might be just enough to satisfy everyone's need.[35] However, one does not have to be a cynic to rule out the feasibility of such an ideal distribution.

Higher levels of production are therefore an obvious necessity; but not so much because it will provide a larger base for public distribution, as because the dynamics of production will help improve the entitlement of all the rural groups through the structural processes described earlier. However, a couple of qualifications to this statement should be noted before proceeding further.

Firstly, it is easy to show that, even with a considerable increase in the rate of food production, the incomes of the poor may not rise enough to eliminate hunger. Khan (1985) has recently given a quantitative demonstration of this argument through an empirical model linking production with income distribution. It is indeed clear that, given the existing endowment distribution and continued demographic pressure, no 'feasible' rates of food production can eliminate hunger in the near future. This naturally turns one's attention to the need for changing the 'endowment distribution' as well as for containing the rate of population growth. But this does not obviate the need for stepping up the rate of food production. A higher rate of growth may not be *sufficient* to *eliminate* hunger, but will at least be *necessary* to *reduce* it.[36]

[35] Note that per capita calorie intake was estimated to be 1,943 calories per day in 1981/2 (INFS 1981/2) while per capita requirement according to one estimate is 2,020 calories (World Bank 1985a). Given the margin of error that is likely to be involved in both these estimates, it is perhaps fair to conclude that requirement and availability match each other reasonably well at the aggregate level.

[36] It follows from this observation that any comprehensive discussion of the strategies for eliminating hunger should also involve discussion of the political strategy for bringing about changes in 'endowment distributions'. Lack of competence on the part of the author is the principal reason for not venturing into this field.

But will it be *sufficient* to *reduce* hunger? This is where the second set of qualifications come in. We have pointed out earlier that growth can certainly occur in a manner which will not only fail to reduce hunger, but may even accentuate it. If, for instance, all the growth is concentrated on the lands of large farmers who decide to switch over to mechanized cultivation, then both small peasants and wage labourers may experience increasing hunger. Mechanization however is very unlikely to be adopted extensively in Bangladesh agriculture, given the cheap labour and fragmented holdings prevailing there. But the possibility of large-farmer bias in the pattern of growth cannot be ruled out. We have seen earlier that the past history of technological transformation in Bangladesh agriculture does not indicate any such bias. But whether the past pattern will continue into the future is very largely a function of present policy. It is in this light that we intend to review the present orientation of long-range food strategy in Bangladesh.

In the past, the diffusion of modern technology has been brought about largely through heavy subsidization of two crucial inputs, fertilizer and irrigation, combined with extensive government control in the distribution of these inputs. In contrast, price support for farm output has played a negligible role. A foodgrain procurement system has of course been in operation for a long time, but it was geared essentially to meeting the needs of a subsidized public foodgrain distribution system (PFDS). Accordingly, the objective was to procure a target quantity of foodgrain at a price which would be low enough to avoid an excessive fiscal burden on account of PFDS. Whether that price would provide an incentive to the producers to expand production was not a matter of explicit concern. One other element of policy was government ownership of the major irrigation assets such as large-scale river-control projects as well as power pumps and deep tubewells. Only the small irrigation equipment such as shallow tubewells and hand tubewells was sold to the private sector. The publicly owned irrigation equipment used to be rented out to groups of farmers at a subsidized fee.

All these policies have recently undergone an almost complete reversal, beginning in the late 1970s and gaining momentum in the 1980s. The emerging policy regime can be characterized by the following features: (1) withdrawal of input subsidies, (2) instituting a compensating price support programme, (3) a relatively free market for determining both input price and consumer price of foodgrain, (4) distribution of fertilizer through private traders, and (5) private ownership of irrigation equipment (all kinds of tubewells and power pumps), with large-scale irrigation projects being financed and executed by the public sector.

How is this strategy going to affect the growth and pattern of foodgrain production and, through it, the evolution of food entitlement? Let us begin by looking at the implications of the policy of withdrawing input subsidy.

We have argued elsewhere that the main rationale for providing input subsidy in Bangladesh agriculture lies in the fact that it helps to ease the credit

THE FOOD PROBLEMS OF BANGLADESH 337

constraint faced by the small farmers (Osmani and Quasem 1985). The adoption of HYV technology raises the working capital requirements for cultivation as the farmers have to pay for fertilizers and irrigation charges before they reap the harvest. This cost however cannot usually be covered through institutional credit to which they have very little access (Table 9.5). It has been estimated for instance that no more than 10 per cent of the fertilizer cost of small farmers is financed out of institutional credit (Hossain 1985c).

Under the circumstances, the small farmers are left with the option of either borrowing from the informal credit market or drawing upon their own meagre resources. In the first case, they are usually forced to pay an exorbitant rate of interest and in the second they apply high subjective rates of discount on future income in view of their subsistence level of present consumption. In either case, both equity and efficiency are adversely affected. An interesting piece of evidence in this regard is provided by a recent survey (Hossain 1985b). It shows that at the current level of fertilizer application, the marginal value product (MVP) of fertilizer is considerably higher than its price, in fact much higher than can be accounted for as the interest cost at the official rate of interest. There are several alternative ways in which such a differential could conceivably arise.[37] In the first place, there could have been a binding constraint of fertilizer supply which would force the farmers off their demand curve. But it has been shown by Quasem (1985) through an analysis of the stocks and sales of the fertilizer-distributing agency (BADC) that supply of fertilizer was not generally short of demand (barring some occasional localized shortages) in the recent years, including the period to which the above survey results relate. Secondly, the observed divergence could be a consequence of farmers' risk aversion in a situation of uncertainty. In fact, the uncertainty involved in the use of an unfamiliar input, and the resulting divergence between its MVP and price, has been the traditional argument for subsidizing an input in the early stage of adoption. The proponents of 'subsidy withdrawal' however argue that after two decades of experience with modern technology, the farmers are now well aware of its benefits and do not need subsidy any more.[38] If this argument is accepted, then the only other plausible explanation of the observed divergence would be in credit constraint.[39] Under the usual maximizing assumptions, the divergence would then imply either that the effective cost of fertilizer is very high (because the farmers have to borrow from the informal credit market) or that the effective MVP is low (because the small farmers draw upon

[37] Note that price here refers to the actual market price paid by the farmers and not the official subsidized price. The divergence is therefore a real one and not a consequence of using the wrong prices.

[38] Arguments of this kind frequently appear in various World Bank documents urging the government of Bangladesh to withdraw input subsidy. For a comprehensive documentation of the World Bank view and its arguments, see Osmani and Quasem (1985).

[39] The other possibility, namely the uncertainty due to the vagaries of nature, is not particularly relevant in the case of HYVs which are grown mostly under controlled irrigated condition.

their own resources and hence apply a high subjective rate of discount). It will then be necessary on the ground of economic efficiency to remove the credit constraint so that the price of input can be equated with its nominal MVP. One way of doing it is to provide input subsidy which will ease the credit constraint by the simple expedient of reducing the need for credit.[40]

However, it may be argued that the best answer to the credit problem is to solve it directly by providing more credit to the small farmer instead of going through the roundabout way of subsidizing inputs. That is indeed true, in principle; but in reality credit programmes for small farmers have proved notoriously unsuccessful almost everywhere in the developing world. Until an institutional mechanism can be found for successful targeting of credit to the small farmers, input subsidy is necessary to deal with the credit constraint, albeit as a second-best strategy.[41]

We have already noted that the high levels of input subsidy offered at the early stage of 'Green Revolution' in Bangladesh probably explain why the small farmers could participate at least proportionately in the adoption of new technology. But the subsidies have been reduced at a rapid rate in recent years.[42] It is sometimes argued that the withdrawal of subsidy would not affect the farmers since they, especially the small farmers, do not receive the benefit of subsidy anyway. The basis of the argument is that the farmers usually buy their fertilizer not directly from the official distributing agency but from private dealers who lift fertilizer at the subsidized price and allegedly sell to the farmers at a higher price as dictated by supply and demand.[43] But this is really

[40] If uncertainty due to the use of an unfamiliar input is thought to persist and contribute to the divergence between price and MVP, then of course the case for subsidy is further strengthened.

[41] It may be mentioned in this context that the Grameen Bank experiment (see n. 21 above) seems to have found an effective institutional method of reaching the poor in the non-farm sector. One might naturally ask why this method cannot be extended to the farm sector as well. The Grameen Bank has already made a beginning in this direction, but it is still too early to assess the results. There would however appear to be some intrinsic problems of agricultural credit which the Grameen Bank approach might come up against. It is well known that one of the keys to the success of the Grameen Bank is the system of weekly repayment of loans. The poor people, who are under the constant pressure of immediate consumption, find it so much more convenient to repay their loans if they are to repay in small instalments over an extended period of time. This process is facilitated if they also have a continuous flow of income. Repayments can then be made regularly out of current income, obviating the need for first accumulating and then drawing down a savings balance. Most of the activities in the non-farm sector are in fact of this 'point-input continuous-output' type. In contrast, agricultural operations are more akin to 'point-input point-output' type. Output is harvested at a point in time; and the small farmers are hardly capable of converting a 'point output' into a 'continuous income' by phasing out the sale of crops over an extended period. The discipline of weekly repayment in this case is likely to come up against a very strong time preference for current consumption.

[42] For instance, urea, the most widely used fertilizer in Bangladesh agriculture, used to enjoy a subsidy of 58% in the late 1960s; and even as late as 1975/6, the rate was 52%, but it fell to a mere 4% in 1982/3.

[43] Field information on actual prices paid by the farmers reveals that they do generally pay a premium over the official price, but a fairly small one. It is also found that the small farmers sometimes pay more than the large farmers, but again the difference is not a striking one. For details of the evidence, see Osmani and Quasem (1985).

a non-argument; it represents a confusion over the relevant concept of subsidy. The market price, as determined by supply and demand, may of course be regarded as one notion of unsubsidized price, and by that criterion the farmers may not be receiving any subsidy. But when the government of Bangladesh and its advisers propose to withdraw subsidy, they take the cost of procurement as the unsubsidized price; and it turns out that actual market prices have always remained far below the cost of procurement (Osmani and Quasem 1985).

In other words, the scarcity premium reaped by the dealers was lower than the rate of subsidy and to that extent the farmers have indeed shared the benefit of subsidy. One implication of this fact is that if the subsidy is removed and the official price is set at the cost of procurement, the resulting price increase will be too high to be absorbed into the scarcity margin. Consequently, the market price will have to rise and, as indicated by some recent estimates of elasticity,[44] this will have a substantial dampening effect on the demand for fertilizer.

Of course, the net effect will depend also on what has been happening to the other determinants of fertilizer demand, one of them being the price of food crop. As it happens, however, the price of crop has failed completely to keep pace with the rising price of fertilizer. As a result, the fertilizer–paddy price ratio has trebled from 0.74 in 1971/2 to 2.03 in 1983/4. The growth-retarding effect of this price disincentive has recently been demonstrated by Osmani and Quasem (1985). The subsidies have been reduced most drastically in the second half of the post-Liberation period and it is in this half that the intensity of fertilizer application on individual crop varieties has come to a standstill after exhibiting a rapid growth in the preceding years. It is also in this subperiod that yield improvement in individual crop varieties has made a negative contribution to the overall growth of foodgrain production, while it had made the biggest contribution to growth in the earlier period.

Growth of course has still occurred and the average application of fertilizer per unit of land has still risen as irrigation facilities have made it possible to shift from local to improved varieties of seeds which are more intensive in the use of fertilizer and have a higher level of yield.

But even this process is now being threatened by the policy of privatization and subsidy reduction that is being followed in the irrigation sector. There is ample evidence that privatization of irrigation equipment has added to the cost of irrigation on top of the effect of subsidy reduction.[45] Private owners of irrigation equipment charge a higher rate to its users than that generally paid by the groups renting publicly owned equipment and the area irrigated per machine is correspondingly lower for the privately owned ones. At the same time, the sale of irrigation equipment is also facing increasing difficulty. After

[44] These estimates seem to lie between −0.7 and −0.8. For details of estimation procedures, see Hossain (1985b) and Osmani and Quasem (1985).

[45] For substantiation of the empirical statements made in this paragraph, see Osmani and Quasem (1985).

the initial burst of privatization, the market for new equipment seems to have shrunk considerably. This is quite understandable when one realizes that after the initial purchase by larger farmers (of whom there are not very many), the smaller ones are finding it harder to pay the price, especially as the rate of subsidy is being scaled down.

Clearly, all these developments have a potentially restrictive effect on both overall production and the small farmers' participation in it. However, one may recall that the current policy package does at least in principle provide an antidote to all this in the form of a compensating price support programme. The foodgrain procurement system is being increasingly reorganized as a price support programme, as the procurement price is now being consciously set at a level that is expected to cover the cost of production and also leave a margin of profit. If effective, this should in principle be able to neutralize the accentuation of credit constraint caused by the happenings on the input side. This it will achieve by ensuring a higher price for the marketed surplus and thus offsetting the effect of a high rate of interest or subjective discount.

But there are serious limitations to this policy: it is simply irrelevant for subsistence farmers who do not have any marketable surplus and positively harmful to the deficit farmers who are net buyers in the market. According to some calculations, no more than 30 per cent of the farmers will derive any substantial benefits from an output price support programme (Ahmed 1981). The rest will not only fail to derive any benefit, they will in fact be worse off as the credit constraint gets tightened by the policies on the input side such as withdrawal of subsidy and privatization of irrigation equipment. Further diffusion of HYV technology will then be concentrated on the lands of the rich peasants, while the poor peasants become increasingly marginalized and eventually alienated from land. Man-made policies will thus combine with underlying structural forces to hasten the proletarianization of an already marginalized peasantry.

The stage is thus being set for a neatly polarized agrarian structure by concentrating incentive in the sphere of large farmers and driving the small peasants out of the production nexus. In the mean time, privatization of fertilizer trade and creation of irrigation entrepreneurs will help in the process of primitive capital accumulation. Thus the various components of the prevailing long-range food strategy appear to derive their unifying logic from an underlying development strategy that aims at the capitalist transformation of Bangladesh agriculture.

All the issues that are raised by the prospect of such a transformation cannot obviously be discussed within the confines of this chapter. But at least its implications for the evolution of food entitlement ought to be mentioned.

It is immediately obvious that the small peasants, marginalized and eventually driven out of land, will suffer a decline in food entitlement unless alternative employment opportunities are opened up. But the prospects of such alternative opportunities are not very bright either. It has been estimated that during the rest of the century the rural labour force will grow at the rate of around 3 per cent a year. Even with a 3.7 per cent growth in production, a rate that has not on average been achieved in recent years, agriculture can absorb no more than a quarter of the additional labour force (World Bank 1983). There is therefore already a strong tendency to aggravate the excess supply of agricultural labour. If the proletarianization of the peasantry adds to this natural increase in labour supply, there can only be an all-round reduction in wage and employment per person, with its obvious implications for food entitlement.

Nor does non-farm employment opportunity hold out any better hope. We have noted earlier that the non-farm sector is already severely stretched to provide residual employment for those being thrown out of the agricultural sector. An exodus into this sector will only serve to bring down further the entitlement of the poor engaged in this sector. Such an all-round impoverishment and the resulting shrinkage of effective demand may even constrain the process of capitalist growth itself, unless of course the 'capitalist dynamism' is sustained by exporting food while people within the country go hungry.

9.7.   *Summary and concluding remarks*

Our aim in this chapter was to seek illumination on three questions pertaining to the food problems of Bangladesh: first, what are the processes perpetuating the food deprivation of the great majority of the masses; secondly, has Bangladesh achieved over time a greater degree of immunity from the sudden failures of food entitlement leading to famines; and finally, what hopes do the current food policies hold out for the elimination of endemic hunger?

On the first question, we started with the premise that, in a food-dominated production structure, as happens to obtain in rural Bangladesh, the long-term food entitlement of all sections of people depends crucially on the pace and pattern of food production. Yet one finds that, despite positive growth in per capita food production, the food entitlement of a great majority shows no visible signs of improvement during the post-Liberation period. Various alternative hypotheses were considered to explain this phenomenon. In particular, we tried to investigate whether the very pattern of growth was immiserizing, or whether the rate of growth was inadequate to offset the immiserizing force of demographic pressure operating within a system of private property ownership. The available empirical evidence seems to support the latter hypothesis. It is the slow rate of growth rather than a 'distorted' pattern of growth in food production that has been historically responsible for persistent contraction in the food entitlement of the masses. Also, it was argued that the proximate cause of slow growth was sluggish investment in agriculture and the resulting failure to convert a huge pool of surplus manpower into productive farmland capital. No attempt was made however to go beyond the proximate cause and to explore how the rate of investment has in fact been constrained by various factors such as the prevailing social structure, incentive systems, and the political economy of public sector decision making. Consideration of these issues, vital as they are, would have broadened the scope far beyond the limitations of a single chapter.

On the issue of vulnerability to famines, it was noted that, since the famine of 1974, the country has successfully avoided similar disasters despite the recurrence of potential threats, especially in 1979 and 1984. We have argued however that this success does not unfortunately indicate any inherent improvement in the country's immunity from famines. The proximate reason why famine did not occur in 1979 and 1984 was that anticipated loss of food crops could not generate a speculative price spiral, as it did in 1974. Strong government intervention through the public foodgrain distribution system served to dampen the speculative hoarding of foodgrain, whereas in the famine year of 1974 speculation was in fact fuelled by a thoroughly inadequate and unreliable public intervention. But it is important to note that intervention was made possible in 1979 and 1984 only by the existence of two fortuitous circumstances. One was a congenial aid atmosphere and the other was an unexpectedly large foreign exchange reserve which together made it possible to import a record amount of foodgrain to feed the public distribution system. Since neither of these factors can be relied upon to prevail every time a crisis occurs, there is no ground for inferring from the recent success stories that the economy has acquired any genuine resilience against the threats of famine.

The final issue we addressed was the implication of prevailing food policies for the evolution of food entitlement in the future. The focus was on the likely impact of these policies on the pace and pattern of growth in food production. It was of course recognized that, in the absence of fundamental changes in endowment distribution, no feasible rate or pattern of growth can possibly eliminate the scourge of hunger in the face of an increasingly adverse land–man ratio. Accordingly, the focus was on the role of food policies in containing rather than eliminating long-term hunger. Our analysis shows that even the limited goal of containing long-term hunger is unlikely to be accomplished by the pursuit of food policies currently being implemented. The various components of the existing food strategy mutually reinforce each other to concentrate incentives and opportunities among the relatively well-off farmers. This is likely to alter the historical pattern of a fairly equitable diffusion of modern technology, making it increasingly difficult for the small farmers to benefit from further gains in productivity. In the face of unabated demographic pressure, the failure to improve the productivity of land will hasten the impoverishment of small farmers and quicken the pace of landlessness. As they swell the ranks of agricultural labour and non-farm workers, adding to the natural increase of labour supply in these sectors, there is likely to occur an all-round contraction in the entitlement of the rural poor.

If the food policies are to contain rather than accentuate the process of entitlement contraction, a minimal requirement is to ensure an equitable diffusion of modern technology so that the proletarianization of the peasantry can at least be retarded. A chief obstacle to be overcome in this regard is the credit constraint faced by the small farmers. Input subsidies and public provision of capital assets should form essential ingredients of any food strategy aimed at overcoming this constraint.[46]

[46] For a fuller account of the author's views on the appropriate strategies for both farm and non-farm sectors in rural Bangladesh, see Osmani (1985).

References

ABDULLAH, A. A. (1985), 'Three Notes on Fertilizer Subsidy Removal in Bangladesh' (revised), mimeo (Dhaka: Bangladesh Institute of Development Studies).

AHMAD, Q. K. (1985), 'Food Shortages and Food Entitlements in Bangladesh: An Indepth Enquiry in Respect of Selected Years', mimeo (Rome: FAO).

——and HOSSAIN, M. (1985), 'An Evaluation of Selected Policies and Programmes for the Alleviation of Rural Poverty in Bangladesh', in Islam, R. (ed.), *Strategies for Alleviating Poverty in Rural Asia* (Dhaka: Bangladesh Institute of Development Studies; Bangkok: ILO/ARTEP).

AHMED, R. (1981), 'Agricultural Price Policies under Complex Socioeconomic and Natural Constraints: The Case of Bangladesh', Research Report 27 (Washington, DC: IFPRI).

ALAMGIR, M. (1980), *Famine in South Asia: Political Economy of Mass Starvation in Bangladesh* (Cambridge, Mass.: Oelgeschlager, Gunn & Hain).

BEATON, C. H. (1983), 'Energy in Human Nutrition', *Nutrition Today*, 18.

BIDS (1981), 'Rural Industries Study Project: Final Report', mimeo (Dhaka: Bangladesh Institute of Development Studies).

——and IFPRI (1985), *Development impact of the Food-for-Work Program in Bangladesh: Summary* (Dhaka: Bangladesh Institute of Development Studies; Washington, DC: IFPRI).

CHEN, L. C., HUQ, E., and D'SOUZA, S. (1981), 'Sex Bias in the Family Allocation of Food and Health Care in Rural Bangladesh', *Population and Development Review*, 7.

CLAY, E. J., and KHAN, M. S. (1977), 'Agricultural Employment and Unemployment in Bangladesh: The Next Decade', mimeo (Dhaka: Bangladesh Agricultural Research Council).

CSS (1980), 'Report on Barisal Area III Project: Agrarian Structure and Trends', mimeo (Dhaka: Centre for Social Studies, University of Dhaka).

HOSSAIN, M. (1981), 'Land Tenure and Agricultural Development in Bangladesh', VRF Series No. 85 (Tokyo: Institute of Developing Economies).

——(1984a), 'Employment and Labour in Bangladesh Rural Industries', *Bangladesh Development Studies*, 12.

——(1984b), 'Increasing Food Availability in Bangladesh: Constraints and Possibilities', Technical Paper 'A', Food Strategy Review Exercise, mimeo (Dhaka: Ministry of Agriculture, Government of Bangladesh).

——(1984c), 'Credit for the Rural Poor: The Grameen Bank of Bangladesh', Research Monograph No. 4 (Dhaka: Bangladesh Institute of Development Studies).

——(1984d), 'Productivity and Profitability in Bangladesh Rural Industries', *Bangladesh Development Studies*, 12.

——(1984e), *Employment Generation through Cottage Industries: Potential and Constraints* (Bangkok: ILO/ARTEP).

——(1985a), 'A Note on the Trend of Landlessness in Bangladesh', mimeo (Dhaka: Bangladesh Institute of Development Studies).

——(1985b), 'Fertilizer Consumption, Pricing and Foodgrain Consumption in Bangladesh', in BIDS/IFPRI, *Fertilizer Pricing Policy and Foodgrain Production Strategy in Bangladesh*, vol. ii (Dhaka: BIDS; Washington, DC: IFPRI).

——(1985c), 'Agricultural Development in Bangladesh: A Historical Perspective', paper presented at a joint seminar of Bangladesh Economic Association and the International Food Policy Research Institute held in Dhaka.

——RAHMAN, A., and AKASH, M. M. (1985), 'Agricultural Taxation in Bangladesh: Potential and Policies', Research Report No. 42 (Dhaka: Bangladesh Institute of Development Studies).

INFS (1975/6), *Nutrition Survey of Rural Bangladesh 1975–76* (Dhaka: Institute of Nutrition and Food Science, University of Dhaka).

——(1981/2), *Nutrition Survey of Rural Bangladesh 1981–82*, (Dhaka: Institute of Nutrition and Food Science, University of Dhaka).

KHAN, A. R. (1976), 'Poverty and Inequality in Rural Bangladesh', Working Paper (Geneva: ILO).

KHAN, Q. M. (1985), 'A Model of Endowment-Constrained Demand for Food in an Agricultural Economy with Empirical Applications to Bangladesh', *World Development*, 13.

MATIN, K. M. (1986), 'Bangladesh and the IMF: An Exploratory Study', Research Monograph No. 5 (Dhaka: Bangladesh Institute of Development Studies).

McHENRY, D. F., and BIRD, K. (1977), 'Food Bungle in Bangladesh', *Foreign Policy*, 27.

MOF (1986), 'The Existing System of Public Foodgrain Distribution in Bangladesh and Proposal for Restructuring', Draft Report, prepared by Beacon Consultants for the Ministry of Food, Government of Bangladesh, mimeo (Dhaka).

MUQTADA, M., and ALAM, M. M. (1983), *Hired Labour and Rural Labour Market in Bangladesh* (Bangkok: ILO/ARTEP).

OSMANI, S. R. (1982), *Economic Inequality and Group Welfare* (Oxford: Oxford University Press).

——(1984), *Food and the Nutrition Problem: Methodology of Global Estimation* (Rome: FAO).

——(1985), 'Planning for Distributive Justice in Bangladesh', paper presented at the biennial conference of the Bangladesh Economic Association, Dec., Dhaka.

——and CHOWDHURY, O. H. (1983), 'Short Run Impacts of Food for Work Programme in Bangladesh', *Bangladesh Development Studies*, 11.

——and DEB, N. C. (1984), 'Demand for Rural Industry Products in Bangladesh', mimeo (Dhaka: Bangladesh Institute of Development Studies; Bangkok: ILO/ ARTEP).

—— and QUASEM, M. A. (1985), 'Pricing and Subsidy Policies for Bangladesh Agriculture', mimeo (Dhaka: Bangladesh Institute of Development Studies).

——and RAHMAN, A. (1984), *A Study on Income Distribution in Bangladesh* (New York: Department of International Economic and Social Affairs of the United Nations Secretariat).

QUASEM, M. A. (1985), 'Supply and Distribution of Fertilizers in Bangladesh', in BIDS/IFPRI, *Fertilizer Pricing Policy and Foodgrain Production Strategy in Bangladesh* (Dhaka: BIDS; Washington, DC: IFPRI).

RAHMAN, A. (1979), 'Agrarian Structure and Capital Formation: A Study of Bangladesh Agriculture', unpublished Ph.D. dissertation, University of Cambridge.

RAHMAN, M. (forthcoming), 'Socio-economic Determinants of Poverty in Rural Bangladesh', ongoing Ph.D. dissertation, Institute of Statistical Research and Training, University of Dhaka.

RAVALLION, M. (1985), 'The Performance of Rice Markets in Bangladesh during the 1974 Famine', *Economic Journal*, 95.

SEN, A. K. (1981), *Poverty and Famines: An Essay on Entitlement and Deprivation* (Oxford: Oxford University Press).

——(1985), *Commodities and Capabilities* (Amsterdam: North-Holland).

SOBHAN, R. (1979), 'Politics of Food and Famine in Bangladesh', *Economic and Political Weekly*, 48.

SRINIVASAN, T. N. (1983), *Malnutrition in Developing Countries: The State of Knowledge of the Extent of its Prevalence, its Causes and its Consequences* (Rome: FAO).

UNICEF/FREPD (1981), *The Situation of Children in Bangladesh* (Dhaka: University of Dhaka).

USDH (1962–6), *Nutrition Survey of East Pakistan* (Washington, DC: Department of Health, Education and Welfare).

World Bank (1983), *Bangladesh: Selected Issues in Rural Employment* (Washington, DC: World Bank).

——(1984), *Bangladesh: Economic Trends and Development Administration*, vol. ii: *Statistical Appendix* (Washington, DC: World Bank).

——(1985a), *Bangladesh: Food and Nutrition Sector Review* (Washington, DC: World Bank).

——(1985b), *Bangladesh: Economic and Social Development Prospects* (Washington, DC: World Bank).

10

The Elimination of Endemic Poverty in South Asia

Some Policy Options

Kaushik Basu

10.1. *Introduction*

In this age of mammoth scientific achievements we have the necessary
technology, raw material, and skills to grow all the food we need. We also have
a transport system—or at least the capacity to build up the transport system
—which will carry the food to everybody. Nevertheless we have failed to do so,
and persistent mass poverty is a part of twentieth-century life. That this
appears shocking to most of us shows that we have an inherent tendency to
underestimate the complexities of social and political engineering. The oft-
heard view that removing poverty is not difficult at all and our failure is merely
because of vested interests or lack of willingness among powerful people
reflects a misunderstanding of the word 'difficult'. Given that vested interests
are a part of the world, as also are powerful and uncaring people, it is indeed a
difficult task. In designing policies, it is important to recognize this.

  This work is a contribution to the problem of formulating policies to combat
persistent poverty, while recognizing that there are interests and incentive
structures which need to be overcome or tiptoed past. The context of almost all
the analysis will be South Asia, in particular, Bangladesh, India, and Sri
Lanka.

  The study begins by considering the issue of basic needs provision.[1] In order

I am grateful to T. C. A. Anant, Elias Dinopoulos, Jean Drèze, Keith Griffin, Subblah
Kannappan, Sunil Sengupta, and Susan Watkins for discussions. I thank Surjit Bhalla for the
unpublished papers and monographs on Sri Lanka he has sent me, though I am sure he will
disapprove of the use to which these have been put. This work was done at the Institute for
Advanced Study, Princeton. It would have been difficult to complete it without the excellent
support provided by the Institute.

  [1] The definition of 'basic needs' can be controversial. As Streeten (1984: 973–4) notes, 'The
ILO considers employment a basic need; Sidney Webb included leisure. High on the list, as China
recognized in the six guarantees, is a decent funeral . . .' In common parlance basic needs or
standard of living is taken to mean the availability of basic economic necessities (food, shelter,
clothing, etc.) and minimum standards of health and medical facilities (captured by demographic
data on nutrition, life expectancy, etc.). I take advantage of these conventions and escape having to
provide exact measures and definitions. It is arguable that 'basic needs' should also include indices
of political and social ethos. However, the absence of commonly accepted statistics on these makes
them too difficult for use in any meaningful discussion. For those who are overly enthusiastic
about introducing indices of political and social climate to evaluate 'basic needs' policies, a reading
of how such indices are computed could be sobering: see Taylor and Hudson (1972).

to improve the standard of living of the masses, do we have to wait for the benefits of growth to trickle down or could we adopt 'direct action'? This is the subject matter of section 10.2.

Section 10.3 is a detailed consideration of one aspect of basic needs: the removal of poverty and hunger. South Asia has experimented with myriad schemes for supporting the poorest sections and providing employment to the rural landless labourers, for example, the food-for-work programme and the Employment Guarantee Scheme. These are surveyed briefly and suggestions are made for making them more effective.

Even if we accept the desirability of direct action and also know what programmes and schemes to adopt, the actual implementation of such a policy may be hindered because of political constraints. The subject of political constraints is a difficult one and section 10.4 makes a few preliminary comments on it.

10.2.   *On direct action and 'trickle-down'*

It is an old debate as to whether, in a nation's fight against poverty and deprivation, the aim should be to undertake direct action against these or to strengthen the forces of growth and let the poor benefit from the trickle-down effect. Not only does this debate have important policy-consequences for South Asia, but the varied experience of regions in South Asia provides useful evidence for designing effective policy. From our point of view the most remarkable evidence comes from Sri Lanka and the State of Kerala in India. In terms of economic performance, especially growth rates and per capita incomes, these are backward regions; but their achievements in terms of basic needs and standards of living, captured mainly by health and social statistics, are outstanding.[2] Not surprisingly, the role of direct action in these areas has been extensively written about and debated.[3]

I shall begin by commenting on the Sri Lanka debate, comments on Kerala being reserved for later. The Sri Lankan 'paradox' is well known. In terms of the economic criterion that receives most attention, to wit, the per capita real income, Sri Lanka is a very poor country. But its social statistics—variables which indicate the standard of living or quality of life—are very close to those of advanced industrialized countries.[4] As far as per capita income goes, Sri Lanka ranked exactly on par with only one other country in 1983: Sierra Leone. Both these countries had a GNP per capita of $330 in that year.

---

[2] There are other such examples outside South Asia. These include Costa Rica, Cuba, and China.

[3] See Centre for Development Studies (1975), Fields (1980), Isenman (1980), Richards and Gooneratne (1980), Sen (1981*a*, 1985), Nag (1983), Bhalla and Glewwe (1986), Morrison and Waxler (1986).

[4] All the data cited in this and the next two paragraphs, as well as some additional ones, are presented in Table 10.1. All these statistics, except where specified to the contrary, refer to 1983.

Table 10.1 Inter-country social statistics, *c.*1983

	GNP per capita, 1983 ($US)	Life expectancy at birth, 1983 (years)	Infant mortality rate, 1983 (per 1,000 live births)	Number enrolled in secondary school as % of age group, 1982
Mexico	2,240	66	52	54
Korea, Rep. of	2,010	67	29	89
Pakistan	390	50	119	14
Sierra Leone	330	38	198	12
Sri Lanka	330	69	37	54
China	300	67	38	35
India	260	55	93	30
Bangladesh	130	50	132	15

Source: World Bank (1985).

However, in Sri Lanka life expectancy at birth was 69 years, whereas in Sierra Leone it was 38.

Turning to the geographic area being studied in this paper, which also happens to be culturally comparable to Sri Lanka, we find a similar contrast. In India and Bangladesh, life expectancy in 1983 was 55 and 50 years respectively. In Pakistan, where per capita income at $390 is higher than that of Sri Lanka, life expectancy was only 50. Infant mortality in Sri Lanka was 37 (per 1,000 live births), whereas in India it was 93 and in Bangladesh 132. In terms of the percentage of children of the relevant age group attending secondary school,[5] Sri Lanka with a score of 54 is ahead of India (30), Bangladesh (15), and even China (35). In fact, the only country with a comparable per capita income and with similar standard-of-living indicators is China.

It is possible to find countries with six or seven times Sri Lanka's income with standards of living not markedly different from it. Examples include South Korea, with a per capita GNP of $2,010, and Mexico with $2,240. In all the three standard-of-living indicators discussed so far,[6] Mexico does equally

[5] The reason I have chosen secondary school registration data is because this indicates completion of at least the primary level of education. Primary school registration on the other hand may not be sufficiently informative because of high drop-out rates. For example, in UP initial school enrolment in 1965–6 was much higher than in Kerala whereas towards the end of primary school the situation was completely reversed (Centre for Development Studies, 1975: 122).

[6] One variable which is often taken to indicate living standards and is omitted here is fertility. The usual presumption is that in a poor country a drop in fertility rates reflects improved living standards. A careful scrutiny of Kerala's demographic data, however, seems to jeopardize this presumption. It has been shown (A. M. Basu 1986) that the sharper drop in fertility rates in Kerala has occurred among the landless labourers, suggesting that poverty is sometimes as likely to induce fertility declines as are improved living standards.

well or marginally worse than Sri Lanka. In short, a comparison across countries shows Sri Lanka as an 'outlier': In terms of most social and health indicators, Sri Lanka's actual figures are substantially superior to what we would 'predict' on the basis of its per capita income.[7] For these reasons Sri Lanka is often held up as exemplary for other poor countries and also as proof of the fact that 'public action' can lead to the provision of basic needs and, therefore, to an improvement in the quality of life (see e.g. Jayawardena 1974; Fields 1980; Isenman 1980; Sen 1981a; Caldwell 1986).

This very broad thesis has recently been subjected to a detailed econometric scrutiny and has been the source of much controversy and debate (Bhalla 1988a, 1988b; Bhalla and Glewwe 1986; Sen 1988). Bhalla and Glewwe argued that the existing studies, in particular Fields (1980), Isenman (1980), and Sen (1981a), were flawed because they were based on a comparison across countries at a point of time. This, they showed, led to the 'initial conditions' getting omitted. So they set out to examine Sri Lanka's performance over the period 1960 to 1977. As I have already argued and is clear from Table 10.1, if we look at Sri Lanka's ratio of social indicators to per capita income, it is markedly better than that of almost all other countries. Now in order to net out the effect of 'initial conditions' what needs to be done is this: construct a table similar to my Table 10.1, but replace column 1, which shows per capita income at a point of time, with a column showing changes in per capita income between 1960 and 1978; and similarly replace the other columns with 'changes' in variables from the existing 'values at a point of time'. Does Sri Lanka continue to stand out as a country which has done exceedingly well in improving living standards compared to other countries whose change in per capita incomes is similar to that of Sri Lanka? This is the question that Bhalla (1988a, 1988b) and Bhalla and Glewwe (1986) examine meticulously, and they come out with a clear answer: No. On this they are completely convincing; where they err is in drawing inferences from their finding.

For instance, they treat their finding as evidence that a larger social expenditure need not lead to higher living standards. But to maintain this on the basis of a regression analysis of the kind conducted by Bhalla and Glewwe, it is clearly necessary to have comparative data on *changes* in social welfare expenditure in all the countries appearing in the analysis.[8] Without this we cannot jump to any conclusion about the impact of social welfare expenditure based on the finding that in terms of 'changes' between 1960 and 1978 Sri Lanka is not an outlier. Consequently, the basis of their claim gives way when,

[7] Though I used only a few countries and a few variables to demonstrate this, there are more systematic studies which have established it (Isenman 1980; Sen 1981a).

[8] In the absence of this a second-best option is to confine the study to the early 1960s (instead of 1960–78) because there is some evidence that welfare expenditure was increasing in Sri Lanka in the late 1950s. We could therefore argue that the economy in the early 1960s reflected this increase (which we may suppose was sharper in Sri Lanka than in other countries).

after conducting their econometric exercises, Bhalla and Glewwe announce that they do not have these crucial data on welfare expenditures.

As a matter of fact, the proposition that large social expenditures do not necessarily lead to better standards of living is obvious enough not to require any formal econometric study. This is because money is easy to fritter away. One region with a small expenditure can achieve what another region with a large expenditure fails to because of differences in efficiency or methods of disbursement. Thus in Kerala and West Bengal the volume of medical facilities available is comparable, but utilization is much higher in Kerala (Nag 1983); not surprisingly Kerala performs much better than West Bengal in terms of health statistics. So it is easy to concede that while a certain volume of social expenditure is necessary to improve living standards, it is not a sufficient condition.

The other important question that emerges from this debate is: can basic needs be provided directly or do we have to wait for the trickle-down effects of growth? Bhalla and Glewwe treat their findings as implying that reliance on growth rather than direct action is essential. But to answer the above question we have simply to seek examples where income is low but living standards are high, i.e. do the kind of exercise that Isenman (1980) and Sen (1981a) have done. This, as we have just shown, is the case with Sri Lanka, and, as I show below, is also partly the case with Kerala. Hence, whatever it is that Sri Lanka did has led to its achieving very high levels of provision of basic needs. Clearly this is all we need to show that we do not *have to* rely on growth to mitigate poverty and provide basic needs. To assert that something works, but direct action does not, implies a semantic misunderstanding of the term 'direct action'.

It is possible to argue that the cause of the misunderstanding is that many analysts have labelled whatever the Sri Lanka Freedom Party (the one associated with the Bandarnaikes) did as 'direct action' and have taken the failure of those policies to mean a failure of direct action. I will argue later that despite the equity orientation of the Bandarnaike government its policies were often inappropriate.

Given that direct action is possible, the next question is: what is the appropriate direct action for South Asian countries? Before delving into this general subject, let us take a look at the causes of Sri Lanka's—and later I comment on Kerala—exceptional performance. The main contribution of Bhalla's work is to shift our attention to the period before the 1970s. As it turns out, there is clear evidence of governmental action. In particular, three policies which played important roles are: provision of health facilities, free and compulsory education, and free or subsidized food rations.

Sri Lanka's record in terms of health facilities is good. Richards and Gooneratne (1980) have documented some of these and I note here only a few salient features. It is well known that Sri Lanka's excellent mortality figures owe a lot to the malaria eradication programme of 1946. In one year, between

1946 and 1947, the death rate fell from 20 to 14. As one would expect, there were sharp improvements in infant mortality and life expectancy around the same time. Clearly a malaria eradication programme is a direct welfare activity of the government. More generally, the ratio of doctors and nurses to the total population in Sri Lanka has been high relative to the South Asian experience. In the early 1970s the nurse–population ratio was four times that of India. From the mid-1950s to the early 1970s real expenditure on health services rose steadily.[9]

Despite all this, for a health programme to succeed, it is essential that the people accept what the government offers. It is not sufficient to have a large family planning programme if people are not willing to listen, or a large vaccination centre if people view it as a torture cell. So for a health programme to succeed it is important that people have some education. Isenman's regression analysis confirms the crucial role of literacy in improving life expectancy and infant mortality.[10] Demographers have often stressed the positive relation between literacy among women and infant mortality. Some data suggesting this relation can be found in the Survey on Infant and Child Mortality 1979, conducted by the Office of the Registrar-General in India. This is presented in Table 10.2. The table suggests not only a relation between health and the 0–1 concept of literacy but a monotonic relation, with increasing education resulting in lower mortality.

Table 10.2 Mortality and the education of women in India, 1978

Education of mother	Infant mortality	
	Rural	Urban
Illiterate	145	88
Literate but below primary	101	57
Primary and above	71	47

Source: Office of the Registrar-General of India (1981a).

Given that Sri Lanka has had a long history of free education—dating back to its pre-independence period—it is not surprising that its health programme has been successful. Its education programme is an example of meaningful social expenditure. As Isenman (1980: 239) notes, 'As a result of high expenditures and high enrolment rates at all levels of education, adult literacy increased from 58% in 1946 to 78% in 1971.'

Finally, Sri Lanka has had a comprehensive system of free food rations for

[9] Richards and Gooneratne (1980).

[10] It also probably influences fertility. The World Development Report, 1985, notes that the percentage of married women of child-bearing age using contraceptives in Sri Lanka in 1982 was 55. This compares favourably not only to Bangladesh's 25 but to India's 32.

about 40 years.[11] This has taken the form of providing a certain amount of free rice (and, on occasions, wheat) and some additional rations at a subsidized price. What is unusual about Sri Lanka's rationing system is its comprehensive coverage of the entire population, including the urban *and rural* areas. This is in sharp contrast to India and Bangladesh. It will be argued later that Sri Lanka would have done better to cover a target population, namely those in poverty. Nevertheless, Sri Lanka's system of *total* coverage was better than having a system where only the urban sector has access to rationed foods. There has been a tendency for this to happen in some countries and its deleterious consequence was clearly evident during the Bangladesh famine of 1974. The urban sector, being covered by a rationing scheme, could ensure that a substantial part of the food would be diverted to it. The rural entitlement crisis was thus heightened by the very fact of the rationing scheme (McHenry and Bird 1977; Sen 1981*b*).

Not surprisingly, Sri Lanka's daily calorie intake is much higher than that of India or Bangladesh. Coupled with the fact that poverty in Sri Lanka is less, this suggests that the calorie intake of the poor is superior. The Sri Lankan food ration and subsidy scheme has been noted by several authors as the cause of its greater equality and better nutrition (Jayawardena 1974; Sen 1981*a*). The change in inequality in Sri Lanka over time is a much more controversial subject.[12] In fact, the whole question of changes in economic conditions in the 1960s and 1970s and their connections with the politics of the nation is an interesting and much misunderstood subject. But before going on to that I want to briefly dwell on the other striking example in South Asia of a poor region attaining a high standard of living—the State of Kerala.

The status of Sri Lanka among nations and that of Kerala among the Indian States bear striking resemblances. Kerala is one of the poorer States in India in terms of per capita income and also per capita nutrition (see Centre for Development Studies 1975; Dholakia and Dholakia 1980; Bardhan 1984*a*) —though its nutritional status is probably much better than a direct reading of the data suggests (Centre for Development Studies 1975: ch. 1). In terms of standard-of-living indicators, however, Kerala is markedly ahead of other States and in some ways quite close to advanced industrialized countries. In 1978 literacy in Kerala was 72 per cent as compared to the all-India figure of 39 and Punjab's 47. Infant mortality in Kerala was 39 compared to the all-India

---

[11] This has been largely dismantled in recent years, a point that is discussed later.

[12] It is commonly believed that Sri Lanka's income distribution in 1973 was more equitable than the ones in 1963 or 1953. It has in fact been shown (Fields 1980: 198) that the distribution in 1973 Lorenz-dominates the earlier ones. These facts run into controversy once we look at consumer expenditure data. It can be shown that in terms of this the share of income accruing to the bottom one-fifth of the population fell and the share going to the highest one-fifth rose between 1963 and 1973 (Lee 1977). Lee has argued convincingly that because of sharp relative price changes and a consequent index-number problem, the income data is rendered a less accurate indicator of what happened between 1963 and 1973 than the expenditure data.

Table 10.3 Inter-state social statistics in India, 1978

	Literacy (%)	Male literacy (%)	Female literacy (%)	Infant mortality (per 1,000 live births)
All India	39	50	27	126
Kerala	72	77	66	39
Punjab	47	54	39	103
Uttar Pradesh	33	46	19	167
West Bengal	47	56	35	78 (approx.)

Source: Office of the Registrar-General of India (1981*a*).

average of 126 and Punjab's 103. These statistics and more are presented in Table 10.3.

As in the case of Sri Lanka, Kerala demonstrates that improvement in the standard of living does not have to come via growth. Also, as we look into the factors behind Kerala's remarkable achievement, a lot of the same factors stand out here as in the case of Sri Lanka.

Kerala's educational performance is a direct consequence of progressive government policies. The State has had a long tradition of free primary schooling which has led to high enrolment rates and, more importantly, low drop out rates. These tendencies have been strengthened by the provision of free meals at schools to some categories of students (CDS 1975).[13] Compared to other States, Kerala's performance in terms of *female* literacy is particularly striking, as Table 10.3 shows. This, as argued earlier, helps in the attainment of a better health status.

It seems generally accepted that health facilities are better distributed in Kerala.[14] The State's progressive health policies go far back into history, to the policies of the princely State of Travancore (Panikar and Soman 1984).

A major factor behind Kerala's health statistics is its food rationing scheme. As in the rest of India, subsidized foodgrains are sold in limited quantities to individuals through ration shops. However, whereas, all over India, food rations are essentially an urban feature, in Kerala the coverage is comprehensive, including urban and rural areas. This is again a striking similarity with Sri

[13] The Keralite's general penchant for education is also well known. This partially explains the recent mushrooming of private English-medium schools in Kerala. As a cynical bureaucrat noted, in Kerala you have to simply put up the label 'English Medium', think of a good English name, like John or Mary, prefix it with a 'Saint', and you are in business.

[14] The percentage of population within two kilometres of medical facilities in 1978 is 64 for Kerala compared to the Indian average of 35 (Office of Registrar-General 1981*a*). Percentage of live births unattended by trained medical practitioners in 1978 in Kerala is 38% in the rural sector and 25% in the urban sector. The all-India figures for the same are 42 and 33 (Office of Registrar-General 1981*b*).

Lanka. In Kerala the public distribution scheme reaches 97 per cent of the population; in Sri Lanka, before 1978, 93 per cent of the population was covered. Detailed studies of Kerala (Kumar 1979; George 1979) seem to establish the important contribution of the public distribution system to the citizens' nutrition and health. This is particularly true of the poorer classes.

State-wide data on social expenditure are difficult to get and what little is available presents problems of interpretation. Hence, it is difficult to judge whether social expenditure was high in the case of Kerala. This, however, as argued earlier, is not the crucial question. Clearly the expenditure must have been above a certain level since the provision of free education, subsidized health facilities, and rationed food entails this. Apart from this it is not clear whether Kerala spent little on social expenditure very efficiently or a lot inefficiently. The important point is that Kerala undertook direct action in government activities and this resulted in a relatively higher standard of living than one would expect from its general economic indicators.

What then is the basis of the view that direct redistributive and equity-oriented policies cannot work? One reason must be that policies come in bundles and it is difficult for us to sort out which is the cause of success and which of failure. We have some broad stereotypical notions of different governments: South Korea and Taiwan are *laissez-faire* economies, so if they succeed it is a success of non-intervention. China is a socialist country, so its success indicates the effectiveness of intervention. Reality can be different. For instance, in the case of South Korea and Taiwan, some policies that have been followed by their governments (e.g. land reform) are more radical than those any South Asian government has tried.[15] Given the scope of this essay, I shall concentrate on South Asia and illustrate this point with the example of Sri Lankan politics.

For all practical purposes, Sri Lanka has had a two-party system: the Sri Lanka Freedom Party (SLFP) associated with the Bandarnaikes, and the United National Party (UNP) associated with Senanayake and now Jayawardena.[16] The SLFP is considered the left-of-centre party and the UNP the right. The Sri Lankan electorate is volatile and responsive and regular changes in government have been seen, as follows: 1947–56, UNP in power; 1956–65, SLFP;[17] 1965–70, UNP; 1970–7, SLFP; 1977 onwards, UNP.

Economists, implicitly or explicitly, have taken 1956–65 and 1970–7 (because these were the times when the SLFP was in power) as the periods when 'direct action' was at its peak; failures during these periods have been taken to

[15] See Lee (1981) and in particular Datta Chaudhuri's (1981) essay in that collection. For a very interesting analysis contrasting South Korea and Taiwan, see Scitovsky (1985).

[16] There are several other parties of varying importance and governments have generally been coalitions, but such details are being ignored here.

[17] This is so excepting for a brief period in 1960 when, after a general election in which there were no clear victors, Dudley Senanayake of the UNP was appointed Prime Minister.

be failures of direct governmental action. But politics is a more complex game. A country which espouses socialism within its boundaries may follow a foreign policy of supporting right-wing regimes. Even in a party's domestic policy one can find unexpected mixtures which render easy labelling hazardous.

Note first that Sri Lanka's welfare programmes concerning education, health, and food were in effect during the first UNP government. Also, in 1978 it was the UNP government that made the food rationing scheme more equitable by ruling that only families whose annual income fell below Rs 3,600 would be eligible for free rations.[18] With this progressive move, the total number of beneficiaries fell from 93 per cent of the population to 54 per cent.[19] In retrospect it is clear that this progressive move was but a first step towards dismantling most of the public distribution schemes Sri Lanka had had. In 1979 the Jayawardena government abolished the rice rations and introduced a food stamp programme in its place. But the value of the food stamp programme was fixed in nominal terms and its real value has unfortunately declined rapidly because of inflation.[20]

As far as the SLFP is concerned, it is vital to distinguish between its two periods of government. During its first reign, that is, 1956–65, it stepped up social expenditure sharply—from about 5.3 per cent of GNP to 12.8.[21] It passed the Paddy Lands Act (1958), to increase security of tenure, and undertook many other domestic measures.

The second period, 1970–7, was very different.[22] The government's foreign policy was now more radical (e.g. it established diplomatic relations with several Communist countries), but its domestic rule was inefficient and inequitable. There was first of all considerable instability, including that stemming from the Communist insurgency of 1971, which the Prime Minister, Mrs Bandarnaike, put down ruthlessly. Unemployment was on the increase and money wages began to slip behind the price index. The real downturn came in 1973–4 with a severe failure of food crops and also as a consequence of the general international slump. Calorie intakes fell and health indicators deteriorated slightly. In addition, welfare expenditures were on the decline. Real expenditure on health programmes was probably falling, but, more

[18] Marginal adjustments were made for family size (Edirisinghe 1986).

[19] From full coverage of the population, in 1972 Mrs Bandarnaike ruled that income tax payers would not get rationed food. The effect of this was negligible (Edirisinghe 1986).

[20] The full consequence of this cannot as yet be judged but, based on some preliminary evidence, Jayanntha (1985: 47) has noted in his lucid monograph on Sri Lankan politics, 'Available evidence suggests that the nutritional status especially of infants and children under two years has deteriorated significantly.' Regarding why this did not erode the popularity of the UNP government (judging by some by-election results), he observes, 'These groups though vulnerable are not articulate or politically organized. Moreover malnutrition is often not recognized by the mother . . . Thus increased malnutrition alone . . . may not be translated into overt forms of political discontent.'

[21] Bhalla (1988a).

[22] See Jayanntha (1985) for an excellent account.

importantly, the size of the population per doctor or assistant medical practitioner was rising: from 3,800 in 1971 to 4,250 in 1976.[23] As Richards and Gooneratne (1980: 152) note, 'This coupled with drug scarcities and rising costs must indicate a recent deterioration in levels of medical care.' Government expenditure on education as a percentage of GNP also fell, from 4.3 in 1970 to 2.7 in 1977.[24] It is not surprising, therefore, that a study of change during the 1970s does not show up Sri Lanka in a particularly favourable light.

The final issue that I want to discuss in this section is the larger macroeconomic one of the alleged trade-off between growth and equity. If we do go in for the kind of basic needs policy discussed above, do we have to sacrifice growth? A lot of traditional thinking presupposes the existence of such a trade-off, though several authors have challenged this presupposition (a particularly vehement and clear case was made by Myrdal 1970).[25] There are two reasons why a simplistic view of a growth–equity trade-off may be wrong. First, it is reasonable to assert that, even if there is a relation between growth and equity, it is not a 'functional' one but in the nature of a 'correspondence', whereby a set of values of growth is compatible with each level of equity. Though in this case there may be a *potential* trade-off, this may not be of any immediate concern to the economy. This would be true of an economy which is functioning below its 'possibility frontier' in the growth–equity space. This is the view that I take here: in most LDCs there is sufficient slack for them to have more of both equity and growth.

A second and more fundamental criticism (one which is not pursued here) is to deny any relation between growth and equity in an economy. The absence of any relation between two variables may at first sight seem difficult to imagine but there are plenty of examples of this in economics. For example, it is meaningless to talk of the relation between price and supply in a traditional monopoly. If this happened to be true of growth and equity, then we would not be able to talk of a trade-off, immediate or potential. There can be other, more philosophical problems. For instance, one could argue that the only growth–equity combination that *can* occur in a country is the one that actually *does* occur. The question of what rates of growth are compatible with a different level of equity may then be meaningless because a different level of equity may be logically inconsistent with the other given features of the country.

One reason for the widespread belief in a trade-off is that policies often come in bundles: the government that enhances controls (an act which often has a negative impact on growth) is the one that has a more radical poverty-removal programme (which brings about greater equity). On the other hand a government like the one formed by Jayawardena tends to cut controls and minimize expenditure on basic needs programmes.[26] It is this policy bundling which

---

[23] Richards and Gooneratne (1980).   [24] Bhalla (1988*a*).   [25] See also Sen (1981*a*).

[26] There are important exceptions to this, as just discussed in terms of Sri Lanka's experience between 1971 and 1977.

may give us an exaggerated view of trade-offs, in particular the false view that an increased social spending must result in sluggishness of growth.

The amount of slack in most LDCs is large. The fact that a country takes up an activity x with zeal therefore does not mean that there will be less of activity y.[27] (Of course, we may nevertheless lament that the zeal is for x and not for y.) Parents who curb a child's zeal for sports, in the belief that this will help him become a scientist, will usually be disappointed. A better strategy for the parents would be to try to develop the child's enthusiasm for science.

Given the political structure of South Asian governments, there is an inherent tendency for them to indulge in controlling activities: licensing, price-setting, and fixing trade tariffs and quotas. These often encourage inefficiencies and curb growth, but the established domestic businesses have a vested interest in this structure of controls which makes it very difficult to dismantle it. Every time some import restriction is removed and consumers find they can buy some product cheaper and of better quality, one hears cries of dumping and 'foul'. There is much to be gained on the growth front by lowering trade restrictions and allowing prices to play a more important role;[28] and these policies need not be a curb on basic needs policies. In fact in the long run basic needs policies may actually be helped by these.

Bhagwati (1985) has argued that the problem with a large basic needs programme is not that in itself we cannot have it or it will not be beneficial; but simply that we may not be able to sustain such a programme for long. Indeed Sri Lanka was under severe fiscal strain in the 1970s. To ensure the sustenance of poverty alleviation programmes, we need some concomitant policies. We need to bolster growth so that the government has adequate resources for its programmes. What I have just been arguing is that it is not necessary to prune the poverty alleviation projects in order to have growth. Growth can be bolstered through a different set of policy instruments while continuing with the same basic needs policies. Of course, we may have to try to restrict the recipients of government support to the really needy.[29] This, as we have seen in the case of Sri Lanka, is a difficult task; but it is essential for keeping the fiscal burden manageable. This subject is discussed in the next section. Thirdly, what can be implemented or sustained depends on the political climate of a nation. This is discussed in section 10.4.

In the next section I narrow the focus from basic needs policy in general to a part of it: the provision of food and the combating of poverty. This narrowing

[27] Scitovsky's (1985) study shows that Taiwan is ahead of Korea in terms not only of equity and standards of living but also (albeit marginally) of growth and economic performance. What comes out of this study is that Taiwan's growth rate instead of having been curtailed by its greater equity was probably aided by it. For a detailed cross-country study of growth and equity, see Ahluwalia (1976).

[28] I have discussed some of these issues in several short articles in the *Indian Express* and in a longer essay in the *Statesman* of 5 Nov. 1985.

[29] As Ahluwalia (1974) emphasizes, the very purpose of a support programme is to exercise selectivity.

down reflects the scope of this chapter and is not meant to suggest the unimportance of the other features of a basic needs programme.

10.3. *Poverty alleviation programmes*

South Asia has seen a plethora of schemes for alleviating poverty and acronyms have multiplied faster than one can count. Popular programmes include: food-for-work (FFW); Employment Guarantee Scheme (EGS); food ration and subsidy schemes; food stamps; nutrition programmes like Tamil Nadu's noon-meal scheme; Integrated Rural Development Programme (IRDP); credit support schemes like the Grameen Bank in Bangladesh. Of these, the IRDP and Grameen Bank, while very different from each other, are also very different from the other schemes and on these I offer only a few remarks. Programmes like FFW and food rations are more directly concerned with attacking the problem of food entitlement and unemployment and these are of central interest in this section.[30] I shall however begin with a few comments on programmes which provide some credit support.

IRDP is an important programme in Bangladesh and India. In India 15 million people were meant to be assisted by it during the Sixth Five Year Plan.[31] The motivation for the programme arose out of a feeling that the earlier anti-poverty policies were piecemeal and needed consolidation and that they were working mainly as subsidy schemes on which the poor were likely to get chronically dependent. The aim of IRDP was, therefore, to offer a combina tion of subsidies and credit to poor households so as to bolster their asset position and enable them to have a higher income and become self-sufficient. The scheme was supposed to help the poorest sections of the rural sector. 'Poor' was now being defined differently from what was conventional. First, the household, instead of each individual, was being treated as a unit. Secondly, poverty was not defined in terms of landholdings, but in terms of the family's income from all sources. If this was below a certain level the family was considered eligible for support from IRDP. While this is, in principle, a better criterion for selecting the needy, it is also one which makes the problem of identifying the beneficiaries more acute.

Studies of the functioning of IRDP in India so far reveal that it has been very successful in terms of the target number of beneficiaries. But the average amount of investment that each beneficiary received was only about half of the planned investment of Rs 3,000 per family at 1979–80 prices. Also, in terms of

---

[30] Also omitted from the purview of the present paper are more structural reforms like land redistribution. Programmes like the EGS and FFW do not usually require structural changes and, as Herring and Edwards (1983) rightly observe, they may even help ossify existing structures.

[31] For critical assessments, see Sundaram and Tendulkar (1985*a*, 1985*b*) and Bandyopadhyay (1985). A general survey of poverty programmes in South Asia is contained in Islam and Lee (1985).

the objective of reaching the poorest people, the achievement of IRDP is doubtful, though no definitive study on this is available.

The targeting problem was, to a certain extent, preordained because of some inconsistencies in the planned objectives of the project. While (1) it was supposed to benefit the poorest, (2) it was also expected to assist families so as to push them above the poverty line. There is some ambiguity about objective (2). Two alternative elucidations of (2) are: (a) the number of families that cross the poverty line should be maximized. (b) A family which is assisted ought to be assisted sufficiently to cross the poverty line. Under both interpretations (2) conflicts with (1). With (b) the conflict is indirect and stems from the fact that during the process (over time) of assisting a family, it may cease to be the poorest. The conflict between (1) and the first interpretation is direct. If we want to maximize the number of families that cross the poverty line, we should choose as beneficiaries families which are close to the poverty line. This would, of course, conflict with objective (1). The incompatibility between (1) and (2) is very marked in practice. Sundaram and Tendulkar (1985a) have shown that, given some assumptions, if the average amount of benefit per family disbursed during the first three years of the Sixth Five Year Plan had gone to the poorest 30 per cent of the rural population, then none of the IRDP beneficiary households would have crossed the poverty line, that is, objective (2) would have remained completely unsatisfied.

Though we have to wait for more detailed empirical research, there are some grounds for maintaining that the poorest people were not reached. For one, there were other objectives which militated against this happening. For instance, the so-called 'cluster approach' which was adopted by IRDP meant that its assistance would go to areas where credit institutions existed and there was 'the capacity to absorb credit to the extent envisaged' (Sundaram and Tendulkar 1985b: 209). Further, since a part of the IRDP package consists of assistance with credit, it would face the difficulties which credit support policies face in general in trying to reach the very poor.[32] I am in sympathy with Rath's (1985) argument that, though credit and subsidy for self-employment are important, we cannot ignore the need for massive programmes for creating public and private employment (see also Dantwala 1985 and Hirway 1985). Consequently, the waning of official interest in India for such schemes (see Rath 1985) is unfortunate. A similar sentiment is expressed by Dandekar (1986: A-100): '. . . while the possibilities of creating self-employment should be explored, the main reliance will have to be on offering wage-employment'. He rightly observes that this does not mean a perennial dependence because the 'more thrifty, provident, and enterprising' among the beneficiaries of an

---

[32] In general the 'very poor' tend to raise problems quite distinct from the ones associated with the poor. Can the very poor be helped so as to become permanently self-sufficient? Are they in a position to avail themselves of the benefits provided for the poor? Such questions need investigation (see Lipton 1983).

employment scheme are likely to 'set themselves up' in the long run and become independent.

Before turning to employment programmes, let us take a brief look at pure credit support policies which have also been tried over a long period in South Asia. In India, the coverage provided by institutional credit has steadily increased (thereby hopefully diminishing the hold of the legendary rural money-lender). But nevertheless the credit policy has been far from a success. The main reason is that institutional credit has failed to reach the poorest people, who have by and large remained dependent on the unorganized sector, i.e. on private money-lenders.[33] Hence it is possible that institutional credit, instead of having alleviated the condition of the poorest, has merely bolstered the position of the not-so-poor. The reason for this is sufficiently deep as to imply that it cannot be corrected by merely doctoring the credit programmes. The main problem of providing organized credit to the poor is the recovery of loans. The village money-lender has a variety of methods for ensuring repayment[34] which are not open to the manager of the bank sent from the nearest city to provide rural credit. Apart from the problem of absconding from repaying, there is the genuine problem of bankruptcy. The very poor who borrow to survive may well find themselves with no liquidity at the time of repayment. The private money-lender may then 'bond' them, that is, acquire a right over their labour for a long enough period to recover the loan.[35] It is this knowledge which gives the money-lender the confidence to lend to the poor. Clearly this option is not open to government-run banks. Moreover, the rich and influential have the ability to divert to themselves the organized-sector low-interest credit; and even if their repayment record is poor they continue to get loans (see e.g. Bhende 1986). It is for these reasons that a credit scheme is very unlikely to be able to confer benefits on the poorest sections.

The Grameen Bank of Bangladesh however seems to provide a counter-example. Established in 1983, it is a successor to the Grameen Bank Project which was launched in 1976 by Muhammed Yunus, an economics professor at Chittagong University. It is considered one of the most successful rural credit schemes in South Asia. The Grameen Bank is a public sector credit institution and its aim is to provide loans to the poor on reasonable terms, the idea being that of enabling the poor to become self-sufficient. A member of any household owning less than half an acre of cultivable land can avail himself of the services of the Grameen Bank. The workers of the bank actually search for poor people who need financial support but are too ignorant or diffident actively to seek credit. Paradoxically it has done well exactly where other schemes have

---

[33] The problem seems to be similar for Bangladesh (Khan 1972; Rahman 1979).

[34] The use of personalized relationship and collateral has been discussed in Bhaduri (1977) and Basu (1984a, 1984b).

[35] This, as is well known, may be long enough to cover the lifetime of the borrower and may even spill over to his children who would then be born into bondage.

floundered. Its repayment record is excellent. Studies done in the early 1980s show that only 1 or 2 per cent of all outstanding loans were overdue (Siddiqui 1985; see also Ahmad and Hossain 1985). Secondly, its targeting has been quite good. According to a 1983 survey, a vast majority of loanees owned no agricultural land (for detailed tables, see Siddiqui 1985: 175). Another striking feature of the Grameen Bank is the prominence of women among the borrowers. In 1980, 39 per cent of the borrowers were women and by late 1984 the figure had risen to 54 per cent (Hossain 1985: 12).

A part of the Grameen Bank's success lies in its organizational structure. For example, the manager of a new branch has to survey the concerned villages for two months without subordinates. This ensures first-hand knowledge and direct involvement. The Grameen Bank is, in part, a co-operative. It organizes credit recipients into groups and helps them build up their own savings for emergencies. The group is useful in preventing defaults by applying 'social' pressure on individuals to stick to schedules. This co-operative aspect of the bank may have had other indirect benefits. It has, for instance, been found that an increasing amount of credit is being taken from the bank for co-operative ventures like purchasing equipment for irrigation which would benefit a group or buying rice hullers or even leasing market-places (Ahmad and Hossain 1985). According to Hossain (1985: 12–13), among the main causes of the Bank's good record are the 'close supervision of the activities in the field by the managing director' and the dedication of the bank workers, 'most of whom have taken the job as providing services to the poor rather than simply as an income earning opportunity'. In the context of the present chapter the important question is: to what extent can such a credit programme be replicated elsewhere?

In the early 1980s the Grameen Bank was a small project with plans for vast expansion through the 1980s. In May 1980 the bank had 24 branches. By February 1987 this had grown to 298 and loans had been disbursed to about 250,000 households. The plan was to keep up the expansion for some more years.[36] With such expansion it will of course lose the personal touch; and the robustness of its organization and its relevance for large countries, like India, will only then be fully tested. However, its success thus far is good reason for other South Asian countries to examine the viability of such a credit programme.

More direct methods of enhancing the food entitlements of the poor are the EGS or FFW and food rations or food stamps. These have had a fair measure of success in the Indian subcontinent. Food-for-work in Bangladesh was begun in the wake of the 1974 famine. The programme has run mainly on food received as aid—primarily from the US. In the first year of the programme,

---

[36] See Ahmed (1986) for a discussion of the prospects of the Grameen Bank and the impact of credit availability on employment. He argues that in the long run technology upgradation will be necessary for fully realizing the benefits of a credit programme.

32,000 tons of wheat were disbursed through the programme and 8.6 million man days of work were created. In 1982–3, approximately 371,000 tons of wheat were used to create 101 million man days of work. The FFW programme is computed to have created jobs equivalent to only 2–3 per cent of the total annual unemployed labour time in Bangladesh. Also, it has been estimated that 30 per cent of the workers came from households owning more than half an acre of land (Ahmad and Hossain 1985).

In India FFW (which was subsequently renamed the National Rural Employment Programme, NREP) was begun in April 1977, with the objective of creating jobs, creating durable infrastructure, and using up the surplus grain which had accumulated with the government.[37] In this respect India differed from other countries; its programme was not based on food received as aid.[38] In 1978, 12 lakh tonnes of wheat were used and 286 million man days of jobs were created.[39] Though the programme was running fairly successfully it got mired in political controversy and was somewhat tarnished. First of all the programme caused a certain amount of alarm because it was having the sort of impact it was intended to have: a study of the Planning Commission found that, of the twenty Districts surveyed, six had experienced a significant upward movement of wages. This was undesirable from the point of view of rich landlords and may have been a factor behind the loss of official enthusiasm for FFW. Secondly, FFW became the source of Centre–State conflicts and this resulted in a curb on foodgrain supplies to several States, including West Bengal (for a discussion, see Basu 1982).[40] In terms of economic efficiency, where the programme has really floundered is in its effort at creating infrastructure. While it did create a certain amount of employment, it was usually unproductive. But indeed the sheer fact of doling out food may be of value.

The rice ration scheme or the provision of food stamps[41] are methods of

---

[37] Contrary to the official proclamation, this last 'objective' is not really an objective. The availability of surplus grain simply makes it easier to fulfil the real objectives of employment and income transfer and production.

[38] FFW or some variant of it has been used in several LDCs, e.g. Tunisia, Morocco, and Egypt. Tunisia is also one of the few countries where FFW began without foreign support, though within a few years food shortages developed and it had to use US wheat.

[39] India's FFW had an important precursor in the EGS which had been in operation since 1972 in Maharashtra. It was merged with the FFW programme when the latter was started. For a study of the EGS, see Dandekar (1983).

[40] The original organization structure of the FFW was as follows. The Centre supplied foodgrains to the State governments, which were responsible for setting up labour intensive projects in the rural regions. The States had considerable freedom in terms of the actual execution of projects. They could, for instance, pay wages purely in terms of foodgrain or pay partly in foodgrains and partly in cash.

[41] The food stamp programme, as implemented in Sri Lanka, is something in between a free rice ration scheme and a negative income tax. A recipient of food stamps can exchange them for a certain range of food items, including rice. Members of households which earn less than Rs 300 per month were eligible. Adults received stamps worth Rs 15 per month and children a little more (see Edirisinghe 1986).

doling out food and, as I have argued in the previous section, they have played an important role in raising living standards in Sri Lanka and Kerala. Ideally FFW and rice rations should be used as complementary schemes because their points of strength are very different. FFW, properly executed, can provide a self-selection device for picking out the poor and also it has the advantage of being productive. Its main disadvantage *vis-à-vis* a rice ration scheme is that it discriminates against the old and the disabled. Since the old and disabled are easier to identify, one possibility is to have free rations restricted to them and an FFW open to all and hopefully, because of its self-selection property, utilized only by the poor.

For countries as large as India and Bangladesh, the problem of selecting the poor is so important that reliance on FFW seems natural. If too many non-deserving people rely on such governmental support, the burden on the exchequer may be unbearable. To get the full advantage of an FFW we need to organize it very skilfully. To bring out the salient features of FFW, I present some simple analytics.

The difference between an FFW and a food ration scheme is that they alter entitlements differently. Suppose a person earns z rupees from a day's labour;[42] and that his daily non-labour income is Rs v. Let y denote his total income. Thus

$$y = z + v$$

Let p be the price of the foodgrain in the open market. In the absence of a price support scheme, his budget set is given by $y0A$ is Fig. 10.1. Now let us consider two alternative support programmes.

Food ration scheme: let us suppose that a free rice ration of R units is given. Then this person's budget set becomes $0yCB$. Here and below I assume that the transaction cost of reselling food is prohibitive.

Food-for-work: now suppose that instead of a food ration scheme food-for-work is started where foodgrains worth G units are given in exchange for a day's labour. Then his budget set is $0vDE$.

So what these schemes do is alter the entitlements of individuals. The interesting feature of FFW is that z will vary between individuals. If for a person z is sufficiently high, then his food-for-work budget set becomes a subset of $0yA$ (see Fig. 10.1) and he would prefer not to avail himself of the opportunity of FFW. It is easy to check that the FFW budget set is subsumed in the normal budget set if

$$G < z/p. \qquad (10.1)$$

Hence a person will certainly not work for FFW if condition (10.1) is true. (If 10.1 is false he may or may not work.) It is clear therefore that those who have

---

[42] I am assuming that a day's labour is an indivisible unit. That is, a worker does not face a choice between hours of leisure each day and daily income.

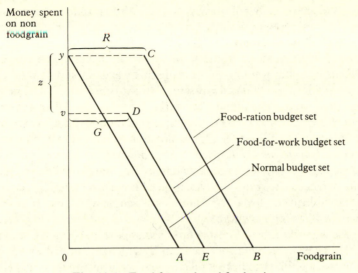

Fig. 10.1. Food for work and food ration

access to a well-paid labour market or high productivity in their own farms (basically a high z) will not participate in FFW projects. This is the self-selection property of FFW.

There is one problem. A person with a high non-labour income, but low z, may nevertheless come to work for FFW and clearly we would not like to have such people. There are two mitigating factors. First, manual labour is considered demeaning for anybody who has access to other income, especially a large non-labour income. Thus for reasons of status, those with a sufficiently high v are unlikely to come. Secondly, it is quite possible that v and z are positively correlated: it is the richer people who have access to well-paid labour markets. This may be briefly captured by asserting

$$z = z(v), \ z'(v) > 0.$$

In that case it is clear that if a person's v is large, (10.1) will be satisfied and the FFW programme will be spared the labours of such a person.

A controversial matter concerning FFW is the level of wages that ought to be paid to the labourers.[43] It is a widely held view that the wages paid on FFW ought to be higher. It will, however, be argued here that both on grounds of keeping the self-selection property sharp and *also for ethical reasons* the wage paid at FFW sites, i.e. G, should be kept as low as possible (in a sense made clear below).[44]

This seems to be a surprising recommendation if our objective is to remove

[43] Dandekar and Sathe (1980); Basu (1981, 1982); Panda (1981).
[44] I argued this in Basu (1981) and the next few paragraphs draw heavily on that paper.

poverty. But such a feeling of surprise arises from an implicit 'headcount' view of poverty. This comes out clearly from Dandekar and Sathe's (1980) study of FFW and EGS in Maharashtra. They found that 90 per cent of the people working on this scheme continue to be below the poverty line despite such work. From this they went on to conclude that wages should be raised. In the case of Bangladesh, Ahmad and Hossain (1985: 80) observed that wages paid to FFW workers were substantially below the officially stipulated wage rate. 'It has been shown that about 56 per cent of the workers did not know about the stipulated wage rate. Those who know do not bargain lest they do not get the jobs at all as *there are many others who are unemployed and would be too willing to take them up on the offered terms and conditions*' (my italics).[45] It is the italicized part which suggests why underpayment need not be unethical, since that will make it possible to employ a larger number of people who are needy enough to be willing to work for a low wage.

Suppose we subscribe to a headcount view of poverty[46] and try to minimize this. Then, given a total stock of foodgrain X, which is to be disbursed through the FFW, we would try to heap it on people so as to ensure that the maximum number of people cross the poverty line. But clearly our more intuitive normative penchant (as opposed to one formally derived from trying to minimize the headcount index) would be to spread out X over the poorest people, even if that leaves the numbers on the two sides of the poverty line the same. Fortunately, according to some more sophisticated measures, this will register a decline in poverty.

To formalize this argument suppose X is the total amount of grain available for giving out as wages in a FFW. For simplicity I am assuming that wages are paid entirely in terms of food grain. Let L be the number of labourers supplying their labour to FFW. As usual, we assume

$$L = L(G), L'(G) > 0 \qquad (10.2)$$

This supply curve of labour is depicted in Fig. 10.2.

Given a wage of G, the maximum number that can be employed, which may be labelled 'potential employment', is given by X/G. The relation between G and potential employment is depicted in Fig. 10.2. Clearly this is a rectangular hyperbola. What is being recommended here is that G should be minimized subject to $L(G) > X/G$. Let the solution of this be defined by G^*. This is easily seen to be given by the point of intersection of the two curves in Fig. 10.2. G^*, it is being argued here, is the wage that we should aim to offer.[47]

[45] See Bandyopadhyay (1985: 137) concerning underpayment in FFW in India.

[46] For a critique of such a view of poverty see Sen (1988: ch. 3 and Appendix C).

[47] The actual execution of this may not be as easy as it appears. In Afghanistan, wages were set so low, in an effort to maximize the spread, that the projects were perennially short of labour. In Lesotho the wage was set so high that landowners were quitting working on their own land to work at FFW sites.

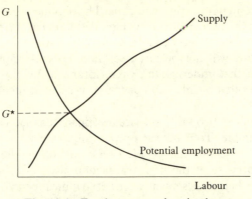

Fig. 10.2. Employment and optimal wage

As I have argued in Basu (1981) on the basis of some Planning Commission data (Project Evaluation Organization 1979) it seems likely that the wage that has been paid in India is above G^*. A similar claim seems to be possible for Bangladesh on the basis of Ahmad and Hossain's paper.

It has already been argued that G^* is more equitable (in the sense of ameliorating poverty) than a higher wage. G^* has another advantage. It sharpens the self-selection property of FFW since from (10.1) it follows that, as G becomes smaller, the wealthier (in terms of labour income) will be less inclined to come for FFW jobs, thereby paving the way for the poor to take these up.

The above analysis implies that there are three ways of raising the wage: (1) by improving the opportunities open to the labourers (by, for example, having infrastructural investments in the rural sector. This would raise the supply curve in Fig. 10.2). (2) By assigning a larger food stock for distribution through FFW. This raises the 'potential employment' curve. (3) By simply deciding to set G above G^* and maintaining an excess supply of labour. What I have argued above is that we should raise wages via methods (1) and (2); option (3) ought not to be normally used. It may be used only if we can devise some additional selection criterion whereby the poorest among the job applicants are selected. Here and elsewhere it ought to be kept in mind however that accurate targeting of benefits may itself be an expensive exercise and there may be times when it is suboptimal to perfect one's marksmanship in this respect.[48]

Finally, I make some brief comments on the form of wage payment. Should this be paid in cash or kind? In other words, should we have an FFW programme or a cash-for-work programme? I do not want to give a firm answer

---

[48] Reutlinger (1984) has suggested a method of computing the relative efficiency of giving aid in the form of different goods, which takes into account the delivery cost. A similar exercise should be possible whereby the efficiency of transferring income to the poor via different schemes is computed, taking into account the cost of organizing the schemes.

here but merely point out the pros and cons. The popular argument for paying in food grains is to encourage the poor to have better nourishment even if that is not what they would do with the same amount of income. The ethical strength or weakness of this will not be discussed here. I will simply evaluate the positive argument that underlies this prescription, namely, that payment in foodgrains ensures that people will not fritter away their income on 'useless' consumption.

The weakness of this proposition becomes apparent as soon as we recognize that money is fungible. To make the proposition as strong as possible before attacking it let me assume that people cannot sell off foodgrains earned as wages (perhaps because of the high transaction costs of selling such small quantities). Nevertheless, as soon as we grant that most people will have some income from other sources (i.e. other than what they earn from FFW), it follows that the portion of that other income which they would have spent on food they can now spend on other things given that their food supply now comes from the FFW project. In other words, the fact of paying wages in food does not mean that food consumption will go up by that amount and it may not in fact go up at all. A little calculation shows that, given the actual facts of FFW in India (see Basu 1981, it is the case that the *form* of payment is unlikely to affect the volume of consumption of food. The evidence from Bangladesh suggests that payment in wheat does not affect significantly the *volume* of foodgrain consumption, but it does tilt its *composition* in favour of wheat (Osmani and Chowdhury 1983).

An important case for payment in food stems from the recognition of some political constraints, which apply especially to India. In the Indian economy, thanks to several compulsions including those emanating from the agrarian lobby, it seems likely that the food procurement policies of the government will continue for some time. If wages are paid in foodgrain at rural works programmes then the procured grain—or at least a part of it—will get earmarked for use in FFW. If, on the other hand, wages are paid in cash, the government will soon be looking for avenues for selling this grain. Once the grain gets converted into cash, it is unlikely that it will be used for the poor. Given the forces around government—and this is the central point of Griffin's paper (Griffin 1985)—it is more likely to get spent on amenities for the urban middle class. One may object here that if a government is inclined to do so, it will do so anyway. But the logic of large organizations like government does not work that way. The same 'end' may be infeasible by one route but by another route it may just be possible to tiptoe past vested interests.

The subject of political constraints has been mentioned several times, but in passing. It is an important issue in food policy but also a difficult one to write about; and so I reserve only a brief section for it.

10.4. *Optimal policies and political constraints*

Keith Griffin (1985) has pointed out in a lucid essay on the state of poverty in Asia that the problem of poverty can be largely eliminated through 'purposeful government intervention'; but 'given the class basis of the state, a question arises about the possibility of effective action'. He argued correctly that, in most South Asian countries, governments are closely in alliance with the wealthier sections of society. These people therefore guide policy to their advantage. The government's rhetoric is meant for the poor who are not near enough to see the actual policies, and the actual policies are inclined to help the already wealthy who keep a close watch on them. More disturbing is Gunnar Myrdal's (1970) accurate observation that not only policies but even the perception of truth can deviate in favour of the dominant classes.

There is a danger in pushing this kind of an argument too far. Though such a charge cannot be levelled against Griffin or Myrdal, several radical and conservative writers have been *too* successful in explaining the backwardness of LDCs, in the sense that their models leave no chinks for changing the situation. If such an all-encompassing explanation was valid, then there would be no point in making policy recommendations.

More formally, what I am claiming is that if a model of an economy is constructed in which every agent knows what is in his own interest and acts to achieve it, then 'advice' can have no role in affecting the 'outcome' of such an economy. This is the case with the Arrow–Debreu model of general equilibrium. There is no provision here for 'advice' to change any agent's behaviour. Let us call an agent whose actions can be altered by *some* advice an 'open end' of a model. If we want to construct a model and make recommendations, the model must be one which has open ends. In some conventional models the government is treated as an open end. If however we treat the government as either completely subservient to certain class interests or comprising of fully informed individuals with well-defined objectives, we lose the open end and policy advice becomes redundant again. In reality there is scope, however slender, for influencing the outcomes of economies.

First note that people do not always act selfishly and our hope for more equitable policies lies in the fact that altruism, anger, envy, or the influence of writings can lead us to work against our own interest. Secondly, the rich constitute a group. Consequently, even though a particular policy may be in their own interest, they may fail to implement it because their individual rationality may be incompatible with their group rational behaviour. In short, within their own class they may interact as in the Prisoner's Dilemma.

Finally, even though governments do exhibit class bias, there are chinks in the system, which can be exploited to divert resources to the poor. A government or a Minister chooses his policy bundle subject to several constraints. Some of these are, however, unusual constraints in that they may be political in character: certain powerful lobbies could make some policies impossible to implement. How much of a government's preference or ideology is revealed in its choice of policies depends on how restrictive these constraints are. Given the several lobbies that surround South Asian governments[49] the room for manœuvre must indeed be small. Hence two Finance Ministers with very different ideologies would draft budgets which are not too different (otherwise at least one of them would cease to be Finance Minister). In brief, South Asian economies are Finance Minister neutral—or almost so. This makes it clear that if government policies are to be influenced, instead of trying to alter the government's preference, our aim should be to alter the constraints. The poorer sections have to be made more demanding and more conscious of their rights.

There is an interesting self-referential reason why some downtrodden groups are so dormant. Note first that if all members of a group, H, consider it unreasonable to demand a larger share of the cake then, given that a government is always under severe pressure to make concessions to different groups lobbying for more, it will indeed be reasonable not to give H a larger cut. After all H is not pressing for more and others are. Hence each individual member of H will be right in supposing that it is unreasonable to ask for a larger share. If however each member of H chooses to be unreasonable and demands more, the government may find it in its own interest to concede to the group's demand. Also, the government would be able to persuade the other lobbies that it has to concede to H, because of its large 'voice'. In other words, it would no longer be an unreasonable demand to ask for more.[50] This is where the media can play a major role. They can influence our view of what is acceptable. And, as has just been argued, what is acceptable depends, at least in part, on what we consider to be acceptable.

10.5. Concluding remarks

The aim of this chapter was to evaluate policies for combating persistent and mass poverty in South Asia. In so doing it was necessary to go into some general analytical questions and to comment on existing debates. Though most of the empirical discussions were based on India and Sri Lanka, it is hoped that the analysis and policy suggestions which emerged will be of interest for the larger problem of poverty in the Third World.

The chapter began with the question as to whether 'direct action' for mitigating the poverty problem could be fruitful or would it be necessary to wait for the benefits of growth to 'trickle down'. It was argued that direct action

---

[49] Bardhan (1984b) has argued that Indian policy making is a compromise of the interests of three dominant classes: the industrial bourgeoisie, wealthy farmers, and the bureaucracy.

[50] Using the idea of self-fulfilling conjectures I have tried to show in a different context (Basu 1986) how certain unwanted political power structures could be sustained by a web of reinforcing beliefs among individuals.

was possible and desirable. To pursue this objective it was not necessary to sacrifice growth. Different policy instruments are available for achieving higher growth and greater equity. Given the enormity of this problem my comments were, perforce, in the nature of an overview. Several subthemes would have to be the subject of much more detailed research. The present chapter pursued in greater depth one particular subtheme—that of poverty alleviation programmes in rural South Asia.

Several schemes, for example, food-for-work and the Integrated Rural Development Programme, were commented on. However, it ought to be mentioned that, while I have analysed the schemes separately, in designing a full anti-poverty policy it will be essential to evaluate the whole package together. This is because poverty has many dimensions[51] and it will be necessary to use more than one programme to mitigate poverty,[52] and the value of one particular programme may depend on what else is being implemented. Some complementarities, for example, that between food-for-work and food rationing, were discussed in this chapter but a more systematic evaluation of *packages* will have to be undertaken in future.

The last part of the chapter was devoted to the politics of anti-poverty programmes. The brevity of section 10.4 reflects the difficulty of the subject, not its unimportance. Political constraints do not necessarily arise out of the wilful machinations of groups and lobbies but could be the inadvertent consequence of a multitude of individuals, each acting atomistically and in his own interest. This makes political constraints difficult not only to overcome but even to understand; and this subject must loom large in any agenda for research on poverty.

[51] See Rodgers (1976) for a discussion of the concept of poverty viewed as a 'multivariate phenomenon'.

[52] There is a semantic problem here in that we may think of a combination of programmes as yet another programme. This would render the claim that *one* programme can never be sufficient erroneous. The defence against this criticism is that the expression (one programme) is being used here to describe one member of the existing menu of anti-poverty schemes.

References

AHLUWALIA, M. S. (1974), 'The Scope for Policy Intervention', in Chenery *et al.* (1974).

——(1976), 'Inequality, Poverty and Development', *Journal of Development Economics, 3.*

AHMAD, A. K., and HOSSAIN, M. (1985), 'An Evaluation of Selected Policies and Programmes for the Alleviation of Rural Poverty in Bangladesh', in Islam (1985).

AHMED, H. (1986), 'Rural Landless in Bangladesh: An Enquiry into the Economic Results of Grameen Bank', mimeo (Oslo: Institute of Economics).

BANDYOPADHYAY, D. (1985), 'An Evaluation of Policies and Programmes for the Alleviation of Rural Poverty in India', in Islam (1985).

BARDHAN, P. K. (1984a), *Land, Labour and Rural Poverty: Essays in Development Economics* (New York: Columbia University Press).

——(1984b), *The Political Economy of Development in India* (Oxford: Basil Blackwell).

BASU, A. M. (1986), 'Birth Control by Assetless Workers in Kerala: The Possibility of a Poverty-Induced Fertility Transition', *Development and Change*, 17.

BASU, K. (1981), 'Food for Work Programmes: Beyond Roads that Get Washed Away', *Economic and Political Weekly*, 16.

——(1982), 'Food for Work: Some Economic and Political Consequences', *Economic and Political Weekly, Review of Agriculture*, 17.

——(1984a), *The Less Developed Economy: A Critique of Contemporary Theory* (Oxford: Basil Blackwell).

——(1984b), 'Implicit Interest Rates, Usury and Isolation in Backward Agriculture', *Cambridge Journal of Economics*, 8.

——(1986), 'One Kind of Power', *Oxford Economic Papers*, 38.

BHADURI, A. (1977), 'On the Formation of Usurious Interest Rates in Backward Agriculture', *Cambridge Journal of Economics*, 1.

BHAGWATI, J. N. (1985), 'Growth and Poverty', Occasional Paper No. 9 (East Lansing, Mich.: Center for Advanced Study of International Development, Michigan State University).

BHALLA, S. S. (1988a), 'Is Sri Lanka an Exception? A Comparative Study in Living Standards', in Srinivasan and Bardhan (1988).

——(1988b), 'Sri Lanka's Achievements: Fact and Fancy', in Srinivasan and Bardhan (1988).

——and GLEWWE P. (1986), 'Growth and Equity in Developing Countries: A Reinterpretation of the Sri Lankan Experience', *World Bank Economic Review*, 1.

BHENDE, M. J. (1986), 'Credit Markets in Rural South India', *Economic and Political Weekly*, Review of Agriculture, 21.

CALDWELL, J. C. (1986), 'Routes to Low Mortality in Poor Countries', *Population and Development Review*, 12.

Centre for Development Studies, Trivandrum (1975), *Poverty, Unemployment and Development Policy: A Case Study of Selected Issues with Reference to Kerala* (New York: United Nations ST/ESA/29).

CHENERY, H., AHLUWALIA, M. S., BELL, C. L. G., DULOY, J. H., and JOLLY, R. (1974), *Redistribution with Growth* (Oxford: Oxford University Press).

DANDEKAR, K. (1983), *Employment Guarantee Scheme: An Employment Opportunity for Women* (Bombay: Orient Longman).

——and SATHE, M. (1980), 'Employment Guaranteee Scheme and Food-for-Work Program', *Economic and Political Weekly*, 15.

DANDEKAR, V. M. (1986), 'Agriculture, Employment and Poverty', *Economic and Political Weekly, Review of Agriculture*, 21.

DANTWALA, M. L. (1985), ' "Garibi Hatao": Strategy Options', *Economic and Political Weekly*, 20.

DATTA CHAUDHURI, M. K. (1981), 'Industrialization and Foreign Trade: The Development Experiences of South Korea and the Philippines', in Lee (1981).

DHOLAKIA, B., and DHOLAKIA, R. (1980), 'State Income Inequalities and Inter-state Variations in Growth of Real Capital Stock', *Economic and Political Weekly*, 15.

EDIRISINGHE, N. (1986), 'The Food Stamp Program in Sri Lanka: Costs, Benefits and Policy Options' (Washington, DC: IFPRI).

FIELDS, G. S. (1980), *Poverty, Inequality and Development* (Cambridge: Cambridge University Press).

GEORGE, P. S. (1979), 'Public Distribution of Foodgrains in Kerala: Income Distribution Implications and Effectiveness' (Washington, DC: IFPRI).

GRIFFIN, K. (1985), 'Rural Poverty in Asia: Analysis and Policy Alternatives', in Islam (1985).

HERRING, R. J., and EDWARDS, R. M. (1983), 'Guaranteeing Employment to the Rural Poor: Social Functions and Class Interests in the Employment Guarantee Scheme in Western India', *World Development*, 11.

HIRWAY, I. (1985), ' "Garibi Hatao": Can IRDP Do It?' *Economic and Political Weekly*, 20.

HOSSAIN, M. (1985), 'Institutional Credit for Rural Development: An Overview of the Bangladesh Case', *Bangladesh Journal of Agricultural Economics*, 8.

ISENMAN, P. (1980), 'Basic Needs: The Case of Sri Lanka', *World Development*, 8.

ISLAM, R. (ed.) (1985), *Strategies for Alleviating Poverty in Rural Asia* (Bangkok: ILO).

——and LEE, E. (1985), 'Strategies for Alleviating Poverty in Rural Asia', in Islam (1985).

JAYANNTHA, D. (1985), 'Sri Lanka: The Political Framework (1947–84)', mimeo (Washington, DC: World Bank).

JAYAWARDENA, L. (1974), 'Redistribution with Growth: Some Country Experience —Sri Lanka', in Chenery *et al.* (1974).

KHAN, A. R. (1972), *The Economy of Bangladesh* (London: Macmillan).

KUMAR, S. K. (1979), 'Impact of Subsidized Rice on Food Consumtpion in Kerala' (Washington, DC: IFPRI).

LEE, E. (ed.) (1981), *Export Led Industrialization and Development* (Bangkok: ILO).

LEE, E. L. H. (1977), 'Rural Poverty in Sri Lanka, 1963–73', in International Labour Organization, *Poverty and Landlessness in Rural Asia* (Geneva: ILO).

LIPTON, M. (1983), 'Poverty, Undernutrition and Hunger', World Bank Staff Working Paper No. 597 (Washington, DC: World Bank).

McHENRY, D. F., and BIRD K. (1977), 'Food Bungle in Bangladesh', *Foreign Policy*, 27.

MORRISON, B. M., and WAXLER, N. E. (1986), 'Three Patterns of Basic Needs Distribution within Sri Lanka: 1971–73', *World Development*, 14.

MUKHOPADHYAY, S. (ed.) (1985a), *The Poor in Asia: Productivity-Raising Programmes and Strategies* (Kuala Lumpur: Asian and Pacific Development Centre).

——(ed.) (1985b), *Case Studies on Poverty Programmes in Asia* (Kuala Lumpur: Asian and Pacific Development Centre).

MYRDAL, G. (1970), *The Challenge of World Poverty* (London: Allen Lane).

NAG, M. (1983), 'Impact of Social and Economic Development on Mortality: Comparative Study of Kerala and West Bengal', *Economic and Political Weekly*, 28.

Office of the Registrar-General of India (1981a), *Survey on Infant and Child Mortality 1979* (New Delhi: Government of India).

——(1981b), *Levels, Trends and Differentials in Fertility 1979* (New Delhi: Government of India).

OSMANI, S. R., and CHOWDHURY, O. H. (1983), 'Short Run Impacts of Food For Work Programme in Bangladesh', *Bangladesh Development Studies*, 11.

PANDA, M. K. (1981), 'Productivity Aspects of Wages in Food for Work Programme', *Economic and Political Weekly*, 16.

PANIKAR, P. G. K., and SOMAN, C. R. (1984), *Health Status of Kerala* (Trivandrum: Centre for Development Studies).

Project Evaluation Organization, Planning Commission (1979), *A Quick Evaluation Study of Food for Work Programmes* (New Delhi: Government of India).

RAHMAN, A. (1979), 'Usury Capital and Credit Relations in Bangladesh Agriculture: Some Implications for Capital Formation and Capitalist Growth', *Bangladesh Development Studies*, 7.

RATH, N. (1985), ' "Garibi Hatao": Can IRDP Do It?' *Economic and Political Weekly*, 20.

REUTLINGER, S. (1984), 'Project Food Aid and Equitable Growth: Income Transfer Efficiency First!' *World Development*, 12.

RICHARDS, P., and GOONERATNE, W. (1980), *Basic Needs, Poverty and Government Policies in Sri Lanka* (Geneva: International Labour Office).

RODGERS, G. B. (1976), 'A Conceptualisation of Poverty in Rural India', *World Development*, 4.

SCITOVSKY, T. (1985), 'Economic Development in Taiwan and South Korea: 1965–81', *Food Research Institute Studies*, 19.

SEN, A. K. (1981a), 'Public Action and the Quality of Life in Developing Countries', *Oxford Bulletin of Economics and Statistics*, 43.

——(1981b), *Poverty and Famines: An Essay on Entitlement and Deprivation* (Oxford: Oxford University Press).

——(1985), *Commodities and Capabilities* (Amsterdam: North-Holland).

——(1988), 'Sri Lanka's Achievements: How and When?', in Srinivasan and Bardhan (1988).

SIDDIQUI, K. (1985), 'An Evaluation of Grameen Bank Operations', in Mukhopadhyay (1985b).

SRINIVASAN, T. N., and BARDHAN, P. K. (ed.) (1988), *Rural Poverty in South Asia* (New York: Columbia University Press).

STREETEN, P. (1984), 'Basic Needs: Some Unsettled Questions', *World Development*, 12.

SUNDARAM, K., and TENDULKAR, S. D. (1985a), 'Anti-poverty Programmes in India: An Assessment', in Mukhopadhyay (1985a).

————(1985*b*), 'Integrated Rural Development Programme in India: A Case Study of a Poverty Eradication Programme', in Mukhopadhyay (1985*b*).

TAYLOR, C. L., and HUDSON, M. C. (1972), *World Handbook of Political and Social Indicators* (New Haven, Conn., and London: Yale University Press).

World Bank (1985), *World Development Report* (New York: Oxford University Press).

NAME INDEX

SUBJECT INDEX

Africa 155–93, 197–233, 281–302
  agriculture: policy options 215–29;
    problems and constraints 198–215
  economic performance 155
  food situation trends 282–91
  imports and exports 197
  institutions and policies 8–9
  role of industry 290–302
  undernourishment 155–93; extent of 8,
    159–62; indicators of 156–93
  see also individual countries
agricultural equipment 10, 291–8
  production 291–3, 296
  research and development 293–7
agricultural processing 10, 298–300, 302
agriculture
  Africa 8–9, 9, 197–233, 236–76, 240
  Brazil 98, 100–3
  co-operatives 222, 228–9
  employment in 217–18
  mechanization 288, 318
  per capita production 197, 198, 282
  and poverty 137–8
  role in development 215–18
  taxation 47
  terms of trade 34–7, 208–9
  wage earning groups 287, 289
aid climate 331–2
anthropometric
  evidence 163–8, 169, 183–8, 310
  norms 191–2
Argentina 124

Bangladesh 10–11, 307–43, 364, 366
  credit 316, 325 n., 336–8, 359, 361–2
  famine 327–32
  food entitlement contraction 312–27
  food-for-work 362–3
  hunger 308–12
  IRDP 359
  life expectancy 349
  public food distribution system
    (PFDS) 330–1, 333–5, 336
basal metabolic rate (BMR) 160, 188–9,
  190–1
basic needs provision 11, 347, 358–68, 371
BELINDIA 99–100
black market 254
body mass index (BMI) 163, 186, 188, 189
Brazil 93–116
  agriculture 98, 100–3
  crossover time 120, 145

development history 94–6
ecological debt 103–4
housing 113–14
income distribution 94 n., 97–8, 106–7,
  115
industrial structure 97–8, 115
infant mortality 114
land tenure 101, 103, 115
life expectancy 111–12
malnutrition 108–10
poverty: extent of 104–6; food 124; and
  growth 6–7, 145–8; rural 140–3;
  urban 125
racial relations 114–15
social profile 96, 104
social programmes 115–16
two gear economy 100
unemployment 111
urbanization 95, 102–3, 135
bureaucracy 213
Burkina Faso 295

calories
  availability estimates 157–8, 168, 170–4
  distribution 179–82, 182
  intake estimates 158–9
  as intermediate goods 181
  normal requirement 177–9, 182, 188–91,
    309–11
  see also food
capitalism, peripheral, dependent or
  retardatory 93
cash-crops 246
Chad 217
childrens' growth 128–9
Chile 125, 127, 145
China 4–5, 15–53
  communes 18–20, 37, 51
  Cultural Revolution 20, 48
  distribution of food 38–47, 47–51
  famine 28–33
  famine and state policy 51–2
  five-guarantee households 48–9
  Great Leap Forward 5, 18, 29, 31
  household responsibility system 20
  institutional framework 18–21, 355
  land distribution 18
  national food supply 21–3
  nutrition 24–6
  official statistics 23 n.
  physical geography 15–16
  pre-reform food policy 33–8